International Research Group on Authoritarianism and Counter-Strategies (ed.)
Global Authoritarianism

The work on this volume was coordinated by
Börries Nehe, Ailynn Torres Santana, Fathima Nizaruddin, Inés Durán Matute, Sabrina Fernandes, Khanyile Mlotshwa, and Jeffrey G. Karam.

This open access publication was enabled by the support of POLLUX – Informationsdienst Politikwissenschaft

and a network of academic libraries for the promotion of the open-access-transformation in the Social Sciences and Humanities (transcript Open Library Community Politik 2022).

Vollsponsoren: Freie Universität Berlin – Universitätsbibliothek | Staatsbibliothek zu Berlin | Universitätsbibliothek der Humboldt-Universität zu Berlin | Universitätsbibliothek Bielefeld | Universitätsbibliothek der Ruhr-Universität Bochum | Universitäts- und Landesbibliothek Bonn | Staats- und Universitätsbibliothek Bremen | Universitäts- und Landesbibliothek Darmstadt | Sächsische Landesbibliothek Staats- und Universitätsbibliothek Dresden (SLUB) | Universitäts- und Landesbibliothek Düsseldorf | Universitätsbibliothek Frankfurt am Main | Justus-Liebig-Universität Gießen | Niedersächsische Staats- und Universitätsbibliothek Göttingen | Universitätsbibliothek der FernUniversität in Hagen | Staats- und Universitätsbibliothek Carl von Ossietzky, Hamburg | Gottfried Wilhelm Leibniz Bibliothek - Niedersächsische Landesbibliothek | Technische Informationsbibliothek (TIB Hannover) | Universitätsbibliothek Kassel | Universitätsbibliothek Kiel (CAU) | Universitätsbibliothek Koblenz · Landau | Universitäts- und Stadtbibliothek Köln | Universitätsbibliothek Leipzig | Universitätsbibliothek Marburg | Universitätsbibliothek der Ludwig-Maximilians-Universität München | Max Planck Digital Library (MPDL) | Universität der Bundeswehr München | Universitäts- und Landesbibliothek Münster | Universitätsbibliothek Erlangen-Nürnberg | Bibliotheks- und Informationssystem der Carl von Ossietzky Universität Oldenburg | Universitätsbibliothek Osnabrück | Universitätsbibliothek Passau | Universitätsbibliothek Vechta | Universitätsbibliothek Wuppertal | Vorarlberger Landesbibliothek | Universität Wien Bibliotheks- und Archivwesen | Zentral- und Hochschulbibliothek Luzern | Universitätsbibliothek St. Gallen | Zentralbibliothek Zürich

Sponsoring Light: Bundesministerium der Verteidigung | ifa (Institut für Auslandsbeziehungen), Bibliothek | Landesbibliothek Oldenburg | Ostbayerische Technische Hochschule Regensburg, Hochschulbibliothek | ZHAW Zürcher Hochschule für Angewandte Wissenschaften, Hochschulbibliothek

Mikrosponsoring: Stiftung Wissenschaft und Politik (SWP) - Deutsches Institut für Internationale Politik und Sicherheit | Leibniz-Institut für Europäische Geschichte

The **International Research Group on Authoritarianism and Counter-Strategies** is an initiative of the Rosa-Luxemburg-Stiftung that brings together more than 20 scholar-activists from across the Global South to share and exchange ongoing research on the Authoritarian Right and strategic responses from the Left.

International Research Group on Authoritarianism and Counter-Strategies (ed.)
Global Authoritarianism
Perspectives and Contestations from the South

[transcript]

Sponsored by the Rosa-Luxemburg-Stiftung with funds of the Federal Ministry for Economic Cooperation and Development (BMZ) of the Federal Republic of Germany.

Bibliographic information published by the Deutsche Nationalbibliothek
The Deutsche Nationalbibliothek lists this publication in the Deutsche Nationalbibliografie; detailed bibliographic data are available in the Internet at http://dnb.d-nb.de

This work is licensed under the Creative Commons Attribution 4.0 (BY) license, which means that the text may be remixed, transformed and built upon and be copied and redistributed in any medium or format even commercially, provided credit is given to the author. For details go to https://creativecommons.org/licenses/by/4.0/
Creative Commons license terms for re-use do not apply to any content (such as graphs, figures, photos, excerpts, etc.) not original to the Open Access publication and further permission may be required from the rights holder. The obligation to research and clear permission lies solely with the party re-using the material.

First published in 2022 by transcript Verlag, Bielefeld
© International Research Group on Authoritarianism and Counter-Strategies (ed.)

Cover layout: Maria Arndt, Bielefeld
Translation: »Foreword« by Verónica Gago translated by Joel Scott for Gegensatz Translation Collective; »(Re)Thinking Authoritarianism in Democracy: The Public Denunciation of State Violence During the Pandemic in Argentina 2020-21« translated by Michael Dorrity and Joel Scott for Gegensatz Translation Collective
Copy-editing: Eve Richens and Rowan Coupland for Gegensatz Translation Collective
Printed by Majuskel Medienproduktion GmbH, Wetzlar
Print-ISBN 978-3-8376-6209-2
PDF-ISBN 978-3-8394-6209-6
EPUB-ISBN 978-3-7328-6209-2
https://doi.org/10.14361/9783839462096
ISSN of series: 2702-9050
eISSN of series: 2702-9069

Printed on permanent acid-free text paper.

Contents

Preface 7

Foreword
Verónica Gago 9

Introduction
International Research Group on Authoritarianism & Counter-Strategies 13

Embedded Authoritarianism
Sovereignty, Coloniality, and Democracy in Latin America
Pedro Salgado 25

Hindu Majoritarianism and Authoritarian Shifts in the Age of Informational Capitalism in India
Fathima Nizaruddin 41

Right-Wing Authoritarianism Against Nature
The Latin American Context
Sabrina Fernandes 57

Neoliberal Authoritarian Urbanism
A Comparative Study of New Patterns of Urban Development in Brazil and Turkey
Aysegul Can and Hugo Fanton 77

Authoritarian Neoliberalism from Below
Subjectivity and Platform Capitalism in Argentina and Brazil
Fábio Luís Franco and Gustavo Robles 99

Reconfiguration of the Regime of Impunity and Authoritarian Statecraft in Turkey
Hülya Dinçer 119

Anti-feminist Meeting Points in Latin America
Religious Neoconservatism, Authoritarian Neoliberalism, and Beyond
Ailynn Torres Santana 139

Exploring the Colonial and Apartheid Roots of Urban Authoritarianism in Postapartheid South Africa
Khanyile Mlotshwa 159

(Re)Thinking Authoritarianism in Democracy
The Public Denunciation of State Violence During the Pandemic in Argentina 2020–21
Julieta Mira 179

Authoritarianism and Developmentalism Framing 'Progressive' Governments in Mexico and Argentina
Inés Durán Matute and Mariano Féliz 197

Agrarian Neoliberalism, Authoritarianism, and the Political Reactions from below in Southern Africa
Boaventura Monjane 219

Factors of Resilience and Constraint in the Myanmar Resistance Movement
Nwet Kay Khine 239

Contentions and Contradictions
The Rise of Duterte's Authoritarianism with Fascist Tendencies Amidst the Hegemonic Crisis of (Neo)Liberal Democracy in the Philippines
Verna Dinah Q. Viajar 261

Production of Activism under Authoritarianism
Insights from the Rights-Based Civil Society in Turkey
Ülker Sözen 281

Contributors 297

Preface

This volume is the product of three years of collective work at the International Research Group on Authoritarianism and Counter-Strategies (IRGAC), an initiative founded in 2019 by the Rosa-Luxemburg-Stiftung (RLS) in Berlin, Germany to support critical research on authoritarianism in and from countries of the so-called Global South. The IRGAC assembles more than 20 scholar-activists from Argentina, Brazil, Cuba, Mexico, Zimbabwe, Mozambique, Egypt, Palestine, Lebanon, Turkey, Iran, India, Myanmar, and the Philippines, who were granted postdoctoral research fellowships of up to three years by the RLS.

The group's goal is to combine in-depth studies of national, regional, and local processes of socioeconomic transformation and politics with a global perspective that recognizes and analyzes the universal manifestations of authoritarian capitalism and universalizing processes that lie behind the rising tide of authoritarianism. At the same time, we propose an internationalist perspective on local and regional counter-strategies, a perspective that, while discussing alternative paths and concrete, popular resistances, explores their potential to pave the way for internationalist emancipatory transformative strategies.

Ever since our first gathering in late 2019, the group has worked together closely on- and offline, not only to regularly discuss our research and sharpen our theoretical, conceptual, and methodological tools to understand the manifold manifestations of global authoritarianism, but also in a series of concrete collective endeavors. In this respect, the research group collectively curates its website, www.irgac.org, where we regularly publish our findings as well as a series of other, non-academic articles on authoritarianism around the world. Likewise, the group has held seminars and public workshops, and organized a major international conference ("Contesting Authoritarianism: Perspectives from the South") in Berlin in May 2022.

Work on *Global Authoritarianism: Perspectives and Contestations from the South* began back in 2020 with a collective editorial process organized by an editorial committee. Since then, each article has been written, read, discussed, and re-written several times in an incredibly rich, open, and informative dialogue between scholar-activists from across the world. Although, due to reasons of timing, not all of the people that participate in IRGAC contributed an article to this volume, their perspectives are nevertheless an integral part of it, as its production has been an inherently collective process in which we constantly place the diversity of perspectives within the group into a highly productive tension. In this sense, the making of this volume is part of our ongoing effort to develop critical theories from the South in a collective and decentralized manner – with all the difficulties and potential that this implies.

Our work benefited greatly from the peer-review process this volume went through, for which we counted on the support of the Rosa-Luxemburg-Stiftung's Academic Advisory Board as well as its wider network of scholars. We would like to thank them wholeheartedly for their critical reading and helpful comments. We also want to thank our colleagues and comrades from Al.Berlin, Academy in Exile, the Arnold-Bergstraesser-Institut Freiburg, the Berlin Graduate School Muslim Cultures and Societies, bi'bak, the Center for Middle Eastern and North African Politics, the International Center for Development and Decent Work, Forum Transregionale Studien and OFF University for their trust and solidarity, for fruitful discussions and many joyous moments.

Börries Nehe
IRGAC coordinator

Foreword

Verónica Gago

This book presents a constellation of terms for describing a pressing problem that we could sum up as follows: What are the dynamics of capitalist violence today? There are myriads names, concepts, and categories for the political characterization of what is happening today: authoritarianism, the New Right, right-wing extremism, neoconservativism, neo-fascism; with each term also forming plurals with a concluding "s". The urgency of understanding the manifestations of forms of sexism, racism, and classism as generalized affects that are crystallized in structures of power while also being encouraged by these structures is the first port of call when it comes to making sense of the current crisis. This task, which is a central part of all debates, requires efforts of characterization, of diagnosis, and of political strategy if we are to adequately name these phenomena. This collective work forms part of this saga.

There are two issues that ought to be emphasized in relation to this *multiplication* of categories. The first of these has to do with the fact that ascribing multiple names to a *reactionary* phenomenon illustrates that the phenomenon is responding to diverse realities and geographies at a particular historical moment. But it also highlights a second issue: that we must think *from within* historical conjunctures in order to produce concepts, include specificities, and broaden our capacity to find names for current events, accounting for their multiple determining factors. It is a procedure that runs contrary to the one that has been used all too often, namely of beginning by constructing a single concept and applying it to the rest of the world from a single primary location, in order to then measure the extent to which this category fits or does not fit with each manifestation.

If today these categories fail to attain the homogeneous unity they once had, it is because they are subjected to a provincialization of the Eurocentric rationalizations that produced theories which "spilled over" to other parts of the planet and which, for this very reason, guaranteed a unified origin and manifested as a set of clear and distinct definitions. As such, this multiplication does not reflect a simple lack of agreement or a volatility in the modes of conceptualization, but a categorical destabilization which responds to the effort to truly take seriously the notion that there are no central and peripheral experiences in theoretical practice.

Breaking out of the paradigm of smooth and definitive categories which can later be applied or interpreted in places which then go on to "embody" or "adjust" them, exposing imperfect "cases", is not just a conceptual shift, it also implies a shift in the way that we think of theory itself.

In this book, there has been an explicit decision to define the problems from the perspective of the Global South (a category that is itself contested). But I would stress that this is not in order to provide a compilation of peripheral cases, not an exercise in shedding light on a neglected portion of the map, but forms part of a *general* analytical perspective which requires us to: 1) reveal colonial vectors, their currency, and their political memories; 2) refute methodological nationalisms in order to frame the analysis within a world economy; 3) question the modernizing ideals of progress and capitalist development; 4) foreground the questions of gender, ethnicity, and race rather than framing them as cultural epiphenomena; and 5) dismantle the passivization of the subaltern groups.

This is a mode of analysis which, as well as emphasizing the divisions between North and South, also repositions them outside of a static division between different continents in order to read the *multi-layered* forms in which this division prospers: souths within the metropoles of the North, norths within the regions of the South. This allows us to delineate the global logic of capitalism *as well as* the debates around mobility sparked by the trajectories of migrants, both decisive issues when it comes to understanding recent modifications of both urban space and non-urban and rural spaces. This proposition is also important when it comes to re-plotting the coordinates of key elements of modernity, such as war and colonialism, in which they take on new features and are played out in different landscapes and territories under the banner of the neoliberal era. At the same time, it is necessary—as has been done here—to more astutely outline the relationships between elements that seem unrelated, but are not: for example, religious fundamentalisms that propagate theologies of prosperity with algorithmic forms that order the exploitation of labour "without bosses", to name just two.

Another key aspect that this work also illustrates is the urgency of *systematizing* the multiple manifestations of this phenomenon, both in its definitions and its varying proportions. Reading the book, we can gain a detailed picture of a certain *convergence* of elements that enables us to conceptualize the phenomenon of these "new" authoritarianisms as a combination of transformations in our political systems, in our states, and in the dynamics of governmentality, but also in the subjectivities and affects that are engendered, in the forms of organizing labour, and in the extractivist tendencies of neoliberalism. The various dimensions of these authoritarianisms are not merely a matter of semantics or reflective of an array of perspectives that can be picked and chosen in order to approach the phenomenon. On the contrary, they are an expression of the complexity of the subject that we must analyse if we are to gain an understanding of how these economic, political, cultural, ideological, and subjective issues are articulated and reinforced. Or to put it more directly: why has capitalism always employed the strategy of segmenting and "autonomizing" these issues, as if they originated from independent spheres? The task we are faced with comprises no more and no less than fostering the emergence of a diagnostic framework for identifying the authoritarian, reactionary, and fascist forms—in their repetition and difference—to which contemporary capitalism makes recourse today in order to prop itself up.

In this sense, these debates are strongly linked with efforts to name the various mutations of neoliberalism, and with the attempts to think through its original, "primitive" violence in order to bring to light genealogies that broaden the frameworks of Euro-Atlantic analyses. There have also been debates about this kind of proliferation of neoliberalism as a rationality and mode of governance that is capable of taking on multiple adjectives as it goes along, chameleon-like, adapting to and recycling the attacks on its legitimacy. Nevertheless, we are not dealing with an apparatus that is always triumphant, with aimless mutations. Neoliberalism's alliances with conservativism and various forms of authoritarianism merely give the lie to its propaganda of combatting violence by way of technologies of control that are growing ever more sophisticated, as well as exposing the intensification of the violence without which these modulations of control cannot function.

We must not forget that the violence of the arena we are confronting is the result of an attempt to shore up neoliberalism in the face of a crisis of political legitimacy that has been sparked by the transnational feminist movement, the forms of insubordination of the LGBTQI movements, the antiracist political practices of migrants, which represent forms of concrete politics that dispute neoliberalism both in its analysis of the crisis and in the way it approaches and confronts precarity on the labour market and more general, existential forms of precarity. These are the struggles that attack the structure of capitalist subordination and exploitation at a sensitive and strategic point: right where neoliberalism comes together with reactionary forces in the regime of the family, on the issues of sexuality, on judgements on who deserves social benefits, forms of non-renumerated labour, anti-immigrant legislation, and so on. This is a reality which has only accelerated with the progression from pandemic to war.

For both discussions, however, we cannot look at structural effects without keeping in mind the way they interweave "from below", given that in this interrelation, a battlefield opens up that is plagued by ambiguities and tensions. The reactionary mood we are witnessing here is being managed from above, taking form in the victorious governments of the right and extreme right; but it also operates from below, disputing the terrain of the subjectivities engendered in the neoliberal cycle and in its specific production of affects.

In my opinion, one of the most important contributions made by feminist debates has been repositioning the term war, talking about a "state of permanent war" against certain bodies and certain territories as a definition of contemporary neoliberalism. This allows us to understand a form of neoliberal violence that becomes authoritarian because it has not been subsumed in apparatuses of subjective pacification, because it has been contested and resisted. This highlights the need to renew our vocabulary and articulate a strategic notion of war that describes a situation which is no longer defined by two clearly identifiable sides in a single arena of conflict (even if this feminist debate was the precursor to the arena of war of 2022).

Finally, there is no doubt that the methodology of this book is linked to its political proposition: a mode of investigation that is militant and rigorous, capable of crystallizing collective debates and of offering a cartography of current issues from an internationalist perspective. Its wager also lies in proposing a geography that once again discusses dependency, forms of subordination and exploitation, ecologies of territories and knowledge systems, the racist legacies of state forms, and the ways that capital metabolizes that which combats it. From my point of view, the initiatives of militant investigation develop a kind of sensitivity in composing statements and resolving conflicts. It's a form of action: it is not a mode of analysis that is devoid of imagination, and even less of calling on others to act. Understood in this way, militant investigation is less a thematization (in the sense of constructing an agenda) and more a question of method, and of a practical commitment. The gravity of the themes discussed here demands nothing less.

Introduction

International Research Group on Authoritarianism & Counter-Strategies

Conceptualizing Authoritarianism

For the last decade and a half, we have been witnessing a worldwide resurgence of reactionary nationalist, racist, anti-feminist, and religious discourses and movements, as well as rapid authoritarian transformations of political systems in all regions of the world. These can broadly be characterized as a further deepening of the non- and anti-democratic features of neoliberal capitalist states and societies, including the expansion of their punitive and repressive nature and increasing state and para-state practices of violence, neutralization of resistance, and marginalization of subordinate groups. Nevertheless, these ideological elements and political practices converge in specific and often very diverse amalgams, and although there are wild dreams of a "nationalist International" (Matteo Salvini), more often than not there seem to be more differences and disputes than commonalities between authoritarian actors.

This means that we are facing a worldwide phenomenon ('global authoritarianism'), which on closer inspection, however, does not in fact show up as global, but as heterogeneous and fragmented. Critical knowledge production and Left politics, which take an international and internationalist perspective, are therefore confronted with a variety of political as well as theoretical and conceptual problems. Thus, the central question arises whether and how these often very different authoritarianisms can be productively conceived of together, if at all: where are the convergences, connections, and parallels between these processes of authoritarian transformation worldwide? Does the current phase differ appreciably from other, preceding phases of authoritarian capitalist rule, such as those we can periodically observe in Europe, Latin America, West Asia and North Africa, Southeast Asia, and numerous other regions? And if so, in what way, i.e. what facets and dimensions actually give this authoritarian phase its specificity?

The difficulty of conceptualizing authoritarianism is further aggravated by its increasing ideological usage in Western mainstream discourse, which places it in opposition to the ideal of 'liberal democracies' (usually reserving the term for regimes that enter into conflict with Western powers). So the question arises whether the concept of authoritarianism can provide us with anything more than a formal description of what, in the worst case, is seen merely as a 'deviation' from the ideal liberal model of the state.

We consider that it can, but this requires acknowledging, as Pedro Salgado argues, that "liberal values are not mutually exclusive with authoritarian practices, but simply rearrange them around a different conception of political subjectivity" (in this volume). Likewise, as the Brazilian sociologist Florestan Fernandes pointed out, under capitalist democracy, the "authoritarian element is intrinsically a structural and dynamic component of preservation, strengthening and expansion of the 'capitalist democratic system'" (2019, 45). In this sense, Julieta Mira shows how authoritarian institutional practices are embedded within democratic regimes, and Hülya Dinçer in her text points towards the often processual authoritarian transformation when discussing Turkey's transition towards "autocratic legalism" and the systematic creation of "legal black holes" for arbitrary authoritarian rule.

Thus, a critical global perspective on authoritarianism implies both to acknowledge its inherent inscription and embeddedness in (post)colonial capitalist states and societies, and to think of it in historically and geographically specific terms, as Inés Durán Matute and Mariano Féliz develop in this book. In this sense, we consider that the concept does not compete with other, sometimes more specific accounts—be they fascism or Bonapartism, authoritarian populism or authoritarian neoliberalism—but rather allows us to build a conceptual arc between the concrete and necessarily specific expressions of a global trend towards an increasingly weaponized regime of capital accumulation coupled with processes of de-democratization and brutalization of social and political practices and relations.

At the core of the current authoritarian turn of global capitalism lies a shared experience of a world in crisis—a multifaceted or 'civilizational crisis', as some observers write. The ecological crisis coincides with overlapping national, regional, and international political crises, a global crisis of representation and, by extension, of the legitimacy of (neo-)liberal democracies, massive economic dislocations, and a long train of closely related migration, health, social, and other crises, all of which seem to be reinforcing each other constantly. The effects of these crises are globally very uneven, while at the same time they contribute to deepening global inequality. In the face of this general collapse, which had a first spectacular expression in the financial crisis of 2008/9, and has recently gained much pace with the pandemic and the Russian attack on Ukraine, neoliberal capitalism seems to have definitely lost its hegemonic aura. But instead of experiencing its end—as many hoped we would when powerful emancipatory movements interrupted the political scene in the aftermath of the financial crisis—we are witnessing a zombie version of neoliberalism: stripped of its liberal imagery and promises (for an institutional rule of law, open market economy, liberal social values, and a better future), but so deeply inscribed in political, social, and economic practices that there really seems to be *no alternative*—neither from below, nor from above.

In the face of the rise of European fascism, Antonio Gramsci (1971) famously observed that "if the ruling class has lost its consensus, i.e. is no longer 'leading' but only 'dominant'", the masses "no longer believe what they used to believe previously": "The crisis consists precisely in the fact that the old is dying but the new cannot be born; in this interregnum a great variety of morbid symptoms appear" (1971, 275–76). The diverse expressions of authoritarianism can be fruitfully analysed as such symptoms. We should add, though, that not only the masses, but also the ruling classes have lost their 'beliefs'—or, as Mike Davis bluntly puts it:

> Everyone is quoting Gramsci on the interregnum, but that assumes that something new will be or could be born. I doubt it. I think what we must diagnose instead is a ruling class brain tumour: a growing inability to achieve any coherent understanding of global change as a basis for defining common interests and formulating large-scale strategies. (Davis 2022)

In this sense, the multifaceted crisis and its concrete local expressions caused contradictions and heavy upheavals within global capitalism, as well as within the nationally and regionally dominant groups who struggle over which path to take. In the absence of a viable popular alternative to this mess, authoritarianism can thus be seen as a contingent response of the dominant classes to the crisis and their own inability or unwillingness to articulate a new hegemonic project (see Demirovic 2018) —or rather, as a diverse and often contradictory *set of responses* whose common denominator is their anti-democratic and frenetically neoliberal character. This is not to say—as many simplified accounts that focus on 'leader figures' do—that authoritarianism is solely a top-down project directed 'against the (otherwise immaculate) people'. Rather, as Gustavo Robles and Fábio Franco remind us in their contribution to this volume, we have to take into account that it is also produced "from below", as neoliberal rationality systematically destroys bonds of social solidarity and produces authoritarian subjectivities who permanently demand competition, performance, and flexibility from themselves and others, while nowadays it has little more to offer than precarization, hyper-exploitation, and a state of permanent individual and collective anxiety.

Current authoritarianisms build on this. In its *authoritarian populist* guise, it operates through an active regressive mobilization of the individuals and the 'masses' through traditional and renewed radical Right narratives—based on imagined neocolonial ethnic, racist, sexist etc. identities—combined with an open radicalization of neoliberal values (such as competitiveness, recklessness, self-management, capitalization etc.). Hatred is channelled towards the political and liberal cultural 'elites', the 'others', 'losers' and perceived competitors, but also towards everyone who dares to question the supposedly 'natural order of things', and the individual and collective imperfectness and weaknesses that may stand in the way of unhindered accumulation. In her contribution, Ailynn Torres Santana discusses this intimate relationship of contemporary anti-feminist and neoconservative discourses and authoritarian politics in Latin America and elsewhere.

Nevertheless, the noise that authoritarian populists are creating should not divert our attention from the authoritarian transformations happening within liberal democratic regimes led by liberal (conservative or social democrat) governments, who increasingly rely on politics of control and discipline rather than consent-building, let alone material concessions to the dominated. Such developments, for which the EU and its core countries offer good examples, have been discussed under the concepts of *authoritarian neoliberalism* and/or *statism*. Often more clearly in line with prior phases of neoliberalism, authoritarian neoliberalism nevertheless constitutes a qualitative change in that it rapidly deepens its anti-democratic nature and expands practices such as

> the repeated invocations of 'the market' or 'economic necessity' to justify a wide range of restructurings across various societal sites ... the growing tendency to prioritize constitutional and legal mechanisms rather than democratic debate and participation, the centralization of state powers by the executive branch at the expense of popular participation and other nodes of governance, the mobilization of state apparatuses for the repression of oppositional social forces at a range of scales, and the heightened pressures and responsibilities shifted onto households by repeated bouts of crisis and the restructuring of the state's redistributive mechanisms. (Bruff and Tansel 2019, 2)

But more often than not, the differentiation between these variants is more one of perspective rather than of its actual character. Thus, what mainstream discourse presents as opposing poles—liberal democracy vs. authoritarianism—is in fact deeply intertwined and overlapping, as authoritarian populists are *also* neoliberal-statist, while authoritarian (neo-)liberals *also* rely on reactionary discourses (against migrants, unions, 'welfare bums', and the like). Aesthetic differences aside, they are both part of a reactionary global culture war from the far right, and they share their absolute commitment to neoliberal forms of exploitation and governance, which are hermetically shielded against popular interference.

Perspectives from the South

Thus, authoritarianism is not located in an identifiable space, but rather, traverses political, economic, and social relations and structures in a heterogeneous manner—globally, but also within states and societies. Acknowledging this leads to implications such as a critical revision of the spatial categories with which we analyse the authoritarian transformations worldwide. In this sense, the perspectives discussed in this book do not only concern the Global South and the authors do not split the geographies and political processes examined on a north-south axis. They acknowledge the widening North-South divide. But this disparity is not simply between countries (if it ever was); it also exists between and within communities on a smaller scale.

In various academic circles, there is an ongoing discussion on the meaning, usage, applicability, and analytical usefulness of the *Global South* as a critical term. The World Bank's low- and middle-income nations in Africa, Asia, Oceania, Latin America, and the Caribbean are usually referred to as the Global South by certain academics and many non-governmental organizations (NGOs). This description just represents the most recent one in a long line of catch-all terms that are meant to identify, categorize, and describe the 'poorer portions of the world'. Some academics and activists continue to adopt this nation-state-focused definition, while others have criticized it. In this edited volume, we prefer to embrace the term and hopefully deterritorialize it for a more holistic understanding of it. "There are Souths in the geographic North and Norths in the geographic South", as Anne Garland Mahler put it (2018, 32). Following from this, the book contains an astonishing chapter on the intertwined relationship between the North and South in terms of extractivism under capitalism, and the effects of Global North country policies in the South (see Sabrina Fernandes, in this book).

It is not a new practice to employ ideas to characterize and categorize regional disparities and uneven economic development. After World War II, when many nations gained their independence from colonial authority and started to be the focus of international 'development' aid, this tendency persisted and gained popularity (Dados and Connell 2012). The phrases 'developed' and 'underdeveloped' (or 'developing') became popular ways to categorize the globe (Clarke 2018). As many people have pointed out, this terminology was problematic for a number of reasons, including the narrow focus it implied on economic growth and levels of industrialization; the implication that there was a universal measurement of 'development' and that national development could be evaluated against this (Western) standard; and the assumption that "development" would help "traditional societies" to catch up with "modern ones" (Kothari et al. 2019).

Thus, the renewed appeals from academics and activists for a 'non-Western' interpretation of global concerns, poverty, and inequality, as well as for a deeper comprehension of the regional, national, or locally-based experiences and struggles do not come as a surprise. In connection with this, scholars who were interested in understanding and mapping geopolitical processes and relationships as well as those who wanted to call attention to political conflicts being fought outside of the 'Western' world started using the term 'South'. In contrast to earlier phrases that othered the 'poorer portions of the world', the term's inspiration originated, in large part, from the South and was intended to centre the South. This is the main intention of this book in using the term as well.

According to Jessica Schafer et al. (2017, 7), the phrase has become more popular over the past ten years in the development and academic communities because it appears "able to incorporate the centrality of historical and contemporary patterns of wealth and power into a loosely geographically defined concept". The concept of 'Global South' is more than just a metaphor for underdevelopment, as Nour Dados and Raewyn Connell (2012, 13) point out. It highlights a long history of colonialism, neo-imperialism, and economic and social transformation that maintains significant inequalities in living conditions, life expectancy, and access to resources. This issue is also widely discussed in the book within chapters focusing on authoritarianism from a colonial perspective (see Salgado, this book) and authoritarian urban practices during and after Apartheid in urban South Africa (see Mlotshwa, this book). Thus, the phrase challenges the elitism of Western political science and emphasizes geopolitical linkages and processes while also giving researchers and activists a platform to analyse the particulars of problems, processes, and conflicts at a local, regional, or global scale. By examining subaltern agency and oppression and connecting localized conflicts to the dynamics of global power systems and dominant social groupings across spatial scales, researchers have adopted the term 'Global South'. However obscure, clouded, and vague the term Global South may be, the researchers and authors of this book decided to embrace it as a way to address power relations and dynamics of exploitation and domination, and to empower the continuing struggles and resistance in a neocolonial world order.

Countering Authoritarianism and Building Alternatives

Countering authoritarianism often involves a combination of two or more factors, such as: denouncing and raising awareness of the situation; building campaigns to gather local strength and/or solidarity from abroad; mobilization methods that range from demonstrations and occupations to armed resistance; and community-building and active construction of alternatives beyond/in spite of the state. A counter-strategy is not merely practical, but also requires theoretical engagement to understand the nature of what is being opposed. Thus, the social actors in opposition to authoritarianism often return to the question of whether they are facing fascism, neo-fascism, a neoliberal version of authoritarian urban practices, the deepening relationship between colonialism and modern capitalism, or the development of new techniques of control and ideological influence, among others, to evaluate and re-evaluate their own counter-strategies. They also do so by learning from similar confrontations in other places and times. In this fashion, the researchers behind this book also hope to contribute to the devising of counter-strategies, not only through awareness, but also by engaging with this learning process.

Learning from other places is important in order to build common counter-strategies that can reverberate in the region and, hopefully, lead to consolidation and continuation. The current phase of authoritarianism is not the sum of simply coincidental events, but reflect the level of sharing and collaboration between various actors, especially on the far right. The case of India is exemplary, since pillars of Hindutva can also be linked to Nazism and Italian Fascism, while today the use of social media platforms to spread hate and violence under Modi is also key to promoting disinformation and far-right ideology in other parts of the world (see Nizaruddin, this book). In the Myanmar case, digital connections offer a counterpoint. The military junta's crackdown on people's financial accounts affected fundraising strategies by the opposition. As a response, resistance groups began to seek donations through video platforms with the support of diaspora communities that also use their own access to social media platforms to denounce the dictatorship and circumvent the censorship faced by those in Myanmar (see Nwet Kay Khine, this book).

Of course, resistance to authoritarianism also runs into its own contradictions. One of these contradictions can be found in the modalities through which activism is produced by the civil initiatives that are integrated with transnational civil society networks, while these modalities are not independent from neoliberal labour relations and global power inequalities, as the case of the rights-based civil society in Turkey exemplifies (see Sözen, this book). Furthermore, opposition can be fragmented and it is expected that people will fight over different political projects as the alternative to be presented. Because of this, it is necessary to note that different levels of authoritarianism are embedded in both Right and Left forms of government. Issues around developmentalism and megaprojects help to highlight its persistence under progressive governments to secure capital accumulation, as is the case with Mexico and Argentina (see Durán Matute and Féliz, this book). This has implications for social movements and other political actors associated with these governments and helps to reveal the limits of treating elections as the main form of combatting authoritarianism. Yet, cases such as the Philippines show that there are instances where methods of radical left resistance have become stale, and parliamentary tactics have actually led to some success recently (see Viajar, this book).

Housing and land struggles should also be observed for they not only reveal continuities of authoritarianism across different regimes, but they also help to connect people over more immediate common projects where demands are made to the state, but also built in spite of it. The authoritarian facet of neoliberal urbanism in Brazil and Turkey can be compared, but the movements in each country can also learn from each other (see Can and Fanton, this book). Soweto residents would protest over housing even on election day, in South Africa, where other movements, as well as in Mozambique and Zimbabwe, have been able to organize hundreds of thousands of farmers around matters tied to land reform (see Mlotshwa and also Monjane, this book). Since demanding is not enough, movements often have to find ways to implement projects that give meaning to the struggle, such as through agroecology, which demonstrates capacity for community-building and politicization. In a way, new social dynamics arise due to the informality of certain types of resistance as forms of negotiating the tensions with and against authoritarianism from the state.

The different situations analysed in this book, from Latin America to Southeast Asia, highlight that the struggle against authoritarianism is not simply about toppling regimes, but essentially connected to world-making. Authoritarianism can become entrenched in ideologies and the regimes they inspire, but it is also a tool for advancing unjust projects and shaping mentalities in freer societies. This versatility makes authoritarianism a long-standing characteristic of political projects both on the Left and Right and, as such, the counter-strategies to it must also be versatile and focused on connecting opposition to alternative hegemonies. As argued by Rodrigo Nunes, it is not about having an ideal model that can be replicated, but understanding that collective processes, in this case ones tied to emancipatory goals, work best ecologically, that is, by "making the most of plurality" (2021, 286). Attending to the various contradictions at play is part of the task, and the chapters in this book add to a body of analysis that helps to identify the dangers of authoritarianism after, during, and before they become concrete so that this knowledge can be translated into sharper and perhaps even faster courses of action.

Reconsidering Disciplinary Boundaries and Mitigating Geographic Limitations

This book results from several conversations, workshops, and conferences between scholars and activists, including those who wrote the chapters below and many others who participated in various discussions from the birth of IRGAC to the moment of writing this introduction. Three conversations are of special relevance here. The first materialized within and between the inaugural cohort of IRGAC fellows in 2019 and only moments before the global pandemic changed the nature of in-person conversations and meetings. The second emerged from different articles and pieces in English and many other languages published on the IRGAC website, discussed in closed and open conferences, and considered with different cohorts of IRGAC fellows, including the Middle East and North Africa cluster that joined the group in April 2021. The third emerged from informal and formal conversations between the editorial committee, the programme director, and staff of IRGAC, and other units at the RLS. These conversations paved the way for a discussion of authoritarianism and different counter-strategies that draw on the lived experiences of societies and people living in the South and others moving between various localities across geographic regions. In many ways, these chapters below reflect the intended and expected theoretical and empirical messiness that accompanies open-ended discussions of authoritarianism and ways to understand new forms of such political systems across both the Global North and South. Furthermore, they also emphasize the need to reconsider and even reimagine why existing explanations of authoritarianism in, from, and within the South are neither exceptional nor satisfactorily conceptualized.

In many ways, this book is an appreciation of the complexity and expected confusion that emerges with unpacking theoretical concepts and finding real-world evidence to validate claims that speak of different struggles, whether through reflecting on the ordinary lives of individuals in extraordinary situations and taking into account why and how such authoritarian practices remain a relevant scope of study. The book is an interdisciplinary, intersectional, and multifaceted treatment of authoritarianism that moves beyond disciplinary boundaries and considerations, and one that truly challenges geographic limitations in producing knowledge on contentious issues. To this end, we will highlight three important points on methodology and sources.

First, this book brings to the fore the voices of scholars, activists, and researchers to analyse the different faces of authoritarianism in the South. While considering the importance of inviting scholars primarily to write, analyse, and reflect on different forms of authoritarianism and counter-strategies in the South, we are aware of the limits of such conversations within the academy. Hence, we sought to rectify some of the issues related to scholarly echo chambers by challenging and even pushing against the artificial boundaries between scholars and activists. While we acknowledge that these are not monolithic categories and in other words, some scholars are not activists and many activists are not scholars, we are further contesting the artificial boundaries that separate activism from the academy and vice versa by hosting conferences and panels that truly engage with different milieus outside of the strict confines of the academy. By bridging the different types of knowledge in different geographic locations, this book discusses some pressing debates that unpack authoritarianism and highlights the need for combining abstract theoretical insights and real-world evidence to provide a holistic account that pushes beyond the theory-reality divide.

Second, this book includes analytical reflections from the lived experiences and different meetings and exchanges between the contributors and many others at different events. The gist of these encounters and exchanges is focused on providing practical reflections and insights on the different manifestations of authoritarianism and the various forms of resisting such practices, whether through the creation of transnational networks or sustaining existing local coalitions that constantly seek to challenge the existing status quo. Due to the COVID-19 global pandemic, much of the writing and editing of the book happened through virtual outlets. While this approach could have limited the potential of conversations that otherwise unfold at in-person events, the editors and the contributors mitigated the distance by ensuring that workshops and conferences—whether online or later in-person—would not disrupt the quality of the contributions below and the overall labour of bringing this book to life. While the book is published in English, several contributors wrote their chapters in their native language and in some instances these were later translated into English. Importantly, the coeditors and contributors are working diligently to ensure that future editions of the book will reach a wider audience and one that transcends the English-speaking world.

Finally, this book is among the first in the broader literature on authoritarianism to exclusively bring together scholars and activists from different corners of the world. This forms an important step in bringing to the fore knowledge production from the South and giving priority to scholars to engage with each other in developing important insights beyond mainstream explanations. By centring the knowledge and experiences of scholar-activists in the South, this book is a vital contribution to the scholarly debates and serves as an invitation to make more space for knowledge production in wider academic and disciplinary publications that challenge South-North and South-South divides, geographic limitations, and disciplinary silos. Importantly, the book highlights the value of inter- and multidisciplinary approaches and methodologies. The diversity in academic training and insights did not impede a cohesive and engaging conversation throughout the book that cuts across strict disciplinary norms. While the book's framing engages with how political scientists, economists, and historians conceptualize and examine authoritarianism, the chapters below are not geared toward engaging with strict methodological and disciplinary concerns. For instance, some chapters engage with deep theoretical debates to demonstrate the rise or vivid features of authoritarianism, and others look deeper into recent struggles that show the various forms of counter-strategies and struggles in conversation with other revolutionary situations. This book is the result of scholar-activist engagement with the problem of authoritarianism, so we urge the reader to take in its academic rigour, but to also interpret it politically. There is, after all, the hope that matters of authoritarianism will one day be the concern of studies of the past, rather than analysis that also deals with the present and future, as is the case for us today.

References

Bruff, Ian, and Cemal B. Tansel (2021), *Authoritarian Neoliberalism: Philosophies, Practices, Contestations*, London: Routledge.

Clarke, M. (2018), "Global South: what does it mean and why use the term?" University of Victoria, 8 August, available at https://onlineacademiccommunity.uvic.ca/globalsouthpolitics/2018/08/08/global-south-what-does-it-mean-and-why-use-the-term/. Last accessed on 28 July 2022.

Dados, N., and R. Connell (2012), "The Global South", *Contexts*, vol. 11, no. 1, pp. 12–13.

Davis, Mike (2022), "Thanatos Triumphant", NLR Sidecar, 7 March, available at https://newleftreview.org/sidecar/posts/thanatos-triumphant. Last accessed on 28 July 2022.

Demirovic, Alex (2018), "Autoritärer Populismus als neoliberale Krisenbewältigungsstrategie", *Prokla: Zeitschrift Für Kritische Theorie*, vol. 48, no. 190, pp. 27–42.

Fernandes, Florestan (2019), *Apontamentos Sobre a "Teoria Do Autoritarismo"*, São Paulo: Expressão Popular.

Gramsci, Antonio (1977), Quaderni del Carcere, Quaderni 3, $34, Turin: Giulio Einaudi editore, pp. 311–12; (1971) Selections from the Prison Notebooks, edited and translated by Quintin Hoare and Geoffrey Nowell-Smith, London: Lawrence & Wishart.

Kothari, A., A. Salleh, A. Escobar, F. Demaria, and A. Acosta (2019), Pluriverse: A Post-Development Dictionary, New Delhi: Tulika Books.

Mahler, A. G. (2018), From the Tricontinental to the Global South: Race, Radicalism, and Transnational Solidarity, Durham, NC: Duke University Press.

Nunes, Rodrigo, Neither Vertical nor Horizontal: A Theory of Political Organization, London: Verso Books.

Schafer, J, P. Haslam, and P. Beaudet (eds.) (2017), "Meaning, Measurement, and Morality in International Development", Introduction to International Development, Don Mills: Oxford University Press.

Embedded Authoritarianism[1]
Sovereignty, Coloniality, and Democracy in Latin America

Pedro Salgado

Introduction

To engage with authoritarianism in the Global South entails more than accounting for its historical, economic, social, and geopolitical particularities. Rather, perhaps precisely in order to be able to address such particularities, it is necessary to move a step back and reassess the assumptions about government, political regimes, and the exercise of sovereign power that are embedded within the notion of authoritarianism itself. The argument presented in this chapter is that contemporary definitions of authoritarian regimes, especially those presented in relation to the Latin American context, are premised on an understanding of sovereign states that assumes (sometimes unproblematically) the liberal democracy as its standard or optimal form. I draw from the literature on international historical sociology an alternative understanding of the relation between statehood and authoritarianism.

A history of the states-system that ties the notion of modernity to the spread of liberal values and political forms misses the role played by colonial rule and imperialism in said history, as well as in liberal political theory itself. By assigning coloniality as the centrepiece of a narrative of international history, we must acknowledge that liberal values are not mutually exclusive with authoritarian practices, but simply rearrange them around a different conception of political subjectivity. In other words, the transition to a liberal order does not bring an end to authoritarian politics, which continues to be the foundation of sovereignty. The notion of the Global South itself is premised upon the coloniality of the modern world-system, understood as the contemporary legacies of colonial rule that continue to shape it. To avoid the structural reductionism that simply describes such legacies as permanent and constant features of global politics, it is important to

---

[1] I would like to thank the comradely rounds of discussion with my IRGAC colleagues for the formulation of the argument presented here, especially to Inés Durán Matute for the comments made on previous versions of this paper.

acknowledge not only the enduring role of coloniality, but also how it is upheld by specific geopolitical strategies.

One of the results of adopting such a broad historical lens is that it becomes difficult to point out a recent or current rise of authoritarian politics. At the same time, it does not imply a denial of all political changes over the past 30–40 years. Instead, it places such changes in a broader context, as a reconfiguration of how political power is organized and exercised over a longer period. Specifically, their relation with neoliberalism is brought into question, being conceived not as an outcome of a neoliberal agenda, but as co-constitutive with it. Additionally, understanding the particularities of authoritarianism in the Latin American context does not only entail uncovering the specific ways in which neoliberal reforms take place and the effects produced by them in each particular case. Instead, such particularities themselves can be grounded upon the geopolitically-differentiated notions of political subjectivities produced through colonial domination. Ultimately, by disrupting the dichotomy between liberal democracy and authoritarianism, the argument presented here traces the problem of authoritarianism back to the idea of sovereignty and sovereign states as a core element of modernity, which presents a different set of challenges.

Before those can be finally addressed, the chapters' argument is developed in two steps. First, I engage with two interpretations of authoritarianism that present it in opposition to liberal democracies. One is found in contemporary institutionalist political science (Levitsky and Ziblatt 2018; Przeworski 2019; Albright 2018), and the other draws from the Poulantzian Marxist tradition of state theory (Poulantzas 1975; 2000) in order to provide an interpretation of the current crisis (Bruff 2014; Tansel 2017). As a second step, the argument moves further back in history to establish the shift towards modern sovereignty and colonial domination as the basis for the creation of geopolitically-differentiated categories of political subjects. By bringing the subject into question, this disrupts the assumption of liberal democracy as a standard form of politics, and, more importantly, reveals the authoritarian practices upon which it is premised (Quijano 2000; Bhambra 2007; 2014; Wood 1991). This concludes with a reflection on how an analysis of authoritarianism from the perspective of coloniality has influenced the narrative of Latin American politics over the past few decades.

Authoritarianism *versus* Democracy

The conception of authoritarianism that presents it in opposition to democracy can be traced back to the earliest steps of political philosophy, where establishing the distinctions between types of states, regimes, and laws was carried out in taxonomical style. Montesquieu, for instance, grounds his anti-absolutist reasoning in

The Spirit of Laws on a characterization of despotism as a regime based on fear and obedience to the will of the ruler, and not on honour and virtue (which are traits of well-regulated monarchies and republics) (Montesquieu 1989, 21–30). This notion of despotism relying on the image of a ruler that deals with the people or citizens as a master does with his slaves is not only already present among classical thinkers, but is also associated with the 'East' or 'Asia'. While this excurse cannot address modern political philosophy in detail (see Wood 2012), it helps me establish the key argument I am presenting to the current literature on authoritarianism (one of the categories to replace despotism in political thinking throughout the centuries) and democracy. These taxonomies of governments and regimes often rely (admittedly or not) on the idea that each nation or people is imbued with a natural propension (a 'spirit', in Montesquieu's terms) towards one particular type of state. The suggestion I develop here is that 'Latin America' (and perhaps even the 'Global South' as a whole) can be placed alongside these identities associated with peoples, nations, and their political forms.

Starting with the liberal institutionalist literature, we see that democracy is described in procedural terms, and degrees of authoritarianism are identified through the measure in which particular regimes distance themselves from this model (Dahl 1998; Linz 2000; Levitsky and Way 2010). This generates the notion that building such democracies is a matter of fostering the correct kind of institutions, which can be achieved through "external democratizing pressure" and "linkage to the West" (Levitsky and Way 2010, 40–46). In the absence of these incentives and strong institutions, there is a constant danger that situations of crisis might trigger a regime change:

> When we think about democracy what we fear is the prospect that some political forces would successfully claim that the only way to remedy some already occurring disasters – economic crises, deep-rooted divisions in society, breakdown of public order – is to abandon political liberty, unite under a strong leader, and repress pluralism of opinions, in short autocracy, authoritarianism, or dictatorship, whatever one wants to call it. (Przeworski 2019, 14)

It has recently become clear that such crises might even be, to some extent, created precisely with the purpose of attacking and subverting democratic institutions. Steven Levitsky and Daniel Ziblatt (2018, 3) argue that this corrosion of democracy is not usually carried out "in spectacular fashion", with military coups and a clear and distinctive institutional rupture. More often than not, the crisis of democracy is insidious, a long and slow process carried out by elected leaders themselves in slow and "barely visible steps". This realization brings two dangers, that are admittedly linked to the reasons for the publication of their bestseller, *How Democracies Die*. First, the idea that even the most stable of Western democracies are vulnerable to being taken over by authoritarian leaders. In other words, strong democratic institutions and linkages to (or even being at the core of) the West might not be enough to ensure the stability of a (liberal) democracy. Even the United States (after Trump) and the UK (seeing UKIP's role during the Brexit campaign) not only are vulnerable to this but might as well be in the advanced stages of such a process. As Levitsky and Ziblatt admit in the book's very first paragraph (2018, 1), one never thought that the processes observed in Latin America, Asia, or the Europe of the 1930s could take place in fully-developed liberal democracies.

Second, precisely because this corrosion of democracy takes place in "barely visible steps", it is hard to build a consensus about which stage such attacks on institutions are in at any given point, or even (in some cases or stages) whether they are already under way or not, which make it harder for political actors and for institutions themselves to decide on how to respond. Since there is not the clear proclamation or institutional rupture that one would expect from the classical coup d'état, the dividing lines between democracy and authoritarianism become blurred. And while the literature has been concentrating efforts on providing guidelines for such an identification (Levitsky and Ziblatt 2018, 21; Albright 2018, 253), such guidelines themselves seem to presume the fully-functioning liberal democracy as the ideal type against which 'populist' or 'fascist' leaders and movements are identified. The fact that democracies in Latin America have seldom conformed to such standards has never led to questions about the underlying assumptions about what one expects from the state and its relation to other social actors, and the histories of such relations in a broader global and geopolitical context (Antunes de Oliveira 2020, 10).

The liberal approach to the current 'crisis of democracy' thus relies on the idea that the rise of authoritarianism entails a corruption of democratic values and institutions, and it does so without questioning the expectations placed upon democratic institutions. Questioning such expectations entails bringing these state forms into their social and geopolitical contexts. This movement is at the core of the argument made here. It moves away from an analysis of the state and state institutions in abstraction, grounding them in global networks of social power. In other words, this means moving further from political science and into the fields of historical sociology and global political economy. This move helps to bridge the analytical gap represented by the differences between the Global North and South in a way that goes beyond acknowledging the particularities of the state in the Global South.

By looking at these states and societies in an integrated manner, through a global lens, the transnational effects of imperialism and coloniality in processes of state-formation and the construction of said democratic or authoritarian 'spirits' become more evident. The effects of imperialism and colonialism in the formation of nationalist sentiments are present across the Global North and South alike. By seeing geopolitical domination as a factor that only appears on one side of the colonial divide, we erase the fundamental role it has played in processes of state-formation in the Global North. Consequently, it is also possible to demonstrate how the dividing line between authoritarianism and democracy is thinner than this liberal literature allows. First, because the ways in which liberal democracy relies on authoritarian practices for the control of its 'undesirables' echo the notion that the first few 'modern states' were, at the same time, colonial empires. Second, in drawing the connection between such early modern empires and liberal democracies through their geopolitical contexts we find a continuous reliance on the superexploitation of labour and the management of surplus populations elsewhere (Marini 1991; Bhattacharyya 2018).

Since such an argument echoes very clearly a conception of the state as part of a broader (geo)political configuration of class-based rule, it is drawn to a dialogue with the Marxist literature on the topic. But rather than trying to encompass all of Marxist state theory, my argument here merely points out that some of the recent contributions in this field also incur problems that are similar to those pointed to above. Namely, the conception of democracy and authoritarianism in mutually exclusive terms, through a study of states and societies that considers them in a kind of abstract isolation, to which international politics is added as an additional later stage in the analysis. Specifically, I am addressing here a type of structural account that establishes a connection between different stages or forms of capitalist development and their corresponding political form, while these different 'stages' of development are actually co-constitutive.[2] I am referring here especially to the literature on "authoritarian neoliberalism" (Bruff 2014; Tansel 2017). The point is not to reject the notion altogether, but to disentangle some of the theoretical premises that stand in the way of their claims that:

> As opposed to enshrining an ossified separation of liberal democracy and authoritarianism, we maintain that it is important to recognize that state responses to the economic and political crises of capitalism can—and increasingly do—assume similar forms both in formal democracies and in traditionally defined authoritarian regimes. (Tansel 2017, 11)

Identifying authoritarian neoliberalism as a "historically specific set of capitalist accumulation strategies" (Tansel 2017, 6) is in itself an important contribution to

---

2   The critique posed here is therefore aimed at the absence of an international dimension of capitalism at the core of the analysis offered by this literature. This is precisely the point raised by scholars affiliated with dependency theory and world-systems theory (Marini 1991; Sotelo Valencia 2019; Antunes de Oliveira 2019; Wallerstein 1983). I would still claim that the geopolitical dimension of strategies of accumulation is undertheorized in such accounts, but such an argument would extend beyond the limits of this paper. Still, it is important to acknowledge a literature that deals with the problem I am raising here in a different way.

recent developmental trajectories on a global scale. However, the identification of this historical specificity with a "post-2007 shift to more authoritarian forms of neoliberalism" (Bruff 2014, 120) returns to a problem of periodization that has already been pointed out by some critiques (Ryan 2018). By ascribing the increasingly authoritarian and antidemocratic tendencies of neoliberalism to the post-2007 period, one creates precisely the kind of divide that Cemal Burak Tansel aims to avoid. My contribution to this critique is to add that such a distinction is not only temporal, but it also carries a necessary geographical component. This separation between neoliberalism 'as usual' and its specifically authoritarian moment is based on Nicos Poulantzas's conception of authoritarian statism, which is clearly developed from the standpoint of advanced capitalist societies:

> I shall deal here only with the dominant (or, in more dignified language, the developed) capitalist countries, above all Europe and the United States. Of course, these changes affect every capitalist country insofar as they have their origin in the current phase of international reproduction of capitalism. But given the deepening division between dominant and dominated countries of the imperialist chain – a result of the internationalization of capitalist relations – we cannot engage in general theorization about the contemporary State covering transformations in these countries as a whole. Thus, in the zone of dominated countries, for example in Latin America, we are witnessing the emergence of *a new form of dependent State* [emphasis in original] which, itself manifested in diverse regimes, involves significant points of dissimilarity with the new form of State in the dominant countries. (Poulantzas 2000, 204)

The phenomenon of authoritarian statism (upon which Ian Bruff grounds his notion of authoritarian neoliberalism) is clearly circumscribed by Poulantzas to developed capitalist states. Whatever is taking place in the Global South (or "in the zone of dominated countries"), despite the global connections clearly established by capitalism itself, is explicitly excluded from Poulantzas's attention, because these states and societies (or "social formations", in Poulantzian terms) find themselves in different 'phases' of capitalist development. The fact that the geopolitical connections between these uneven stages of development are only considered post-hoc is precisely what turns the problem of periodization into a question of geographical separation between liberal democracies and authoritarian regimes (or "new forms of dependent state"). In other words, these analyses result in fixing authoritarian regimes in time (the past) and space (in non-Europe).

The Poulantzian framework adopted by Bruff therefore reproduces the problem identified among liberal scholars, which consists in the identification between liberal democracy and developed capitalist states. Tansel is careful to consider the international networks upon which neoliberalism has relied since the beginning (with its inherent authoritarian tendencies). However, they are simply added to the

Poulantzian state-centric framework described above, without drawing the necessary implications about how the construction of liberal democracies relies on a series of authoritarian practices both domestically and internationally. To account for the inherent coloniality of these geopolitical connections and their role in shaping authoritarianism and liberal democracies, they must be allowed to disrupt the assumptions of any clear empirical separation between the two.

Modern Sovereignty and Embedded Authoritarianism

The point is then to demonstrate that there is no such clear rupture between democracy and authoritarianism. The narrative to which I now turn establishes this distinction as a product of the modernity discourse, in which modern states are distinguished from pre-modern ones by their distinctively democratic form. In this logic, authoritarian institutions are the remains of the *ancien régime* or whatever appears as its equivalent in a particular historical experience, being, therefore, indications of an incomplete or imperfect process of modernization. Both Liberal and Marxist traditions conceive of such transition towards modernity through the notion of a 'bourgeois revolution', which has been critically reassessed in other works (Comninel 1987; Wood 1991; Teschke 2005; Salgado 2020). Rather than return to this argument here, I will start by presenting the transition towards modern state sovereignty not as a conceptual rupture with the legacies of absolutism, but as a result of the appropriation of absolutist sovereignty by a different type of ruling class with its own accumulation strategies—which consequently led to an alternative conception of political institutions and collective subjectivities.

This transition towards political modernity also presents its own problems of periodization. While usually associated with the Enlightenment and the revolutions of the late 18th century in the United States, France, and Haiti, historical sociologists point to the political changes in England in the 17th century (encompassing the English Civil War and the Glorious Revolution) as the earliest case of a change in state structures resulting from a (violent) change in the social composition of governing forces. The struggles between propertied classes against the Crown had been taking place since the beginning of that century and culminated in the transition of sovereign rights from the King to Parliament. A coalition of the country's ruling capitalist and landowning elite secured control over decisions regarding taxation, jurisdiction, use (and financing of) military power, and foreign policy. Sovereignty was then no longer the personal attribute of a ruler but was enacted by Parliament as an abstract representation of the nation and its people (Teschke 2003, 252–55).

However, even though the sovereign was of a different nature, sovereignty itself—the monopoly over the use of force, jurisdiction, taxation, and general coercion and its legitimation—did not change immediately. The different rationale behind its exercise is consolidated in the transition to the 18th century, with a clear difference between Britain and other European powers already being clear in the Treaty of Utrecht in 1713 (Teschke 2020). This created the conditions of geopolitical competition through which such transformations are adopted by other states (culminating in the revolutions in the US and France). Consequently, it makes this general shift in the exercise of sovereignty one that does not subvert the centralized and authoritarian character to which it was associated under absolutism. This is not to say that there were no decidedly anti-authoritarian alternatives raised during the period. However, these attempts to radically transform sovereignty in a popular and more horizontal direction (as was the case with the Levellers, the Jacobins, and in a sense, with Haitian revolutionaries) suffered tragic fates of differing natures. So, although the exercise of sovereignty is clearly transformed in this transition to modernity, such a transition cannot be implicitly associated with a move away from authoritarian rule.

These new practices of sovereign authority play a crucial role in the expansion of capitalism throughout the globe (Wood 2003), but their more important aspect (for the object of this chapter) is the rise of the nation as the legitimation of sovereign power. Sovereignty is still centralized (although not personified) and exercised through a body of representatives that correspond to an abstracted collective will associated with this idea of a culturally-homogenous nation (Anderson 2006; Buzan and Lawson 2015). The construction of such homogeneity draws upon a variety of context-specific elements, but one of its more general aspects is certainly the geocultural identities established through colonial domination (Dussel 1985; Quijano 2000). The coloniality of power described by Aníbal Quijano corresponds to the way in which different subjectivities are constituted by racial categories formed according to specific regimes of labour control, and to their place within colonial structures of geopolitical domination. Therefore, constructing the nation as a homogenous cultural identity implies a series of violent processes and disputes within these colonial powers themselves, but one that also takes place within a context in which a fundamental difference is created between such powers and the victims of their colonial domination throughout the world.

The colonial foundations of modernity that survive far beyond direct colonial domination (through Eurocentric conceptions of the world and racially-differentiated subjectivities, for instance) are understood as coloniality. This lens is essential for addressing any conception of the Global South, since the experience of colonial domination is the cornerstone that makes such a category possible. Precisely because the concrete colonial legacies in each case vary according to their experience of colonial domination, the notion of Global South is itself limited in terms of how exactly this common experience unites such a variety of cases. The key for maintaining such broad categories (like 'coloniality' and 'Global South') in an analytically useful way is to mobilize them not only as a set of particularities, but to give them meaning that goes beyond the empirical. The categories employed in the analysis must themselves take coloniality into account, rather than being formulated from the starting point of an abstract society with no geopolitical ties beyond itself (Bhambra 2007; 2014; Rosenberg 2016). Of course, this is not to say that coloniality is itself a structural condition from which we are able to derive logical conclusions about types of state and political organization. The geopolitical strategies employed in the exercise of such domination are varied, so that the implications for the way in which the resulting subjectivities are produced from the exercise of colonial power in each scenario must be allowed to vary accordingly. History still matters.[3]

Authoritarianism in Latin America: Colonial and Neoliberal

How to take coloniality into account in an analysis of Latin American authoritarianism? The analytical impact of coloniality is twofold. First, it highlights the fact that those changing practices of sovereignty, which in the Latin American context correspond to the long political disputes in the 19th and early 20th centuries, did not shy away from reinforcing their colonial enterprises. In the words of Miguel Centeno and Agustin Ferraro (2013, 3), the institutional transformations in this period never truly rejected "colonial ways of life". They actually became more closely integrated into capitalist networks of accumulation and became a key element in shaping the international states-system (Wood 2003; 2012; Bezerra, Salgado, and Yamato 2019).[4]

Second, the colonial lens denounces how the notion of cultural homogeneity is presented as a condition of the possibility for democracy, which legitimates the violent exclusion of alternative political subjectivities through practices of bordering and policing (Bhattacharyya 2018; Ferguson and McNally 2015). These sovereign powers are necessarily premised on authoritarian practices, as long as they are required to reinforce an idea of 'nation' through the exclusion of those who do not 'belong'. Quijano highlights the devastating effects of this form of legitimation in

---

3   I explore the contributions of historicism for the framework of coloniality proposed by the Latin American decolonial tradition in the essay "Anti-Eurocentric Historicism: Political Marxism in a Broader Context" (Salgado 2021).

4   A similar argument is presented by Florestan Fernandes (2019), as has already been highlighted by our colleague Sabrina Fernandes (2021). However, Florestan still seems to admit the possibility of a non-authoritarian sovereignty, as one of the key elements in his argument about the Brazilian bourgeois revolution is a differentiation between "classic bourgeois revolutions" and those that remain incomplete and result in an "autocratic form of bourgeois rule" (F. Fernandes 2008, 337–48; Salgado 2021, 273–74)

racially-divided societies to the point of making this form of nation-state "impossible" (Quijano 2000, 565–70), while others point out in more detail how this plays a role in the social composition of property regimes (Bhandar 2018; Smith 2008). In fact, both can be brought together through the critique of liberal democracies as regimes designed for the rule of propertied elites and capital accumulation (Wood 1991; 1995; Sitrin and Azzellini 2014). In that sense, if property rights are explicitly designed along racial lines, the exclusion of the dispossessed from politics also implies a movement towards the cultural homogeneity required by nationalism. Authoritarianism can be said to be embedded in the practice of sovereign power precisely because such exclusion has been a common aspect of statehood in the region since the formal declarations of independence in the early 19th century.

However, to simply speak of an embedded authoritarianism as a constant of Latin American states is dangerously close to an essentializing transhistorical view of the region. By bringing coloniality in, it is somewhat tempting to leave all the explanatory power to this concept, which results in that notion of 1492 as the eternal present which the entire region is condemned to repeat endlessly. It was pointed out earlier that bringing such a broad historical perspective makes it harder to speak of a recent 'authoritarian turn'. To avoid such reductionism, it is necessary to encompass the ways in which the exercise of such authoritarianism changes across time, along with the practices of sovereign power.

In a closer dialogue with Tansel and Bruff, even if one does not entirely agree with the characterization of "neoliberal authoritarianism" proposed by them, the influence of neoliberalism over the region during the past 30 or 40 years cannot be neglected. But it also cannot be conceived as an authoritarian era which follows the 'pink tide', through a resurgence of the far right. Even if neoliberalism as a whole is framed as an authoritarian project, it cannot be said to have brought authoritarianism back (as it never left). The neoliberal project in Latin America coincides in many cases with violent military dictatorships (Chile being the main example) and continued throughout the 1990s with the region's redemocratization (Collor and Cardoso in Brazil, Menem and De la Rúa in Argentina, Fujimori in Peru, et al.). The difference between its dictatorial and democratic versions cannot be described through the absence or presence of authoritarianism. Instead, it must be understood as a change in how the authoritarian exclusion of subaltern (dispossessed, racialized) subjects from institutionalized politics operates.[5]

The most important implication for this argument is perhaps that all progressive governments in the regions associated with the pink tide also relied upon these

---

5   For a more detailed discussion on different manifestations of colonial legacies in development projects from neoliberal to progressive governments in Latin America, see the chapter by Inés Durán Matute and Mariano Féliz in this volume.

authoritarian practices to some extent. This becomes clear when addressing the issues raised by the critiques of a neo-extractivist model of development in Bolivia (McKay 2020) or how Brazil under Partido dos Trabalhadores (PT) governments carried out extensive infrastructural projects with huge environmental implications (the Belo Monte dam being the most notorious among them) under the banner of modernization and progress. In many cases throughout the region, armed forces were mobilized by left-wing governments against urban and rural protests. The political situation deteriorated especially after the commodity crises in the 2010s resulted in austerity politics being mobilized, with variations from case to case, by these left-wing governments. The situation is aptly described by Jeffery Webber (2017): "the last day of oppression, and the first day of the same".

These regimes still mobilized the state apparatus to isolate key elements of political decision-making from democratic scrutiny, exacerbating the exclusion of subaltern subjects from institutionalized politics. Despite the reduction of poverty, the "new Latin American left did not challenge the underlying class structures of its societies or the systems of capitalist accumulation that fundamentally reproduce the basic patterns of simultaneous wealth and poverty, of luxury among misery" (Webber 2017, 104–5). There were many important achievements in this period. The point is made here not as a denial of their relevance, but as a discussion about the inherent limitations presented by how they rely on violence against peasants and native populations, or by imposing strict limits around what is or is not subjected to democratic oversight. The existing attempts of improving and enhancing direct participation through social assemblies and popular consultation were designed in ways that can be abandoned before reverting to the more traditional decision-making structures of the state or that can be disciplined and controlled by the ruling social forces. This form of including subaltern populations through invitations from the sovereign effectively conditions their political participation to the 'domestication' of their radical transformative projects in the name of order precisely because, otherwise, it can be easily reversed. This remains clear by how easily the important achievements of the period were erased by the subsequent political growth of the Right in the region through a series of elections and coups. This is therefore not a return to a previous state of authoritarianism, but a continuation of the exclusion of subaltern subjects through the mobilization of sovereign power against its subjects in innovative (and sometimes more explicit) ways.

Conclusion: Towards Decolonial Democracies?

By assuming a spatiotemporal distinction between democratic and authoritarian countries—that corresponds to the West/non-West, developed/underdeveloped countries, or Global North/South—we accept the underlying assumption that authoritarianism is somehow connected to an incomplete or failed transition towards modernity. It is important to return to the discussion about the origins of sovereign power, encompassing both its absolutist roots and its ties to colonial domination as a geopolitical aspect. This centres the notion of sovereignty on the exercise of territorial authority and the production of different political subjectivities that are tied to the idea of nation (and exclusion from it) as a means of legitimating sovereignty. In doing so, it becomes clear how this modern conception of democracy is insufficient to move away from authoritarianism, as the latter remains a constitutive part of modern sovereignty. It remains possible to imagine democratic forms of political organization by addressing their challenges and recovering alternative (including pre-modern) conceptions of democracy and politics. In any case, the challenge entails imagining alternatives to the current conception of sovereign power, by rethinking the use of 'nation' as a basis for its claim of legitimacy (García Linera 2014; Öcalan 2016), and/or by challenging the notion of sovereignty itself in favour of establishing a popular alternative (Bookchin 2015; Rancière 2014).

We have been accustomed to thinking of capitalism and the exploitation of workers as one of the core challenges to the establishment of egalitarian societies, and the roles of racism, sexism, and other forms of structural violence as instrumental in creating conditions for such exploitation. Any conception of democracy that aims to destabilize such modern/colonial structures of exclusion, inequality, and exploitation must also be able to destabilize our current understanding of sovereignty. Of course, this challenge presents many potential ramifications such as questions about alternative forms of subjectivity, the role of the nation, and the possibility of global politics beyond (or even without) the existence of sovereign statehood. But all of these can only be addressed once sovereign power is no longer seen as part of the solution but is instead acknowledged as a form of political organization which cannot be separated from its authoritarian origins and practices.

References

Albright, Madeleine (2018), *Fascism: A Warning*, New York: Harper Collins.
Anderson, Benedict (2006), *Imagined Communities: Reflections on the Origin and Spread of Nationalism*, Kindle edition, London: Verso.
Antunes de Oliveira, Felipe (2019), "Development for Whom? Beyond the Developed/Underdeveloped Dichotomy", *Journal of International Relations and Development*, vol. 23, no. 4, pp. 924–46, available at https://doi.org/10.1057/s41268-019-00173-9. Last accessed on 22 June 2022.

Antunes de Oliveira, Felipe (2020), "Democracy in the Prison of Political Science", *International Political Science Review*, pp. 1–14, available at https://doi.org/10.1177/0192512120932435. Last accessed on 22 June 2022.

Bezerra, Gustavo A. de G., Pedro Salgado, and Roberto V. Yamato (2019), "Escravismo Atlântico No Século XIX: A Construção Do 'Internacional' No Mar", *Monções*, vol. 8, no. 15, pp. 424–57.

Bhambra, Gurminder (2007), *Rethinking Modernity: Postcolonialism and the Sociological Imagination*, Basingstoke: Palgrave Macmillan.

Bhambra, Gurminder (2014), *Connected Sociologies*, Kindle edition, London: Bloomsbury Academic.

Bhandar, Brenna (2018), *Colonial Lives of Property: Law, Land, and Racial Regimes of Ownership*, Durham; London: Duke University Press.

Bhattacharyya, Gargi (2018), *Rethinking Racial Capitalism: Questions of Reproduction and Survival*, Kindle edition, London; New York: Rowman & Littlefield.

Bookchin, Murray (2015), *The Next Revolution: Popular Assemblies and the Promise of Direct Democracy*, edited by Debbie Bookchin and Blair Taylor, Kindle edition, London: Verso.

Bruff, Ian (2014), "The Rise of Authoritarian Neoliberalism", *Rethinking Marxism*, vol. 26, no. 1, pp. 113–29.

Buzan, Barry, and George Lawson (2015), *The Global Transformation: History, Modernity and the Making of International Relations*, Cambridge: Cambridge University Press.

Centeno, Miguel, and Agustin Ferraro (2013), *State and Nation Making in Latin America and Spain*, Kindle edition, Cambridge: Cambridge University Press.

Comninel, George C. (1987), *Rethinking the French Revolution: Marxism and the Revisionist Challenge*, London; New York: Verso.

Dahl, Robert A. (1998), *On Democracy*, New Haven; London: Yale University Press.

Dussel, Enrique (1985), *Philosophy of Liberation*, translated by Aquilina Martinez and Christine Morkovsky, New York: Orbis Books.

Fernandes, Florestan (2008), *A Revolução Burguesa no Brasil: Ensaio de Interpretação Sociológica*, Rio de Janeiro: Editora Globo.

Fernandes, Florestan (2019), *Apontamentos sobre a "Teoria do Autoritarismo"*, São Paulo: Expressão Popular.

Fernandes, Sabrina (2021), "Florestan Fernandes: Explaining Authoritarianism Beyond the Fascist Experience", *IRGAC*, available at https://www.irgac.org/2021/1064/. Last accessed on 22 June 2022.

Ferguson, Susan, and David McNally (2015), "Precarious Migrants: Gender, Race and the Social Reproduction of a Global Working Class", *Socialist Register*, vol. 51, pp. 1–23.

García Linera, Álvaro (2014), *Plebeian Power: Collective Action and Indigenous, Working-Class and Popular Identities in Bolivia*, Leiden; Boston: Brill.

Levitsky, Steven, and Lucan A. Way (2010), *Competitive Authoritarianism: Hybrid Regimes after the Cold War*, Cambridge: Cambridge University Press.

Levitsky, Steven, and Daniel Ziblatt (2018), *How Democracies Die*, Kindle edition, New York: Broadway Books.

Linz, Juan J. (2000), *Totalitarian and Authoritarian Regimes*, Boulder: Lynne Rienner Publishers.

Marini, Ruy Mauro (1991), *Dialéctica de La Dependencia*, 11th edition, Mexico City: Ediciones Era.

McKay, Ben (2020), "Food sovereignty and neo-extractivism: limits and possibilities of an alternative development model", *Globalizations*, vol. 17, no. 8, pp. 1386–1404.

Montesquieu (1989), *The Spirit of the Laws*, edited by Anne M. Cohler, Basia C. Miller, and Harold S. Stone, Cambridge: Cambridge University Press.

Öcalan, Abdullah (2016), *Democratic Nation*, Cologne: International Initiative Freedom for Abdullah Öcalan, available at http://ocalan-books.com/#/book/democratic-nation. Last accessed on 22 June 2022.

Poulantzas, Nicos (1975), *Political Power and Social Classes*, London: Verso.

Poulantzas, Nicos (2000), *State, Power, Socialism*, London: Verso.

Przeworski, Adam (2019), *Crises of Democracy*, Cambridge: Cambridge University Press.

Quijano, Aníbal (2000), "Coloniality of Power, Eurocentrism, and Latin America", *Nepantla: Views from South*, vol. 1, no. 3, pp. 533–80.

Rancière, Jacques (2014), *Hatred of Democracy*, London: Verso.

Rosenberg, Justin (2016), "Uneven and Combined Development: 'The International' in Theory and History", *Historical Sociology and World History: Uneven and Combined Development over the Longue Durée*, edited by Alexander Anievas and Kamran Matin, London; New York: Rowman & Littlefield, pp. 17–30.

Ryan, Matthew (2018), "Interrogating 'Authoritarian Neoliberalism': The Problem of Periodization", *Competition and Change*, vol. 23, no. 2, pp. 116–37, available at https://doi.org/10.1177/1024529418797867. Last accessed on 22 June 2022.

Salgado, Pedro (2020), "The Transition Debate in Brazilian History: The Bourgeois Paradigm and Its Critique", *Journal of Agrarian Change*, vol. 21, no. 2, available at https://doi.org/10.1111/joac.12394. Last accessed on 22 June 2022.

Salgado, Pedro (2021), "Anti-Eurocentric Historicism: Political Marxism in a Broader Context", *Historical Materialism*, vol. 29, no. 3, pp. 199–223.

Sitrin, Marina, and Dario Azzellini (2014), *They Can't Represent Us! Reinventing Democracy from Greece to Occupy*, London: Verso.

Smith, Roberto (2008), *Propriedade Da Terra & Transição: Estudo Da Formação Da Propriedade Privada Da Terra e Transição Para o Capitalismo No Brasil*, 2nd edition, São Paulo: Editora Brasiliense.

Sotelo Valencia, Adrián (2019), *Subimperialismo e Dependência Na América Latina: O Pensamento de Ruy Mauro Marini*, São Paulo: Expressão Popular.

Tansel, Cemal Burak, ed. (2017), *States of Discipline: Authoritarian Neoliberalism and the Contested Reproduction of Capitalist Order*, London; New York: Rowman & Littlefield.

Teschke, Benno (2003), *The Myth of 1648: Class, Geopolitics, and the Making of Modern International Relations*, London: Verso.

Teschke, Benno (2005), "Bourgeois Revolution, State Formation and the Absence of the International", *Historical Materialism*, vol. 13, no. 2, pp. 3–26.

Teschke, Benno (2020), "The Social Origins of 18th Century British Grand Strategy: A Historical Sociology of the Peace of Utrecht", *The 1713 Peace of Utrecht and Its Enduring Effects*, edited by Alfred H.A. Soons, 120–55. Leiden; Boston: Brill.

Wallerstein, Immanuel (1983), *Historical Capitalism*, London: Verso.

Webber, Jeffrey (2017), *The Last Day of Oppression, and the First Day of the Same: The Politics and Economics of the New Latin American Left*, Kindle edition, Chicago: Haymarket Books.

Wood, Ellen Meiksins (1991), *The Pristine Culture of Capitalism: A Historical Essay on Old Regimes and Modern States*, London: Verso.

Wood, Ellen Meiksins (1995), *Democracy against Capitalism: Renewing Historical Materialism*, Cambridge: Cambridge University Press.

Wood, Ellen Meiksins (2003), *Empire of Capital*, London: Verso.

Wood, Ellen Meiksins (2012), *Liberty and Property: A Social History of Western Political Thought from Renaissance to Enlightenment*, London: Verso.

Hindu Majoritarianism and Authoritarian Shifts in the Age of Informational Capitalism in India

Fathima Nizaruddin

Introduction

The ascendency of Hindu majoritarianism in India, under the authoritarian leadership of Prime Minister Narendra Modi, coincides with a particular moment in the history of informational capitalism in the country. The term informational capitalism refers to the shift from industrial capitalism to conditions of production and accumulation that increasingly rely on datafication, platformization, and algorithmic ways of extracting profit (Cohen 2019). While it would be simplistic to attribute the emergence of a competitive authoritarian regime in India (Manor 2021) to the shifts caused by informational capitalism, to understand the manner in which they strengthen Hindu majoritarian subject formations that enabled and continues to sustain the current regime under Modi, such shifts need to be mapped. This chapter will argue that the term *bhakt* (devotee), which in contemporary India is often employed to characterize ardent supporters of Modi and Hindu majoritarianism, can be used to understand such subject formations.[1] What role do social media platforms and the broader configurations of informational capitalism play in enabling the production of bhakts? How does a Hindu majoritarian ecosystem of hate that uses misinformation, extreme speech (Udupa and Pohjonen), and violence, utilize digital platforms in the process of this production? How do these attempts strengthen the current authoritarian turn in India and what could the future implications of this authoritarian turn be? I will argue that it is possible to attempt to answer these questions by acknowledging the role of the process of circulation in producing meaning and subject positions. The following sections of this chapter will expand on this argument by relying on Sara Ahmed's (2014) contention that various affects, including hate, manifest in the process of circulation. Linking this argument with the broader history of Hindu majoritarianism in India will help us to understand the transformation of the circulatory networks of this form of

---

1 The term *bhakt* which can be translated as 'devotee' has different connotations. In this chapter, I am referring to its use within discussions on Hindu majoritarianism in India.

majoritarianism with the arrival of informational capitalism and the significance of such transformation in the enabling of authoritarianism. The conceptualization around circulation that this chapter deploys is part of an effort to map the changes caused by informational capitalism in specific contexts, as part of a larger trajectory of links between communication practices and socio-political processes. As other scholars have argued, the 'online' is formed by political and historical experiences that are also always 'offline' (Banaji and Buckingham 2013). Therefore, in order to ascertain how digital platforms and the broader terrain of informational capitalism contributed to the emergence of an authoritarian regime in India, there is a need to first understand the role of Hindu majoritarianism and its ecosystem of hate in enabling this regime.

Situating the Role of Hindu Majoritarianism within the Authoritarian Turn in India

The Hindutva ideology, which came into being in colonial India, holds together a diverse set of actors who contribute to the consolidation of Hindu majoritarianism in contemporary India. This right-wing ideology has significant links with Italian Fascism and Nazism (Leidig 2020). It situates Hindus as those who regard India as their 'holy land' on account of them being the followers of religions which originated in India: this logic places Muslims and Christians in the country as outgroups. Definitions of Hindutva range from formulations that treat it as a political ideology that is exclusivist (Kanungo 2016) to arguments that link it with ethnonationalism (Zia 2020) or political religion (Frykenberg 2008). This chapter relies on a framework that approaches Hindutva as a variant of right-wing extremism (Leidig 2020). While Hindu religious tropes remain central within Hindutva mobilizations, rather than any theological commitment to religion, these tropes have more to do with efforts to form an ethnonationalist "Hindutva based Hindu identity" (Nizaruddin 2020) which locates the Brahmanical upper caste way of life as the only permissible way of being in India (Basu 2021). There are scholars (Aloysius 1994) who argue that the Hindutva mobilizations and the practices around them are part of an effort by the powerful minority of upper castes to narrate a majoritarian 'Hindu' identity that aims to restrict struggles against the severe caste-based inequalities and divisions within what is perceived as the Hindu community. In these mobilizations, Muslims emerge as the chief outgroups; the history of the partition of colonial India into Hindu and Muslim majority nation states and the colossal tragedy of violent riots around this partition play an important role in this framing of Muslims as outgroups.[2]

---

2   Hindutva groups participated in these violent riots, see: Leidig 2020 and Gupta 2007.

The Sangh Parivar or Sangh family of organizations have been the most significant proponents of the Hindutva ideology in independent India; Rashtriya Swayamsevak Sangh (RSS), the key organization within this 'family' has several parallels and historical links with Italian Fascism.[3] Bharatiya Janata Party (BJP) which currently holds an absolute majority in the lower house of the Indian parliament is the electoral face of Sangh Parivar. It can be argued that the current electoral success of BJP is a result of a careful consolidation of a so-called Hindu vote bank with the help of a Hindutva ecosystem of hate that targets Muslims. This consolidation has a long history and it was only in the 1990s that a Hindu majoritarian party—in this case the BJP—gained enough votes to emerge as the single largest party in the election and formed the central government.[4] Circulations from the Hindutva ecosystem of hate that constantly reiterate the distinctions between Hindus and Muslims were integral to the rise of BJP. Along with misinformation, hate speech and extreme speech, violence is also a central part of these circulations. These circulations and the ease of mobility that they have under the Modi government, can be used to differentiate the current authoritarian situation in India from the earlier 'emergency period' when civil liberties were suspended.[5] Scholars like Balmurli Natrajan have argued that Hindutva politics is "inherently authoritarian since it makes continual demands on citizenry backed by threats and punitive actions" (Natrajan 2022, 304). The current situation in India, where the space for opposing the Hindutva politics is very limited, points to the validity of this argument (Banaji 2018). So, it is not surprising that, under a Hindutva leader like Modi who enjoys an electoral mandate that no other BJP prime minister has seen before, India is witnessing an authoritarian shift. This shift is also characterized by the emergence of a Hindu majoritarian state that locates Muslims as the chief outgroups in the country (Gudavarthy 2019). The subject position of the Hindutva and/or Modi bhakt that emerges from the sites of engagements around the Hindutva ecosystem of hate in contemporary India, plays an important role in this majoritarian turn and its authoritarian manifestations. In the next section, I will delineate some of the key features of this ecosystem of

---

3   The term Sangh Parivar is used to denote the 'family' of Hindutva organizations that are at the centre of Hindu majoritarian politics in contemporary India. RSS, the central organization within this family, can be characterized as a "Hindu nationalist paramilitary organization", see: Roy 2021. The constituents of this 'family' range from the trade union Bharatiya Mazdoor Sangh (BMS) to Vishwa Hindu Parishad (VHP) or the World Hindu Council. VHP played a major role in the mobilizations in the 1980s and 1990s that led to the demolition of the mosque Babri Masjid, see: Leidig 2020.
4   This was a coalition government.
5   The official 'emergency' period in India during the 1970s, when democratic rights were suspended, was declared by the-then Prime Minister Indira Gandhi, who belonged to the Congress party which is perceived as a centrist party in the Indian context.

hate and track its transformation under the conditions provided by the ascent of informational capitalism when social media and online platforms emerged as important players in defining the contours of the communication landscape in India.

Consolidation of the Hindutva Ecosystem of Hate

Hate has been a central affect within Hindutva mobilizations since the colonial times. The locus of Hindutva politics lies in the definition of the Muslim as the 'enemy' (Natrajan 2022) and the carving out of a Hindu majority in opposition to this 'enemy'. Within the scheme of this politics, as Gyan Prakash points out, the project is not to create a theocratic Hindu state but to "expunge the minorities altogether from national life" (Prakash 2007, 178). So, circulation of various narratives of hate and violence that target Muslims who are defined as the principal outgroups have been an integral part of this project. Some of the central themes of these narratives include accounts about a mythical 'Hindu past' before the arrival of Muslim rulers (Karner 2005), the 'danger' of a 'Muslim take over' of contemporary India through the 'population growth' of Muslims and conversions (Singh 2021), the 'dangerous virility' of Muslim men which is perceived as a threat to Hindu women (Tyagi and Sen 2020), and the positioning of Muslims as the killers of the cow, which is considered as a sacred animal by a large section of Hindus (Mukherjee 2020). After India's independence, the territorial dispute between India and Pakistan over the region of Kashmir, as well as the alleged loyalty of Indian Muslims towards the 'enemy state' of Pakistan, and discourses that link Muslims with terrorism have been important motifs within the Hindutva ecosystem of hate (Prakash 2007; Omar 2021). Most of these narratives have their roots in existing schisms and mistrust between communities in a very diverse country which has witnessed a colossal scale of violence between Hindus and Muslims during the partition of colonial India into the nation states of India and Pakistan. The actors within the Hindutva ecosystem of hate, which in independent India consists mainly of those with varying amounts of affiliations to the Sangh Parivar group of organizations, have consistently worked to deepen such existing divisions and mistrust (Brass 2003). Circulatory networks that used various forms of communication including print, video, audio-cassettes, processions, marches, speeches, as well as embodied travel, political mobilizations, and violence were crucial for this ecosystem of hate (Nizaruddin 2020). The strong grassroots presence of Rashtriya Swayamsevak Sangh (RSS), the central organization that is at the heart of the Sangh Parivar group of organizations, has played an important role in sustaining and expanding these circulatory networks. RSS aims to situate India as a Hindu *rashtra* or nation (RSS undated; Nizaruddin 2022).[6]

The most important mobilization leading to the current expansion of the Hindutva ecosystem of hate was the Ram Janmabhoomi agitation. This agitation, aimed at demolishing the 16th century mosque Babri Masjid in order to build a temple to the Hindu god Ram, was spearheaded by the Sangh Parivar group of organizations.[7] By using the trope of *yatra* which in the South Asian context signifies pilgrimage or journey, these organizations were able to transform the lifeworld of the nation by forming various interactive sites that allowed the circulation of hate that targeted Muslims, portraying them as so-called aggressors. The rath yatra (chariot journey) undertaken by BJP leader L. K. Advani, in a van that was fashioned as a chariot in 1990, was a key part of the mobilization that transformed BJP's electoral chances by deepening the existing fault lines between Hindu and Muslim communities.[8] This form of embodied travel across various states of India was a public performance that expanded the circulatory networks of the Hindutva ecosystem of hate by allowing the flow of narratives, media forms, and bodies that targeted the so-called Muslim 'other'. The wave of riots across India in the 1990s, that took place around the Ram Janmabhoomi agitation and the circuit of the rath yatra in which many people were killed, substantiates the argument that Sangh Parivar groups use violence as a form of communication (Banaji 2018).

So, in the early 1990s or even the late 1980s, before the logic of informational capitalism began to have a significant impact on everyday interactions in India, an information order was already in place that allowed Hindutva groups and especially BJP and other Sangh Parivar organizations to create a framework within which even those who opposed these groups articulated their viewpoints (Panikkar 1993; Basu 2021). In other words, even such oppositional articulations used the framework of the Hindu-Muslim divide that the Hindutva groups relied on to consolidate the Hindu majority in their favour. We need to analyse the post-2014 expansion of the Hindutva ecosystem of hate and the role of informational capitalism in this expansion against this background.

---

6 The organization conducts around 57,185 daily meetings in 36,729 places (RSS undated).
7 The claim was that the mosque was built in the exact birthplace of the Hindu God Ram. The mosque was demolished by agitators mobilized by Sangh Parivar in 1992.
8 For a detailed analysis of the significance of yatra in Indian politics and the many yatras mobilized by Sangh Parivar including the ones undertaken by Advani, see: Jaffrelot, 2009.

Transformation of the Hindutva Ecosystem of Hate under Informational Capitalism and a Majoritarian State

The use of online platforms by actors within the Hindutva ecosystem of hate was widespread before 2014. The term 'internet Hindus' was used by journalists and scholars to signify actors who targeted secular liberals and anyone they framed as the enemies of Hindus and/or Muslim sympathizers (Mohan 2015). In terms of political parties, BJP has consistently been more advanced than others at using online media in the process of building a support base in their favour. However, there was a noticeable expansion of this use of online media as well as the Hindutva ecosystem of hate under Modi's reign. As Shweta Desai and Amarnath Amarasingam point out, events in the daily news cycle became a locus from which to spread anti-Muslim hatred (Desai and Amarasingam 2020). One of the most important examples of this was the circulation of the narrative of 'CoronaJihad' during the first phase of the COVID-19 lockdown in India. During this period, an incident of a COVID-19 outbreak in a Muslim organization's mosque and headquarters became the focal point around which to build a narrative of CoronaJihad, which accused Muslims of waging a war against the country by spreading the COVID-19 virus. Along with Hindutva actors on social media platforms, a section of the mainstream media, as well as BJP leaders and those associated with the Hindutva ecosystem of hate, contributed to a rapid circulation of this narrative across the country which led to the boycott of Muslim vendors in some areas (Nizaruddin 2021). While the circulations of hate that targeted Muslims around the narrative of CoronaJihad received widespread attention internationally, this was just one instance within a continuum of such targeting under the rule of Modi. In fact, hate has become a central affect within the nation's lifeworld and anything ranging from an advertisement that shows a Hindu woman with her Muslim mother-in-law (Kapur and Mohsina 2020) to the attack on an Indian military convey in the disputed territory of Kashmir could become the focal point for such circulations of hate (Desai and Amarasingam 2020).

What specifically is the role of informational capitalism in bringing about this scenario? With the arrival of digital platforms, the operations within the Hindutva ecosystem of hate have changed significantly. It is possible to locate such changes by using the lens of remediation. The term remediation signifies the way in which old and new media forms influence each other; when a new media form arrives, an older media often transforms itself rather than becoming extinct (Bolter 2007). The newer media form can also draw from the existing tropes of older media forms. In the case of circulatory processes within the Hindutva ecosystem of hate, they have undergone considerable transformation because of the widespread availability of smartphones in India after 2013 (Banaji et al. 2019). Circulation of misinformation and spectrums of extreme speech, including what can be classified as hate speech, has been a central activity within this ecosystem of hate. With the arrival of platforms like WhatsApp and Facebook, such platforms have become key sites for these circulations. The use of these and other digital platforms by Hindutva groups needs to be situated within the context of the existing misinformation ecology in contemporary India.

In popular parlance in India, the term 'WhatsApp University' is used to denote the avalanche of misinformation that circulates through WhatsApp, the most popular mobile instant messaging platform in India which has over 400 million users (Roy 2018). For example, it is possible to enquire jokingly to a friend or a colleague who gives a new piece of misinformation whether they learnt it from WhatsApp University. While it is certainly true that content flows across diverse digital platforms in the current conditions of informational capitalism, the popularity as well as particular affordances of WhatsApp make it a significant platform within the misinformation ecology in India. The circulations of the so-called WhatsApp University in India are very varied and they are not limited to Hindutva circulations. However, actors from the Hindutva ecosystem of hate contribute to a significant portion of such circulations (Sharma 2020). Though WhatsApp is an important platform for the circulation of misinformation and extreme speech for Hindutva groups, actors from such groups have a considerable presence in several other digital platforms as well (Mohan 2015). In fact, the digital capacities of the Hindutva ecosystem of hate are so formidable that they can be compared to a distribution engine that works with precision (Sundaram 2020). The precision of this distribution engine has certainly increased the circulatory capacities of the Hindutva ecosystem of hate.

A brief outline of some of the key actors who contribute to such capacities can help to create understanding about how this ecosystem of hate has transformed under the conditions provided by the arrival of informational capitalism. Currently, such actors can be divided into the following categories: (1) a section of BJP workers and leaders; (2) actors belonging to the various Sangh Parivar organizations including RSS; (3) fringe Hindutva groups who may or may not have links with the Sangh Parivar group of organizations including BJP; (4) Hindutva sympathizers; (5) Hindutva 'entrepreneurs' (Udupa 2018); (6) paid trolls with links to the BJP Information Technology wing (Chaturvedi 2016); (7) corporate or IT firms who are alleged to have been involved in the spread of misinformation to consolidate a Hindu vote bank in favour of BJP; (8) cyber troops (Campbell-Smith and Bradshaw 2019); (9) aspiring and established 'hate stars' (Sundaram 2020); (10) small content producers who can be hired by anyone who aspires to be an influencer including those who aspire to be Hindutva hate stars (Nizaruddin 2021); and (11) online Hindutva platforms such as OpIndia (Kritika 2020).⁹

The first four categories have traditionally been active within the Hindutva ecosystem of hate. Their use of online platforms can be situated as an extension or even remediation of their already existing activities. The later categories have emerged within the landscape provided by informational capitalism. The rise of hate stars needs to be placed in the context of the emergence of the majoritarian state as well. In contemporary India, the targeting of Muslims through acts of hate speech or violence is an easy way to become prominent within the ranks of Hindutva groups and sympathizers. Arjun Appadurai (2019) has termed this syndrome aspirational hatred. For aspiring as well as established hate stars, online media is an important means to build a support base and popularity. Some of these hate stars or groups affiliated with them also participate in acts of violence, they often film and circulate recordings of such acts of violence through digital platforms (Mukherjee 2020).

Violence has been an important component of the Hindutva circulations since the colonial era. With the emergence of a majoritarian state under Modi, this violence has escalated and the ability of perpetrators to act with impunity has increased. The lynching of Muslim men across several states in India, especially in the context of so-called 'cow protection', is an example of this. So-called cow protection groups target Muslims and Dalits who are accused of transporting cows for slaughter. In fact, in the context of the lynchings of Muslim men including the ones around cow protection, scholars have argued that Muslim men have become the *homo sacer* in India, meaning it is possible to attack, perpetrate hate crimes, or even kill them without serious legal consequences (Ahmad and van der Veer 2022). Certain social media platforms, especially WhatsApp, are used to co-ordinate acts of violence that target Muslims (Nizaruddin 2022).

The digital distribution engine of Hindutva groups and the broader Hindutva ecosystem of hate provide sites of engagement that contribute to the production of the subject position of the bhakt, that is integral to the functioning of the authoritarian regime of Modi. As mentioned earlier, the term bhakt, which can be translated as devotee, describes a category of blind supporters of Modi and the Hindutva narratives. Nisha Mathew has argued that under Modi, India is transforming into a bhakt nation. Mathew suggests that this transformation draws on certain aspects of the traditions of 'bhakti' devotionalism in medieval South Asia (Mathew 2021). In the case of this emerging bhakt nation, "followers are redefining their identities around Modi as their guru, leader and 'deity'" (ibid., 5). Within the configurations of Hindutva, bhakts are not a uniform category and they can

---

9   This is not an exhaustive categorization. More empirical work is needed to expand these categories.

range from upper middle-class people residing in gated communities in cities to underemployed lower middle-class youth for whom forwarding Hindutva WhatsApp messages is a way to earn extra money (Mukherjee 2020). They play a major role in circulating Hindutva narratives across various platforms. The ubiquity of these narratives in the lifeworld of the country works performatively to solidify the perceived consensus around the authoritarian trend under Modi.

The ubiquitous iterations from the Hindutva ecosystem of hate limit the scope of permissible articulations in India. Those who oppose the authoritarian measures of the government are termed anti-nationals or Muslim sympathizers. Within online spaces, those who attempt to articulate such opposition face severe backlash, ranging from trolling to deplatforming. The lacunae in moderation practices that are created by the working practices of information capitalism (Cohen 2019) help to configure such a backlash. For example, within these moderation processes, the labour of the users is crucial. The digital distribution engine of Hindutva groups, who are able to use the labour of a critical mass of users, finds it easier to target those who are perceived as the so-called enemies of the nation.[10] This limiting of permissible articulations is also achieved through the use of the state's law and order apparatus, as well as vigilante violence perpetrated by Hindutva groups. For example, those who oppose the Modi regime, ranging from academics and activists to ordinary people, can find themselves at the receiving end of violence or legal action that results in imprisonment (Goyal 2021). Altogether, as mentioned earlier, the limiting of iterations that oppose the logic of Hindutva and the proliferation of narratives from the Hindutva ecosystem of hate, translates into a perceived consensus in favour of authoritarian transformations under Modi within the lifeworld in India.[11] Against the framework of this argument that links the expansion of the Hindutva ecosystem of hate with current authoritarianism in India, it will be useful to delineate some of the specific socio-political processes that facilitate this expansion under the conditions provided by informational capitalism. In this context, Sara Ahmed's proposition becomes relevant that, like other affects, hate is also "an effect of the circulation between objects and signs" (Ahmed 2014, 45). This proposition about the affective economy of hate contends that "hate is economic, and it does not reside positively in a sign or body" (Ahmed 2014, 59). So, if hate manifests itself in circulation, then in the Indian context, conditions for such circulation have

---

10   Here Farman's argument becomes important, regarding how—with the increased popularity of digital networks and especially smartphones—the embodied spaces that we inhabit are produced by material as well as virtual means, see: Farman 2012.
11   Protest movements ranging from the ones against the discriminatory citizenship amendment act (Kaur and Dyuti 2020) to the farmers' movement in India continue to create fissures within this perceived consensus.

increased manifold since 2014. The following section will outline the entanglements of informational capitalism with these conditions for circulation.

Situating the Conditions for Circulation of Hate in Contemporary India

Julie Cohen's argument that "communicative spaces produced by platform-based, massively intermediated information infrastructures are not neutral spaces" can be used to understand how the current trajectory of informational capitalism contributes to the ease of circulation of Hindutva hate that targets the Muslim minority in India (Cohen 2019, 107). These communicative spaces that are optimized for engendering "cascade based diffusion, polarization and relativization" privilege crowd-based judgements in pursuit of greater profits, and in turn open up the possibility of creating powerful mobs (Cohen 2019, 88). In the Indian context, such communicative spaces enhance the circulatory capacities of the Hindutva ecosystem of hate. Several participants within this ecosystem were capable of forming polarized crowds through various means and it made the remediation of such capacities in the communication spaces created by informational capitalism an easy task for them. As I have mentioned earlier, even before the advent of digital platforms, circulations from this ecosystem were able to reach ubiquity, as the case of the mobilizations that led to the demolition of Babri Masjid show. However, the arrival of informational capitalism certainly increased the speed of such circulations. This increase could be situated in the context of the enhancement of the network-making power (Castells 2009) of Hindutva groups in a media landscape that saw major transformations under the sway of informational capitalism.

Globally, individual nation states are seen as key stakeholders in controlling the ease of circulation of hateful content within communicative spaces created by digital platforms (Nizaruddin 2022). However, the example of India demonstrates that such assumptions become irrelevant in a majoritarian state, where the ruling party has a stake in maintaining a polarized environment to consolidate a vote base of majority voters by situating a specific minority as dangerous. In such situations, digital platforms can become vital for the circulation of hate that targets such minorities. Many technology companies make statements about their intention to contain circulations that target minorities (Fung 2020). However, the current mode of functioning of informational capitalism where technology companies are able to function without any real accountability (Suzor 2019) means that companies can continue to make such statements without any matching structural changes. Companies also often align themselves with the interests of authoritarian rulers to ensure ease of operation in various countries (Cohen 2019). In the case of India, the exit of India's Facebook policy chief Ankhi Das over a controversy about favouritism towards the ruling party (Horwitz and Purnell 2020) shows the existence of such aligning of interests. So, under the present mode of functioning of informational capitalism, the emergence of a majoritarian state can seriously enhance the circulatory capacities of actors who target minorities. In the case of India, hate could even be situated as a tool of Hindutva governmentality. This in turn makes those who oppose the government a target of such hate and they get positioned as Muslim appeasers. Thus, one of the main permissible positions available to avoid being targeted becomes that of the bhakt or devotee. As I have argued before, this seriously undermines democratic modes of functioning and contributes to an authoritarian turn.

Conclusion

The manner in which the Hindutva groups in India were able to use the conditions produced by informational capitalism to configure an authoritarian transformation in the country shows the need to confront the current logic of operation of this informational capitalism. While several socio-political factors contributed to an authoritarian transformation in India, the production of the subject position of the citizen as bhakt is integral to building a consensus around this transformation. The circulations produced by the Hindutva ecosystem of hate aim at consolidating such a subject position. The current logic of operation of informational capitalism has certainly contributed to the precision of the digital distribution engine of this ecosystem. Any reversal from the present scenario to a more democratic mode of governance will require a reordering of the current circulatory regime in the country. This will require a serious engagement with strategies that can challenge the current workings of informational capitalism that have contributed to this circulatory regime.

References

Ahmad, Irfan, and Peter van der Veer (2022), "Muslim Bare Life in Contemporary India", *The Nation Form in the Global Age: Ethnographic Perspectives*, edited by Irfan Ahmad and Jie Kang, Cham: Springer International Publishing, pp. 127–52, available at https://doi.org/10.1007/978-3-030-85580-2_5. Last accessed on 7 June 2022.

Ahmed, Sara (2014), *The Cultural Politics of Emotion*, Edinburgh: Edinburgh University Press, 2nd Edition.

Aloysius, G. (1994), "Trajectory of Hindutva", *Economic and Political Weekly*, vol. 29, no. 24, pp. 1450–52.

Appadurai, Arjun (2019), "A Syndrome of Aspirational Hatred Is Pervading India", *The Wire*, 10 December 2019, available at https://m.thewire.in/article/politics/unnao-citizenship-bill-violence-india. Last accessed on 7 June 2022.

Bagchi, Suvojit (2019), "Number of Shakhas Has Doubled in 10 Years: RSS Leader", *The Hindu*, 15 August 2019, available at https://www.thehindu.com/news/national/number-of-shakhas-has-doubled-in-10-years-rss-leader/article29096977.ece. Last accessed on 7 June 2022.

Banaji, Shakuntala (2018), "Vigilante Publics: Orientalism, Modernity and Hindutva Fascism in India", *Javnost – The Public*, vol. 25, no. 4, pp. 333–50, available at https://doi.org/10.1080/13183222.2018.1463349. Last accessed on 7 June 2022.

Banaji, Shakuntala, Ram Bhat, Anushi Agarwal, Nihal Passanha, and Mukti Sadhana Pravin (2019), "WhatsApp Vigilantes: An Exploration of Citizen Reception and Circulation of WhatsApp Misinformation Linked to Mob Violence in India", *LSE*, 11 November 2019, available at https://blogs.lse.ac.uk/medialse/2019/11/11/whatsapp-vigilantes-an-exploration-of-citizen-reception-and-circulation-of-whatsapp-misinformation-linked-to-mob-violence-in-india/. Last accessed on 7 June 2022.

Banaji, Shakuntala, and David Buckingham (2013), *The Civic Web: Young People, the Internet and Civic Participation*, Cambridge, MA; London: MIT Press.

Basu, Anustup (2021), "Hindutva 2.0 as Information Ecology", *Spaces of Religion in Urban South Asia*, edited by István Keul, London; New York: Routledge.

Bolter, Jay David (2007), "Remediation and the Language of New Media", *Northern Lights: Film & Media Studies Yearbook*, vol. 5, no. 1, pp. 25–37, available at https://doi.org/10.1386/nl.5.1.25_1. Last accessed on 7 June 2022.

Brass, Paul R. (2003), *The Production of Hindu-Muslim Violence in Contemporary India*, New Delhi: Oxford University Press.

Campbell-Smith, Ualan and Samantha Bradshaw (2019), "Global Cyber Troops Country Profile: India", *Oxford Internet Institute, University of Oxford*, available at https://demtech.oii.ox.ac.uk/wp-content/uploads/sites/93/2019/05/India-Profile.pdf. Last accessed on 7 June 2022.

Castells, Manuel (2009), *Communication Power*, Oxford: Oxford University Press.

Chatterji, Angana P, Thomas Blom Hansen, and Christophe Jaffrelot (2019), "Introduction", *Majoritarian State: How Hindu Nationalism Is Changing India*, edited by Angana P Chatterji, Thomas Blom Hansen, and Christophe Jaffrelot. New York: Oxford University Press.

Chaturvedi, Swati (2016), *I Am a Troll: Inside the Secret World of the BJP's Digital Army*, New Delhi: Juggernaut Books.

Cohen, Julie E. (2019), *Between Truth and Power: The Legal Constructions of Informational Capitalism*, Oxford: Oxford University Press.

Desai, Shweta, and Amarnath Amarasingam (2020), "#CoronaJihad: COVID-19, Misinformation, and Anti-Muslim Violence in India", *Stong Cities Network*, available at https://strongcitiesnetwork.org/en/wp-content/uploads/sites/5/2020/06/CoronaJihad.pdf. Last accessed on 7 June 2022.

Farman, Jason (2012), *Mobile Interface Theory: Embodied Space and Locative Media*, New York: Routledge.

Frykenberg, Robert E. (2008), "Hindutva as a Political Religion: An Historical Perspective", *The Sacred in Twentieth-Century Politics: Essays in Honour of Professor Stanley G. Payne*, edited by Roger Griffin, Robert Mallett, and John Tortorice, London: Palgrave Macmillan UK, pp. 178–220, available at https://doi.org/10.1057/9780230241633_10. Last accessed on 7 June 2022.

Fung, Brian (2020), "Facebook Will Label More Controversial Content and Tighten Advertising Policies – CNN", *CNN Business*, 26 June 2020, available at https://edition.cnn.com/2020/06/26/tech/facebook-zuckerberg-content-ad-policies/index.html. Last accessed on 7 June 2022.

Kritika (2020), "OpIndia Loses Ads after UK-Based 'Stop Funding Hate' Campaign", *TheQuint*, 29 May 2020, available at https://www.thequint.com/news/webqoof/opindia-loses-ads-after-uk-based-stop-funding-hate-campaign. Last accessed on 7 June 2022.

Goyal, P. (2021), "Bhima Koregaon case: Three years of legal and rights violations", *Newslaundry*, 2 January, available at https://www.newslaundry.com/2021/01/02/bhima-koregaon-case-three-years-of-legal-and-rights-violations. Last accessed on 4 July 2022.

Gudavarthy, Ajay (2019), *India after Modi: Populism and the Right*, New Delhi: Bloomsbury India.

Gupta, Dipankar (2007), "Citizens versus People: The Politics of Majoritarianism and Marginalization in Democratic India*", *Sociology of Religion*, vol. 68, no. 1, pp. 27–44, available at https://doi.org/10.1093/socrel/68.1.27. Last accessed on 7 June 2022.

Horwitz, Jeff, and Newley Purnell (2020), "Facebook Executive Supported India's Modi, Disparaged Opposition in Internal Messages", *The Wall Street Journal*, 30 August, available at https://www.wsj.com/articles/facebook-executive-supported-indias-modi-disparaged-opposition-in-internal-messages-11598809348. Last accessed on 4 July 2022.

Jaffrelot, Christophe (2009), "The Hindu Nationalist Reinterpretation of Pilgrimage in India: The Limits of Yatra Politics", *Nations and Nationalism*, vol. 15, no. 1, pp. 1–19, available at https://doi.org/10.1111/j.1469-8129.2009.00364.x. Last accessed on 7 June 2022.

Kanungo, Pralay (2016), "Public Hinduism and Hindutva", *Hinduism in the Modern World*, edited by Brian A Hatcher, New York; London: Routledge.

Kapur, Roshini, and Nazneen Mohsina (2020), "India: Trolls from a Hindu Nationalist Fringe with a Majority Complex", *The Interpreter*, 16 November, available at https://www.lowyinstitute.org/the-interpreter/india-trolls-hindu-nationalist-fringe-majority-complex. Last accessed on 7 June 2022.

Karner, Christian (2005), "Writing Hindutva History, Constructing Nationalist Religion", *Writing History, Constructing Religion*, pp. 205–26, Hampshire: Ashgate Publishing.

Kaur, R., and A. Dyuti (2020), Reclaiming the sublime: The (un)making of the people's constitution in India, *HAU: Journal of Ethnographic Theory*, vol. 10, no. 3, pp. 716–25, available at https://doi.org/10.1086/712220. Last accessed on 4 July 2022.

Leidig, Eviane (2020), "Hindutva as a Variant of Right-Wing Extremism", *Patterns of Prejudice*, pp. 1–23, available at https://doi.org/10.1080/0031322X.2020.1759861. Last accessed on 7 June 2022.

Manor, James (2021), "A New, Fundamentally Different Political Order: The Emergence and Future Prospects of 'Competitive Authoritarianism' in India", *Economic and Political Weekly*, vol. 56, no. 10, available at https://www.epw.in/engage/article/new-fundamentally-different-political-order. Last accessed on 7 June 2022.

Mathew, Nisha (2021), "Bhakt Nation: The Return of the Hindu Diaspora in Modi's India", *History and Anthropology*, vol. 0, no. 0, pp. 1–18, available at https://doi.org/10.1080/02757206.2021.1946049. Last accessed on 7 June 2022.

Mohan, Sriram (2015), "Locating the 'Internet Hindu': Political Speech and Performance in Indian Cyberspace", *Television & New Media*, vol. 16, no. 4, pp. 339–45, available at https://doi.org/10.1177/1527476415575491. Last accessed on 7 June 2022.

Mohsina, Nazneen (2020), "Hindutva Vigilantism: Online Hate, Offline Harms", *Global Network on Extremism & Technology*, 22 October, available at https://gnet-research.org/2020/10/22/hindutva-vigilantism-online-hate-offline-harms/. Last accessed on 7 June 2022.

Mukherjee, Rahul (2020), "Mobile Witnessing on WhatsApp: Vigilante Virality and the Anatomy of Mob Lynching", *South Asian Popular Culture*, vol. 18, no. 1, pp. 79–101, available at https://doi.org/10.1080/14746689.2020.1736810. Last accessed on 7 June 2022.

Natrajan, Balmurli (2022), "Racialization and Ethnicization: Hindutva Hegemony and Caste", *Ethnic and Racial Studies*. vol. 45, no. 2, pp. 298–318, available at https://doi.org/10.1080/01419870.2021.1951318. Last accessed on 7 June 2022.

Nizaruddin, Fathima (2020) "Resisting the Configurations for a Hindu Nation", *HAU: Journal of Ethnographic Theory*, vol. 10, no. 3, available at https://doi.org/10.1086/711891. Last accessed on 7 June 2022.

Nizaruddin, Fathima (2021), "Role of Public WhatsApp Groups Within the Hindutva Ecosystem of Hate and Narratives of 'CoronaJihad'", *International Journal of Communication*, vol. 15, no. 0, p. 18.

Nizaruddin, Fathima (2022), "Institutionalised Riot Networks in India and Mobile Instant Messaging Platforms", *Asiascape: Digital Asia*, 9 (1-2).

Omar, Mohammad (2021), "The Muslim 'Threat' In Right Wing Narratives: A Critical Discourse Analysis", *SOAS South Asia Institute Working Paper Series 2021*, London: SOAS.

Panikkar, K. N. (1993), "Religious Symbols and Political Mobilization: The Agitation for a Mandir at Ayodhya", *Social Scientist*, vol. 21, no. 7/8, pp. 63–78, available at https://doi.org/10.2307/3520346. Last accessed on 7 June 2022.

Prakash, Gyan (2007), "Secular Nationalism, Hindutva, and the Minority", *The Crisis of Secularism in India*, Durham, NC: Duke University Press, pp. 177–88, available at https://doi.org/10.1515/9780822388418-011.

Roy, Sandip (2018), "WhatsApp—India's Leading University", *The Hindu*, 7 July 2018, available at https://www.thehindu.com/society/whatsapp-indias-leading-university/article24358591.ece. Last accessed on 7 June 2022.

Roy, Srirupa (2021), "Target Politics: Digital and Data Technologies and Election Campaigns-A View from India", *Media and the Constitution of the Political South Asia and Beyond*, edited by Ravi Vasudevan, pp. 595–659, Delhi: SAGE Publications, available at https://spectrum.sagepub.in/book/media-and-the-constitution-of-the-political-ravi-vasudevan-9789354790768/14?fbclid=IwAR0CaLSOkiYU2WRU4Oah8cnyrNB2l-UEpoLTV8oa2W_8hFxOS9VJJEjzwHc. Last accessed on 7 June 2022.

RSS (undated), "Basic FAQ on RSS", *Rashtriya Swayamsevak Sangh*, available at https://www.rss.org/Encyc/2017/6/3/basic-faq-on-rss-eng.html. Last accessed on 7 June 2022.

Sharma, Betwa (2020), "CAA: RWA Whatsapp Groups Are Filling Up With Pro-Govt. Hate Again", *HuffPost India*, 1 January, available at https://www.huffingtonpost.in/entry/caa-whatsapp-messages-targeting-muslims_in_5eob07fae4b0843d360b745c. Last accessed on 7 June 2022.

Singh, Rahul (2021), "Deflating the Bogey of a Rapidly Growing Muslim Population", *The Tribune*, 31 October, available at https://www.tribuneindia.com/news/comment/deflating-the-bogey-of-a-rapidly-growing-muslim-population-332190. Last accessed on 7 June 2022.

Sundaram, Ravi (2020), "Hindu Nationalism's Crisis Machine", *HAU: Journal of Ethnographic Theory*, vol. 10, no. 3, pp. 734–41, available at https://doi.org/10.1086/712222. Last accessed on 7 June 2022.

Suzor, Nicolas P. (2019), *Lawless: The Secret Rules That Govern Our Digital Lives*, Cambridge; New York: Cambridge University Press.

Tyagi, Aastha, and Atreyee Sen (2020), "Love-Jihad (Muslim Sexual Seduction) and Ched-Chad (Sexual Harassment): Hindu Nationalist Discourses and the Ideal/Deviant Urban Citizen in India", *Gender, Place & Culture*, vol. 27, no. 1, pp. 104–25, available at https://doi.org/10.1080/0966369X.2018.1557602. Last accessed on 7 June 2022.

Udupa, Sahana (2018), "Enterprise Hindutva and Social Media in Urban India", *Contemporary South Asia*, vol. 26, no. 4, pp. 453–67, available at https://doi.org/10.1080/09584935.2018.1545007. Last accessed on 7 June 2022.

Udupa, Sahana, and Matti Pohjonen (2019), "Extreme Speech and Global Digital Cultures—Introduction", *International Journal of Communication*, vol. 13, no. 0, pp. 3049–67.

Zia, Ather (2020), "The Haunting Specter of Hindu Ethnonationalist-Neocolonial Development in the Indian Occupied Kashmir", *Development*, vol. 63, no. 1, pp. 60–66, available at https://doi.org/10.1057/s41301-020-00234-4. Last accessed on 4 July 2022.

Right-Wing Authoritarianism Against Nature
The Latin American Context

Sabrina Fernandes

The most recent wave of authoritarian right-wing governments in the 21st century has led to a series of setbacks in quality of life, civil liberties, and human rights. The Donald Trump government was marked by white supremacist discourse, climate denialism, and threats of war. In India, Narendra Modi pits the country against the Muslim population. In Latin America, the return of the far-right after a period of progressive governments known as the 'pink tide' is marked by conservatism and neoliberal reforms. Whereas the United States and Bolivia have moved on from these far-right authoritarian governments, the reality of authoritarianism remains to different degrees in Latin America. In Brazil, Jair Bolsonaro promotes guns and deforestation under a nationalist Christian motto: "Brazil above everything, God above everyone". In Chile, the prospects of a new constitution and a progressive government offer hope in a historical context of privatized water and the repression of social movements. Iván Duque's Colombia is marked by the assassination of community leaders and struggles in territories that are under pressure from extractivism; thus, Gustavo Petro and Francia Márquez face an arduous journey as the country's first leftist government.

The authoritarian aspects of these governments require thoughtful examination and not all of them could be classified easily under the term fascism. In fact, current scholarship struggles to find appropriate terminology that would aid in drawing comparisons and identifying particular phenomena. We speak of the far right, the alt-right, the fascists, neofascists, and proto-fascists (Traverso 2019 and Webber 2020). Overt authoritarianism, however, seems to be a common trend throughout these categories, though it is not much simpler to define. What is also noteworthy is how these authoritarian experiences do not only affect human society, but also affect other species and the natural environment as a whole. Climate change and the ecological crises associated with this age—often named the Anthropocene—constitute an environment of heightened conflict over territory, raw materials, and the primacy of the capitalist market that refuses to acknowledge the imminent danger of social and natural collapse.

There is important literature that helps to identify and analyse the relationship between the authoritarian right and the destruction of nature (Malm and the Zetkin Collective 2021; Forchtner 2020). Although, given the sheer dimensions of the subject and the different dynamics involved, more research is required, especially from the perspective of the Global South and the different dynamics of destruction and spoliation in the periphery of capitalism. For instance, 21st century ecofascism and its anti-immigrant politics is more perceptible and widespread in the Global North, especially in the way it frames particular people as victims (Thomas and Gosink 2021, 42), but its likelihood of occurring in the Global South depends on adapting values and practices to dependence on aggressive extractivism and the dispossession of local communities.

Drawing from Latin American examples, but with support from literature focused on the United States and Europe, this chapter offers a brief theoretical primer for understanding the various forms of authoritarianism against nature popular among right-wing forces in the context of the Global South. It begins by establishing the relationship of nature to capitalism—and how it varies according to global inequalities—in order to show how authoritarianism, particularly right-wing authoritarianism, is an important element of the destruction of nature and oppression of peoples in the Global South for the sake of capital accumulation. Capitalist pressure and other forms of domination, such as racism, xenophobia, neocolonialism, and conservatism, walk hand in hand with authoritarianism. Once we add centuries of extractivism, colonialism, dependent capitalism, and underdevelopment, a special set of characteristics that constitute the phenomenon of authoritarianism against nature in Latin America and the Global South more generally arises.

Nature under Capitalism

One primary characteristic of capitalism is its perception of nature as a body of resources, free to be utilized as raw materials for the upkeep of basic necessities and the production of commodities. Although there are costs associated with labour and machinery for the extraction of raw materials from nature, these materials do not cost anything themselves as no exchange-value is attributed to them at the point of extraction. Karl Marx explains in Volume III of *Capital* that the value of nature's production is not acknowledged within the capitalist system and, therefore, natural elements enter capitalist production as "free gifts" (Marx 1981; Burkett 1999, 92). This allows capitalism to appropriate nature's production as its own and cheapens the cost of the commodity cycle. While this is the general approach, it is also true that, in practice, capitalists profit by cheapening nature in other ways, such as in the industrial production of meat, which involves both the appropriation of animals' bodies and the employment of very cheap and precarious human labour (Patel and Moore 2017, 4).

Today, a capitalist corporation may have to pay royalties and concession rights to the state to be able to exploit mineral resources, water, wood, and oil. It could, on the other hand, purchase land once and, for a fixed initial price, exploit natural resources until depletion. There is also the matter of direct dispossession and the stealing of land, through practices of territorial enclosure, invasion or, in some cases, free state-sanctioned exploitation of resources in public or Indigenous territory. Whether a price is paid or not, the principal act of the appropriation of nature is still free as costs are not transferred to nature but to a third party that grants rights or holds rights over a territory. Fauna, flora, and inorganic parts of nature are utilized and reduced to their role as resources so they can be exploited and upkept for further exploitation or human enjoyment—which can also be a commodified activity. This reduction to resources is part of the appropriation process and also important for artificially detaching human society from the rest of nature (Clark and Foster 2010). A key aspect of capitalist modernity is its treatment of humans as separate from nature, as its tamers or overlords (Dussel 1985, 114).

When ecological concerns are divorced from an interpretation of the capitalist appropriation of nature, more common negative impacts of production are normalized as natural outcomes that cannot be prevented: an iron ore mine, for example, is expected to leave a trail of pollution. Environmental racism plays a role as it enmeshes already politically marginalized peoples in a system of environmental degradation that treats their communities and territories as sacrifice zones (Lerner 2012, 312; Herculano 2008). The system of appropriation of nature is designed to normalize everyday impacts in sacrifice zones, including through legal devices, and it is only required to be accountable when it comes to major events of ecocide and human rights abuse. Since major events are treated as exceptions and/or accidents, they can be approached from the economic perspective of externalities, fines, and compensations that do not actually change the structure of natural exploitation, let alone interrupt it in favour of an alternative system of production of goods and services.

The current system of industrial extractivism, wherein materials are extracted on a large scale with little regard for socioecological impact, operates precisely this way. Capitalism's growing demand for raw materials makes it appear as if environmental impacts are a normal occurrence and cannot be prevented, or only prevented in the most extreme exceptions. Martin Arboleda explains that Chilean towns impacted by mining "tend to be intensive on energy, logistics, and mining infrastructure, they are usually burdened by high levels of air, water, and noise pollution, a feature that dramatically impacts public health and the quality of life more generally" (Arboleda 2020, chapter 3). The social and environmental costs are the price that is paid in the name of development, although the unequal exchange of these resources and reproduction of precarious working and living conditions in the Global South often means that the costs in Latin America are borne for the benefit of European, North American and, more recently, Chinese markets. Even the advancement of technology geared towards renewables and climate transition can mean more exploitation in the Global South, since the race for so-called green minerals tends to expand previous sacrifice zones but now, under the discourse that these activities serve the greater good of transition (Zografos and Robbins 2020, 543; Pérez 2021). This is referred to as 'eco-extractivism' (Núñez et al. 2019). Then, whenever one speaks of alternatives in a post-extractivist scenario, it sounds as if it is impossible to supply such materials without sacrificing entire ecosystems and communities.

Horacio Machado Aráoz refers to extractivism as a system of "modern colonial mining" (Machado Aráoz 2018, 21). Little about right-wing authoritarianism in Latin America can be understood without looking at the patterns of mining exchange between the region and the rest of the world. If we consider ecological exchange as a whole—including here aggressive agribusiness and its monocrops and the connection between transnational capital and territorial control—the picture of capitalist dependence coupled with violence and the dispossession by Latin American states of their own people becomes even clearer. Colonial expansion over the past centuries also included biological expansion, and the way landscapes were merged, altered, and destroyed and species were rearranged or made extinct comprises a phenomenon understood by Alfred Crosby as ecological imperialism (Foster and Clark 2004; Crosby 1986). With the advancement of capitalism, the need to analyse the perception and usage of nature as highly political also became a matter of survival. The relationship of production between humans and nature that was mediated by necessity in most places expands through trade, systemic exploitation, and a growing appetite for resources. In fact, nature is reduced to sectors of resource extraction and human enjoyment. Whereas dependence on nature is acknowledged for matters of production, the limits of this dependence are not.

Enrique Dussel argues that a political interpretation of nature happens all the time and is informed by contrasts such as those between the periphery and the centre of capitalism, the different social classes, the various political systems, and how a particular mode of production treats and interacts with nature (Dussel 2011). The capitalist system has transformed nature and its systems so deeply that collapse has become a daily phenomenon. However, this collapse is not uniform. Since the periphery of the system is more affected as sacrifice zones and through patterns of ecological imperialism, to understand the relationship between capital and nature in the Global South requires a particular political interpretation of nature itself. If impacts are unequal and the economic rationale is also based on an 'international division of natural exploitation', we must also examine how authoritarian practices that involve environmental destruction and attacks on communities and their territories at the periphery of capitalism differ from what happens at the core. Whereas the capitalist system causes a metabolic rift with nature on a global scale, the ways in which it operates in the Global South favour a normalization of authoritarian practices and regimes in order to secure the stream of profits that flows from the margins to the centre.

The Global South's Metabolic Rift

It is important to note that to speak of how capitalism severs the link between humans and nature is to speak of social metabolism and the metabolic rift caused by capitalist production (Foster and Holleman 2014). The sociometabolic perspective entails the understanding of human society as part of and dependent on nature—possibly interdependent too when we consider human creation and regeneration, such as through Indigenous co-creation of the Amazon rainforest over thousands of years. We can speak of humans *and* nature and humans *in* nature, while combatting the capitalist hierarchy that forces humans *out of* nature in a pattern of total crisis.[1]

István Mészáros spoke of sociometabolism directly when referring to the material conditions of production and reproduction. In his book *Beyond Capital*, he argued the following about capitalism's relationship to nature:

> It is in the nature of capital that it cannot recognize any measure by which it could be restrained, no matter how weighty the encountered obstacles might be in their material implications, and no matter how urgent—even to the point of extreme emergency—with regard to their time scale. For the very notion of 'restraint' is synonymous with *crisis* in the conceptual framework of the capital system. Neither the degradation of nature nor the pain of social devastation carries any meaning at all for its system of social metabolic control when set against the absolute imperative of self-reproduction on an ever-extended scale. This is why in the course of historical development capital not simply *happened* to fatefully overreach itself on every plane—even in its relationship to the basic conditions of social metabolic reproduction—but sooner or later was *bound* to do so. (Mészáros 1995, 173)

More specifically, the discussion and concept of the metabolic rift is important for the context of authoritarianism against nature because it is often the sociometabolism of sacrifice zones that is interrupted with the help of authoritarian forces. These sacrifice zones exist everywhere, as one can see from the state violence perpetrated against the Wet'suwet'en nation that resists the laying of

---

1   For a defence of the metabolic rift theory and how the language of humans and nature does not make it necessarily dualistic, please see Malm 2018.

a pipeline in their territory in British Columbia (Dhillon and Parrish 2019). The colonial nature of the Canadian state affects marginalized peoples domestically, who are supposed to bear the damage done in their territory for the sake of fossil capital, while it also supports the advancement of Canadian multinationals so involved in extractivism in Latin America that in almost every place there is a potential sacrifice zone. Todd Gordon and Jeffrey Webber show that "in Latin America and the Caribbean, Canada was the largest investor nation in the [mining] sector, and four countries—Australia, Canada, the United Kingdom and the United States—accounted for 74 percent of mergers and acquisitions from 2000 to 2015" (Gordon and Webber 2019, 8). The pattern of unequal ecological exchange does not prevent the creation of sacrifice zones in the North, but surely contributes to their normalization and ubiquity in the South.

The theory of the metabolic rift proposes that a system powered by constant accumulation, namely the capitalist system today, leads to an irreparable rift between humans and nature due to the pressure placed on nature's metabolism by society's demands. Resources are extracted without care for the integrity of nature's metabolism and, as a consequence, human society is impacted too. A metabolic rift may occur in the transfer of nutrients from one area to another, as in Karl Marx's original analysis in Volume III of *Capital*, or it can amount to a global phenomenon that, under the tools of ecological imperialism, involves "environmental degradation and ecologically unequal exchange" (Clark and Foster 2009, 317). When taking international trade into account, the unequal ecological exchange becomes visible alongside negative trade balances, with countries at the periphery unable to really afford imports even after many years of excess exports (Hornborg and Martinez-Alier 2016, 331). When Brazil and Argentina rely heavily on the export of primary goods, they reinforce the unequal movement of such goods from the periphery to core countries (Dorninger and Eisenmenger 2016).

Unequal ecological exchange takes place via the exploitation of materials and destruction of biomes in one place for the benefit of another place, usually better positioned in regard to both capitalist and geopolitical power. Globally, this is extended through ecological imperialism, as a subset of imperial power that includes but is not limited to:

> the pillage of the resources of some countries by others and the transformation of whole ecosystems upon which states and nations depend; massive movements of population and labour that are interconnected with the extraction and transfer of resources; the exploitation of ecological vulnerabilities of societies to promote imperialist control; the dumping of ecological wastes in ways that widen the chasm between centre and periphery; and overall, the creation of a global 'metabolic rift' that characterizes the relation of capitalism to the environment, and at the same time limits capitalist development. (Foster and Clark 2004, 187)

Where the metabolic rift is an integral part of the local economy and deeply embedded in trade patterns that match economic and unequal ecological exchange, a set of vulnerabilities to authoritarianism develops. Much can be justified, legalized, or hidden when a country's fate and development is said to depend on it. In addition, the structure of dependent capitalism in the Global South means that national elites organize themselves in autocratic ways that already disregard principles of liberal democracy in order to reproduce the economic conditions that favour this class (F. Fernandes 2019), primarily by keeping labour cheap and nature cheaper or free. As such, a place need not be governed by extreme forms of authoritarianism to lead to constant environmental degradation and the destruction of life-sustaining systems that are also interconnected with race, class, gender, and other structures of oppression. Rather, a degree of authoritarianism is enmeshed in daily life, benefitting the continuation of the system of exploitation. In the early 2000s, this meant the heavy repression of demonstrators against the privatization of water in Bolivia, whereas in Brazil, the advancement of agribusiness has come at the expense of campesino, Quilombola, and Indigenous communities. In fact, although this text analyses right-wing authoritarianism, it is worth highlighting that the economic structure in the Global South also means that even progressive governments tend to engage with authoritarian practices in order to secure extractive and development projects with their partners (Svampa 2019, 1).

Latin America's Authoritarian Rifts

Under capitalism, Florestan Fernandes explains, the "authoritarian element is intrinsically a structural and dynamic component of preservation, strengthening and expansion of the 'capitalist democratic system'" (F. Fernandes 2019, 45). The system needs authoritarian practices in order to maximize profits and production, allowing for the super-exploitation of labour, repression against opponents and unwanted groups, and the continuous robbery of nature. Thus, it is a matter of whether this authoritarianism is practiced in particular spheres, local, and/or global, or becomes the dominant expression of the regime. Since countries in the Global South are subject to dynamics of colonialism and capitalist dependence that maintain levels of instability and underdevelopment, authoritarianism not only functions as a more common expression of everyday politics, but is also entrenched in imperialist relations and interventions that range from coups that establish dictatorships to dealings in favour of the extractive industries that risk the survival of entire communities.

These relations show that authoritarianism is established from both the inside of a nation and also from the outside. The United States has been involved in a series of war incursions and special forces interventions abroad connected to fossil fuels, including in Latin America. Scholars offer many examples of this, such as how, throughout the years, the CIA helped to train paramilitary forces involved in territorial conflict in Colombia, oil companies lobbied for further US military presence in the region (Scott 2004, 100), and "special warfare manuals" even advocated for the "harsh treatment of civilians" (Stokes 2005, 60). Doug Stokes argues that authoritarian states were seen as partners that could further US interests in Latin America, adding to a broader scenario that Michael Watts refers to as petroimperialism (Stokes 2005, 58; Watts 1999, 7). Ecological imperialism has a natural affinity with authoritarianism because it speeds up processes of resource extraction while "hindrances" such as community resistance and territorial protections can be easily suppressed.

The mainstream discussions about authoritarianism often frame it as deviations from liberal democracy (F. Fernandes 2019). This perspective tends to equate fascism and communism, while it holds liberal democracy as the highest standard, hiding its limitations, like the defence of capitalism and the necessary domination it exercises to exploit peoples and nature. In practice, liberal democracy leaves the door open for fascism according to convenience, especially when there is a crisis. For Stuart Hall, this means a swing to the Right as a way to respond to the crisis, while social democracy renders the Left too disorganized to respond (Hall 1979, 16). In the case of Brazil, liberal parties and groups chose to support Jair Bolsonaro's campaign, aware of the threat of authoritarianism, in opposition to the return of the Workers' Party (PT) and its attempts to couple progressive social policies with actions that favour the Brazilian capitalist class. The parliamentarian coup against the Dilma Rousseff government is a good example of how it is possible to defend liberal democracy and use its devices to oust a legitimate president legally, but with false charges, in order to replace her with a more authoritarian leader with a clear project of austerity.

Since different regimes and different governments may produce different combinations and layers of authoritarianism, three elements must be highlighted: (1) under authoritarianism, power is exercised through coercion, or the threat of coercion, and consent is used to legitimize and maintain coercion; (2) capitalism is prone to authoritarian tools and actions, but authoritarianism is the entrenchment of these tools as a way of governing; (3) this power is exercised to maintain hierarchies and exclude the oppressed from the possibility of popular power.

Authoritarianism against nature acts against peoples and the environment, maintaining the metabolic rift in particular territories for the sake of resource extraction, land grabbing, and territorial control, and to be able to negatively impact ecosystems without much external pressure and regulation. Thus, it entails very racist, gendered, and xenophobic authoritarian acts of expulsion of peoples and repression of dissenting groups. Since authoritarianism against nature ensures patterns of unequal economic and ecological exchange for the benefit of capital circulation, it goes hand in hand with imperialist interests and tends to strengthen nationalism and borders in some places while it weakens self-determination claims and sovereignty in others.

The dispossession of Indigenous peoples and the appropriation of their territories comprise one of the clearest examples of authoritarianism against nature, including both environmental destruction and violence against human communities, that continues to take place in liberal democracies and is normalized because of capitalist appetite for land and raw materials. Colonization entails violence against Indigenous communities in order to access territory but also to sever the link between community and territory that historically conditions a more balanced relationship with the natural environment (Crook, Short, and South 2018). Land grabbing and forced urbanization also aid capital by adding to the labour force and its reserve army. Genocide against Indigenous and traditional communities goes hand in hand with ecocide. Alongside patriarchy, racism, and ethnic violence, these tactics fit into a particular perspective of development concerned with economic growth (Malheiro, Porto-Gonçalves, and Michelotti 2021).

Because of this, the task of understanding authoritarianism against nature must consider at least three political regimes: (1) authoritarian far-right expressions, mainly in fascism and its ecofascist correlative, (2) authoritarian practices under liberal democratic regimes that involve both right-wing and progressive/moderate left-wing governments, and (3) socialist Left engagement with authoritarianism—both historical and by governments that propose a socialist transition today.

This paper is concerned with the right-wing expressions under (1) and (2), and it must be stressed that a direct interest in the upkeep and deepening of the capitalist system and repression of anticapitalist ideas and practices falls within the political spectrum of the Right. This spectrum ranges from a moderate Right that generally accepts liberal democracy and its negotiation with capital to overt far-right authoritarianism that combines attacks on people's rights with a strong capitalist orientation. Centre-left and progressive groups under (2) help to maintain capitalism as well and may oppose direct anticapitalist action, but in this case, are not about the furthering of capitalism, but rather projects of conciliation and/or reformism that restrain the search for alternatives within the system. This perspective of conciliation is connected to the centre-left's general acceptance of the terms of liberal democracy—primarily the legitimacy of private property and the capitalist market—and its maintenance of capitalist infrastructures. It shows, for example, the limits of moderate Left experiences in Latin America under the pink tide governments, when the advancement of social rights was negotiated alongside capitalist growth and the strengthening of particular sections of each country's elites (Webber and Carr 2013; S. Fernandes 2019).

For the Right, these conciliations imply profit reduction, regulation, and other concessions that stand in the way of the type of free-rein capitalist system it envisions. Thus, centre-right governments seek to legitimize their authoritarian actions through liberal institutions—the legal system and mass incarceration—or by treating them as exceptional cases—imperialist war abroad or torture in the name of fighting terrorism. Far-right expressions, such as fascism, have a strong capitalist component, even if some of them may challenge free-market policies in favour of protectionist nationalist approaches (Konder 2009). They still assert private property, while having strong ethnonationalist—often white supremacist—and authoritarian values that tend to be mobilized in an "us versus them" framework (Forchtner 2019). Far-right forces end up incorporating authoritarianism in the very core of their project, as is the case of overt repression under the military dictatorship that governed Brazil between the 1960s and the 1980s, or the defence of white nationalism and strong borders that unites fascists in the United States and Europe.

In the economic relations between central and peripheral countries in the capitalist system, the periphery is a major source of natural resources and, therefore, the negatively impacted party in the system of unequal ecological and economic exchange. The Global South, as the sum of peoples and territories at the margins of the system, has to bear the brunt of authoritarian practices by its own elites and the elites in the Global North. Whether there is a leftist or a right-wing government, the paradigm of development in Latin America is still embedded in a logic of dependence. Even when strategies geared towards import substitution industrialization were implemented to boost domestic industry, they failed to overcome a general state of underdevelopment due to both internal and external factors (Hira 2007; Love 1990) and still contributed to environmental pressures.

This dynamic has long been explored in Marxist dependency theory (MDT) and studies on development and underdevelopment. Latin American industrialization was done in such a way that the strong concentration of land in the hands of a few permitted labour to be overexploited in both rural and urban areas (Marini 2013, 67). The tenets of industrialization were set according to the demands of foreign capital, so that the local capitalist class was devoid of a national project of capitalist development. The rule of thumb was—and still is—to maximize profits through very cheap labour and access to raw materials and rights to exploitation that could be purchased at a very low cost or even taken. Because of this, underdevelopment is not simply a status or innate characteristic of countries under dependent capitalism but the result of ongoing economic and political relations.

Although traditionally MDT does not provide an analysis embedded in ecological considerations, a critique of extractivism in Latin America expands its potentiality and helps to identify patterns of underdevelopment connected to the reduction of nature to a free gift. Thea Riofrancos explains that MDT led to a struggle between "nationalist-developmentalist versus revolutionary paths to development"

(Riofrancos 2020, 235). Whereas the latter acknowledges that the national elites will not bring about development, a critical position on extractivism builds on a critique of imperialism and expands the conversation by troubling assumptions over extractivism and industrialization that have constrained the Left to a monolithic approach to development (Riofrancos 2020, 15).

Understanding the context of dependence is essential for avoiding the mistake of treating environmental destruction in the Global South as a simple issue created by poor environmental consciousness, lax regulations, or irresponsible leaders. Dependence influences and moulds how authoritarianism against nature operates at the margins of capitalism, where sacrifice zones and ecocide are the norm rather than the exception. Fostering environmental degradation in one place while national parks are valued and protected elsewhere is part of the global capitalist project. A marked characteristic of ecological imperialism today is that it not only exploits nature heavily in the Global South but also creates, as Camila Moreno suggests, mechanisms for existing alongside growing environmental concerns through negotiations and compensations that are seen as assets in projects of "New Development", as suggested by Camila Moreno (2012, 57). Carbon credit schemes are only one of the ways through which false compensation for ecocide is sold—as if that were even possible—in dollars or the creation of protected units around the world. This also impacts marginalized communities in the Global North whose habitat is invaded by mining initiatives geared towards traditions of green technology while the same companies or even the state contributes to a green fund for protecting a limited piece of tropical forest somewhere else (S. Fernandes et al. 2021). This further normalizes authoritarian practices of dispossession and violence in sacrifice zones through eco-extractivism and a model that proposes remedying the ecological crisis without fixing the metabolic rift and regulating with nature; that is, without challenging the capitalist system.

The link between ecological imperialism and extractivism makes it acceptable for Canadian mining companies to destroy biomes and encroach on Indigenous territories in Brazil, Bolivia, and at home, while governments justify these actions through a need for resources for development and growth and offer limited conservation initiatives that function as olive branches (Gilchrist-Blackwood 2020). Contradictions like this become even more apparent when dealing with far-right governments.

Canada's Belo Sun Mining Corp has long planned to open an open-pit gold mine in the Brazilian Amazon, but the project only became viable under Jair Bolsonaro's presidency, when entities responsible for Indigenous protection actually liaised with miners and against Indigenous leadership (Arsenault 2021). After the outset of war in Ukraine, the Bolsonaro government pushed this agenda further, justifying it as a necessity for the fertilizer industry, since Brazil imports a great deal of its fertilizers from Russia (Brant and Sassine 2022). This is one example of how a cycle of dependence leads to sacrifice zones and sacrifice communities that are easily discarded and/or violated, especially when authoritarian tendencies are already established in the political landscape. Brazilian agribusiness relies heavily on fertilizers because of its monocrop model of production, so mining activities in key Indigenous territories become justifiable in order to sustain industrial agriculture. The Bolsonaro government continues to weaken deforestation safeguards while it sets targets for deforestation reduction through offsetting and other market mechanisms that attract Brazilian agribusiness and financial institutions (Horn and Fernandes 2021). Bolsonaro's government offers denialism of two kinds, the anti-science positions that deny that there is a crisis, but also the kind of denialism that serves to discredit environmental movements and to remove protections and eventually make way for corporations and market-based solutions to environmental crises (Moreno et al. 2021; Horn and Fernandes 2021).

These denialisms are promoted in the context of a fascist imaginary, national chauvinism, promotion of a ferocious capitalism tied to neoliberal reforms, defence of the interests of the extractive bourgeoisie, and growing practices of institutional racism and white supremacist ideology. Matters of exclusion and death became even more prominent during the COVID-19 pandemic, with Jair Bolsonaro's promotion of an authoritarian political tripod focused on "guns, virus, and soy" (S. Fernandes 2021). Bolsonaro's anti-ecological perspective is not simply an irrational display of far-right conspiracy theories about climate change, though these are certainly present in *bolsonarismo* as well as most major far-right movements today (Malm and the Zetkin Collective 2021, 279). This rationale serves to make room for the almost unlimited exploitation of labour and resources by foreign capital and lucky members of the national capitalist class. With bolsonarismo, lobbying for ecocidal proposals became easier, especially when the very notion of territory is encircled by ideas of private property, to be bought and sold. This goes beyond the perspective on neoextractivism espoused by progressive governments or a traditional approach to developmentalism in Brazil. With the authoritarian far-right, the point is simply to maximize gains and leave no stone unturned. The nationalist rhetoric operates as a legitimacy tool when, in fact, borders and sovereignty will be sold to the highest bidder without concern for community and environmental impact.

Although the Bolsonaro government is openly anti-ecological, other cases of right-wing authoritarianism in Latin America create similar dynamics. The tenure of Jeanine Áñez, the interim president of Bolivia after the 2019 coup, was short but intense. The far-right forces in government shared many characteristics with bolsonarismo, such as Christian fundamentalism. Although the progressive government of Morales was heavily criticized for furthering extractivism, carrying its own authoritarian contradictions under liberal democracy, it tried to negotiate this process with redistributive policies that advanced the country's fight against poverty.

Añez's authoritarianism was of a different degree, with overt use of violence, the spreading of fear in Indigenous and campesino communities, and an open politics of ecocide. Pablo Solón highlights this difference:

> Morales' MAS government was indeed allied to the agribusiness sector, which it had given broad concessions for years before the change in government. The Añez government was not only allied to agribusiness, it was deeply entrenched in the business [itself] and directly represented agribusiness interests in pursuing new, even more expansive policies. (Solón 2020)

Far-right authoritarianism provides an opportunity to advance capitalist interests without much concern for impact or negotiation with local actors as was necessary in the experiences of the pink tide in Bolivia, Brazil, Ecuador, and Venezuela. This is advantageous for the commodity markets and states seeking large amounts of natural resources from the Global South. There are fewer obstacles to extractivism, monoculture agribusiness, polluting industries, and fossil capital when Indigenous and campesino communities are not political subjects valued by the far-right, and violence against them is not only normalized but actually promoted. This is a problem that afflicts such communities throughout Latin America, such that Brazil and Colombia are among the most dangerous countries in the world for environmentalists (Global Witness 2021). With the pink tide, some of this improved through dialogue with social movements and some protections. With right-wing governments, treatment of these groups ranges from a general state of disregard for the impacts caused to them, to a clear directive towards ecocide. In this spectrum of authoritarianism, one can see how the right-wing government of Iván Duque in Colombia is complicit in the institutional persecution of local leaders that are also targeted by paramilitary groups in territorial disputes. Meanwhile, Jair Bolsonaro is engaged in the direct promotion of violence in rural areas, with efforts to arm the land-owning class, and the criminalization of social movements such as the Landless Workers' Movement (MST). Both cases involve governments established by a history of militia groups with far-right tendencies (Manso 2020; Maciel and Rojas 2021).

Fossil capital necessitates intense extractivism to increase commodity production, doing so by negotiating with the developmentalist Left in the Global South, by creating mechanisms of compensation under green capitalism, or by heightening exploitation to optimal levels with the far right. Far-right authoritarianism gets the job done a lot faster and the scenario of ecological imperialism and dependent capitalism in the Global South creates fertile soil for fossil capital to exacerbate previous contradictions and eventually take everything. As argued by Andreas Malm and the Zetkin Collective, "it remains hard to imagine a transposition whereby fossil capital would fight its rearguard battles from the left while the right executed its destruction" (Malm and the Zetkin Collective 2021, 476).

Yet, an important distinction is that the alliance between fascism and the destruction of nature can take on a 'green' appearance too, especially in the Global North. Streams of 'ecological fascism', shortened to ecofascism, appear in Europe and in the United States with a defence of pristine national forests and lakes, an appeal to 'blood and soil' arguments that lead white people to make claims to territory as if they were Indigenous communities, anti-immigrant rhetoric, and discourse that blames the poor and the foreign for pollution, environmental destruction, and even climate change itself (Taylor 2019; Boggs 2019). With ecofascism, the conspiracy theory is not about denying the existence of climate change but rather to manipulate the scientific explanation for authoritarian racist objectives, arguing that the poor of the Global South have way too many children, lack environmental consciousness, and will put pressure on the Global North's resources. By denying or distorting the root causes, ecofascism also promotes scientific denialism, even if different from the kind that claims that there is no global warming or that the Amazon rainforest is not at risk, as Bolsonaro would say. Ecofascism recognizes the crisis but is not about saving the Earth, instead deciding who gets to survive on a dying planet. Thus, it mobilizes the climate agenda in authoritarian ways against nature and peoples tightly connected to it. Further, it normalizes discussions over decarbonization and energy transition in the North without any consideration for the provenance of materials and the sharing of important technologies. This is a path for ensuring ecological imperialism and unequal ecological exchange from the Global South to the Global North, in ways that guarantee white supremacist control of ecosystems for richer countries. It is no surprise that although ecofascism is still marginal, there is ample room for its growth in imperialist countries particularly as the ecological crisis escalates.

Ecofascism in the Global North means not only strong borders in Northern countries, but a race to secure resources to transition faster for their own means without any challenge to their own mode of living. Green capitalism needs to sell false solutions to the climate crisis in order to replace commodities, leaving the imperial mode of living of the Global North unchanged (Brand and Wissen 2021, 157). However, this is only possible because the Global North will continue to steep materials in the exploitation of nature elsewhere, particularly in the Global South. An example is the exploitation of one of the key green minerals, lithium, that impacts Chilean and Argentinian environments. Nevertheless, the Global North is still focused on individual electric vehicles rather than a system overhaul. This creates a convenient opportunity both for green capitalist approaches to transition in rich liberal democracies and for authoritarian far-right governments that promote ecocidal extractivism in peripheral countries. It could be, however, even more devastating if ecofascism manages to take the lead in places like Germany, France, Austria, and the United States and furthers practices tied to ecological imperialism. Its advancement may also aid in the creation of pockets of ecofascism within Global

South countries by contributing to an elitist and segregationist view of environmental protection, which could lead to what Daniel Aldana Cohen terms an "eco-apartheid" (Aldana Cohen, 2019).

Towards a Framework of Authoritarianism against Nature

The majority of the literature available on this subject helps to identify standard cases where far-right ideology causes ecological destruction. However, it is important to consider the differences in phenomena of the Global North and the Global South. This means that authoritarianism against nature in the South is embedded in a history of unequal ecological exchange and unequal economic exchange between the periphery and the centre of capitalism that creates and normalizes sacrifice zones for the benefit of industrialization, in places like Latin America, that support or create the mode of living in the United States and Europe. These elements, together, add to a framework for understanding how ecocide and violence against peoples connected with the protection of nature is not the same at the centre and at the margins of capitalism. In fact, there may be conflicts between the interests of workers in Canada and in Bolivia, in ways similar to conflicts between many who live in urban areas in Canada and First Nations communities opposing pipelines in their territories. The difference is that when dealing with geopolitical arrangements and the differences in development in the system of dependent capitalism, ecological imperialism is also a situation that sets authoritarian practices apart in the richer and the poorer countries.

To understand these different expressions of authoritarianism against nature is to be able to map out trends and threats under the already existing ecological crisis. In the case of the Global South, the situation is even more critical due to climate debt, underdevelopment, and the ways that mainstream environmentalism is failing to consider how the South will transition into carbon neutrality when the technologies and resources to do so continue to be concentrated in the North.

This chapter focuses on Latin America for its analysis of how expressions of right-wing authoritarianism connect to capitalism's demand for resources and cheap labour, creating sacrifice zones for the benefit of affluent areas. Yet, authoritarianism against nature in the Global South and the Global North may take on even more sinister characteristics when considering the combination across different political projects and practices. There is need for a broader framework that may help to generate a better understanding of the authoritarian phenomena that further the metabolic rift and prevent transition into a society where the metabolism between humans and nature is regulated and reconciled. Today, the different faces of fossil fascism in the South are not detached from new enclaves of ecofascism in the North. However, as the ecological crisis heightens, the danger of ecofascism may grow in the periphery as local elites look for ways to protected themselves, while fossil capital attempts to reinvent itself in places like Europe.

References

Arboleda, Martín (2020), *Planetary Mine: Territories of Extraction under Late Capitalism*, Brooklyn, NY: Verso Books.

Arsenault, Chris (2021), "Canadian Firm's Proposed Gold Mine in Amazon Rainforest a Step Closer to Reality, CEO Says", *CBC News*, 28 March, available at https://www.cbc.ca/news/world/belo-sun-brazil-gold-bolsonaro-amazon-indigenous-environment-rainforest-business-1.5963002. Last accessed on 30 June 2022.

Aldana Cohen, Daniel (2019), "Eco-Apartheid Is Real", *The Nation*, 26 July, available at https://www.thenation.com/article/archive/green-new-deal-housing-climate-change. Last accessed on 07 July 2022.

Boggs, Kyle (2019), "The Rhetorical Landscapes of the 'Alt Right' and the Patriot Movements", *The Far Right and the Environment: Politics, Discourse and Communication*, London: Routledge, pp. 293–309.

Brand, Ulrich, and Markus Wissen (2021), *The Imperial Mode of Living: Everyday Life and the Ecological Crisis of Capitalism*, Brooklyn, NY: Verso.

Brant, Danielle, and Vinicius Sassine (2022), "Governo Faz Ofensiva Para Liberar Mineração Em Terra Indígena – 07/03/2022 – Mercado – Folha", *Folha de São Paulo*, 7 March, available at https://www1.folha.uol.com.br/mercado/2022/03/governo-faz-ofensiva-para-liberar-mineracao-em-terra-indigena.shtml. Last accessed on 30 June 2022.

Burkett, Paul (1999), "Nature's 'Free Gifts' and the Ecological Significance of Value", *Capital & Class*, vol. 23, no. 2, pp. 89–110.

Clark, Brett, and John Bellamy Foster (2009), "Ecological Imperialism and the Global Metabolic Rift: Unequal Exchange and the Guano/Nitrates Trade", *International Journal of Comparative Sociology*, vol. 50, no. 3–4, pp. 311–34.

Clark, Brett, and John Bellamy Foster (2010), "The Dialectic of Social and Ecological Metabolism: Marx, Mészáros, and the Absolute Limits of Capital", *Socialism and Democracy*, vol. 24, no. 2, pp. 124–38, available at https://doi.org/10.1080/08854300.2010.481447. Last accessed on 30 June 2022.

Crook, Martin, Damien Short, and Nigel South (2018), "Ecocide, Genocide, Capitalism and Colonialism: Consequences for Indigenous Peoples and Local Ecosystems Environments", *Theoretical Criminology*, vol. 22, no. 3, pp. 298–317.

Crosby, Alfred W. (1986), *Ecological Imperialism: The Biological Expansion of Europe, 900–1900*, Cambridge: Cambridge University Press.

Dhillon, Jaskiran, and Will Parrish (2019), "Exclusive: Canada Police Prepared to Shoot Indigenous Activists, Documents Show", *The Guardian*, 20 December, available at https://www.theguardian.com/world/2019/dec/20/canada-indigenous-land-defenders-police-documents. Last accessed on 30 June 2022.

Dorninger, Christian, and Nina Eisenmenger (2016), "South America's Biophysical Involvement in International Trade: The Physical Trade Balances of Argentina, Bolivia, and Brazil in the Light of Ecologically Unequal Exchange", *Journal of Political Ecology*, vol. 23, no. 1, pp. 394–409.

Dussel, Enrique (1985), *Philosophy of Liberation*, New York: Orbis Books.

Dussel, Enrique (2011), *Filosofía de La Liberación*, México: Fondo de Cultura Económica.

Fernandes, Florestan (2019), *Apontamentos Sobre a "Teoria Do Autoritarismo"*, São Paulo: Expressão Popular.

Fernandes, Sabrina (2019), *Sintomas Mórbidos: A Encruzilhada Da Esquerda Brasileira*, São Paulo: Autonomia Literária, available at https://doi.org/10.1017/CBO9781107415324.004. Last accessed on 30 June 2022.

Fernandes, Sabrina (2021), "Ecological Imperialism and Jair Bolsonaro's Agenda in Brazil", *New Politics*, vol. 18, no. 3.

Fernandes, Sabrina, Eduardo Gudynas, Michael Löwy, René Rámirez Galegos, and Thea Riofrancos (2021), "Extractivismo y Soberanía En América Latina", *Jacobin América Latina*, 11 January 2022, available at https://jacobinlat.com/2022/01/11/extractivismo-y-soberania-en-america-latina-2/. Last accessed on 30 June 2022.

Forchtner, Bernhard (2019), "Far-Right Articulations of the Natural Environment", *The Far Right and the Environment: Politics, Discourse and Communication*, London: Routledge.

Forchtner, Bernhard (ed.) (2019), *The Far Right and the Environment: Politics, Discourse and Communication*, London: Routledge.

Foster, John Bellamy, and Brett Clark, (2004), "Ecological Imperialism: The Curse of Capitalism", *Socialist Register*, vol. 40, no. 1, pp. 186–201.

Foster, John Bellamy, and Hannah Holleman (2014), "The Theory of Unequal Ecological Exchange: A Marx-Odum Dialectic", *Journal of Peasant Studies*, vol. 41, no. 2, pp. 199–233.

Gilchrist-Blackwood, Aidan (2020), "Canadian Exceptionalism, Greenwashing Imperialism: The State, Energy Transition, and the (Contested) Discursive Legitimation of Mining Sector Extractivism", Master's Thesis, McGill University (Canada).

Global Witness (2021), "Global Witness Reports 227 Land and Environmental Activists Murdered in a Single Year, the Worst Figure on Record | Global Witness", Press Release, 13 September, available at https://www.globalwitness.org/en/press-releases/global-witness-reports-227-land-and-environmental-a ctivists-murdered-single-year-worst-figure-record/. Last accessed on 30 June 2022.

Gordon, Todd, and Jeffery Roger Webber (2019), "Canadian Capital and Secondary Imperialism in Latin America", *Canadian Foreign Policy Journal*, vol. 25, no. 1, pp. 72–89.

Hall, Stuart (1979), "The Great Moving Right Show [1979]", *Marxism Today*, pp. 374–92, available at https://doi.org/10.1215/9781478002413-019. Last accessed on 30 June 2022.

Herculano, Selene (2008), "O Clamor Por Justiça Ambiental e Contra o Racismo Ambiental", *Revista de Gestão Integrada Em Saúde Do Trabalho e Meio Ambiente*, vol. 3, no. 1, pp. 1–20.

Hira, Anil (2007), "Did ISI Fail and Is Neoliberalism the Answer for Latin America? Re-Assessing Common Wisdom Regarding Economic Policies in the Region", *Brazilian Journal of Political Economy*, vol. 27, no. 107, pp. 345–56.

Horn, Claudia, and Sabrina Fernandes (2021), "Brazil's Far-Right Government Is Using COP26 to Greenwash Its Image", *Jacobin Magazine*, 12 November, available at https://jacobinmag.com/2021/11/brazil-jair-bolsonaro-government-cop26-greenwashing-carbon-market-climate-crisis. Last accessed on 30 June 2022.

Hornborg, Alf, and Joan Martinez-Alier (2016), "Ecologically Unequal Exchange and Ecological Debt", *Journal of Political Ecology*, vol. 23, no. 1, pp. 328–33.

Konder, Leandro (2009), *Introdução Ao Fascismo*, São Paulo: Expressão Popular.

Lerner, Steve (2012), *Sacrifice Zones: The Front Lines of Toxic Chemical Exposure in the United States*, Cambridge, MA: MIT Press.

Love, Joseph L. (1990), "The Origins of Dependency Analysis", *Journal of Latin American Studies*, vol. 22, no. 1–2, pp. 143–68, available at https://doi.org/10.1017/S0022216X00015145. Last accessed on 30 June 2022.

Machado Aráoz, Horacio (2018), *Potosí, El Origen Genealogía de La Minería Contemporánea*, Quito: Editorial Abya-Yala.

Maciel, Camila, and Luz Rojas (2021), "Iván Duque Representa Uma | Podcast | Rádio Brasil de Fato", *Brasil de Fato*, 24 May, available at https://www.brasildefato.com.br/2021/05/24/ivan-duque-representa-uma-ultradireita-miliciana-afirma-ativista-colombiana. Last accessed on 30 June 2022.

Malheiro, Bruno, Carlos Walter Porto-Gonçalves, and Fernando Michelotti (2021), *Horizontes Amazônicos*, São Paulo: Expressão Popular; Fundação Rosa Luxemburgo.

Malm, Andreas, and the Zetkin Collective (2021), *White Skin, Black Fuel: On the Danger of Fossil Fascism*, London: Verso Books.

Manso, Bruno Paes (2020), *A República Das Milícias: Dos Esquadrões Da Morte à Era Bolsonaro*, São Paulo: Todavia.

Marini, Ruy Mauro (2013), *Subdesenvolvimento e Revolução*, Florianópolis: Insular.

Marx, Karl (1981), *Capital: Volume III*, London: Penguin Books.

Mészáros, István (1995), *Beyond Capital: Towards a Theory of Transition*, New York: Monthly Review Press.

Moreno, Camila (2012), "Green Economy and Development(alism) in Brazil", *Inside a Champion: An Analysis of the Brazilian Development Model*, Rio de Janeiro: Heinrich Böll Foundation.

Moreno, Camila, Fábio Pacheco, Larissa Packer, Mariana Vecchione, and Maureen Santos Campos (2021), *O Brasil Na Retomada Verde: Integrar Para Entregar*, Brasília: Grupo Carta de Belém, available at https://br.boell.org/sites/default/files/20 22-02/CARTA-DE-BELEM_PUBLICACAO_RETOMADA-VERDE4.pdf. Last accessed on July 07 2022.

Núñez, Andrés, Enrique Aliste, Alvaro Bello, and Juan Pablo Astaburuaga (2019), "Eco-Extractivismo y Los Discursos de La Naturaleza En Patagonia-Aysén: Nuevos Imaginarios Geográficos y Renovados Procesos de Control Territorial", *Revista Austral de Ciencias Sociales*, no. 35, pp. 133–53.

Patel, Raj, and Jason W Moore (2017), *A History of the World in Seven Cheap Things*, Oakland: University of California Press.

Pérez, Alfons (2021), *Green Deals in a Time of Pandemics: The Future Will Be Contested Now*, Barcelona: Icaria Editorial.

Riofrancos, Thea (2020), *Resource Radicals: From Petro-Nationalism to Post-Extractivism in Ecuador*, Durham, NC: Duke University Press.

Scott, Peter Dale (2004), *Drugs, Oil, and War: The United States in Afghanistan, Colombia, and Indochina*, Lanham: Rowman & Littlefield Publishers.

Solón, Pablo (2020), "Why Lucho & David Won the Bolivian Elections", *Systemic Alternatives*, 19 October, https://systemicalternatives.org/2020/10/19/why-lucho-david-won-the-bolivian-elections/.

Stokes, Doug (2005), *America's Other War: Terrorizing Colombia*, London: Zed Books.

Svampa, Maristella (2019), *Neo-Extractivism in Latin America: Socio-Environmental Conflicts, the Territorial Turn, and New Political Narratives*, New York, NY: Cambridge University Press.

Taylor, Blair (2019), "Alt-Right Ecology: Ecofascism and Far-Right Environmentalism in the United States", *The Far Right and the Environment: Politics, Discourse and Communication*, London: Routledge, pp. 275–92.

Thomas, Cassidy, and Elhom Gosink (2021), "At the Intersection of Eco-Crises, Eco-Anxiety, and Political Turbulence: A Primer on Twenty-First Century Ecofascism", *Perspectives on Global Development and Technology*, vol. 20, no. 1–2, pp. 30–54, available at https://doi.org/10.1163/15691497-12341581. Last accessed on 30 June 2022.

Traverso, Enzo (2019), *The New Faces of Fascism: Populism and the Far Right*, London: Verso.

Watts, Michael J. (1999), "Petro-Violence: Some Thoughts on Community, Extraction, and Political Ecology", Berkeley Working Papers, WP 99–1, Institute of International Studies, University of California, Berkeley.

Webber, Jeffery R. (2020), "Late Fascism in Brazil? Theoretical Reflections", *Rethinking Marxism*, vol. 32, no. 2, pp. 151–67.

Webber, Jeffery R., and Barry Carr (2013), *The New Latin American Left: Cracks in the Empire*, Lanham: Rowman & Littlefield Publishers.

Zografos, Christos, and Paul Robbins (2020), "Green Sacrifice Zones, or Why a Green New Deal Cannot Ignore the Cost Shifts of Just Transitions", *One Earth*, vol. 3, no. 5, pp. 543–46.

Neoliberal Authoritarian Urbanism
A Comparative Study of New Patterns of Urban Development in Brazil and Turkey

Aysegul Can and Hugo Fanton

Introduction

Over the last few decades, massive and usually state-led urban redevelopment and housing projects have been implemented all over the world, with more intensity in the Global South, and alliances between entrepreneurs and state authorities have produced new urban policies that combine the evictions of poor people from their territories and the private appropriation of land in favour of capital accumulation processes. What has become known as "neoliberal urbanism" (Smith 1996 and 2002; Brenner 2004; Peck and Tickell 2002) refers to the urban specificities of a macroeconomic process, in which the dominant accumulation pattern promotes a "market-oriented regulatory restructuring" (Peck et al. 2009), in unequal and heterogeneous social, political, and institutional settings.

In this context, which dates back to the profound transformations in the relations between market, state, and society since the mid-1970s, cities have become veritable "institutional laboratories for a variety of neoliberal policy experiments" (Peck et al. 2009, 58), that embrace fiscal austerity (Hall 2019), public-private partnerships (Rolnik 2015), property redevelopment accompanied by increasing financialization (Aalbers et al. 2020; Fix 2015), and state repression associated with new strategies of private appropriation of space (Rolnik 2015).

It should be noted that although these phenomena have a broad spatio-temporal spectrum—we are talking here about a global phenomenon which has advanced over at least four decades—in order to properly understand the processes of neoliberalization it is necessary to investigate their general foundations and, at the same time, to carry out "a systematic inquiry into their multifarious institutional forms, developmental tendencies, diverse sociopolitical effects and multiple contradictions" (Peck et al. 2009, 51).

While urban neoliberalism in the Global South and North has exhibited general common features since at least the 1980s, in a post-2008 crisis context there have been some changes in the ways in which neoliberal urbanism is implemented in certain localities. One of the fundamental changes that we observe is an authoritarian turn in urban politics, accentuating coercive means by state and private actors in the imposition of market interests on urban space, while systematically weakening mechanisms that allow the urban poor and marginalized population to defend their interests. This chapter focuses on this dramatic restructuring of city governance in the Global South which we conceptualize as neoliberal authoritarian urbanism (NAU), a restructuring of urban development around the promotion of market-led urban policies and increasing global spatial financialization.

Contemporary expressions of what David Harvey (2003) calls "accumulation by dispossession" are spatialized in an environment where finance and real estate sectors control the urban production according to their interests. As the state, "with its monopoly of violence and definitions of legality, plays a crucial role in both supporting and promoting these processes" (Harvey 2003, 74), it becomes crucial to analyse the forms of the organization of power that correspond with this pattern of capital accumulation, both in terms of the general economic dynamics of each social formation, and the specific ones—urban, rural, industrial, financial, etc. We will analyse the specificity of urban policies—the NAU—based on the intertwining of "neoliberal urbanism" with the concept of "authoritarian neoliberalism" (Tansel 2017; and Bruff 2014).

This chapter aims to shed light on processes of neoliberal urban regeneration/redevelopment during the implementation of increasingly oppressive, authoritarian, and profit-driven urban policies in the specificity of Brazil and Turkey. The two countries were chosen to investigate the extent of transnational—global—capital's reach and influence based on their seeming difference in culture, governance, urban policy, and location. The choice is based on the understanding that both countries have undergone profound political crises in a post-2008 context, with a significant authoritarian turn. In the Brazilian case, we refer to the coup of 2016 and the rise of Jair Bolsonaro, an autocratic leader with fascist tendencies (Singer 2021). In the case of Turkey, the choice is in reference to the institutional changes promoted by the AKP, that fostered an extreme concentration of power. We understand that such changes in the relations of hegemony had profound impacts on urban dynamics, producing an accentuation of coercion that led us to develop the concept of NAU.

We employ the approach of comparative urbanism, based on research conducted in dialogue and with similar methodological tools, such as conducting content analysis of urban policy documents, legislation, and laws, documentary surveys of civil society organizations, and press publications. The chapter concludes with a discussion of how the notion of neoliberal authoritarian urbanism is important for understanding the current phase of the capital accumulation process via urbanism in cities, in a dynamic present, and in different realities in the Global

South. And, furthermore, that the crises of liberal democracy and the rise of authoritarianism share a common denominator.

'Accumulation by Dispossession' and 'Authoritarian Neoliberalism', Shaping NAU

Under neoliberalism, urban governance is driven by value creation, in which physical infrastructure, housing, transportation, and sanitation become means of capital accumulation: "the aim is to create sufficient synergy within the urbanization process for monopoly rents to be created and realized by both private interests and state powers" (Harvey 2001, 103). The emergence of finance-led urban policy is enabled through the reorganization of urban space according to the interests of capital reproduction. Through governance structures, private property rights and mortgage finance are pushed onto poor populations by state-finance coalitions. Land reforms are conducted, implementing property rights in situations where property-led systems coexisted with other forms of tenure, and global finance, nation state, and local governments integrate into an alliance in cities in favour of land privatization and the creation of financial assets based on urban development (Santos 1996; Aalbers et al. 2020).

The extensive literature on "neoliberal urbanism" points to such trends by emphasizing market-driven state initiatives, especially financial ones, with consequent restructuring of regulatory frameworks, territorial development patterns, and socio-political alliances (Peck et al. 2009). Furthermore, "urban real-estate development—gentrification writ large—has now become a central motive force of urban economic expansion, a pivotal sector in the new urban economies" (Smith 2002, 447).

Although such patterns are still present in the urban environment, it is important to note the inflections present in a post-2008 crisis context. The institutional transformations of neoliberalism in the 1990s and early 2000s sought some degree of coordination of interests between dominant and subordinate classes. The sharp growth of private indebtedness that led to the US housing bubble indicates just that, as it implied the active involvement of different actors in that process, such as sectors of the middle classes and various categories of investors, from small owners to large real estate funds, that turned homes into a financial asset in the mortgage market. Amidst market initiatives to restrict urban policy, some theorists demonstrate that there was also "the deployment of community-based programmes and shadow-state initiatives to combat social exclusion; the promotion of new forms of coordination and interorganizational networking among previously distinct spheres of local state intervention" (Peck et al. 2009, 64) and other initiatives to sugarcoat the pill and promote some degree of legitimacy.

We argue here that this is precisely what has changed. The rise of so-called 'authoritarian populism' and its implications in everyday politics has transformed urban dynamics, and therefore we should give specific attention to the urban implications of the latest authoritarian turn—even though authoritarian populism as a concept was coined over 40 years ago by Stuart Hall, in 1980. In the literature of political economy and also in urban studies, the emergence of more authoritarian neoliberal regimes has been the subject of discussion since the mortgage crisis in 2008 (Adaman and Akbulut 2021; Rodrik 2017; and Rolnik 2019). Some other scholars also noted that neoliberalism as a furthering of free market logic started to reach into every part of society, emphasizing economic agendas and development as the only worthy human activity (Madra and Adaman 2014; Adaman and Akbulut 2021; and Bruff and Tansel 2018). This view highlighted neoliberalism as a specific structure for governance.

The concept we present here of neoliberal authoritarian urbanism is based on an effort to identify, in a more accurate way, "the contemporary mechanisms of neoliberal governance" (Tansel 2017, 3). We followed closely the elaborations of Cemal Burek Tansel and Ian Bruff who emphasize the tendencies accentuating the coercive dimension as "strategies for the reproduction of capital-in-general" (Ayers and Saad-Filho 2014, 4). By using the term neoliberal authoritarian urbanism, we analyse the urban governance part of that neoliberal structure.

The notion of authoritarian neoliberalism expresses "a transformation of the 'normal' operation of the capitalist state" and a "qualitative shift from the intrinsic 'illiberal' propensities of neoliberalism" (Tansel 2017, 3), which operates through legal, coercive, and administrative mechanisms to limit the public dimension of the state—or the realms of consent building—the sphere of popular action and resistance (Bruff 2014, 116), and the "escalation in the state's propensity to employ coercion and legal/extra-legal intimidation" (Tansel 2017, 3).

Also important is the relationship established by the concept between the political form of organization of power and neoliberalism as a regime of capital accumulation. There is an "embodied condition whereby authoritarian neoliberalism subjects individuals, collectives and populations to economic, financial and corporeal discipline" (Tansel 2017, 4). Following Bruff, the governance mechanisms under authoritarian neoliberalism are "increasingly preemptive" (2014, 123), imposing austerity measures or restructuring the space "towards protecting the pillars of neoliberal accumulation" (Tansel 2017, 4). Thus, the concept stresses "a *qualitative* change in how state power is wielded by dominant groups in order to maintain hegemony—specifically, via a range of coercive and legal measures that aim to insulate the state from popular contestation" (Fabry and Sandbeck 2018, 3).

With this chapter we want to contribute to this discussion by contextualizing the "relationship between the changing political terrain of neoliberalism and the new modes of authoritarian governance" in the urban environment (Fabry and

Sandbeck 2018, 3). We understand that there is a correspondence between current patterns of urban governance and neoliberal authoritarianism, in an urbanism marked by the accentuation of coercion and legal administrative mechanisms that favour the reproduction of capital in urban space and restrict the space for popular action and resistance.

This is precisely why we base the NAU concept on Harvey's political economy and his formulation that the capitalist "inability to accumulate through expanded reproduction on a sustained basis has been paralleled by a rise in attempts to accumulate by dispossession" (Harvey 2003, 64), with the resulting relationship between space and capital accumulation. The concept is based on the principles of a Marxian "description of primitive accumulation [which] reveals a wide range of processes", such as commodification and privatization of land, suppression of rights to the commons, processes of appropriation of assets, usury, and debt. "The state, with its monopoly of violence and definitions of legality, plays a crucial role in both backing and promoting these processes" and operates continuously in the reproduction of capitalism, meaning all "the features of primitive accumulation that Marx mentions have remained powerfully present within capitalism's historical geography up until now" (Harvey 2003, 186).

The direct relationship that urbanism establishes between capital accumulation and space makes urban policy one of the main forms and manifestations of accumulation by dispossession. Spatial power is necessary to take, make, and dominate in the most literal sense (Centner 2008) the reproduction of capital. Consequently, spatial capital can be defined as "all resources accumulated by an actor enabling him or her to benefit, according to their strategy, from using society's spatial dimension" (Lévy and Lussault 2003, 124). Spatial capital is a factor in social differentiation, and also an indicator of social inequality. It shows the patterns of privileged consumption rather than collective consumption and emphasizes that cities are places of struggle as Manuel Castells demonstrated (Castells 1977, 2000, and 2001).

The ability to take and make space not only gives different groups 'holding power' over negotiations and control over space, but also the capacity to mould space through different practices and moments. Harvey adds that although Bourdieu refers to individualized processes—as individuals floating, almost like atoms, "in a sea of structured aesthetic judgments"—concepts such as "collective symbolic capital" linked to urban spaces express the competitive dynamics that now predominate in cities. The aim of Paris, Berlin, New York, Istanbul, or São Paulo is to "raise their quotient of symbolic capital and to increase their marks of distinction so as to better ground their claims to the uniqueness that yields monopoly rent" (Harvey 2001, 103).

In this context, we expose and analyse the cases of Turkey and Brazil, with emphasis on the correlation between urban governance and capital accumulation. The cases explored demonstrate the spatial dimension of capital reproduction, and how this directly impacts the lives of impoverished city inhabitants. The commodification of territories, the dispossession of the commons, and their reappropriation by capital produces, as a combined effect, the urban spoliation of thousands of people and neoliberal advance as a logic of social (de)integration. For this, the state is a central agent, since it organizes the power mechanisms necessary to spatialize capital, in the conformation of what we call here neoliberal authoritarian urbanism.

Turkey, Brazil, and the Rise of NAU

In the last 30 years, the neoliberal urban policies implemented in Turkey and in Brazil have not only increased their policies of land grab and speculation, but also dispossession by capital accumulation (Serin et al. 2020; Rolnik 2015; and Aalbers 2020). This situation has led to many massive urban regeneration and redevelopment projects, and brutal processes of eviction. Naturally, this increase in neoliberal urban policies is associated with a world economy that has been changing since the 1970s. Countries in the Global North experienced the withdrawal of industrial production and therefore a decrease in the primary circuit of capital (Merrifield 2014). Speculation on real estate that works as a secondary circuit of capital started to increase, and capital has shifted over to this, as the primary circuit of capital slowed down. Henri Lefebvre (1996) and Harvey (2005) have talked about these changes and unpacked them many times. This rise in the real estate sector has been the driving factor of urbanization in the Global South (Lees et al. 2015). Urban regeneration and redevelopment projects, and state-led gentrification, started to become perceived as a 'quick fix' for transforming the urbanized areas in Southern countries that needed to catch up economically with their Northern counterparts. This change in economy helps improve the understanding of urbanization, not only in the South but also in the North as well. As Loretta Lees, Hyung Ban Shin, and Ernesto López-Morales put it:

> Given that the rise of the secondary circuit of the built environment and the real estate sector is geographically uneven, it is important to understand the geographically and historically uneven ways in which various agents of capital investment, as well as the functions of a range of state apparatuses and hegemonic ideologies, have contributed to both the safeguarding and reproduction of (often speculative) investment in the built environment. (Lees et al. 2015, 449)

These features that are present in both countries are analysed here. We can speak of a rise of 'neoliberal urbanism', that focuses on the commodification of space through mostly profit-led projects and urban decisions resulting in the crisis context of 2008. In the following years, however, by distinct and not concomitant processes, there was an authoritarian rise in both countries. Here, we will seek here to analyse how urban governance was affected and what the similarities and differences are in the two contrasting national contexts.

We now turn to a brief discussion of neoliberal urbanism in Turkey and Brazil respectively. Following that, NAU in both countries and how this affects their major cities will be discussed.

Neoliberal Urbanism in Turkey and Brazil

In Turkey, the neoliberal era primarily began in the 1980s. However, it was the 2001 economic crisis that significantly increased neoliberalization as a whole. The economic crisis of 2001 was the biggest one in the history of the republic and Turkey responded to this crisis with widespread neoliberalization, including a significant increase in the real estate sector and privatization (Serin et al. 2020). In the case of Istanbul, this resulted in opening up many state-owned and other forms of land to development through various changes and additions in urban laws and regulations. The Turkish state played two roles in the increasing capital accumulation through urban development: firstly, the national state was the one regulating land use, planning laws, and regulations, and also designating resources; and secondly, it was the body actually constructing the developments and developing the land (Serin et al. 2020).

Another thing that happened in the 1980s was that the Housing Development Administration (TOKI) was established in 1984, with the goal of generating cheap housing. However, TOKI quickly evolved into a highly influential government agency with broad authority over practically every element of the housing market. TOKI was initially an institution that provided low-cost housing with cheap mortgages and low monthly instalments but these houses were for sale and this institution did not create any rental social housing. Most of the working class in Turkey did not have enough financial power, savings, or security to commit to a 10–20-year contract. After its foundation, laws and regulations helped TOKI gain the power to become the biggest land speculator and real estate developer in the country. This authority is now somewhat shared with another important governmental institution, the Ministry of Environment, Urbanization and Climate Change (Can, publication forthcoming).

Turkey began to have a growing—but also very unequal—economy by changing urban and municipal law, providing subsidies and tax exemptions to private construction companies, increasing financialization of the housing market, and finally beginning to implement massive urban regeneration, renewal, redevelopment, and infrastructure projects (Yardimci 2020). In Turkey, urban regeneration became a legal term in 2004, and the extended power of TOKI only expedited the centralized application of neoliberal urban politics (Batuman 2013). Many state-led urban redevelopment projects and TOKI-built social housing buildings drove disadvantaged city residents to either leave the neighbourhood and be pushed farther out to the peripheries, or to take out mortgages and become indebted to the state or state-backed banks. This new strategy was extremely different from the traditional Turkish urbanization paradigm, which relied on overlooking squatting and instead advocated for total and full commercialization of the urban landscape (Keyder 2010; Batuman 2015; and Kuyucu and Unsal 2010).

In all Turkish cities, without any citizen engagement in the decision-making and execution process, large regions and neighbourhoods were classified as urban regeneration/renewal areas (Batuman 2015). Squatter areas were targeted initially, but subsequently deteriorating inner-city regions became the focus of urban regeneration efforts (Batuman 2015). As neoliberal urban policies grew more prevalent, formerly destitute and 'undesirable' but historically significant regions of Istanbul's inner city became increasingly valuable, attracting domestic and foreign investment—Tarlabaşı, Bomonti, Sulukule, Talimhane, and so on (Can 2021). Newly constructed high-rise apartments and luxury shopping malls all suggested that the real estate and construction sector was becoming a lucrative capital venture environment, as Neil Smith previously remarked (2002, 446). As a result of both this shift in policy and transition, an ever-expanding and hastily designed urban sprawl has formed, complete with endless shopping malls, vacant high-rise apartment buildings, and massive mosques. Official documents—such as Turkey's Vision 2023—and the creation and implementation of urban megaprojects have helped Istanbul become the metropolis that local and international investors have flocked to as Turkey's growing global city (Dogan and Stupar 2017).

In the Brazilian context, the state is also configured as a fundamental agent in the process of spatial formation of cities in favour of capital interests. Throughout the 20th century, accompanying the industrial expansion, state investment in the urban environment was "a factor of intense differential land valuation" (Kowarick 2000, 23). Under neoliberalism, the state began to combine this with its role in the process of financialization of urban space by promoting financialized investment mechanisms and the transformation of urban land into a financial asset.

Starting in the 1990s, Brazilian national and local governments implemented the 'structural adjustment' of the Washington Consensus, with the adoption of focalized urban policies, as advocated for by international financial organizations, especially the World Bank (WB), the International Monetary Fund (IMF), and the Inter-American Development Bank (IADB). This included the creation of "private financial intermediation agencies (enclave agencies), legally independent and responsible for implementing projects and raising funds in the market"; public-private partnerships (PPPs) in urban regeneration projects, gentrification and urban services and infrastructure concessions by private companies; and "the raising of funds in the national and international credit market", with the issuance of public bonds to finance urban projects. This set of measures constituted public action and urban development under the growing control of finance (Arantes 2006, 75).

With monetary stabilization and the advance of financialization, private indebtedness was presented as a housing solution for the middle and upper-income sections of society (Castro 1999, 135). Another consequence of neoliberal urbanism was the "articulation between local real estate developers and national investors" to promote "the construction of new office towers and multi-purpose complexes, which would be rented by multinational companies" (Fix 2011, 121). Excluded from any market alternative, the most vulnerable sectors began to occupy informal settlements, which led, for example, to a 52 percent growth in the number of houses in favelas in São Paulo from 1991–96 (Pasternak 2002, 8).

The rapprochement between the real estate circuit and the capital market gained new energy from the Real Estate Financing System and the Real Estate Investment Funds (FII), created by law in 1993. The novelty of this mechanism lies in the possibility of "pooling resources for investments, without fragmenting the ownership of real estate" (Fix 2011, 126). This is advantageous when stimulating the construction of large commercial towers and malls, as it allows each of the investors to "become the owner of a certain number of quotas" (Fix 2011, 126). In addition, it allows the "attracting [of] investors who were not necessarily interested in using the property. That is, facilitating the untying of use from ownership", so that the development could be deployed as "a financial asset with greater liquidity, placed alongside others in an investor's portfolio" (Fix 2011, 126).

In the 2000s there was a political shift during the election of the Workers' Party (PT) to occupy the Presidency of the Republic, first with Luiz Inácio "Lula" da Silva—2003–10—and then with his successor Dilma Rousseff—2011–16. It is commonly understood that the new 'developmentalism' in Brazil between 2003–14 that the PT's support of economic policies directly affected urban dynamics. The main used examples are the Growth Acceleration Program (PAC), launched in 2007 to stimulate growth by infrastructure investments, and the My House My Life programme (MCMV), which began in 2009 as a measure to mitigate the internal effects of the international financial crisis, and has considerably increased the volume of resources for financing social housing.

During Lula and Rousseff's governments, there was a significant set of measures in place that were in line with the interests of the construction business and that impacted directly on the cities' dynamics. In addition to the above-mentioned programmes, a special tax regime applicable to real estate developments was adopted, the National Treasury's budget allocated resources to be directed towards the sector, real estate credit was extended, interest rates reduced, and an intensive use of the National Bank for Economic and Social Development resources was given to stimulate the sector. Politically, the articulation of the businessmen with public agents at different levels and spheres, by participating in economic policymaking bodies and in the financing of electoral campaigns, should also be emphasized.

Despite this correspondence between market interests and the policies adopted, there was an accentuation of the consensual component in the coercion-consensus dynamic of the relation between the state and the popular classes in the period. This can be exemplified by: the greater participation of labour income in the national gross aggregate value, resulting from full employment policies and an increase in the minimum wage (Rugitsky 2017; Serrano and Summa 2018); the creation of specific urban policies for the popular classes, such as the My House My Life programme (Rolnik 2015; Maricato 2015); and the mechanisms of participatory democracy that have expanded popular participation in the elaboration and management of public policies (Fernandes 2007; Avritzer 2010; and Dagnino 2014), among others.

Thus, the cities experienced an intensification of the struggles that opposed different forces involved in urban politics. The contradictions spanned themes such as the dispute over land and budget between businessmen and social movements, the definition of criteria for prioritization of income bands in the allocation of resources, the rise of real estate speculation and the degree of state participation in the process involving housing production, and the actions of different popular social and political groups (Rolnik 2015).

As part of this context, homeless social movement organizations[1] broadened their social bases and acted in different ways, which make up a historically shaped 'repertoire of interactions' which constitute political-institutional relations, party disputes, parliamentary representation, and negotiation strategies with local and national executive powers. In addition, direct actions such as public manifestations and occupation of empty land and properties in different spaces of the cities, including in central and highly valued areas. The interaction of movements with antagonistic forces and state power involves "much more than formal experiences of institutionalized participation: they also include other practices of dialogue and conflict" permeated by "a tension between the principles of autonomy and political effectiveness" (Tatagiba et al. 2011), which permeates their political and social relations.

However, as a consequence of the 2008 economic crisis the dispute over the macroeconomic management of the country increased when several sectors of the business community started to shift in political terms. Their movement was related to items such as the worsening of the economic crisis in the domestic environment,

---

1 In Brazil, since the 1970s and 1980s, there have been emerging urban social movements organizing with the homeless population to advocate for the right to housing. They are known as homeless movements, such as the National Union for Popular Housing (UNMP) and the Homeless Workers' Movement (MTST).

the advance of state intervention in response to the crisis, the degree of financialization of the economy and of the productive sector, the diminishing rates of profit, the fall in direct investment, pressure over the labour market, and the intensification of the social political struggles and labour union activities (Singer 2018). The change in the political stance of business leaders, along with the absence of organization and massive resistance of the working classes in defence of Rousseff's measures, resulted in a judicial-parliamentary coup in 2016 and in the election of Jair Bolsonaro in 2018. In the conceptualizations of the period after Rousseff's fall, authors such as André Singer, Alfredo Saad Filho, and Lecio Morais emphasize two combined aspects: the ruling classes' definite break from the social pact established in the constitution of 1988; and the growing coercive forms used to exercise power and implement an extreme orthodox neoliberalism. This is the Brazilian political form of authoritarian neoliberalism, which accentuated the mechanisms of coercion in the organization of power in favour of market interests after the 2016 coup, while excluding the popular classes from access to public policies.

The NAU in Turkey and Brazil

A construction boom began in the early 2000s in Turkey and as its biggest city and economic capital, Istanbul was affected the most by this boom. The number of construction companies founded doubled and direct investment in housing increased significantly, from USD 6 million to USD 987 million between the years 2004 and 2008 (Balaban 2012). Project-based development in the form of megaprojects, private neighbourhood projects, public-private urban regeneration projects, and so-called social housing projects have become the mainstream ways of providing housing in Turkey and in Istanbul and, therefore, the main tools for furthering the neoliberal transformation of local and urban governance in Istanbul (Perouse 2013; Serin et al. 2020; and Kuyucu and Unsal 2010). A web portal called Yeni Projeler (New Projects) lists a number of projects—2,115 to be exact—in Istanbul by 2018 (Yeni Projeler 2018).

The AKP heavily relied on the tools of authoritarian neoliberalism and developmentalism by utilizing extractive sources such as mining, energy, and construction (Adaman and Akbulut 2021). Through this developmentalism, the AKP garnered popular support and created an image of a 'strong and benevolent state' (see Koch and Valiyev 2016). The urban megaprojects, ever-growing in size, also have the aim of nation-building and the manufacturing of consent from society (Can 2020 and 2013). As the biggest and richest city in Turkey, Istanbul, of course, was subject to the majority of these changes and projects. Especially in the last decade, this urban transformation and the scale of these top-down urban projects has reached unprecedented levels. Having said that, the biggest difference is that the public tenders for all these projects used to be distributed somewhat equally between private companies. However, in line with the increasingly non-democratic forms of governance in Turkey, nowadays, most tenders are only given to pro-government companies. In addition, this ever-shrinking circle of pro-government businesses are able to engage in never-before-seen projects and benefit from them at the maximum level (Oktem 2019). This contributes to the authoritarian nature of urban administration in Turkey. As Kerem Öktem explains skilfully in his chapter:

> This business model is facilitated by "Turkey's exit from democracy" (Öktem and Akkoyunlu, 2016), the increasing centralisation of powers in the hand of the president, and the progressive erosion of the rule of law, allowing for the realisation of real estate and infrastructure projects that would otherwise have failed environmental impact assessments and/or municipal oversight or would not have been allowed within the framework of existing zoning plans (Lovering and Türkmen, 2011). With Turkey's increasingly authoritarian drift since around 2011, a coup attempt on 15 July 2016, and the regime change to a hyper-presidential system in June 2018, the construction sector has morphed into one of the economy's few remaining growth engines. (Öktem 2019, 299)

The most renowned mega projects are Istanbul Airport—the third airport—Yazuv Sultan Selim Bridge, and the Çamlıca Mosque, all of which are recent constructions and introduced to the public as being both the biggest and the best (Adaman and Akbulut 2021). These projects managed to garner support from AKP constituencies, usually through the politics of nation building, developmentalism, and growth 'while the whole world is watching us' even though urban megaprojects rarely ever create economic growth or sustainable development for any part of the population, except the ruling elite.

In spite of the insistence by policymakers and both local and national authorities on the fact that most of these urban regeneration and redevelopment projects are proposed and constructed for risk mitigation, earthquake purposes, and with 'significant' social benefit,[2] the fact that they mostly target middle and upper-class people—who increase land speculation and squeeze out the urban poor from any neighbourhood that is remotely central—leads most academics and activists to think that there is a more gentrification-seeking agenda (Can 2020; Islam 2010; and Ucal and Kaplan 2020). However, in spite of these increasing authoritarian practices, there is a growing and important urban resistance against these projects and decisions. Most of the controversial urban projects—like the Tarlabaşı Renewal Project, Sulukule Project, and Kanal Istanbul Project—and authoritarian urban decisions were met with important criticism and resistance, one important example

---

2   For an example of proposed social benefits see the Mayor of Fatih's statements on the Sulukule Project: https://www.hurriyet.com.tr/gundem/fatih-belediye-baskanindan-sulukule-aciklamasi-9779099.

being the Gezi Park protests. This also proved that this increasing neoliberalization coupled with an oppressive approach to urban dissent has resulted in a fundamental reconfiguration of the urban-level hierarchies in which cities are enmeshed, and cities remain crucial theatres for socio-political conflicts as a result (Purcell 2008; Lelandais 2014). In spite of the state's physical and symbolic dominance, social action and resistance within the city aims to modify capitalism's socio-territorial organization at many geographical scales (Purcell 2008; Lelandais 2014).

In Brazil, just like in Turkey, during the past years there has been a significant increase in authoritarian urban policies as well, and as a result many democratic practices were either limited or completely repressed. After the coup against Rousseff in 2016, the national context has changed profoundly, characteristic of a new form of imposition of market interests which accentuate coercion as a key component of politics in general, and urbanism in its specificity. Despite the high growth rates observed between 2005–08, and a rapid economic recovery after the international financial crisis, the political scenario changed profoundly from 2013 onwards. The intensification of social, economic, and political conflicts in the country, especially related to the role of the state in promoting development, resulted in Rousseff's government shifting towards fiscal austerity policies (Serrano and Summa 2018), which were exacerbated by both the Temer and Bolsonaro governments. During the 2000s, Lulism would have initiated a process of change in the country's class structure, reducing the industrial reserve army, which touched the core of national dependent capitalism and caused a repositioning of the dominant classes in favour of a new political-economic agenda (Singer 2018, 18). It seems that the industrialists, who began the decade participating in a national-corporativist arrangement of a neo-developmentalist character, progressively shifted their position in favour of austerity and a reduction of social rights.

In urban policy, it is possible to list a number of elements that support the notion that there has been an authoritarian rise and the conformation of NAU:

- The end of spaces of participatory democracy, with the cancellation of the national conference of cities by the Temer Government in 2017, and the closing, by the Bolsonaro Government, of the National Council of Cities—a space for the formulation of urban policy that involved the participation of social movements.
- The worsening of the criminalization of social movements, with arrests of leaders and repression of mobilizations and occupations. In addition to the arrests of housing movement leaders in 2019, there were assassinations of rural leaders, and two bills—272/2016 and 1595/2019, presented by Bolsonaro's allies with the aim of silencing the opposition, criminalizing social movements and strikes, and restricting fundamental freedoms—are still being processed. The

bills propose broadening the concept of terrorism to include popular mobilizations and demonstrations critical of the government.
- The end of the My House My Life programme and its replacement by a new housing policy that prioritizes construction for the middle classes. The "Casa Verde e Amarela" programme is aimed at subsidizing construction companies and housing production for middle incomes, and to stimulate the creation of financial assets in land regularization processes.
- The dismantling of the land legislation—Law No. 11,977—which adopted a model of full land regularization, with a focus on guaranteeing rights, and the instauration of a new legislation—13,465/17—to encourage land grabbing and land appropriation by the market, which is founded on the formalization of private property titles.
- The privatization of basic sanitation, through the establishment of a new legal framework in the sector—law 14.026/2020—which can be pointed to as a further step towards the commodification of water, one of the main forms of the ongoing process of primitive accumulation, or in Harvey's terms, accumulation by dispossession.
- The exponential increase in evictions and removals, including during the COVID-19 pandemic, with a growth in administrative evictions, i.e. those conducted by the administrative forces of the state without judicial authorization. In one year, from August 2020 to August 2021, there was a 310 percent increase in the number of evicted families in Brazil. There were 19,875 families evicted in this period. In addition, there was a 495 percent increase in the number of families threatened with losing their housing.[3]

Other policies can be listed that exemplify this new authoritarian neoliberal phase, such as the precariousness of public services as a result of the approval of Constitutional Amendment 95, which established a limit for social investments in the country. Neoliberal urbanism in Brazil created a period of intense disputes, which at some moments resulted in achievements by social movements from the perspective of rights. The City Statute and the participatory budget are perhaps the best-known examples of Brazilian urban policy, even during the neoliberal phase, they served as models for the adoption of instruments that imposed limits on the accumulation of capital and guaranteed the right to the city (Fernandes 2007; Avritzer 2010; and Dagnino 2014). These mechanisms, however, were already quite limited by the dominant pattern of accumulation, and were completely annulled by the measures pointed out above that make up the NAU: participatory spheres were closed down, urban development policy was further privatized, housing supply was

---

3   The data can be seen, in Portuguese, here: https://drive.google.com/file/d/1CIZjXacbUDgMq SaidkIpsoba9BF9q8Ju/view?usp=sharing

focused on the highest income households, state and parastatal violence against social movements increased significantly, and the poorest population was made even more vulnerable to evictions and displacements. Accumulation by dispossession becomes widespread through the private appropriation of land and collective goods that conform urban spaces. In the same historical context in which half of the Brazilian population is in a situation of food insecurity, without having enough resources for three meals a day, and unemployment reaches historic highs, the real estate market announces impressive numbers. In 2020, there was a 57.5 percent growth in real estate financing, with BRL 124 billion released by the banks, and a new growth of 113 percent in the first quarter of 2021. According to data from ABECIP—the Brazilian Association of Real Estate Loans and Savings—operations between January and March 2021 reached a record amount of BRL 43.1 billion, with 187,600 units sold.

Capital accumulation is produced by a dynamic that combines state, parastatal, and paramilitary violence against the popular classes, i.e. police operations, and judicial and extrajudicial expulsion of vulnerable populations from where they live, with the reappropriation of land by real estate and financial agents, construction companies, and speculators, among others. With urban governance geared towards private real estate production, for middle and high-income consumption, and the permanent linking of interests between the financial sector, real estate developers, private investors, and the state, the land previously occupied by homeless families becomes an 'asset'.

In both countries there is a remarkable overlap in terms of neoliberal urban policies and practices and the oppressive way they were implemented. Brazil saw some development of social housing before 2013 and the economic agenda was positioned more towards growth. However, after 2013 there have been clear austerity politics which were complemented by neoliberal policies and authoritarian practices. This has been different in Turkey. First of all, despite the increasing political tension between actors, there has not been a major political change in Turkey since 2002 and the urban agenda has so far followed a neoliberal developmentalist path, most of the time at the expense of the vulnerable urban population. In the case of Brazil, social movements have achieved effective mechanisms of participation in the elaboration and management of urban policies, which resulted in public policies with some degree of inclusion that accentuated the legitimation component in the coercion-consensus binomial present in the period of hegemony under neoliberal urbanism. In the case of Turkey, the coercion that already prevailed in the pre-2008 period was progressively accentuated, with increasing concentration of power and state participation in urban development, which allows us to categorize political relations as authoritarian in the recent period.

Certainly, this growth and development has been very unequal, which has been the case in both countries. Especially recently, as most—if not all—of the housing stock has been constructed for the middle or upper-middle class and most schemes for generating money have benefitted the ruling and business elite. In terms of growing resistance and oppressing that resistance, both countries' civil societies followed a similar path where the importance of solidarity and notions of urban justice have been increasing and urban space has been a strategic arena for demonstrating and organizing for such unrest and discontent. Finally, in both countries, urban laws and regulations have been weaponized and modified to fit the needs of housing capital, instead of the population in need of shelter.

Conclusion: Conceptualizing Neoliberal Authoritarian Urbanism

There is a neoliberal authoritarian urbanism which promotes capital accumulation in the city space, a financialized governance structure that combines global market interest and local public and private agents. Since the beginning of the neoliberal era, state-finance-led urban policy has been enabled through the dismantling of pre-existing systems and it advances its frontiers by mobilizing state agents, which dismantle existing social and territorial relations and reorganize them according to market interests. What was once a common space occupied by poor families becomes a commodity offered as a new lifestyle for the upper classes. Neoliberal authoritarian urbanism combines historical urban actors such as owners, developers, builders, banks, and often inhabitants with a continuous acceleration of the role of financial investors associated with an increasingly authoritarian state in the development of large urban projects and real estate developments. This growing articulation between autocratic personalities in state power and private actors imposes new challenges on the understanding of urban space production.

As shown by some commentators, the rapprochement between the real estate sector and finance has become closer and more evident in the various financial innovations that have, in turn, mobilized various capital circuits for the financing of real estate developments, with significant effects on urban territories (Fix 2015; Aalbers et al. 2020). The new authoritarian phase, that distinguishes itself from neoliberal urbanism "marks a significant shift away from consensus-based strategies to a model of governance" (Tansel 2017, 11), in which "dominant social groups are less interested in neutralizing resistance and dissent via concessions and forms of compromise", and produce "the explicit exclusion and marginalization" of the urban poor (Bruff 2014, 116). What we here call neoliberal authoritarian urbanism expresses a new phase of relationship between market and state in the accumulation of capital through urban development. The action of market actors, both global and local, is articulated within authoritarian governance on a national and local scale, no longer as a mere consequence of the known epicentres of dissemination of practices and neoliberal reforms.

There is significant social transformation taking place in Turkey and Brazil. An important part of that transformation is conducted through urban development and there are several common features of regeneration taking place. The neighbourhoods selected for these projects have mostly been areas that are physically deteriorated. Most of the investments and urban policies have been primarily about profit and creating new residential areas for the middle and upper class. Many of the housing investments and housing policies are prepared without including public opinion and with as little information as possible provided to the public. This means that urban planning, which was supposed to be a tool for the public, is reaffirmed as a tool of authoritarian imposition of interests in favour of the business sector and the financially privileged.

Neoliberal urban policies go hand in hand with the increasingly oppressive attitude of the local and national governments of Turkey and Brazil. Both urban governance authorities prioritized the private housing and real estate sector and capital accumulation through the increasing dispossession of the vulnerable urban population. In this regard, the privilege the real estate developers and the middle and upper classes have 'to take and make' space and make it look like 'there was never really any alternative' through the brutal and oppressive displacement processes, with the help of the local and national governments, emphasizes the need for resistance that enables the people to stay in neighbourhoods that are now contested and commodified.

With the rise of NAU and the growing financialization of the global economy, the accumulation of capital through urbanization has imposed itself as a homogenizing pattern globally, despite the profound differences and spatial heterogeneities between the various geographical regions of the world. The countries in focus demonstrate the articulation between state and market in the appropriation of urban space as an accumulation process. Despite their vast differences in terms of culture, language, geography, and state institutions, there is an important overlap in terms of the financialization of the housing market in both countries. Additionally, the fact that both countries' current governments opt to use authoritarian practices to suppress any kind of resistance from the public—while implementing controversial urban projects, especially from the vulnerable urban population, and coddling profit-led companies—supports the idea of this overlap. This oppression makes these locations even more attractive for transnational real estate capital, as international investors understand that they would not have to deal with a public outcry themselves. Additionally, they could benefit from tax exemptions and weakened institutional and bureaucratic checks due to the authoritarian nature of the regimes and these regimes' desire to selectively engage with free market capitalism to stimulate growth.

This is a deepening of the relationship of dependency between state and capital, between the local and the global, which makes it necessary to analyse in combination the transnational structures of the financial market and the role of government-led coalitions in promoting private housing production or megaprojects. The central role of the state in the process of accumulation is shown in public subsidies for low-interest mortgage programmes—the use of public funds to expand financialization, the relationship between state intervention and increasing home ownership rates, and how the states represent the interests of the construction and finance industry.

Thus, we have presented in this chapter the importance of urban dynamics for the understanding of contemporary political phenomena, and vice-versa. The new authoritarianisms are supported by the urban development markets, which in turn accentuate exclusionary dynamics that have historically shaped cities. If this hypothesis is correct, we hope that the category NAU presented here may contribute to the study of these combined phenomena that are profoundly transforming life in cities and imposing new challenges on the working classes, poor, and marginalized populations.

References

Aalbers, M. B., R. Rolnik, and M. Krijnen (2020), "The Financialization of Housing in Capitalism's Peripheries", *Housing Policy Debate*, vol. 30, pp. 481–85.

Adaman, F. and B. Akbulut (2021), "Erdoğan's Three-Pillared Neoliberalism: Authoritarianism, Populism and Developmentalism", *Geoforum*, vol. 124, pp. 279–89, available at https://doi.org/10.1016/j.geoforum.2019.12.013. Last accessed on 24 June 2022.

Arantes, P. F. (2006), "O ajuste urbano: as políticas urbanas do Banco Mundial e do BID para as cidades", *Pós*, no. 20, São Paulo.

Avritzer, L. (2010), "Living Under a Democracy: Democracy and Its Impact on the Living Conditions of the Poor", *Latin American Research Review*, vol. 45, p. 4.

Ayers, A. J., and A. Saad-Filho (2014), "Democracy Against Neoliberalism: Paradoxes, Limitations, Transcendence", *Critical Sociology*, vol. 41, no. 4–5, pp. 597–618.

Balaban, O. (2012), "The Negative Effects of Construction Boom on Urban Planning and Environment in Turkey: Unravelling the Role of the Public Sector", *Habitat International*, vol. 36, no. 1, pp. 26–35.

Batuman, B. (2015), "Everywhere Is Taksim", *Journal of Urban History*, vol. 41, no. 5, pp. 881–907.

Brenner, N. (2004), *New State Spaces*, Oxford: Oxford University Press.

Bruff, I. (2014), "The Rise of Authoritarian Neoliberalism", *Rethinking Marxism*, vol. 26, no. 1, pp. 113–29.

Bruff, I. and B. C. Tansel (2018), "Authoritarian Neoliberalism: Trajectories of Knowledge Production and Praxis", *Globalizations*, vol. 16, no. 3, pp. 233–44.

Can, A. (2013), "Neo-Liberal Urban Politics in the Historical Environment of Istanbul – The Issue of Gentrification", *Journal of Planning*, vol. 23, no. 2, pp. 95–104.

Can, A. (2020), "A Recipe for Conflict in the Historic Environment of Istanbul", *ACME: An International Journal for Critical Geographies*, vol. 19, no. 1, pp. 131–62.

Can, A. (2021), "The Making and Unmaking of Tarlabasi, Istanbul: An Account of Territorial Stigmatisation", *International Development Planning Review*, vol. 43, no. 4, pp. 435–60.

Can, A. (forthcoming), "Increasing Spatial Authoritarianism and Increasing Spatial Resistance: The Struggle for Istanbul", *Spatializing Authoritarianism*, Syracuse: Syracuse University.

Castells, M. (1977), *The Urban Question: A Marxist Approach*, Cambridge, MA: MIT Press.

Castells, M. (2000), *Rise of the Network Society*, 2nd edition, Malden: Blackwell.

Castells, M. (2001), *The Internet Galaxy: Reflections on the Internet, Business, and Society*, Oxford: Oxford University Press.

Castro, C. A. (1999), *Explosão do autofinanciamento na produção da moradia em São Paulo nos anos 90*, thesis, São Paulo: University of São Paulo.

Centner, R. (2008), "Places of Privileged Consumption Practices: Spatial Capital, the Dot-com Habitus, and San Francisco's Internet boom", *City & Community*, vol. 7, pp. 193–223.

Coskun, Y., C. Watkins, and M. White (2014), "Change, Housing Affordability and Public Policies: The Case of Turkey", Working Paper, *ENHR Conference*, 1–4 July, Scotland.

Dagnino, E., and A. C. C. Teixeira (2014), "The Participation of Civil Society in Lula's Government", *Journal of Politics in Latin America*, vol. 6, no. 3, pp. 39–66.

Dogan E., and A. Stupar (2017), "The Limits of Growth: A Case Study of Three Mega Projects in Istanbul", *Cities*, vol. 60, available at https://doi.org/10.1016/j.cities. 2016.09.013. Last accessed on 24 June 2022.

Fabry, A., and S. Sandbeck (2018), "Introduction to Special Issue on 'Authoritarian Neoliberalism'", *Competition & Change*, vol. 23, available at 102452941881382. Last accessed on 24 June 2022.

Fernandes, E. (2007), "Constructing the 'Right to the City' in Brazil", *Social and Legal Studies*, vol. 16, no. 2, pp. 201–19.

Fix, M. (2011), *Financeirização e transformações recentes no circuito imobiliário no Brasil*, PhD Thesis, Instituto de Economia, Universidade Estadual de Campinas, Campinas, available at https://edisciplinas.usp.br/pluginfile.php/4854780/mod_res ource/content/0/Fix_Mariana_D.pdf. Last accessed on 14 July 2022.

Fix, M. (2015), "The Real Estate Circuit and (the Right to) the City: Notes on the Housing Question in Brazil", *Housing after the Neoliberal Turn*, Leipzig: Spector Books.

Hall, S. (1980), "Popular Democratic versus Authoritarian Populism", *Marxism and Democracy*, London: Lawrence and Wishart.

Hall, S. (2019), *Everyday Life in Austerity: Family, Friends and Intimate Relations*, London: Palgrave Macmillan.

Harvey, D. (2001), *Spaces of Capital: Towards a Critical Geography*, Edinburgh: Edinburgh University Press.

Harvey, D. (2003), *The New Imperialism*, Oxford: Oxford University Press.

Harvey, D. (2005), *A Brief History of Neoliberalism*, Oxford: Oxford University Press.

Islam, T. (2010), "Current Urban Discourse: Urban Transformation and Gentrification in Istanbul", *Architectural Design*, vol. 80, pp. 58–63.

Keyder, C. (2010), "Istanbul Into the Twenty-First Century", *Orienting Istanbul: Cultural Capital of Europe?* London: Routledge.

Koch, N., and A. Valiyev (2016), "Urban Boosterism in Closed Contexts: Spectacular Urbanization and Second-tier Mega-events in Three Caspian Capitals", *Eurasian Geography and Economics*, vol. 56, no. 2, pp. 575–98.

Kowarick, L. (2000), *Escritos urbanos*, São Paulo: Editora 34.

Kuyucu, T., and O. Unsal (2010), "'Urban Transformation' as State-led Property Transfer: An Analysis of Two Cases of Urban Renewal in Istanbul", *Urban Studies*, vol. 47, no. 7, pp. 1479–99.

Lees, L., H. B. Shin, and E. Lopes-Morales (2015), *Global Gentrifications: Uneven Development and Displacement*, Bristol: Policy Press.

Lefebvre, H. (1996), "The Right to the City", *Writings on Cities*, Cambridge, MA: Wiley-Blackwell, p. 158.

Lelandais, G. E. (2014), "Space and Identity in Resistance Against Neoliberal Urban Planning in Turkey", *International Journal of Urban and Regional Research*, vol. 38, no. 5, pp. 1785–1806.

Levy, J., and M. Lussault (2003), *Dictionnaire de la géographie et de l'espace des sociétés [Dictionary of geography and the space of society]*, Paris: Belin.

Lovering, J., and H. Türkmen (2011), "Bulldozer Neo-liberalism in Istanbul: The State-led Construction of Property Markets, and the Displacement of the Urban Poor", *International Planning Studies*, vol. 16, no. 1, pp. 73–96.

Madra, Y. M., and F. Adaman (2014), "Neoliberal Reason and its Forms: Depoliticization Through Economization", *Antipode*, vol. 46, no. 3, pp. 691–716.

Maricato, E. (2015), *Para entender a crise urbana*, São Paulo: Editora Expressão Popular.

Merrifield, A. (2014), *The New Urban Question*, London: Pluto.

Öktem K. (2019), "Erasing Palimpsest City", *Routledge Handbook on Middle East Cities*, Routledge Handbooks Online, available at https://www.academia.edu/38018781/Routledge_Handbook_on_Middle_East_Cities. Last accessed on 24 June 2022.

Öktem, K., and K. Akkoyunlu (2016), "Exit from Democracy: Illiberal Governance in Turkey and Beyond", *Southeast European and Black Sea Studies*, vol. 16, no. 4, pp. 469–80.

Pasternak, S. (2002), "Espaço e população nas Favelas de São Paulo. Trabalho apresentado no", *XIII Encontro da Associação Brasileira de Estudos Populacionais*, Ouro Preto, 8 November.

Peck, J., and A. Tickell (2002), "Neoliberalizing Space", *Antipode*, vol. 34, pp. 380–404.

Peck, J., N. Theodore, and N. Brenner (2009), "Neoliberal Urbanism: Models, Moments, Mutations", *SAIS Review of International Affairs*, vol. 29, no. 1, pp. 49–66, available at https://muse.jhu.edu/article/269245. Last accessed on 24 June 2022.

Perouse, J. F. (2013), "Kentsel Donusum Uygulamalarinda Belirleyici Bir Rol Ustlenen Toplu Konut Idaresi'nin (TOKI) Belirsiz Kimligi Uzerine Birkac Saptama", *Istanbul: Mustesna Sehrin Istisna Hali*, Istanbul: Sel Yayincilik, pp. 81–96.

Purcell, M. (2006), "Urban Democracy and the Local Trap", *Urban Studies*, vol. 43, available at https://journals.sagepub.com/doi/10.1080/00420980600897826 . Last accessed on 24 June 2022.

Rodrik, D. (2017), "Populism and the Economics of Globalization", NBER Working Paper No. 23559.

Rolnik, R. (2015), *Guerra dos Lugares: a colonização da terra e da moradia na era das finanças*, São Paulo: Boitempo.

Rolnik, R. (2019), *Urban Warfare: Housing Under the Empire of Finance*, London: Verso.

Rolnik, R. (2020), "The Renewed 'Crisis': Housing Struggle Before and After the Pandemic, *Radical Housing Journal*, vol. 2, no. 1, pp. 2–8.

Rugitsky, F. (2017), "The Rise and Fall of the Brazilian Economy (2004–2015): The Economic Antimiracle", Dept. of economics FEA-USP, working paper series, vol. 29.

Saad Filho, A., and L. Morais (2018), *Brasil: Neoliberalismo versus democracia*, São Paulo: Boitempo.

Santos, M. (1996), *A natureza do espaço. Técnica e tempo – razão e emoção*, São Paulo: Hucitec.

Serin, B., H. Smith, and C. Williams (2020), "The Role of the State in the Commodification of Urban Space: The Case of Branded Housing Projects, Istanbul", *European Urban and Regional Studies*, pp. 1–17.

Serrano, F., and R. Summa (2018), "Conflito distributivo e o fim da "breve era de ouro" da economia brasileira", *Novos estudos*, vol. 37, no. 2, pp. 175–89.

Singer, A. (2018), *O lulismo em crise: Um quebra-cabeça do período Dilma (2011-2016)*, São Paulo: Companhia das Letras.

Singer, A. (2021), "Após marcha troll de Bolsonaro sobre São Paulo, democratas precisam isolar direita lunática", *Folha de S. Paulo*, 18 September, available at https://www1.folha.uol.com.br/ilustrissima/2021/09/apos-marcha-troll-de-bolsonaro-sobre-sao-paulo-democratas-precisam-isolar-direita-lunatica.shtml. Last accessed on 24 June 2022.

Smith, N. (1996), *New Urban Frontier: Gentrification and the Revanchist City*, London: Routledge.

Smith, N. (2002), "New Globalism, New Urbanism: Gentrification as Global Urban Strategy", *Antipode*, vol. 34, no. 3, pp. 427–50.

Tansel, C. B. (2017), "Authoritarian Neoliberalism: Towards a New Research Agenda", *States of Discipline: Authoritarian Neoliberalism and the Contested Reproduction of Capitalist Order*, London: Rowman & Littlefield International, pp. 1–28.

Tatagiba, L., R. Abers, and L. Serafim (2011), "A participação na era Lula: repertórios de interação em um Estado heterogêneo", *Dados*, vol. 57.

Ucal, M., and U. Kaplan (2020), "Housing Prices in a Market under Years of Constant Transformation: A County-Based Analysis of İstanbul", *Entrepreneurial Business and Economics Review*, vol. 8, no. 2, pp. 71–91.

Yardımcı, O. (2020), "State Stigmatisation in Urban Turkey: Managing the "Insurgent" Squatter Dwellers in Dikmen Valley", *Antipode*, vol. 52, pp. 1519–38.

Yeni Projeler (2018), *YeniProjeler.com*, available at: http://www.yeniprojeler.com/konut-projeleri. Last accessed on 24 June 2022.

Authoritarian Neoliberalism from Below
Subjectivity and Platform Capitalism in Argentina and Brazil

Fábio Luís Franco and Gustavo Robles

In recent years, after the decline of the so-called Latin American 'pink tide', it became commonplace to speak of an authoritarian turn or the return of neoliberalism to the region. Undoubtedly, the decline of progressivism as the lingua franca of Latin American politics had given way to governments with a marked right-wing profile, explicitly anti-progressive rhetoric, and aggressive agendas of economic flexibilization (Svampa 2020). The governments of Michel Temer, after a coup d'état, and Jair Bolsonaro in Brazil, or Mauricio Macri in Argentina seemed to reconfigure a new political landscape in Latin America that is somehow reminiscent of the 1990s, the golden age of neoliberalism. But this narrative of the Latin American authoritarian turn rarely considers certain continuities that lie beneath the changes of administration and which are based on slower but constant processes of deployment of what we understand here as neoliberal rationality. Such deployments show the latent continuities between the old progressive years and the new conservative years, whilst letting us understand that authoritarianism is not limited to the lack of the rule of law, nor to the ideological profile of the president in office, nor even to the configuration of the state-form. This is because understanding authoritarianism means also being able to conceptualize manners of production and management of life, manners that involve ideologies and representations of the social world, but also bodily experiences and subjective affections and emotions that are often not directly articulated through public discourses or political actions.

In this chapter, we will explore the subjective dimensions of neoliberal biopolitics (those "manners of production and management of life") by analysing the working conditions in the platform economies in Argentina and Brazil. In our opinion, this approach may shed light on aspects of that authoritarianism spread over society which cannot be fully caught by the narrative of administration changes, and on forms of neoliberal authoritarianism, at a time and in a region in which neoliberalism has lost its seductive power, but not its power to make lives precarious.

As we said, we will focus here on the world of work, fundamentally on what is currently known as the platform economy or gig economies, since from there are visible certain key elements of the biopolitical dimension of authoritarianism that involves the organization of labour processes and production of subjective features. These gig economies represent, at the same time and paradoxically, one of the most recent stages of the technological management of labour and one of the deepest stages of labour precarization, which makes these platform economies a privileged place to observe the coexistence between technology and precarization inherent to the new model of neoliberal accumulation, as well as forms of authoritarianism embedded in the management of subjectivities.

In the framework of the global expansion of capital, countries with high levels of informality and precarity, such as Latin American countries, appear as especially favourable environments for the deployment and expansion of these digital economies, due both to the weakness of their legal frameworks, the difficulties for labour market insertion, and the limited infrastructure required (Hidalgo Cordero and Salazar Daza 2020). Although the platform economy is one chapter in a long history of the precarization of labour and life in the societies of the Global South, it is now updated by technologies that have succeeded in extending its control into zones that had hitherto remained at the margins of the exploitative practices of capital: peripheral territories, along with their survival strategies and sociability networks (Franco 2021). Through the promotion of values such as those of flexibility or autonomy, and due to the convenience of their hiring procedures, these companies are often the most immediate employment option among young people and immigrants—and sometimes the only one available—in contexts of recurring economic crisis and structural unemployment (Antunes 2018). Particularly in Argentina and Brazil, companies such as Rappi, PedidosYa, and Glovo started to emerge between 2016 and 2018 reshaping working conditions as well as implying transformations at the level of workers' subjectivities.

As said, this chapter aims to present an approach to the biopolitical dimension of management and control over the workforce in the platform economies to understand authoritarian continuities in societies from the Global South. Towards that end, firstly we will define neoliberalism as a form of political rationality 'from below' since this micropolitical perspective permits inquiry into the subjectivity dimensions of labour management. Secondly, we will offer some comments on the functioning of algorithmic management and, thirdly, an analysis of the impact of the on-demand platforms on workers' subjectivities based on case studies and other research in Argentina and Brazil. In the last section, we will reflect on some theoretical and political aspects of the connection between authoritarianism and neoliberalism in the field of practices and forms of subjectivization.

Neoliberalism from Above and from Below

The financial crisis of 2008 seems to have exposed the weakness of certain liberal imagery that shaped the political culture of post-war Western societies and, since the 1980s, also of Latin America: an imaginary based on the combination of an institutional rule of law, an open market economy, and liberal values of socialization (Robles 2020a). Nowadays, we witness how this liberal consensus is being challenged by a wave of far-right leaders and political movements around the world, which has led to the question of how to conceptualize the connections between neoliberalism, as the latter phase of the capitalist mode of accumulation, and the (re)emergence of authoritarian and anti-democratic political expressions. However, this discussion had already been present in the first moments of the neoliberal revolution, as shown, for example, in the debate about the "authoritarian statism" after Nicos Poulantzas (2000) towards the end of the 1970s, or about the "authoritarian populism" after Stuart Hall (2007) in the mid-1980s. Currently, and in continuity with those perspectives, the connection between authoritarianism and neoliberalism has been discussed by political theory mainly at macro-political or discursive-ideological levels: in terms, for example, of anti-democratic modifications of the state's structure and functioning (Bruff 2013), of mixtures of authoritarian values and ultraliberal dogmas (Biebricher 2000), of amorphous ideological formations caused by the hegemonic crisis of neoliberalism (Brown 2020), or of neoliberal crisis management strategies (Demirovic 2018).

These multiplicities of perspectives are partly due to the elusiveness of the very concept of neoliberalism, which has become widespread in social sciences to define a new historical period from the 1970s onwards. Despite its condition as a 'newcomer' in social and political thought, multiple approaches and disputes are going around about what neoliberalism means, making it impossible to reach an agreement on its meaning. To give some examples of this situation, in the last decade neoliberalism was defined as a set of ideas on the economy and society (Slobodian 2017), as ways of regimenting the Global South after its decolonization (Borón et al. 1999), as a set of institutional policies carried out by supranational institutions (Harvey 2007), as a de-democratization process (Brown 2015), and as the concrete hegemony of financialization and austerity (Streeck 2013), among others. However, there is a certain line of inquiry that we want to follow up in this chapter that defines neoliberalism as a particular kind of political and practical rationality, since it will allow us, on the one hand, to connect neoliberalism with the ideological production of subjectivities and, on the other hand, to understand its pragmatic functioning beyond the institutional level.

The mentioned perspectives arise from Michel Foucault's 1979 lectures, titled *The Birth of Biopolitics* (2004). There, Foucault defines neoliberalism as a new "art of governmentality" that rules the relation between state, market, and subjects by expanding the market rationality to the entire social field through the generalization of the enterprise model. In this way, neoliberalism is understood as a device that produces practical rationalities, based no longer on exchange but on competition, and modes of subjectivization oriented toward the promotion of human capital. The central point is that this neoliberal understanding of the corporate form as an atom of society has the ideological effect of obscuring the contradiction between capital and labour by transforming the workers into their capitalists. Those ideas have given rise to a research field called 'governmentality studies', which has focused on the techniques, institutions, and reflections on techniques that allow the exercise of specific forms of power over populations (Barry et al. 1996).

Although this research field has produced contributions to inquiry into authoritarian governmentality methods, these contributions have been mostly limited to the analysis of ideas, schools, and theories on authoritarian and racist control over populations (Haidar 2019). On the contrary, our perspective will attempt to directly address the psychosomatic dimensions of biopolitical management in the workplace as, from the neoliberal view, it is up to the individuals to ensure the prosperity of themselves as enterprises: the individuals on their own must invest and manage their capital, improve their skills and competencies, and obtain the income corresponding to their performances. In short, neoliberalism consists of ways of governing through the constant creation and management of freedoms: unlike sovereign regimes, that had tried to constrain the behaviours of subjects, neoliberal governmentality works by setting up a series of technologies, practices, and ideologies that promote free initiative, self-responsibility, and individual self-management. Neoliberalism contains the paradox that its authoritarian premises are included in its definition of freedom (Robles 2020b).

Then, understanding neoliberalism as political rationality allows for light to be shed on the mechanisms of exploitation through a set of everyday tactics of (self-)control and (self-)surveillance, ways of behaving, feeling, and thinking that shape the social world 'from below'. Following this line of thought, Verónica Gago (2014/2017) in her book *La razón neoliberal (Neoliberalism from Below)* coined the concept of "neoliberalism from below" to complement the Foucauldian understanding by bringing up the neoliberal specificities of contemporary Latin American societies. In a simplified topology, neoliberalism "from above" would mean a global accumulation regime associated with transformations at the nation-state level, while "from below" refers to "forms of life that reorganize notions of freedom, calculation, and obedience, projecting a new collective affectivity and rationality" (Gago 2014, 6). This approach is particularly valuable as it tries to explain why neoliberalism is still alive and effective after its crisis of political legitimacy, as she shows through an analysis of the popular and informal economic sectors in Buenos Aires. In Gago's perspective, neoliberalism is always involved in ways of appropriation, alteration, and relaunching from the grassroots, combined and contaminated by local and traditional know-how, communal strategies, local representations, previous experiences, and cultural values.

Unlike Gago, in this text, we will not focus on the pragmatics and agency strategies of the actors, but on the subjective consequences of the algorithmic organization of work. However, this does not prevent us from speaking of neoliberalism analysed "from below" since we are looking for those authoritarian dimensions of neoliberal systems of management. Thus, this understanding of neoliberalism, a type of political rationality that works from below, leads to a central question of our research: the question of subjectivities. Neoliberalism is basically a way of producing subjectivities through permanently demanding competition, engagement, performance, and self-capitalization. In the last few years, many authors have been creating concepts to refer to this connection between the mechanisms of subjectivization and neoliberal transformations, such as the "entrepreneurial self" (Bröckling 2007), the "achievement-subject" (Han 2014), or the "neoliberal subject" (Dardot and Laval 2009). Although most of these reflections were formulated from experiences from industrialized countries and based on consultants, entrepreneurs, and managers as models of "neoliberal subjectivities", they permit us to reflect on the impact of neoliberal transformations on the subjectivities related to precarious working conditions in the Global South.

In this regard, what we want to analyse in the following sections is a phenomenon that has received scant attention: the subjective effects of the working conditions in platform economies. The theoretical and political meaning of this subject lies in the fact that it will allow us to observe the authoritarian deployment of neoliberal governance at the subjective level, that is, techno-political modes of acting on bodies and psyche that are a necessary condition for the functioning of neoliberal governmentality. Furthermore, we will argue that these techno-political mechanisms of management of subjectivities must be characterized as authoritarian insofar as they systematically produce dispossession of subjective autonomy, psychophysical pathologies, and modes of desymbolization through biopolitical mechanisms of the immunization of labour relations.

Algorithmic Governmentality

The location-based platform companies have been growing in Brazil and Argentina since 2015 by feeding on the massive unemployment resulting from periodic capitalist crises and the failure of the developmental model's promises of absorption of workers into the formal labour market. The platform economies can be described, in general terms, as companies based on digital infrastructures (platforms) that operate by connecting, through algorithmic technologies, the demand for service with its supply, and which must be understood as part of an extensive course of capitalist readaptation after the crisis of the industrial mode of production in the 1970s (Srnicek 2016). Then, there is a direct relationship between the crisis of overaccumulation and the falling rate of profit that opened up in the 1970s, and the implementation of the algorithmic management of labour. That crisis led to capital going on the offensive against work for the reduction of labour costs and the participation of workers in the distribution of profits, at the same time commencing a process of financialization and increased investment in intangible capital over physical capital, for example machines and installations (Beniger 1989).

However, the emergence of algorithmics must be understood as a continuity but also as a rupture with previous modes of automation, since algorithmics allows the organization of work without investment in physical capital or the development of complex technologies. Algorithms are basically a cheaper and relatively simple technology of work management that can be defined as computational metrics by which decisions are made automatically according to a given structure. After the 2008 financial crisis and the recent crisis of the pandemic, the implementation of algorithmic management (over the more expensive and complex machine or robotic automation) accelerated and became the model of rationalization, control, and exploitation of labour *par excellence* of post-growth capitalism (Schaupp 2021). These platform economies carry out their activities in the interstices and legal loopholes and are based on an extractivist logic of data, financial rent, and labour force to the point of exhaustion, both physical and mental.

That can be seen in the case of location-based platform companies that have spread to all the cities of the world in recent years. They are companies whose on-demand workers operate in an anonymous position of intermediary between supply and demand that gives these companies their claim to neutrality, i.e. to belong neither to the sphere of production nor to that of consumption and, crucially, to avoid being labelled as employers. By offering seductive gains at the very beginning of their operations, those companies created an army of workers that has not stopped increasing even if the tariffs are frozen and the individual earnings become too little to make ends meet. Therefore, reflecting on the labour dimension of platform economies points to the heart of this new form of capitalist value extraction, since, as Philipp Staab states, these new digital economies are based on the "alliance between the figures of rent-seeking capital and the consumer" to the detriment of the figure of the producer (Staab 2019, 277), i.e. an alliance between financial capital that seeks quick returns and consumer citizens who pursue low-cost profits at the expense of the intensification of labour exploitation.

As has been widely discussed, neoliberalism sets in motion the permanent process of fragmentation of society into a myriad of individuals identified as microenterprises and mobilized by the relentless pursuit of self-valorization, but with the spread of digital platforms, this process has reached new limits. Among the delivery and shipping app workers, can be identified an ongoing process of hyper-individualization arising from the systematic adoption by app companies of "immunization strategies" (Van Doorn 2017). These strategies consist of measures and procedures of subordination, management, and exploitation of workers that on the one hand make it very difficult for the companies to be held legally accountable, and on the other hand, directly and indirectly, intensify the productivity of the deliverers. The immunization strategies are also associated with the "demutualization of risks" that reaches three main and interrelated levels: health risks, financial risks, and epistemic risks (De Stefano 2016). Following this thread, we advocate for the inclusion of subjective risks linked to dimensions of psychosomatic pathologies, as we will discuss further.

Central to these immunization strategies is the invisible nature of algorithmic power through which companies manage to maximize control and management of labour, as well as the flows between supply and demand, anonymously attributing to the indecipherable calculability of software the allocation of bonuses, oscillation in the value of payments, inconsistencies in the distribution of orders, and even arbitrariness in the definition of suspensions. Hence, as Alexandra Mateescu and Aiha Nguyen (2019, 13) explain: technology such as "algorithmic management … can serve to shift existing power dynamics and destabilize employment relationships" in terms of (1) "surveillance and control", which creates new speed and efficiency pressures on workers and removes them from the decision-making; (2) "transparency", that creates power asymmetries difficult to be challenged without knowledge of how these systems work; (3) "bias and discrimination", based on consumer-sourced rating systems that "can introduce biased and discriminatory practices towards workers" (ibid., 2) without the company being responsible for those practices; and (4) "accountability", since algorithmic management is used to "distance companies from the effects of their business decisions, obscuring specific decisions made about how a system should function" (ibid., 14).

These forms of immunization, propitiated and sustained by the mode of operation proper to algorithmic governance, directly affect individual and collective efforts to protect against risks, since they increase the sense of arbitrariness and meaninglessness in everyday work, further weakening workers' security in their ability to interpret the apps and make decisions. This is what can be called 'epistemic risk', which concerns the transformation of uncertainty, arbitrariness, and illegibility into algorithmic work-management mechanisms. Everything is happening as if algorithmic power permanently produces the shuffling of the rules of the digital game, forcing workers to frequently revise their room for manoeuvre and leeway, a situation that can be described as an incessant effort on the part of "partners" to "provisionally manage uncertainty" (Guerra 2021, 212).

This immunization of platform companies begins as early as the signing of the employment contract, where workers are usually defined as "collaborators" or "partners", an expression that seeks to dilute the contradictions between capital and labour by reinforcing the idea of the autonomous and free individual who participates in horizontal labour relations. Companies constantly claim that they are not employers, since the image they intend to give of themselves is, as we said, that of an intermediary between the needs of someone who requires a delivery service (a consumer), with someone who offers a product (for example, a restaurant), and an entrepreneur who offers to transport it (the rider). Appealing to the ideals of individualization of work, entrepreneurship, meritocracy, individual effort, etc., these companies offer an idealized world where there are no bosses, no hierarchies, no fixed schedules, and where the possibility of obtaining a high income depends solely on individual efforts (Diana Menéndez 2019).

As a generalized modus operandi, companies are exempt from the costs and legal obligations imposed by legal labour relations as well as from the burdens of the activities, since it is the 'partners' or 'collaborators' (i.e. the workers) who assume the losses and expenses of their work (traffic accidents, diseases, and contagions during the pandemic, assaults, robberies, vehicle breakdowns, obsolescence or breakage of the smartphone, connectivity problems, etc.). The assumption of costs and burdens by the individual worker also implies, in the absence of the minimum rights and benefits assured by labour legislation, the assumption of health and financial risks. This effectiveness of the platforms in putting their workers outside of the social protection system and assimilating them into the figure of the self-employed entrepreneur is connected not only to the weakness of labour regulation in countries such as Argentina and Brazil but also to the characteristics of algorithmic management which, by depersonalizing the management and control body, fosters an impression of autonomy and flexibility that quickly becomes illusory.

Working in Platform Capitalism

As seen, platform companies manage work tasks through algorithmic immunization mechanisms that take place in day-to-day work, for instance with the immunization of communication flows between the 'partners' and the company, which reduces daily contact between the workers and the company to anonymous notifications and automatic messages. In many cases, communication with the company takes place through call centres located abroad, in countries such as Colombia or Peru, and therefore contact is made with operators who are unfamiliar with the geography and situation of where the workers carry out their tasks, and who can therefore offer few solutions to daily inconveniences. Thus, communication is experienced by the workers as a Sisyphean task, always postponed by unanswered calls, emails that are automatically replied to, or the innumerable intermediate instances in which other precarious workers give standardized explanations to enquiries. Maurício Santos, a driver for a platform company, expresses the following:

> The relationship between the operator and the application is very difficult. You try, but the app gives you ready-made messages; you try with a phone, but it rings and no one answers and, when it answers, sometimes you know more than the person who answers; you call there to ask for guidance, the person asks you questions that make no sense to you ... it's a mess, it's a big mess, and you feel disoriented, and the only solution that comes up is to learn by watching videos on YouTube. (Pessoa Masson and Santos Oliveira 2021)

Cases of temporary suspension or definitive blocking without any justification by the companies, or the so-called *suspensão branca* ('white suspension'), which occurs without the worker knowing that they are being sanctioned, are frequent in this way, in which someone can go for hours or even days without receiving a delivery request without being officially suspended. This can happen for many reasons: receiving bad evaluations, breaching a contractual clause, rejecting a high number of orders, simply because a client complains about something beyond the worker's control, or even in retaliation for having participated in protests or demonstrations against the company (Abílio 2020). Besides that, the arbitrariness of the supposed algorithmic functioning reaches other spheres of the management of platformed labour, such as, for example, the distribution of bonuses for workers who reach a certain goal set by the application. The complaints of workers, in this case, point to the abrupt interruption of delivery requests when someone was close to earning some additional bonus, a practice which causes frustration and spreads distrust of the applications.

Thus, labour tasks in location-based platforms intensify the hyper-individualization of the worker by deepening the spatial decentralization of work as a fundamental condition for full localization. In this sense, performing a just-in-time job means being permanently available to accept tasks that require travel to any place, no matter how far away it may be. This deterritorialization of just-in-time work contributes to the scarcity of opportunities for workers to meet and, therefore, to build emotional and political ties. In this way, workers are at the disposal of the companies all the time, despite only being paid for a fraction of this time: strictly the period concerning the journey from the commercial establishment to the customer's hands. It is increasingly common to find in São Paulo or Buenos Aires, for example, huge groups of delivery people sitting under marquees, grouped in squares or busy streets, concentrating on their smartphones, waiting for an order that may take hours to arrive. The presence of the digital platforms in the workers' lives extends beyond working hours, as the application remains installed on their phones and therefore continues to extract their private data and record their daily activities.

Algorithmic power seeks to individualize the organization of work, something that the workers experience as the condition of being thrown to their fate, as solely and exclusively responsible for their gains and losses, and for survival and resilience strategies. These precarious conditions are aggravated by the structural effects of neoliberalization in countries such as Argentina and Brazil, with weak mechanisms of social protection and state control over companies' compliance with the law, as well as the constant increase in unemployment. This situation of existential anguish is described by Mauricio Santos:

> What surprises me most about working with apps, unfortunately, is the feeling that you're on your own, right? You must figure everything out your way. You don't have support. You try ... you try communication, you try something, but if you don't stop to analyse everything and try to solve it yourself, you will be waiting for a miracle to happen practically, that we are alone. So, it is a feeling of loneliness at the beginning. If you don't overcome this barrier of this feeling of work, you end up with psychological damage. (Pessoa Masson and Santos Oliveira 2021)

This psychological damage is registered by health indicators in Brazil and Argentina. For example, in Brazil depression and anxiety are the second-biggest causes of work-related illnesses and the first for musculoskeletal disorders. Psychic damage is also accompanied by significant organic impacts, as the requirement to work 12 to 14 hours a day leads to bone and muscle injuries, as well as diseases associated with the circulatory system or eating disorders. In the workers' accounts, such anxiety is strongly linked to loneliness, the meeting of productivity targets being met with silence, and lack of interaction with managers or supervisors. When the orders do not arrive, the silence of the phone echoes the silence of the companies and customers; however, when the service arrives and the expected 'ding' of the application notification is heard, the anxiety is related to the impossibility of rejecting the order due to the threat of suspension, even if the distances are enormous, the area is dangerous, or there are bad weather conditions.

As Luciana Kasai, a delivery worker, says:

> We stay in this distress all day long. If it's not distress because there's no rush; it's distress because you must do a lot, you have to rush, because otherwise they'll complain about you, and you'll be the one who suffers. (Pessoa Masson and Santos Oliveira 2021)

Moreover, the strong feeling of uncertainty about the future, accentuated by the epistemological, financial, and health risks we mentioned earlier, makes room for frequent anxiety crises among workers, with their characteristic bodily manifestations, such as insomnia, tachycardia, or panic attacks. As anxiety, according to a Freudian-Lacanian perspective, is understood as a disorder carried out by processes of subjective destitution, we can here identify the existence of 'subjective risks'. Indeed, not having a minimum guaranteed income and job permanence, being shaken every time by a new accusation of arbitrary suspension or cancellation of 'partner' accounts, and the almost complete isolation in the carrying out of work tasks. In sum, the exposure of workers to a multiplicity of risks weakens more and more the confidence and self-esteem that the workers have in themselves. Added to this is the daily exposure to multiple forms of violence, including racial or gender-based violence or xenophobia (frequently concerning immigrant workers), competition among colleagues, and, during a crisis like the coronavirus pandemic, the constant fear of getting infected.

The hyper-individualization of tasks associated with algorithmic work management contributes to intensifying the competitive struggle between workers, encouraging the transformation of ties into a myriad of fragmented competitors who fight among themselves to increase individual profits. This hyper-individualization also expresses a process of "political psychologization of work" in which social problems, such as unemployment or job insecurity, are attributed to personal or psychological causes, such as the worker's lack of entrepreneurial attitudes (Morales Muñoz 2020). The companies dictate the rules, charge commissions (and keep a proportion of the worker's profit), establish forms and times of payment and shipping, and even decide on promotions without consulting the worker, who must assume the costs. One example of such cases would be the '2 x 1' deliveries in the Rappi app, in which the worker must make two deliveries for the price of one. As can be seen, this scheme allows for little autonomy or freedom. Rather than an entrepreneur, this is a digitally precarious worker (Scasserra 2019).

In sum, from the analysis of the experience of work in platform economies, we see that algorithmic control produces effects on the subjectivity of workers, not only through entrepreneurial discourse or through the very organization of tasks in the workplace, but also by encouraging workers to consider themselves in the terms in which the control mechanisms define them, i.e. to monitor their behaviour to meet the company's goals and to extend these conduct norms to their colleagues. Neoliberal societal values such as self-regulation and entrepreneurship are combined with symbolic traditional values such as the struggle for survival and the personal strength to legitimize the model of corporate de-responsibilization. In the pandemic, these values have been explicitly promoted by the platform companies: for instance, in Argentina, the company Rappi launched an advertising campaign to promote its workers as "Rappi Heroes" of the pandemic, to which the Association of Platform Personnel (APP) replied with the statement: "we are not heroes but workers claiming our rights" (Brunetto 2020).

However, despite these attempts at the 'desymbolization' of social bonds and ties of camaraderie among workers, workers have not ceased to experiment with forms of counterstrategies and mutual protection: from sabotage actions, private chat groups, online forums, and the blocking of applications, to more complex practices of cooperative self-organization or different struggles for unionization and recognition as workers, not as 'partners'. Examples of these strategies are the creation of the APP union in Argentina after a series of strikes due to unjustified suspensions in 2018 (Del Bono 2019; Negri 2020); or the delivery workers' strike called *breque dos apps* (apps stoppage) occurring throughout Brazil, which so far has engaged workers in Porto Alegre, Belém, Manaus, Niterói, São Paulo, São José dos Campos, Atibaia, Ribeirão Preto, Jundiaí, Paulínia, São Carlos, etc. Those cases show that digital control over working conditions is not a natural law, but a new space for class struggle. Through various tools of struggle, diverse political experiences, and the participation or disinterest of the big unions, the riders are beginning to become an active political subject under the demand to be recognized as workers with rights.

On Authoritarian Neoliberalism

In Brazil and Argentina, the authoritarian wave that emerged in the last few years has been feeding on the failure of the development promises of social inclusion via consumerism and political rights (Féliz 2021). Instead of that perspective, both the discursive matrices of the Bolsonaro and Macri regimes praise entrepreneurial merits while concurring with the idea of social policies being responsible for national economic crises, whether through the overspending of public funds or by stimulating vagrancy among the population (Catanzaro and Ipar 2017). Based on these justifications, governments have been setting up precarization labour policies combined with the systematic demolition of public funding for social welfare. The wage society linked to the import substitution model no longer exists and the growth of non-wage forms of work, related to the digital economy, is the last expression of this transformation. These platform companies have been developing new strategies of accumulation different from those of the former industrial mode of production, strategies that entangle algorithm management as new practices of governing subjectivities at work, which are at the core of the new neoliberal governmentality.

Indeed, they also promote the reconfiguration of the workers' libidinal economy, that is, of the workers' psychic investments in social models responsible for socializing the individual according to norms of behaviour, moral evaluation, and emotional disposition. That libidinal economy of platform capitalism involves both a configuration of the worker's subjectivity in conformity with those capitalist patterns and a psychic economy, understood as "the contemporary investment—techno-scientific, economic, and social—in algorithmic processes of capturing and using psychic and emotional information extracted from our data and actions on digital platforms" (Bruno et al. 2019, 21). Inversely, the algorithmic power of the platforms not only jeopardizes the psycho-emotional data generated by subjects from their interaction with or through the platforms but also *produces psychological designs* both at behavioural levels and within the subjective dynamics of identification and desire.

Due to such implications, we are convinced that these new techno-political developments should be considered in the current debates on the rise of authoritarianism around the world and on the so-called crisis of democracies. In such debates, the concept of 'authoritarian neoliberalism' has become recurrent as a means of describing an institutional formation under which the reproduction of capital uses the state apparatus to marginalize and repress political and social opposition rather than seeking their explicit consent or co-optation. Some characteristics of authoritarian neoliberalism that are usually pointed out are, for example, the prioritization of legal mechanisms over debates and democratic participation, the centralization of state activity in the executive branch, the increasing use of state repression against opposing political forces, the intervention of the media, etc. (Bruff and Tansel 2019). However, beyond its theoretical productivity, the debates around this concept are often framed in a perspective focused on state functioning or on the ideological-discursive level, perspectives that risk losing pragmatic and biopolitical dimensions of the exercise of power, and which are key dimensions for understanding the persistence of neoliberalism as political rationality in the era of its hegemonic crisis.

Thus, the analysis of the labour market in these platform economies can make visible how neoliberalism survives when no one believes in its heroic tales of progress and welfare anymore. Constant surveillance, evaluation mechanisms, and unjustified suspensions, anonymization of the relationship with the employer, commands from the algorithmic black box, etc. reveal that the authoritarian face of neoliberalism also has its microphysical expression in the world of work, where ideologies of freedom, autonomy, and self-responsibility coexist with the opacity and arbitrariness of algorithmic management. This contradiction between the authoritarian structure of the workplace, as if reproducing a miniature dictatorship of the "private governments" (Anderson 2017) and its ideological legitimization through individualistic values, is one of the silent and persistent phenomena of the current authoritarian regression. This could mean that authoritarianism is not only an expression of the much-mentioned 'crisis of (liberal) democracy' or a crisis of political representation but will also "entail the permutation and crystallization of neoliberal modes of dehumanization involving *new technologies*" (Gambetti 2021). These new technologies and their ideological effects on working subjectivities pose new tasks, both for critical theory and political counterstrategies.

One of these tasks is to overcome the classical dichotomy of consensus versus coercion, ideology versus repression in the authoritarian crisis of neoliberalism. An example of this can be read in *Capital Hates Everyone: Fascism or Revolution* by

Mauricio Lazzarato, where he criticizes the micropolitical approaches of neoliberalism by arguing that, in its current phase, capitalism reproduces itself not only by subjectivizing, producing embodiments, social recognitions, or tacit agreements but also by civil wars, states of exception, class hatreds and repressive violence (Lazzarato 2021). Although many of his observations on the new fascisms are of great value, Lazzarato still maintains a strict dichotomy between ideology and repression to characterize the current authoritarian moment of neoliberalism. This dichotomization is what we wanted to call into question by considering the working conditions of capitalism in the Global South to show that neoliberalism activates ways of subjectivization and ideological discourses that are, at the same time, methods of control, punishment, and surveillance. As an extreme instance of this, we saw recently in São Paulo and Rio de Janeiro how militias have been involved as paramilitary forces of certain platform companies to manage workers through violence and harassment (Liberato 2021). Entrepreneurialism and paramilitary violence work together as the Janus face of new digital capitalism in the Global South.

This workplace-based approach also sheds light on the limits of certain leftist technocratic optimism, which considered that industrial automation and digitalization would lead to a "postcapitalist" society (Mason 2015; Srnicek and Williams 2015). Beyond its fetishization of technology and its misunderstanding of the structural economic trends (Benanav 2021), these perspectives barely focus their analyses on the concrete organization, control, and management of the labour force. Such an analysis would uncover the authoritarian condition of neoliberal governance and, at the same time, would go beyond the liberal understanding of authoritarianism, which conceives it as a conglomerate of values and practices that stand in contrast to the values of modernity—especially liberalism, pluralism, and individualism (Nohlen and Schmidt 1998). In our approach, authoritarianism is neither a kind of 'illiberalism' nor a sociological correlation between authoritarian political choices and factors of social belonging, as the sociologist Seymour Lipset (1959) formulated decades ago through the concept of "working-class authoritarianism". On the contrary, authoritarian neoliberalism rather means the depersonalized digital governmentality of behaviours, desires, and bodies in the name of liberal principles such as freedom, autonomy, or individual responsibility, that work as the structural condition of liberal societies without the legal orbit of the state.

However, a blind spot of the Foucauldian biopolitical approach to governmentality lies in the fact that it does not pay enough attention to the circulation of the libidinal energies linked to the social reproduction of the labour force, nor the psychic malaises caused and exploited by algorithmic management within workplaces. As the analysis of the working conditions in the platform economies showed, a critical theory of authoritarian neoliberalism needs to consider the different expressions and symptoms of anxiety, depression, anguish, and phobias as a social and political phenomenon linked to the new digital phase of neoliberal governmentality

(Exposto and Rodriguez Varela 2021). Algorithmic management, the acceleration of informational processes, the virtualization of social relations, and the alienation of the financialized economy are all facets of neoliberal transformations that impact our subjectivities in the form of psychological and somatic pathologies. Contemporary capitalism puts our subjectivity, desires, emotions, and cognitive capacities to work to produce value under conditions of social and political inequalities and, at the same time, it individualizes and privatizes the costs and burdens of such processes (Safatle 2021). Therefore, the politicization of these psychosomatic malaises is a key part of the struggle against the combination of biopolitical management and meritocratic ideologies carried out by authoritarian neoliberalism.

Conclusions

In this chapter we wanted to approach the relationship between authoritarianism and neoliberalism at the level of practices located in the sphere of labour-management and its impact on the process of subjectivization, taking as an example the working conditions in platform economies in Argentina and Brazil. This analysis has shown that the connection between authoritarianism and neoliberalism works out not only at the level of ideas, political formations, or state regulations but also at the level of the social technologies of control and management of workers' subjectivities. However, we did not pretend to explain the so-called authoritarian turn nor a political analysis of why Macri came to power in Argentina or Bolsonaro in Brazil, since we consider that the connection between the sphere of practices 'from below' and the sphere of macro-political transformations requires multiple epistemological and historical mediations, which go beyond the boundaries of this work and our capacities. Our purpose was rather to shed light on some hidden aspects of the capitalist structural trends that operate as practical rationality and also as symbolic and social conditions for political subjectivization, aspects that should be taken into account when analysing and contesting the current authoritarian turn of neoliberalism.

However, we consider it necessary to keep exploring hypotheses that look for those connections between neoliberalism at the biopolitical level and the sphere of political culture and political transformations. It seems to us that reflection on the change in working conditions and its effects on subjectivities is key to understanding our current political moment. For that, it would be necessary to recover the analysis of the world of work in order to rethink the often mentioned 'crisis of democracy' and the 'authoritarian turn'. This task was recently pointed out by the philosopher Axel Honneth (2021) when he said that "one of the major shortcomings of almost all theories of democracy is to keep forgetting that most members of the sovereign they loudly invoke are working subjects". In this sense, we should venture to explore hypotheses that raise the questions of whether neoliberal precarization, hyper-exploitation, and depersonalized management of labour would not be undermining the symbolic and subjective conditions of democratic relations at the political level; whether the neoliberal governmentality of work is not somehow connected with political apathy and disenchantment, with the attack on solidarities and symbolic bonds, and with forms of de-subjectivization, the symptoms of which we are currently seeing as a political emergence.

References

Abílio, L. C. (2020), "Plataformas digitais e uberização: a globalização de um Sul administrado?" *Revista Contracampo*, vol. 39, no. 1, pp. 12–26, available at https://doi.org/10.22409/contracampo.v39i1.38579. Last accessed on 7 July 2022.

Anderson, E. (2017), *Private Government: How Employers Rule Our Lives (and Why We Don't Talk about It)*, Princeton University Press.

Antunes, R. (2018), *O privilégio da servidão: O novo proletariado de serviços na era digital*, Boitempo.

Barry, A., N. Rose, and T. Osborne, (eds.) (1996), *Foucault and Political Reason: Liberalism, Neo-liberalism, and Rationalities of Government*, UCL Press.

Benanav, A. (2021), *Automation and the Future of Work*, London: Verso.

Beniger, J. (1989), *The Control Revolution: Technological and Economic Origins of the Information Society*, Harvard University Press.

Biebricher, T. (2000), Neoliberalism and Authoritarianism, *Global Perspectives*, vol. 1, no. 1, pp. 1–18.

Borón, A., J. Gambina, and N. Minsburg, (eds.) (1999), *Tiempos violentos: Neoliberalismo, globalización y desigualdad en América Latina*, Buenos Aires: CLACSO.

Bröckling, U. (2007), *Das unternehmerische Selbst: Soziologie einer Subjektivierungsform*, Frankfurt am Main: Suhrkamp.

Brown, W. (2015), *Undoing the Demos: Neoliberalism's Stealth Revolution*, New York: Zone Books.

Brown, W. (2020), *In the Ruins of Neoliberalism*, Columbia University Press.

Bruff, I. (2013), "The Rise of Authoritarian Neoliberalism", *Rethinking Marxism*, vol. 26, no. 1, pp. 113–129, available at https://doi.org/10.1080/08935696.2013.843250. Last accessed on 7 July 2022.

Bruff, I., and C. B. Tansel, (2019), *Authoritarian Neoliberalism: Philosophies, Practices, Contestations*, Abingdon: Routledge.

Brunetto, S. (2020), "Inédita protesta de repartidores de comida en seis países", *Página/12*, 23 April, available at https://www.pagina12.com.ar/261548-inedita-protesta-de-repartidores-de-comida-en-seis-paises. Last accessed on 12 July 2022.

Bruno, F. G., A. C. F. Bentes, and P. Faltay, (2019), "Economia psíquica dos algoritmos e laboratório de plataforma: mercado, ciência e modulação do comportamento", *Revista FAMECOS*, vol. 26, no. 3, available at https://doi.org/10.15448/1 980-3729.2019.3.33095. Last accessed on 7 July 2022.

Catanzaro, G., and E. Ipar, (2017), "Nueva derecha y autoritarismo social", *Revista Anfibia*, available at https://www.revistaanfibia.com/nueva-derecha-autoritari smo-social/. Last accessed on 7 July 2022.

Dardot, P., and C. Laval (2009), *La nouvelle raison du monde: Essai sur la société néolibérale*, Paris: La Découverte.

Del Bono, A. (2019), "Trabajadores de plataformas digitales: Condiciones laborales en plataformas de reparto a domicilio en Argentina", *Cuestiones de Sociología*, vol. 21, pp. 1–14, available at https://doi.org/10.24215/23468904e083. Last accessed on 7 July 2022.

Demirovic, A. (2018), "Autoritärer Populismus als neoliberale Krisenbewältigungsstrategie", *Prokla Zeitschrift Für Kritische Theorie*, vol. 48, no. 190, pp. 27–42.

De Stefano, V. (2016), "Introduction: Crowdsourcing, the Gig-Economy and the Law", *Comparative Labor Law & Policy Journal*, vol. 37, no. 3, pp. 461–470, available at https://ssrn.com/abstract=2767383. Last accessed on 7 July 2022.

Diana Menéndez, N. (2019), "¿Qué hay de nuevo, viejo? Una aproximación al trabajo de plataformas en Argentina", *Revista de Ciencias Sociales*, vol. 3, no. 165, pp. 45–58, available at https://doi.org/10.15517/RCS.VoI165.40064. Last accessed on 7 July 2022.

Exposto, E., and G. Rodriguez Varela (2021), "El giro malestarista de las nuevas teorías críticas y el análisis militante del inconsciente", *Crisis y crítica: Intervenciones en presente sobre el futuro de la emancipación*, edited by A. Prestifilippo and S. Roggerone, Buenos Aires: CLACSO-IIGG/UBA, pp. 249–73.

Féliz, M. (2021), "¿Veinte años no es nada? Neodesarrollismo, movimientos populares y nueva forma estatal en Argentina", *(En)Clave Comahue: Revista Patagónica de Estudios Sociales*, vol. 28, pp. 6–37.

Foucault, M. (2004), *La Naissance de la biopolitique: Cours au Collège de France (1978–1979)*, Paris: Gallimard.

Franco, F. L. (2021), "Neoliberal Platform Capitalism and Subjectivity: A Study of the Hybridization between Labor Platformization and *Viração* in Brazil", *South Atlantic Quarterly*, vol. 120, no. 4, pp. 795–808, available at https://doi.org/10.12 15/00382876-9443350. Last accessed on 7 July 2022.

Gago, V. (2014), *La razón neoliberal: Economías barrocas y pragmática popular*, Buenos Aires: Tinta Limón (English Version: [2017], *Neoliberalism from Below: A Perspective from Latin America*, Durham, NC: Duke University Press).

Gambetti, Z. (2021), "The New Fascist Moment", *Historical Materialism*, 25 June, available at https://www.historicalmaterialism.org/index.php/blog/new-fascist-m oment. Last accessed on 7 July 2022.

Guerra, A. G. (2021), *Infraestruturas, narrativas e imaginários algorítmicos: tecnografando o preço dinâmico da Uber*, dissertation, Universidade Federal de Minas Gerais, available at https://repositorio.ufmg.br/handle/1843/39461. Last accessed on 7 July 2022.

Haidar, V. (2019), "¿Autoritarismo al interior del liberalismo? Entre los aportes de los Governmentality Studies y las posibilidades abiertas por la Historia del Presente", *Conductas que importan: Variantes de análisis de los Estudios en Gubernamentalidad*, edited by A. Avellaneda and G. Vega, Corrientes: EUDENE, pp. 77–105.

Hall, S. (2007), "The Great Moving Right Show", *Selected Political Writings*, Durham, NC: Duke University Press.

Han, B.-C. (2014), *Psychopolitik. Neoliberalismus und die neuen Machttechniken*, Berlin: Fischer Verlag.

Harvey, D. (2007), *A Brief History of Neoliberalism*, Oxford University Press.

Hidalgo Cordero, K., and C. Salazar Daza (eds.) (2020), *Precarización laboral en plataformas digitales: Una lectura desde América Latina*, Quito: Friedrich Ebert Stiftung, available at http://library.fes.de/pdf-files/bueros/quito/17108.pdf. Last accessed on 7 July 2022.

Honneth, A. (2021), "Arbeit, Selbstachtung und Demokratie: Der arbeitende Souverän", *Die Tageszeitung*, 12 June, available at https://taz.de/Arbeit-Selbstachtung-und-Demokratie/!5774633/. Last accessed on 7 July 2022.

Lazzarato, M. (2021), *Capital Hates Everyone: Fascism or Revolution*, MIT Press.

Liberato, L. V. (2021), "A inovadora parceria entre o IFood e as milícias", *Le Monde Dipomatique Brasil*, 23 July, available at https://diplomatique.org.br/a-inovadora-parceria-entre-o-ifood-e-as-milicias/. Last accessed on 7 July 2022.

Lipset, S. (1959), "Democracy and Working-Class Authoritarianism", *American Sociological Review*, vol. 24, no. 4, pp. 482–501, available at https://doi.org/doi.org/10.2307/2089536. Last accessed on 7 July 2022.

Mason, P. (2015), *PostCapitalism: A Guide to our Future*, London: Allen Lane.

Mateescu, A., and A. Nguyen (2019), "Algorithmic Management in the Workplace", *Data & Society*, available at https://datasociety.net/wp-content/uploads/2019/02/DS_Algorithmic_Management_Explainer.pdf. Last accessed on 7 July 2022.

Morales Muñoz, K. (2020), "La valoración de la flexibilidad y la libertad en el trabajo en apps: ¿Los trabajadores de plataforma son sujetos neoliberales?" *Precarización laboral en plataformas digitales una lectura desde América Latina*, edited by K. Hidalgo Cordero and C. Salazar Daza, Quito: Friedrich Ebert Stiftung, pp. 21–37, available at http://library.fes.de/pdf-files/bueros/quito/17108.pdf. Last accessed on 7 July 2022.

Negri, S. (2020), "Condiciones laborales, proceso de trabajo y movilización de los trabajadores en plataformas de reparto en Argentina", *Precarización laboral en plataformas digitales una lectura desde América Latina*, edited by K. Hidalgo Cordero and C. Salazar Daza, Quito: Friedrich Ebert Stiftung, pp. 37–55.

Nohlen, D., and M. G. Schmidt (1998), "Autoritarismus", *Lexikon der Politik*, edited by D. Nohlen, Munich: C.H.Beck, p. 61.

Pessoa Masson, L., and S. Santos Oliveira (2021), "Trajetos e trajetórias invisíveis na cidade", *YouTube*, Fiocruz, UFRJ, and UFF, available at https://www.youtube.com/watch?v=mKoCf338F5c&ab_channel=VideoSaúdeDistribuidoradaFiocruz. Last accessed on 7 July 2022.

Poulantzas, N. (2000), *State, Power, Socialism*, London: Verso.

Robles, G. (2020a), "Sobre la dimensión política del resentimiento", *Castalia: Revista de Psicología de la Academia*, vol. 34, pp. 5–23, available at https://doi.org/10.25074/07198051.34.1756. Last accessed on 7 July 2022.

Robles, G. (2020b), "What does authoritarianism mean in times of coronavirus?" *International Research Group on Authoritarianism and Counter-strategies (IRGAC)*, available at https://www.irgac.org/2020/07/17/what-does-authoritarianism-mean-in-times-of-coronavirus/. Last accessed on 7 July 2022.

Safatle, V. (2021), "A economia é a continuação da psicologia por outros meios: sofrimento psíquico e o neoliberalismo como economia moral", *Neoliberalismo como gestão do sofrimento psíquico*, edited by V. Safatle, N. da Silva Junior, and C. Dunker, São Paulo: Autêntica, pp. 11–38.

Scasserra, S. (2019), "El despotismo de los algoritmos: Cómo regular el empleo en las plataformas", *Nueva Sociedad*, no. 279, pp. 133–40, available at http://library.fes.de/pdf-files/nuso/nuso-279.pdf. Last accessed on 8 July 2022.

Schaupp, S. (2021), *Technopolitk von unten: Algorithmische Arbeitssteuerung und kybernetische Proletarisierung*, Berlin: Matthes & Seitz.

Slobodian, Q. (2017), *Globalists: The End of Empire and the Birth of Neoliberalism*, Harvard University Press.

Srnicek, N. (2016), *Platform Capitalism*, London: Verso.

Srnicek, N., and A. Williams (2015), *Inventing the Future: Postcapitalism and a World Without Work*, London: Verso.

Staab, P. (2019), *Digitaler Kapitalismus: Markt und Herrschaft in der Ökonomie der Unknappheit*. Frankfurt am Main: Suhrkamp.

Streeck, W. (2013), *Gekaufte Zeit: Die vertagte Krise des demokratischen Kapitalismus*, Frankfurt am Main: Suhrkamp.

Svampa, M. (2020), "Lo que las Derechas traen a la región latinoamericana: Entre lo político y lo social; nuevos campos de disputa", *Nuevas derechas autoritarias: Conversaciones sobre el ciclo político actual en América Latina*, Buenos Aires: Fundación Rosa Luxemburgo/Ediciones Aby Yala, pp. 33–77.

Van Doorn, N. (2017), "Platform labor: on the gendered and racialized exploitation of low-income service work in the 'on-demand' economy", *Information, Communication & Society*, vol. 20, no. 6, pp. 898–914. available at https://doi.org/10.1080/1369118X.2017.1294194. Last accessed on 7 July 2022.

Reconfiguration of the Regime of Impunity and Authoritarian Statecraft in Turkey

Hülya Dinçer

Introduction

Impunity is a legal concept defined by the UN Commission on Human Rights as "the impossibility, de jure or de facto, of bringing the perpetrators of violations to account ... since they are not subject to any inquiry that might lead to their being accused, arrested, tried and, if found guilty, sentenced to appropriate penalties, and to making reparations to their victims" (Orentlicher 2005). In that regard, impunity is generally considered to be an exemption of punishment resulting from a "conscious policy" operating through formal legislation or from a "gradual historical indifference", which through "weakness or lack of political will, creates a de facto regime of impunity" (Cohen 1995, 28). It is not only an overall lack of criminal punishment and official acknowledgment of human rights abuses which is created by impunity, but this also leads to the concealment and denial of the truth that perpetuates state violence over the victims (Zur 1994).

From the very early Republic to the present day, impunity for state crimes has been a consistent and systematic state policy in Turkey, deployed with an aim to legitimize state-sponsored violence against marginalized political, religious, and ethnic groups. Political massacres targeting the Alevi community and left-wing militants in the late 1970s, widespread torture and extrajudicial killings carried out before and after the military coup of September 1980, and systematic enforced disappearances and extrajudicial executions during the states of emergency in the 1990s all still remain unaccounted for and their perpetrators have so far largely remained immune to prosecution (Mecellem 2016; Göral et al. 2013; Dinçer 2020; Sevimli et al. 2021).

However, during the ongoing rule of the Adalet ve Kalkınma Partisi (the Justice and Development Party, AKP), some major criminal cases were initiated. Between 2007 and 2010, with the so-called Ergenekon and Balyoz (operation 'Sledgehammer') trials, a large number of high-ranking military officers were put on trial for their alleged involvement in anti-government coup plots (Polat 2011). For a brief period, this evoked hope for families of those tortured, forcibly disappeared, or killed that the military command would also be held responsible for human rights abuses they had been involved in (Avşar et al. 2013).

Subsequently, the constitutional self-amnesty for the wrongdoings of the 1980 military junta was abolished in 2010 by a referendum, and two retired generals—both leaders of the military coup—were put on trial in 2012. This was equally considered to be a significant step towards accountability for past state crimes (Bakıner 2013). Furthermore, encouraged by the initiation of an official peace process in 2012 between the Turkish state and the Kurdish armed movement,[1] public prosecutors had reopened criminal investigations in dozens of cases and issued indictments against some of the high-ranking military officers and middle-ranking members of the military involved in extrajudicial killings and enforced disappearances in the 1990s.

Scholars have interpreted this judicial endeavour to put those military officers on trial as linked to the "redistribution of the power among elite actors, which created a window of opportunity allowing for ongoing legal mobilization to result in prosecutions" (Mecellem 2018, 14), or considered them to be mere political instruments in the conflict between the AKP and the military (Söyler 2015), or judicial manoeuvres (Budak 2015) that were "limited and strategic acts of acknowledgment" that are falling short of "initiating a more comprehensive process of coming to terms with the past" (Bakıner 2013, 16).

The growing trend of judicialization has eventually failed to establish criminal accountability for human rights abuses, as the majority of the cases were closed with the dismissal of the cases or acquittal of the perpetrators (Dinçer 2020). The dramatic end of the peace process in mid-2015,[2] and the resumption of the armed

---

[1] In 2012, peace negotiations had officially been initiated between the leadership of the Partiya Karkerên Kurdistanê (Kurdistan Workers' Party, PKK) and the Turkish state to resolve the long-running armed conflict that had begun in 1984. The process, which was aimed at conflict resolution and mostly referred to as the "resolution process" in Turkey had two essential elements: the peace talks between state officials and the PKK; and the enacting of reforms aimed at democratization and recognition of the cultural and political rights of Kurds (Yeğen 2015).

[2] After three years of negotiations and despite some achievements in the process, the official peace talks were abruptly ended in 2015 following a shift in the balance of power. The aggressive involvement of the AKP government in the escalating war in Syria against Kurdish autonomy also had a decisive impact on the collapse of the peace talks. Although throughout the process the Kurdish political movement insisted upon the establishment of legal mechanisms to strengthen the negotiations, the government was reluctant to enact the necessary reforms and insisted upon total PKK disarmament. The reciprocal loss of confidence by the parties, alongside the increased militarized activities of the government, accelerated the end of the peace process (Savran 2020). Finally, the peace process officially came to an end following the killing of two police officers in Ceylanpınar, a district of Şanlıurfa Province in south-

conflict alongside the shift in political atmosphere towards an entrenched authoritarianism, had a decisive role on the fate of these trials. Consequently, rather than establishing criminal responsibility, these trials themselves served as a legal means to whitewash state crimes and perpetuate violence against the victims and survivors. The failure of the criminal justice system to reckon with the most egregious crimes of the country's history showed once again that impunity has been operating as a pervasive and routine procedure, endorsed by a politically-dependent judiciary.

While not departing from this long tradition, the third term of the AKP's rule, starting with electoral triumph in the June 2011 general election, saw developments such as the radical transformation of the regime of impunity, alongside a new configuration of political power associated with erosion of the rule of law. This paper investigates how the politics of impunity has changed over the last decade, along with a radical transformation of the political regime in Turkey. Following the trajectories of this transfiguration and situating it within the context of authoritarian consolidation in Turkey, it seeks to uncover the political function(s) of impunity for authoritarian statecraft.

Drawing on the analysis of the successive legal interventions in the field of legal accountability, I argue that the reconfigured regime of impunity has played a crucial role in the establishment of a new form of authoritarianism in Turkey. To unpack this argument, the article first scrutinizes critical stages of the regime transformation. It then offers a critical analysis of the legal developments that have reconfigured the regime of impunity over the last decade. It concludes by discussing the ways in which this reconfigured regime of impunity has served to entrench authoritarian rule in Turkey.

Regime Transformation towards an Exceptional State in Turkey

Recent socio-political literature points to a political regime transformation in Turkey from the 2010s onwards, which is characterized by a gradual centralization of political power and a drastic expansion of coercive force over society. The country is witnessing an enormous democratic breakdown with an intense crackdown on constitutional rights and liberties, an exacerbated targeting of political opposition, and the narrowing of civil space. Some describe this transformation as a transition from a semi-democracy into a form of competitive authoritarianism (Esen and Gümüşçü 2016) or to a semi-competitive (Burç and Tokatlı 2020) or electoral autocracy (Bargu 2018), whereas others view it as an emergent new authoritarianism,

---

eastern Turkey. Those who were arrested for the killings were recently acquitted and the perpetrators of the attack are still unidentified.

corresponding to a structural transformation which is unprecedented in Turkey's history (Somer 2016).

While there is no agreement on how to define this emergent regime, the first crucial turning point of the current authoritarian drift is considered by many to be the 2013 Gezi Park protests. The Gezi protests initially began in order to oppose the destruction of Gezi Park in Istanbul under the amended urban development plan and quickly turned into an anti-government uprising, accumulating social unrest and the grievances of different opposition groups. The AKP government's reaction to the protests—excessive and blind police violence—marked the beginning of the new era of a "punitive state" (Kaygusuz 2018, 290). Primarily used as a political weapon against the Kurds, in the aftermath of the Gezi uprising, the law started to be increasingly instrumentalized against all progressive forces as a tool of political repression. Consequently, the freedoms of expression, the press, and assembly were severely restricted.

The emerging conflict within the ruling bloc between the AKP and its long-term political ally, the Gülen movement,[3] was another crucial moment in the regime transformation. The AKP government's struggle to neutralize the plots of the so-called "parallel state"[4] and to "purge" the entire state apparatus of its militants resulted in critical legal reforms between 2013–15. The overall aim of the reforms was the reconfiguration of the state apparatus in order to regain control over bureaucracy, the military, national intelligence, and the judiciary. This series of strategic legal amendments allowed the executive branch to monopolize state power and to

---

3 The Gülen movement is a long-standing religious movement in Turkey which is strongly informed by Turkish nationalism (Tee 2021). Following the doctrine of its religious leader Fethullah Gülen, the Gülen movement was involved in power relations and had succeeded in infiltrating state structures since the 1970s. However, the movement accumulated considerable political power during the AKP era and provided the ruling party with the educated cadre to take over the state bureaucracy, including the security sector, judiciary, and national intelligence (Jongerden 2020). It was the AKP's biggest partner until the early 2010s. Gülenist prosecutors and judges prosecuted socialists and the Kurdish political movement during the 2000s by staging widescale prosecutions on falsified evidence. They also launched the coup plot trials, accusing hundreds of retired and high-ranking active duty members of the Turkish army of attempting to overthrow the AKP government in collusion with secular civil actors (Tee 2021). From 2011 on, the Gülen movement began to challenge the AKP and directly targeted Erdoğan by initiating first the national intelligence and then anti-corruption investigations (Şık 2019). The Gülen movement is now accused of masterminding the July 2016 coup attempt.

4 In the face of the corruption investigations against cabinet ministers and Erdoğan's family members, Erdoğan labelled the Gülen movement as a "parallel state" and branded it "FETÖ" (Fethullah Gülen Terrorist Organization), claiming that its political project was to plot against the democratically elected government.

particularly strengthen its domination of the judiciary and the legislature (Kaygusuz 2018; Oğuz 2017; Yılmaz 2019; Bermeo 2016). The AKP's battle to destroy its former ally, now enemy, has demonstrated how the law can be opportunistically used and misused in line with the party's strategic interests.

The legislative elections of June 2015 were another turning point in the authoritarian escalation. The Pro-Kurdish Halkların Demokratik Partisi (People's Democratic Party, HDP)[5] had enormous success in the elections by obtaining 13 percent of the votes and 80 seats in the Parliament. The AKP, who lost their absolute majority of seats in the Parliament, dismissed the results of the election and created an atmosphere of chaos to justify calling a new snap election in November 2015. Between the elections of June 2015 and November 2015, peace negotiations between the AKP government and the PKK were disrupted and the country was once again dragged into a vicious circle of violence. Emergency practices and securitization discourse intensified after the resumption of armed conflict in south-eastern Turkey and in the aftermath of subsequent ISIS terrorist attacks in different cities, which claimed hundreds of lives. As a result of this re-securitization (Geri 2016; Jongerden 2020), political repression over the opposition increased. The government mobilized the entire state apparatus against its opponents, targeting primarily the Kurdish political movement,[6] which was demonized and stigmatized once again as a national security threat (Jongerden 2020).

From summer 2015 onwards, the government declared blanket and round-the-clock curfews in urban areas of Kurdish cities where self-government had been declared by the Kurdish political movement. The establishment of curfews with a view to eradicating the armed resistance of urban PKK units was reliant on a highly controversial power which could be wielded by provincial governors, allegedly derived from the law on special provincial administration (Ardıçoğlu 2015; European Commission for Democracy through Law 2016). Imposed from mid-2015 to late 2016, the curfews resulted in serious violations of fundamental rights affecting a huge population. Thousands of people living in the cities under curfews were for months deprived of access to basic needs such as medical care, food supplies, electricity,

---

5   The HDP is a pro-Kurdish political party founded in 2011. While endorsing the long political tradition of the earlier Kurdish parties that were judicially repressed and were all disbanded, the HDP declares that it is committed to uniting progressive groups in Turkey, including socialists, feminists, ecologists, Alevis, Armenians, LGBTQ activists, and Kurds. The HDP qualifies itself as an equitable, gender-inclusive, pro-peace party. For the HDP's political programme, see https://hdp.org.tr/en/peoples-democratic-party/8760/.

6   Since the collapse of the peace talks between the AKP government and the PKK in 2015, dozens of HDP parliamentarians, mayors, politicians, and supporters have been systematically targeted, massively persecuted, and imprisoned. An indictment seeking to ban the HDP was submitted to the Constitutional Court in June 2021, see https://hdpeurope.eu/2021/06/constitutional-court-accepts-indictment-seeking-hdps-closure-2/.

water, communication, and education. The disproportionate uses of heavy shelling and lethal force during the security operations resulted in the killing of hundreds of people including civilians, and the injuring of many more (Human Rights Foundation of Turkey 2016; Office of the United Nations High Commissioner for Human Rights 2017).

Marked by a generalized military violence, this period is to be considered as a de facto state of emergency since the curfew measures were adopted 'in an ordinary time', without an official state of emergency being declared in line with the Constitution. By thus overriding the Constitution, the executive made excessive recourse to exceptional powers on the basis of a "pseudo-legal parallel method unprecedented in the history of Turkey" (Göztepe 2018, 9).

The attempted coup d'état in July 2016, by a group within the military who were affiliated with the Gülen movement, represents perhaps the most dramatic shift in the regime's authoritarian consolidation. The coup attempt was successfully repressed by the government, who, on that occasion, did not wait too long to officially declare a countrywide emergency. Declared on 20 July 2016, the state of emergency was finally lifted in July 2018 after being extended seven times. For two years, the country was ruled by way of emergency decrees issued by the executive without being subject to the review of Parliament or the Constitutional Court. Approximately 126,000 civil servants were dismissed from public service as a result of the largest purge to date (Amnesty International 2017, 2018). These included academics, doctors, judges, members of the military, instructors, and security officers, among others. Furthermore, hundreds of civil society associations, workers' unions, media outlets, schools, and companies were shut down and their properties seized by the emergency decrees (Human Rights Joint Platform 2018). Emergency measures were accompanied by a huge legal campaign against democratically-elected Kurdish politicians, including cases of arbitrary arrest and detention, deprivation of deputy status, lifting of parliamentary immunity, and state takeover of south-eastern municipalities by appointing executive trustees (Bargu 2018; Jongerden 2020). The government thus successfully instrumentalized the security crisis generated by the violent coup attempt in order to stage massive purges, crack down on dissent, and annihilate democratic competition.

Meanwhile, legislating through emergency decrees beyond the constitutional limits became the new technique of governance. Apart from imposing punitive measures, the executive usurped the lawmaking power of the Parliament to regulate every single aspect of state/citizen relations through the use of executive decrees. State institutions were profoundly reshaped by structural and permanent legal changes (Akça et al. 2018). Even after the end of the two-year state of emergency, the law enacted in 2018 authorized the executive for three years to preserve emergency powers such as dismissing any public official from office, severely restricting public assemblies due to the potential threat to public order, and extending police custody to up to 12 days for terrorism-related charges (Human Rights Watch 2018). This law was renewed again in 2021. In other words, a permanent state of emergency was installed through ordinary statutes, which dramatically expanded executive discretion beyond the security crisis.

Finally, the constitutional amendment in April 2017 accomplished executive centralization by officially transforming Turkey's political regime into a presidential system. The new regime was structured around the supreme power of an unaccountable president, "a one-person executive dominating the other two branches" (Burç and Tokatlı 2016, 79) in the absence of any institutional checks and balances (Göztepe 2018). The office of the presidency acquired full legislative powers and was granted an array of autocratic powers, including the authority to appoint the majority of the members of key state institutions such as the high judiciary (Bargu 2018).

The failed coup attempt in 2016 and the transition into a presidential regime are considered in the literature to be two critical turning points in the reconfiguration of the political regime in Turkey (Yılmaz 2020). Some scholars argue that these two events gave birth to a new security paradigm and paved the way for the emergence of an "exceptional state" as coined by Poulantzas (Kaygusuz 2018; Oğuz 2017; Kaygusuz and Aydın 2020; Türk and Karahanoğulları 2018).

Poulantzas contends that struggles within the political power and hegemony crisis may result in "exceptional state forms", which essentially rely on coercive state control rather than consent production (Poulantzas 1974; Jessop 2016). One feature of the exceptional state form is the concentration of state power in the executive branch, which tends to exercise power not through law but rather through executive decrees (Boukalas 2014). The lawmaking function of the legislative is thus transferred to the executive, which is not bound by any practical or constitutional limits (Kaygusuz and Aydın 2020).

In the same vein, Boukalas (2014) identifies the expansion of counterterrorism legislation, loss of judicial control over policing apparatus, the augmented importance of the police among state mechanisms, and the lifting of legal boundaries for the executive as key features of the exceptional state form as they appeared in the 2000s. In this respect, scrutinizing the increasing abolition of legal and judicial oversight over executive action, and most importantly over the state security apparatus, is particularly important to decoding the current move towards the exceptional state form in Turkey. By freeing national security practices from legal and judicial oversight, I would argue that the renewed regime of impunity has created the necessary conditions for an unconstrained executive to implement its authoritarian agenda within a permanent state of emergency. In what follows, I attempt to track and critically analyse the recent legal developments underpinning the construction of a new regime of impunity in Turkey.

Entrenching the Security State through the Legal Reconfiguration of Impunity

Starting from the early 2010s, Turkey has seen a legal reconfiguration that has restructured state power around the executive prerogative principle. One crucial aspect of this reconfiguration has been the gradual removal of the legal responsibility of executive agents and the security forces so as to create a legal vacuum for executive power. This phenomenon of "executive aggrandizement" is described by Nancy Bermeo (2016) as a series of institutional changes weakening checks on executive power by elected executives. Richard Ericson rightfully calls the laws that were produced for this purpose as "counter-law" or "laws against law" (Ericson 2007, 207), as they completely disregard the principles, standards, and procedures of criminal law; they also eliminate guarantees of the rule of law and dismantle the constitutional principle of accountability. In Turkey, recent legal initiatives considerably empowered the executive by systematically disabling legal control over its actions and thus broadening the realm of impunity.

The first attempt to neutralize legal oversight over the executive actions was ensured by two legal amendments that brought crucial changes to the law on state intelligence services and the National Intelligence Agency.[7] These amendments subjected Milli İstihbarat Teşkilatı (the National Intelligence Agency, MIT) to the absolute discretion of the prime minister (or now the president, since the transition into the presidential system in 2017), and largely expanded the Agency's powers and exempted intelligence operations from judicial oversight.

In this vein, the MIT was authorized to collect any kind of information, document, or data from all public institutions, private legal entities, and other organizations without having to obtain judicial permission. This unfettered authority of the MIT to access and collect any kind of information clearly overrides the constitutional right to the protection of private data. Moreover, judicial authorities were precluded from collecting or requiring the MIT to submit any document, data, source, or analysis amounting to intelligence information. Under the amended law, those, including civilians, who assisted the MIT's activities and carried out "every kind of demand" as part of the duties and powers given to the MIT would not be held responsible legally or criminally.

Most importantly, the legal amendment granted national intelligence agents quasi-immunity from prosecution for crimes they might have committed in the course of their duties. Under the amended law, public prosecutors were required

---

7   "Law. no. 6278 of 18 February 2012", see https://www.resmigazete.gov.tr/eskiler/2012/02/2012 0218-1.htm;"Law no. 6532 of 17 April 2014", https://www.resmigazete.gov.tr/eskiler/2014/04/2 0140426-1.htm.

to directly notify the head of MIT of any complaint or denunciation involving intelligence personnel. The investigation would be immediately blocked if the MIT declared that allegations were connected to intelligence duties or activities. Hence, the law places the MIT above the prosecuting authority as it is authorized to decide if its own activities should be prosecuted (Human Rights Watch 2014).

According to law, criminal investigation of the head of the Agency, all intelligence agents, and other civil servants tasked by the president for intelligence purposes is conditioned upon a pre-authorization by the president. The public prosecutor is not authorized to subject *ex officio* the alleged wrongdoings of the Agency to judicial scrutiny. A decree-law adopted in 2017 under the state of emergency[8] further made the summoning of MIT agents before the courts conditional upon prior authorization by the head of the Agency; for the head of the Agency this would need to be authorized by the president when either the state's interest or the secrecy of the duty is considered to be at stake.

Accordingly, the Turkish National Intelligence Agency is not to be considered as a legally accountable state institution but rather as a state apparatus which is immune to prosecution and is tasked with implementing the executive's secret priorities above the law. This extra-legal zone created for the 'dark side' of the security apparatus has openly revealed itself in the increase of enforced disappearances and widespread torture after the attempted coup d'état in 2016. At least two dozen persons were reported as having been abducted, tortured, or disappeared for months by MIT agents between 2016 and 2020 (Human Rights Watch 2020).

In March 2015, the government passed its domestic security package in the Parliament. The package amended more than a dozen laws including the law on police powers and duties, the law on meetings and demonstration, the anti-terrorism law, and the Criminal Code. The new legislation significantly expanded the authority and power of the police force to the point that it is considered as an important phase in the institutionalization of an entrenched police state in Turkey (Kaynar 2018; Kaygusuz 2018; Aydın 2015). The law attributed exceptional investigatory powers to the police, which must legally belong to the prosecutor's office. The police's authority to perform body and vehicle searches without a court warrant was expanded in situations deemed to be a flagrant offence. The law further authorized police chiefs to keep a person in custody for 24 hours without a prosecutor's order for crimes involving force and violence during public events and 48 hours for collective crimes. Moreover, the police were given the power to carry out intelligence wiretapping in urgent situations for a 48-hour period (which was 24 hours previously) without a judge's order. The law also widened the authority of the police to use lethal weapons during public demonstrations on wide and open-

---

8   "Decree-law no. 694 of 15 August 2017", https://www.resmigazete.gov.tr/eskiler/2017/08/20170825-13.pdf.

ended terms (Şen 2015) and authorized them to arrest any person considered to be a threat to public order, which entails a high risk of abuse of power. In other words, by legalizing the discretionary margin of the police and the excessive use of force, these provisions reinforced the police state in Turkey and paved the way for unaccountable law enforcement.

Additionally, the law attributed broad investigatory powers—which are constitutionally strictly the duty of prosecutors—to district governors appointed by the executive. This means nothing less than a transfer of judicial authority to the executive, in complete disregard of the principle of separation of powers (Aydın 2015). Finally, district governors were given the authority to order pre-emptive security measures and to largely restrict fundamental rights based on an assumed threat to public order. The exceptional powers conceded to the executive officers aimed in fact at normalizing a de facto state of emergency. The domestic security package thus served to reinforce the prerogatives of the executive and opened up an unprecedented security state era by laying down the legal basis for unaccountable security practices (Kaygusuz 2018).

Reinforced Legal Protections for a Perpetual War

The laws and decrees adopted from 2015 onwards, when first a de facto and then a de jure state of emergency was launched, have introduced a more blatant regime of impunity. Drawing on an aggressive nationalistic narrative and the constant projected threat of a perceived 'enemy', the 'survival of the state' or the 'continuity of the state' became the prevailing official discourse. All kinds of illegal executive actions were framed as legitimate, as long as they were directed at the elimination of threats to national security, and at the survival of the state. In parallel with the rise of this militarized discourse, the legal system began to be overtly instrumentalized to establish a new security regime and to render the regime immune to prosecution for crimes committed in its 'war on terror'. To this end, the government put forward well-structured and manifest legal guarantees against any attempt to hold the executive legally accountable.

One year after the initiation of heavy military operations under curfews in south-eastern Turkey, as of July 2016, the toll of the armed conflict was very heavy, with hundreds of deaths and thousands of wounded. Local prosecutors were reluctant to perform crime-scene investigations and consistently refused or delayed opening investigations into the reported killings by security forces. This reluctance was accompanied by a denial of adequate autopsies or the identification and returning of the bodies to the families (Office of the United Nations High Commissioner for Human Rights 2017, 2018). Finally, in July 2016, a legal amendment was adopted in order to shield security personnel and other state agents participating in the 'fight against terrorism' from prosecution.[9] Several articles of the law on provincial administration were modified to make it more difficult, if not impossible, to bring security agents to justice for the damages incurred and human rights abuses committed during the military operations.

Law no. 6,722 defined the crimes committed in the scope of the fight against terrorism as "military crimes" and conditioned their investigation upon authorization by the relevant ministry and the president. Even the criminal prosecution of the most egregious crimes such as torture and aggravated torture, which must normally be launched ex officio, was subject to authorization by the executive power. In addition to these, a judicial shield was created for all public servants who were involved in planning or prosecuting counter-terrorism operations, including the *Korucular* ('village guards'), a paramilitary force created in 1985 to assist the military forces in the fight against the Kurdish insurgency.[10] Most crucially, a provisional article added to the law provided a retroactive application of the authorization requirement for prosecuting wrongdoing committed during counter-terrorism operations conducted before the adoption of the law. This provision was clearly aimed at retroactively shielding from prosecution those who committed crimes in the most recent period, in which military operations had produced disastrous effects in Kurdish cities. Hence, the law itself engendered a legal vacuum, which guaranteed effective impunity for past, ongoing, and future state crimes. Disabling the existing judicial regime and replacing the autonomy of the judiciary with political discretion eventually created a legal black hole for the executive's campaign for the war on terror.

As Michael Welch (2007) underlines, impunity enhances the risk of perpetuating state abuses in an endless war on terror. It is within the orbit of impunity that a state's security apparatus is emboldened to commit further abuses without fear of being held accountable (ibid., 147). A curtailment of accountability is a global phenomenon when it comes to extrajudicial military practices carried out by states under the guise of fighting terrorism. Hence, Israel's shoot-to-kill policy towards Palestinians is widely sanctioned by the Israeli High Court of Justice (Erakat 2019). In this respect, Noura Erakat (ibid.) underlines that existing laws of armed conflict are constantly being redesigned in order to expand the state's "sovereign right to kill", including, among other things, the narrowing-down of the category of 'civilian' and therefore also of who is entitled to immunity during the conflict. Similarly, Haley Duschinski (2010) shows how extrajudicial executions by Indian soldiers in the Kashmir Valley are officially cast as deaths in "legitimate military encounters" so as to legitimize state violence and render it immune to prosecution. Welch (2007)

---

9   "Law no. 6722 of 14 July 2016", https://www.resmigazete.gov.tr/eskiler/2016/07/20160714-1.htm.

10   For the structure and operation of the village guard system in Tukey, see Özar et al. 2013.

explores the complex legal techniques deployed by the Bush administration after the 9/11 attacks to devise torture as an official policy and to disable existing legal prohibitions. Drawing on evidence from the US war on terror in Afghanistan, Iavor Rangelov and Marika Theros (2019) explore how the pattern of impunity continued after the fall of the Taliban, with legal immunity granted to the local warlords responsible for the most serious war crimes, who were nevertheless seen as indispensable partners in the war.

Rangelov and Theros (ibid., 406) contend that impunity serves an important function in producing a permanent state of emergency, which is essential for the states engaged in the war on terror. In other words, impunity is crucial to create the 'judicial void' within which a permanent state of emergency could operate. The primary political role of impunity is therefore creating a favourable environment for promoting and pursuing the war on terror. As such, "impunity works as a mechanism for reproduction of the war on terror" (ibid., 410), which, in turn, means that rule by exception is intrinsically tied to the entrenched regime of impunity within which the exception will unfold.

Accordingly, exceptional war techniques deployed during the curfews in southeastern Turkey could only become permanent by granting de jure and de facto amnesties, namely by creating an environment that makes it impossible to hold law enforcement agents accountable. With the legal amendment of July 2016, de facto tolerance for arbitrary and excessive use of lethal force in counter-terrorism operations was successfully 'legalized' and institutionalized.

The same amendment also expanded the use of exceptional powers in ordinary times by granting the president unilateral discretionary power to deploy military forces for counter-terrorist purposes on a countrywide scale without the need to declare an official state of emergency. In this context, the military acquired a position of command over all the security forces and was granted tremendous powers in the war on terror. In this setting, exceptional powers are, in practice, transposed within the ordinary laws and become permanent, whereas they actually belong to the legal state of emergency subject to constitutional and legislative oversight.

This logic of power is manifestly based on the spatial and temporal overstretching of the 'executive prerogative' principle and aims at the normalization of emergency powers. If we examine the work of Mark Neocleous (2008) regarding this normalization trend, we may observe that extraordinary powers which are meant to be temporary and restricted "quickly and easily infiltrate the ordinary legal system, becoming regularised as a technique of government" (ibid., 67).

Towards a Sovereign Impunity: Legal Shield for Emergency Powers

As explained above, in the aftermath of the attempted coup d'état in July 2016, a nationwide state of emergency was declared initially for three months, and was renewed seven times before being formally lifted in 2018. Between 2016–18, the country was ruled by emergency decree-laws, which were only later submitted for parliamentary approval. All 37 decrees issued in this period were later legalized and acquired a permanent status. Of particular interest among these emergency decrees regarding accountability are those that amended critical criminal legislation. Some of these amendments considerably eroded legal guarantees against arbitrary detention and potential ill treatment by security forces. For instance, the period a person could be held in custody without charge was extended to up to 30 days under a state of emergency, and the right to unrestricted access to a lawyer while in custody was drastically curtailed.[11] This indeed increased the risk of being subject to torture while in custody, and hampered efforts to produce evidence for establishing torture.

Second and most importantly, a legal shield of immunity was established for state officials and even for civilians who were involved in the suppression of the coup attempt. In this respect, the decree no. 668 dated 8 November 2016, which was later promulgated as law no. 6,755 abolished the "criminal, legal, administrative and financial responsibility of those who made decisions, implemented measures, or fulfilled duties in the context of the state of emergency".[12] This included government agents, ministers, local governors, security forces, and all state employees open-endedly. Those who took action to suppress the violent coup attempt or the subsequent terror incidents were equally excluded from legal and judicial oversight. As such, state officials who ordered or implemented emergency measures would not be held accountable for having used extremely large discretionary powers granted by the emergency decrees. These provisions, which are now incorporated into the ordinary legal order, have basically established an aegis of impunity for governmental action in the context of a state of emergency. To put it another way, a legal space was created for the arbitrary rule of the executive.

Yet another executive decree dangerously expanded the scope of impunity to the actions of civilians who were involved in the suppression of the coup attempt

---

11 Decree-law no. 667, issued right after the attempted coup, allowed the police to hold the suspects of terror-related crimes for up to 30 days without charge. This period was then reduced from 30 to 7 days by the Decree no. 684 with a possible extension to 14 days. See also OHCHR 2017.
12 "Article 37 of Law no. 6755 of 8 December 2016", https://www.resmigazete.gov.tr/eskiler/2016/11/20161124-2..htm.

and the "ensuing events".[13] This legal initiative was totally in line with the statements of the AKP leadership encouraging mass mobilization against potential political threats to the government and the state.[14] The decree brought forward a full and retrospective exoneration for the criminal acts of civilians, including self-organized militia groups who were suspected of playing a key role in suppressing the violent coup attempt. The extremely vague term of "ensuing events" created a very problematic legal grey area where any violent and illicit act perpetrated by the 'angry crowds' could be justified for the survival of the regime. In Turkey's current political context, any political dissent might be placed under the vague qualification of 'terror incidents', which would lead to the criminalization of the regime's opponents and justify violent attacks against them.

With these decrees now being legalized, one can argue that a regime of "sovereign impunity" (Welch 2009) has been established in Turkey with a view to accomplishing executive aggrandizement. Reminding us that all new configurations of power come with unique forms of immunization, Welch (2007, 2009) proposes the concept of sovereign impunity to characterize the political-legal order in the United States after the attacks of 9/11. This reflects a reorganization of power whereby the state crimes committed in the war on terror are rendered completely immune to prosecution. According to Welch, sovereign impunity "is embedded into a newly configured form of power while accentuating its inherent lack [of] accountability" (Welch 2007, 139). In the same vein, along with the reconfiguration of the state regime in the aftermath of the coup attempt, a new regime of impunity has been established in Turkey by strategic legal interventions whose aim, in reality, is to strengthen political domination. This new era is clearly characterized by a blatant and sovereign impunity, which sustains and constantly reproduces an unconstrained executive prerogative.

Conclusion

The last decade has witnessed an increasing trend towards normalizing the exceptional as a feature of the move toward greater authoritarianism in Turkey's political arena. This has occurred most specifically through an accelerated emergency lawmaking that has been aimed at reinforcing executive prerogatives. Consequently, constitutional constraints are loosened: the separation of powers has been severely disrupted while the executive is tremendously empowered. Drawing on Andrew

---

13 "Decree-law no. 696 of 24 December 2017", https://www.resmigazete.gov.tr/eskiler/2017/12/2 0171224-22.htm.

14 For more on the increase in far-right mobilization during the AKP's third term, see Tuğal 2016; Oğuz 2017, pp. 117–19.

Neal's analysis of exceptionalism (2012), it is important to emphasize that this has not happened in the form of a suspension of the law, but through the enactment of legal reforms in an exceptional way, endorsed by a discourse of emergency. The use of autocratic laws to expand the powers of the executive is identified by Javier Corrales (2015) as being a key element of "autocratic legalism".[15] An important feature of the current autocratic legalism in Turkey has been a complete derogation from the rule of law and the creation of 'legal black holes' for the arbitrary rule of the executive through casting out established accountability mechanisms.

The genealogy of recent legal changes studied here demonstrates how the normative basis of the state's 'right to kill' was expanded through gradually disabling judicial constraints over the state's security apparatuses with strategic legal regulations. The analysis has also shed light on how lifting statutory limitations to executive prerogatives through emergency lawmaking permitted the routinization of exceptional powers. The most striking feature of this new era of "sovereign impunity" is that immunity from the law is now not only tolerated, as has historically been the case in Turkey, but it has instead become an officially-sanctioned state policy. Hence, the main argument of this paper is that the removal of executive actions from the rule of law and paralysing judicial control over the security practices is a key feature of and an essential condition for the current regime transfiguration in Turkey towards an exceptional state.

As Welch (2007) points out, every new configuration of power features its own regime of unaccountability. Accordingly, a strategic legal fabrication with a view to building a fortress of impunity for the new regime is the marking feature of the current authoritarian statecraft in Turkey. For a better understanding of how impunity and authoritarianism interplay and are mutually strengthened, we certainly need to dig deeper into the multiple ways in which authoritarian regimes manipulate law and produce new forms of legality to advance their autocratic ends.

References

Akça, Ismet, Süreyya Algül, Hülya Dinçer, Erhan Keleşoğlu, and Barış Alp Özden (2018), When State of Emergency Becomes the Norm: The Impact of Executive Decrees on Turkish Legislation, Istanbul: Heinrich Böll Stiftung, available at https://tr.boell.org/sites/default/files/ohal_rapor_web.pdf. Last accessed on 10 June 2022.

---

15 In his study exploring the mechanisms and the causes of Venezuela's rapid move toward increasing authoritarianism, Corrales (2015) defines autocratic legalism as the use, abuse, and non-use of the law in service of the executive branch. For a comparative analysis on the weaponizing of law by autocratic regimes see Scheppele 2018.

Amnesty International (2017), No End in Sight: Purged Public Sector Workers Denied a Future in Turkey, London: Amnesty International, available at https://www.amnesty.org/en/wp-content/uploads/2021/05/EUR4462722017 ENGLISH.pdf. Last accessed on 10 June 2022.

Amnesty International (2018), "Purged Beyond Return", Amnesty International, 25 October, available at https://www.amnesty.org/en/latest/campaigns/2018/10/turkey-purged-beyond-return/. Last accessed on 10 June 2022.

Ardıçoğlu, Artuk (2015), "Hukuka Uygun Olmayan Sokağa Çıkma Yasağı Hukuka Aykırı Mıdır?" Birikim Dergisi, 27 November, available at https://birikimdergisi.com/guncel/7331/hukuka-uygun-olmayan-sokaga-cikma-yasagi-hukuka-aykiri-midir. Last accessed on 10 June 2022.

Avşar, Gülçin, Koray Özdil, and Nur Kırmızıdağ (2013), The Other Side of the Ergenekon: Extrajudicial Killings and Forced Disappearances, translated by Alex Balistreri, Istanbul: TESEV.

Aydın, Oya (2015), "İç Güvenlik Yasa Tasarısı: Anayasal Düzene Son", Birikim Dergisi, 20 January, available at https://birikimdergisi.com/guncel/1155/ic-guvenlik-yasa-tasarisi-anayasal-duzene-son/. Last accessed on 10 June 2022.

Bakıner, Onur (2013), "Is Turkey Coming to Terms with Its Past? Politics of Memory and Majoritarian Conservatism", Nationalities Papers, vol. 41, no. 5, available at http://dx.doi.org/10.1080/00905992.2013.770732. Last accessed on 23 June 2022.

Bargu, Banu (2018), "Year One: Reflections on Turkey's Second Founding and the Politics of Division", Critical Times, vol. 1 no. 1, pp. 23–48, available at https://read.dukeupress.edu/critical-times/article/1/1/23/139313/Year-One-Reflections-on-Turkey-s-Second-Founding. Last accessed on 10 June 2022.

Bermeo, Nancy (2016), "On Democratic Backsliding", Journal of Democracy, vol. 27, no. 1, pp. 5–19.

Boukalas, Christos (2014), "No Exceptions: Authoritarian Statism: Agamben, Poulantzas and Homeland Security", Critical Studies on Terrorism, vol. 7, no. 1, pp. 112–30.

Budak, Yeliz (2015), "Dealing with the Past: Transitional Justice, Ongoing Conflict and the Kurdish Issue in Turkey", International Journal of Transitional Justice, vol. 9, no. 2, pp. 219–38.

Burç, Rosa, and Mahir Tokatlı (2020), "Becoming an Autocracy under (Un)Democratic Circumstances: Regime Change Under AKP Rule", Erdoğan's 'New' Turkey: Attempted Coup d'état and the Acceleration of Political Crisis, edited by Nikos Christofis, London: Routledge, pp. 75–93.

Cohen, Stanley (1995), "State Crimes of Previous Regimes: Knowledge, Accountability and the Policing of the Past", Law & Social Inquiry, vol. 20, no. 1, pp. 7–50.

Corrales, Javier (2015), "Autocratic Legalism in Venezuela", Journal of Democracy, vol. 26, no. 2, pp. 37–51.

Dinçer, Hülya (2020), "90'lardan Bugüne Türkiye'de Cezasızlık Politikalarının Bilançosu: Savaşın Gölgesinde Adalete Bağırmak", Toplum ve Bilim, vol. 152, pp. 40–72.

Duschinski, Haley (2010), "Reproducing Regimes of Impunity: Fake Encounters and the Informalization of Everyday Violence in Kashmir Valley", Cultural Studies, vol. 24, no. 1, pp. 110–32.

Erakat, Noura (2019), "The Sovereign Right to Kill: A Critical Appraisal of Israel's Shoot-to-Kill Policy in Gaza", International Criminal Law Review, vol. 19, no. 5, pp. 783–818.

Ericson, Richard V. (2007), Crime in an Insecure World, Cambridge: Polity Press.

Esen, Berk, and Sebnem Gümüşçü (2016), "Rising Competitive Authoritarianism in Turkey", Third World Quarterly, vol. 37, no. 9, 1581–1606, available at https://www.swpberlin.org/publications/products/fachpublikationen/Berk_Esen_Rising_competitive_authoritarianism_in_Turkey.pdf. Last accessed on 10 June 2022.

European Commission for Democracy through Law (Venice Commission) (2016), "Turkey – Opinion on the Legal Framework Governing Curfews", opinion no. 842/2016, adopted by the Venice Commission at its 107th Plenary Session, Venice, 10–11 June 2016, Strasbourg: Venice Commission, available at https://www.venice.coe.int/webforms/documents/default.aspx?pdffile=CDL-AD(2016)010-e. Last accessed on 10 June 2022.

Geri, Maurizio (2016), "The Securitization of the Kurdish Minority in Turkey: Ontological Insecurity and Elite's Power Struggle as Reasons of the Recent Resecuritization", Digest of Middle East Studies, vol. 26, no. 1, available at https://doi.org/10.1111/dome.12099. Last accessed on 12 June 2022.

Göral, Özgür Sevgi, Ayhan Işık, and Özlem Kaya (2013), The Unspoken Truth: Enforced Disappearances, Istanbul: Hakikat Adalet Hafıza Merkezi (Truth Justice Memory Centre).

Göztepe, Ece (2018), "The Permanency of the State of Emergency in Turkey: The Rise of a Constituent Power or Only a New Quality of the State?" Zeitschrift für Politikwissenschaft, vol. 28, no. 4, available at https://doi.org/10.1007/s41358-018-0161-0. Last accessed on 10 June 2022.

Human Rights Foundation of Turkey (TİHV) (2016), "Curfews between August 16, 2015 – August 16, 2016 and Civilians Who Lost Their Lives According to the Data of Human Rights Foundation of Turkey Documentation Center", 21 August, available at https://hakikatadalethafiza.org/wp-content/uploads/2016/08/2016.08.21_T%C4%B0HV-16-August-2016-HRFT-Curfews-Fact-Sheet1.pdf. Last accessed on 12 June 2022.

Human Rights Joint Platform (İHOP) (2018), 21 July 2016–20 March 2018: State of Emergency in Turkey, Ankara: İHOP, available at https://ihop.org.tr/wp-content/uploads/2018/04/SoE_17042018.pdf. Last accessed on 12 June 2022.

Human Rights Watch (2014), "Turkey: Spy Agency Law Opens Door to Abuse", 29 April, available at https://www.hrw.org/news/2014/04/29/turkey-spy-agency-law-opens-door-abuse. Last accessed on 10 June 2022.

Human Rights Watch (2018), "Turkey: Normalizing the State of Emergency", 20 July, available at https://www.hrw.org/news/2018/07/20/turkey-normalizing-state-emergency. Last accessed on 10 June 2022.

Human Rights Watch (2020), "Turkey: Enforced Disappearances, Torture", 29 April, available at https://www.hrw.org/news/2020/04/29/turkey-enforced-disappearances-torture. Last accessed on 10 June 2022.

Jessop, Bob (2016), The State: Past, Present, Future, Cambridge: Polity Press.

Jongerden, Joost (2020), "Conquering the State, Subordinating Society: A Kurdish Perspective on the Development of AKP Authoritarianism in Turkey", Erdoğan's 'New' Turkey: Attempted Coup d'état and the Acceleration of Political Crisis, edited by Nikos Christofis, London: Routledge, pp. 200–15

Kaygusuz, Özlem (2018), "Authoritarian Neoliberalism and Regime Security in Turkey: Moving to an 'Exceptional State' under AKP", South European Society and Politics, vol. 23, no. 2, pp. 281–302.

Kaygusuz, Özlem, and Oya Aydın (2020), "Deconstitutionalization and the State Crisis in Turkey: The Role of the Turkish Constitutional Court and the European Court of Human Rights", Turkey's New State in the Making: Transformations in Legality, Economy and Coercion, edited by P. Bedirhanoğlu, Ç. Dölek, F. Hülagü, and Ö. Kaygusuz, London: Zed Books, pp. 41–63.

Kaynar, Ayşegül K. (2018), "Withering Constitutional State? Recent 'Police State' Discussions in Turkey", Research and Policy on Turkey, vol. 3, no. 1, pp. 90–102.

Mecellem, Jessica G. (2018), "Human Rights Trials in an Era of Democratic Stagnation: The Case of Turkey", Law & Social Inquiry, vol. 43, no. 1, pp. 1–33.

Neal, Andrew W. (2012), "Normalization and Legislative Exceptionalism: Counterterrorist Lawmaking and the Changing Times of Security Emergencies", International Political Sociology, vol. 6, no. 3, pp. 260–76.

Neocleous, Mark (2008), Critique of Security, Edinburgh University Press.

Rangelov, Iavor, and Marika Theros (2019), "Political Functions of Impunity in the War on Terror: Evidence from Afghanistan", Journal of Human Rights, vol. 18, no. 4, pp. 403–18.

Office of the United Nations High Commissioner for Human Rights (2017), Report on the Human Rights Situation in South-East Turkey: July 2015 to December 2016, Geneva: OHCHR, available at https://www.ohchr.org/sites/default/files/Documents/Countries/TR/OHCHR_South-East_TurkeyReport_10March2017.pdf. Last accessed on 12 June 2022.

Office of the United Nations High Commissioner for Human Rights (2018), Report on the impact of the state of emergency on human rights in Turkey, including an update on the South-East: January – December 2017, Geneva: OHCHR, available at https://www.ohchr.org/sites/default/files/Documents/Countries/TR/20 18-03-19_Second_OHCHR_Turkey_Report.pdf. Last accessed on 12 June 2022.

Oğuz, Şebnem (2016), "Yeni Türkiye'nin Siyasal Rejimi", Yeni Türkiye'de Kapitalizm, Devlet ve Sınıflar, edited by Tolga Tören and Melehat Kutun, Istanbul: SAV, pp. 81–127.

Orentlicher, Diane (2005), Impunity: Report of the Independent Expert to Update the Set of Principles to Combat Impunity, Geneva: United Nations Commission on Human Rights, available at https://digitallibrary.un.org/record/541829?ln=e n. Last accessed on 12 June 2022.

Özar, Şemsa, Nesrin Uçarlar, and Osman Aytar (2013), From Past to Present—A Paramilitary Organization in Turkey: Village Guard System, translated by Sedef Çakmak, Istanbul: DISA, available at https://dealingwiththepast.org/wp-conte nt/uploads/2015/03/Disa-Paramilitary.pdf. Last accessed on 12 June 2022.

Polat, Necati (2011), "The Anti-Coup Trials in Turkey: What Exactly Is Going On?" Mediterranean Politics, vol. 16, no. 1, pp. 213–19.

Poulantzas, Nicos (2019), Fascism and Dictatorship, Brooklyn: Verso [1974].

Savran, Arin (2020), "The Peace Process between Turkey and the Kurdistan Workers' Party, 2009–2015", Journal of Balkan and Near Eastern Studies, vol. 22, no. 6, pp. 777–92, available at https://www.tandfonline.com/doi/full/10.1080/1944895 3.2020.1801243. Last accessed on 10 June 2022.

Scheppele, Kim L. (2018), "Autocratic Legalism", University of Chicago Law Review, vol. 85, no. 2, pp. 545–83.

Sevimli, Emel A., Esra Kılıç, Gülistan Zeren, Melis Gebeş, and Özlem Zıngıl (2021), İnsan Hakları İhlallerinde Cezasızlık Sorunu: Kovuşturma Süreci, Istanbul: Hakikat Adalet Hafıza Merkezi.

Somer, Murat (2016), "Understanding Turkey's Democratic Breakdown: Old vs. New and Indigenous vs. Global Authoritarianism", Southeast European and Black Sea Studies, vol. 16, no. 4, pp. 481–503, available at https://doi.org/10.1080/146 83857.2016.1246548. Last accessed on 10 June 2022.

Söyler, Mehtap (2015), The Turkish Deep State: Consolidation, Civil-Military Relations and Democracy, London: Routledge.

Şen, Ersan (2015), "6638 sayılı İç Güvenlik Kanunu", Türkiye'de Hukuku Yeniden Düşünmek, edited by Haluk İnanıcı, Istanbul: İletişim Yayınları, pp. 87–103.

Şık, Ahmet (2019), "The Gülen Community and the AKP", interview by Deniz Çakırer, Authoritarianism and Resistance in Turkey, edited by Esra Özyürek, Gaye Özpinar, and Emrah Altındiş, London: Springer, pp. 81–93.

Tee, Caroline (2021), "The Gülen Movement: Between Turkey and International Exile", Handbook of Islamic Sects and Movements, edited by Muhammad Afzal Upal and Carole M. Cusack, Leiden, Boston: Brill, pp. 86–109.

Tuğal, Cihan (2016), "In Turkey, the regime slides from soft to hard totalitarianism", Open Democracy, 17 February, available at https://www.opendemocracy.net/en/turkey-hard-totalitarianism-erdogan-authoritarian/. Last accessed on 10 June 2022.

Türk, Duygu, and Yiğit Karahanoğulları (2018), "Otoriter Devletçilik, Neoliberalizm, Türkiye", Mülkiye Dergisi, vol. 42, no. 3, pp. 403–48.

Welch, Michael (2007), "Sovereign Impunity in America's War on Terror: Examining Reconfigured Power and the Absence of Accountability", Crime, Law and Social Change, vol. 47, no. 3, pp. 135–50.

Welch, Michael (2009), Crimes of Power & States of Impunity: The U.S. Response to Terror, New Brunswick, New Jersey, and London: Rutgers University Press.

Yeğen, Mesut (2015), "The Kurdish Peace Process in Turkey: Genesis, Evolution and Prospects", Global Turkey in Europe, Working Paper no.11/2015, pp. 1–15.

Yılmaz, Zafer (2019), "The Genesis of the 'Exceptional' Republic: The Permanency of the Political Crisis and the Constitution of Legal Emergency Power in Turkey", British Journal of Middle Eastern Studies, vol. 46, no. 5, pp. 714–34.

Yılmaz, Zafer (2020), "Erdoğan's Presidential Regime and Strategic Legalism: Turkish Democracy in the Twilight Zone", Southeast European and Black Sea Studies, vol. 20, no. 2, pp. 265–87.

Zur, Judith (1994), "Psychological Impact of Impunity", Anthropology Today, vol. 10, no. 3, pp. 12–17.

Anti-feminist Meeting Points in Latin America
Religious Neoconservatism, Authoritarian Neoliberalism, and Beyond

Ailynn Torres Santana

The rise of the political Right and the neo-conservative religious expansion feed the current creation and consolidation of anti-feminist discourses and policies. Both processes are deeply related. From a Latin American standpoint, this article will explore how contemporary neoconservative and right-wing politics are assembled into powerful discursive and political devices. At the same time, the article argues the need to politicize and analyse the alliances between religious neoconservatism and the political Left.

Current right-wing forces carry out and/or deepen de-democratizing agendas: they block policies of equality and justice, and they reproduce or authorize the reproduction of policies that are colonial, racist, sexist, and xenophobic, and are devastating to nature.[1] These groups include a myriad of actors and platforms worldwide, not just parties or institutional actors, including religious-based neoconservatives.[2]

The expansion of religious neoconservatism since the 1980s has been due, among other reasons, to the growth of Evangelical actors, alliances forged between Catholics and Evangelicals, the growing activation of "religious citizenships" (Vaggione 2012), and the increasing precariousness of life for large swathes of society who have been abandoned by the state, the traditional Left, and even by social movements. These religious actors have served as material and/or spiritual buffers for the growing precariousness of large social groups and gained ground from a grassroots level. They carry out in unison an advocacy policy 'from above'

---

[1] As analysed within the right-wing populisms, the new right, the radical right, the alt-right, the authoritarian right, 21st century fascism, authoritarian neoliberalism, authoritarian neo-developmentalism, and far-right civilizationism. Each approach has its own categories, emphases, bibliographies, and agents of politicization.

[2] Sometimes they are either one or the other: religious leaders who venture into the electoral arena or join parliaments, or representatives of important economic forces, confessional parties that gain strength in the political arena.

toward states, international organizations, and the media, and create transnational coordination and lobbying platforms (Torres 2020) that reach all political forces, including those on the Left. Likewise, in the face of the greater recognition of the rights of women and LGBTIQ+ people since the second half of the 20th century, and especially since the 1990s, neo-conservative religious expansion is a kind of "reactive politicization" (Vaggione 2009).

Feminist and LGBTIQ+ politics have become increasingly important. Feminism has gained in influence and international coordination, added to its agenda, and expanded its protest repertoires. Therefore, today there are more debates than ever about gender inequality, manifested in policies on sexual and reproductive rights, work and labour markets, public and domestic debts, violence, impoverishment, racial and ethnic exclusions, extractivism, and land defence. Gender has become a kind of "symbolic glue" (Grzebalska, Kováts, and Pető 2017; Kováts and Põim 2015) that holds together disputes about democracy.

All of the above configures a complex and multi-conditional scenario, some angles of which I will examine. I first refer to the arc of contemporary right(s) and current Latin American complexity. Then, I argue that there is a connection between the political Right and religious neoconservatives in producing an anti-feminist and general agenda of de-democratization; my intention is to identify the discursive and political meeting points through which the neoconservative religious neoliberal pact is generated. Finally, I question the relevance of examining the anti-feminist agenda solely in relation to the political Right and highlight the ties between religious neo-conservatives and the Left.

The Right, Neoliberalism, and Authoritarianism in the Latin American Present

Since approximately 2015, Latin America has been centre stage for analyses of contemporary right-wing processes. The previous cycle was defined by the pre-eminence of governments considered progressive—diverse among themselves in terms of agendas and leadership—that shaped what was known as the 'pink tide'. During that period, the lingua franca in Latin America was the amplification of an egalitarian discourse, social inclusion via social platforms and increased consumption, the implementation of heterodox social policies, the promotion of regional integration, and the criticism of neoliberalism (Svampa 2020). These progressivisms also persisted in, and sometimes amplified, the politics of agribusiness and extractive sectors (ibid.).

The pink tide was broken by Mauricio Macri's electoral victory in Argentina, in 2015. Macri represented the rise of a type of anti-progressive, anti-populist project that coagulated in a general policy of neoliberal updating (Stefanoni 2021).

In Brazil, in 2018, Jair Messias Bolsonaro's victory installed in the region the radically undemocratic so-called alternative Right.

The shift to the right, including countries where there was a continuity of right-wing administrations, took place through different means: electoral, in Brazil, Colombia, Argentina, El Salvador, Chile, Uruguay, Ecuador; legislative, the 'No' to the Peace Accords in the referendum in Colombia; coups d'état or parliamentary coups, in Honduras, Bolivia, Brazil, Paraguay; and transitions within the same pink tide field, with Lenin Moreno and Ecuador.

Later, this scenario became more complex. In 2018, Andrés Manuel López Obrador (AMLO), the left-wing candidate in the Mexican elections, assumed the presidency.[3] In Bolivia, after the interim leadership of the neoconservative Jeanine Áñez, the Movement for Socialism (MAS) has returned with the current administration led by Luis Arce. In Argentina, Alberto Fernández won at the polls. In Peru, leftist candidate Pedro Castillo triumphed in 2021, although later, the impossibility of consolidating institutional power was verified. In Chile, the Left won with Gabriel Boric in 2021, and in Colombia, the presidential election of 2022 produced hopeful results for Left politics with the consolidation of an alliance between Gustavo Petro and Francia Márquez. The region has undergone a process of greater heterogenization.

However, there is no longer any indication of a new progressive majority, some examples are the 2021 victory of the Right in the most recent legislative elections in Argentina, the presence of the far-right candidate José Antonio Kast in the second electoral round in Chile in 2021, the radicalization of anti-rights politics in Guatemala, the triumph of neoliberal Guillermo Lasso in Ecuador, the persistence of the Colombian Right as a strong political force, and the deployment of the right-wing government in Uruguay. Simultaneously, right-wing politics is also rising from below, in the actions of social actors working at a grassroots level. The question of where and in what ways the Right is reproduced continues to be important.

A part of these contemporary right-wing forces presents themselves as standard bearers for representational democracy, and respectful, to a certain extent, of institutional frameworks while at the same time promoting heavy-handed policies that promise to restore order (Giordano 2014). Their authoritarian bent, which is not new, is aggravated and reproduced in different ways and on different scales, in despotic, paramilitary, and corrupt state forms that have established a sort of "preventive discipline" (Burak 2017).[4]

---

3   The traditional "leftist" classifier needs to be revised, as well as the expeditious association of progressive pink tide governments with the left. See Svampa 2017, 2018, and 2020, and Hoetmer 2020.

4   It is important to address authoritarian drift and/or repressive shifts—qualitatively and quantitatively different—in countries with long-standing self-defined left-wing govern-

There is also neoliberal transversality[5] in the contemporary right-politics that imply, as Wendy Brown suggests:

> the valorization of unregulated markets for everything and everyone, the conception of human beings as human capital, the disregard for social justice and the common good as totalitarian practices, the privatization of former public goods and the dispossession of welfare states, the reduction of states to instruments of economic growth, etc. (Brown 2020)

Along this line, and although a closer examination of the regional Right reveals differences among them,[6] the Latin American political Right shares other qualities: a "new type of anti-progressivism" (Stefanoni 2021a); a predilection for conspiracy theories; constant colonization of lifeworlds, molecular control, and economization of bodies and nature (Nehe 2020); increased states of emergency, militarization, and securitization, including the promotion of joint manoeuvres or US military bases in the region (Svampa and Terán Mantovani 2019); combination of notions of change with notions of restoration and order, promising ways to return to imagined secure pasts based on family, faith, and national order (Hoetmer 2020); the centrality of the fight against corruption exclusively entrusted to previous progressivisms;[7] the undoing of regional coordination institutions created by progressives and the creation of new ones; the geopolitical oscillation in the relationship with the United States and increased investment and trade commitments with China, and also with Russia and the Pacific; more commodity frontiers; and reconstruction, toward their interests, of an internal enemy in line with the National Security Doctrine (Svampa 2020).[8]

The actors that cement the Right also verify a clear national-conservative path. Their strong conservative imagination updates and expands undemocratic 'traditional values' around the family and sexual morality, combined with the notions of patriotism and an expressed anti-globalism. This imagination is combined with the one displayed by religious neoconservatism. Today, there is a worldwide tsunami

---

ments (Venezuela, Nicaragua, Cuba), which will not be analysed here but are part of the regional panorama.

5 Demirović (2018) and Peck and Tickell (2002) have periodized phases of neoliberalism. The latter warn that the first neoliberal moment promoted a moral-spiritual and neoconservative turn directed against the global social and sexual revolution of 1968.

6 Svampa (2020) details differences between a neoliberal right and a radical right.

7 Anti-corruption struggles have also been used in left-wing political campaigns. See Stefanoni 2021.

8 At the same time, it continues the assassinations of social leaders, especially those tied to human rights and land defense (Svampa 2020). Latin America continues to have the most "prominent" place in this area, both in countries with left-leaning governments such as Mexico and overall, see Global Witness (2021).

of cults, communities of faith, churches, and citizenry—especially the Evangelicals—that participates in the imagination and politics of the Right. Religious leaders and institutions increasingly influence institutional, legislative, and political structures and trajectories; they configure, traverse, and mutually comprise them.

Is the connection between the authoritarian neoliberal right-wing and the religious neoconservatism configured as mere similarity or is it a related phenomenon? I will reflect on this question from a Latin American standpoint. The examples of countries mentioned below serve only as a sample of larger processes, embedded in different scales—local and community, intranational, national, regional, and global. Each fact mentioned has its own path, plot, and conditions of possibility; here they serve to show a general scale, from above, of the assemblages that connect neoconservatism and the neoliberal Right.

The Neoliberal Right and Neoconservatism: Anti-feminist Crossovers

The assemblages connecting religious neoconservatisms and the political Right have been growing since the global crisis of 2008 (Gago and Malo 2020) and strengthened since 2013 (Corrêa 2018 and Torres 2020a). These encounters occur in different ways. The analysis of these pathways shows how and in what ways sexual and gender politics articulate broader political processes, and helps us understand the place that anti-feminism occupies within contemporary politics.

Assemblage 1: Anti-progressivism and Anti-communism

Authoritarian neoliberals and religious neoconservatives both produce a strongly anti-progressive narrative and defend it in different ways. For neoconservatives, especially Evangelicals, Latin American progressivism defended a gender agenda (Semán 2021) which is incompatible with the religious values that should regulate the social collective.[9] Indeed, Latin American progressivisms advanced in the institutionalization of gender rights, and their guarantees, related to labour, women's political participation, and gender-based violence. However, several progressive governments defended conservative positions on sexual morality, abortion, and gender identity, maintaining a very inconsistent or contradictory stance regarding sexual and gender policies.

---

9   The tension between Evangelism and progressivism articulated around gender is more contingent than historical. Semán argues that in Argentina and other countries, Evangelicals were ahead of Catholicism in terms of women's equality and even in matters related to sexual diversity. Nowadays, they radically changed their position on those topics, see Semán 2021.

The political Right—beyond their diversity—ties their anti-progressivism with anti-communist rhetoric and closes ranks against their predecessors, progressivism, the Left, and centre-left (Giordano 2014). The most radical right groups express an explicit "right-wing pride" (Stefanoni 2021a). Pink tide governments are described as communist and propagators of "cultural Marxism",[10] and it is argued that they share politics with feminist and LGBTIQ+ groups. For example, the 2018 Brazilian electoral campaign that ended with Bolsonaro's victory combined an anti-Workers Party agenda[11] with a conservative, markedly anti-feminist moralization and anti-corruption platform (Bringel 2020). Another example can be seen in Colombia, where the political Right and religious neoconservatives linked a discourse of opposition to 'cultural Marxism' and the 'homosexualization' of the country during the referendum for the 2016 Peace Accords. In 2019, the HazteOir organization awarded its annual award to one of the most prominent anti-rights neoconservatives at a global level, the Argentine Agustín Laje, for "denouncing gender ideology, radical feminism and cultural Marxism" (ACI 2019) in its well-known publication *The Black Book of the New Left* (Márquez and Laje 2019). So far, anti-progressive/anti-communist politics intersect with potent anti-rights sexual and gender politics with an anti-feminist core. As Paulo Ravecca argues (Ravecca et al. 2022), sometimes Marxism and feminism are described as natural allies—which implies thinking of them as separate entities—and other times as a single force with different manifestations and moments (Ravecca et al. 2022).

The Madrid Charter, an initiative created in 2020 by VOX, the ultra-conservative Spanish political force known for its radical anti-feminist stance, is a recent joint effort between religious and political neoconservatives. The initiative warns against 'the advance of communism' and the 'serious threat to prosperity' that feminism represents. The document mentions Cuba, the São Paulo Forum, and the Puebla Group, among others, as examples of aspirations to unite against the leftist totalitarianism that infiltrates centres of power to impose their agenda. It has been signed by the well-known religious neoconservative Amparo Medina, general coordinator of *Red Vida y Familia* in Ecuador, as well as by deputies, mayors, former presidents, and political figures from more than a dozen countries, the majority from Latin America.

---

10 The political right traces the antecedent of this cultural Marxism to the theorizations of the Frankfurt School in the 1930s and, in particular, to its dissemination in the uprisings in the 1960s with radical movements, see Gago 2019.

11 Referring to the onslaught of the political right against the Workers Party (Partido dos Trabalhadores).

Assemblage 2: 'Reverse Anti-colonialism' and 'Anti-neoliberalism'

We can also observe the convergence between authoritarian neoliberal rights and religious neoconservatisms in "reverse anti-colonialist" rhetoric (Roth 2020), where gender issues are central. This narrative argues that the gender agenda is anachronistic with respect to national values and that it responds to foreign powers' attempts to re-colonize (Gil 2011).

Again, in Colombia during the referendum for the Peace Accords in 2016, the deputy Ángela Hernández alleged that the national Ministry of Education was attempting a "homosexual colonization" by wanting to impose the criteria of a minority community on the country (El Tiempo 2016). Dale O'Leary, a conservative Catholic journalist and an active lobbyist at the Vatican, consistently argues that gender is "a neo-colonial tool of an international feminist conspiracy" (Gago 2019). Meanwhile, in Costa Rica, the ultra-conservative candidacy of evangelical pastor Fabrizio Alvarado in the 2018 presidential elections polarized the campaign with his rejection of same-sex marriage, while denouncing the country's subjection to international organizations and norms (El País 2018). In Chile, and especially after the social outbreak in 2019, the Republican Party also sustained this sovereigntist, anti-globalist rhetoric, which shields national politics from international organizations and denounces their intervention in 'moral issues' or migratory matters (Campos 2021).

A recent platform of explicit convergence in this regard is the well-known Geneva Consensus, launched in October 2021, that has thirty-six signatory countries, including Brazil and Guatemala. This Consensus, signed by ministers and senior government representatives, claims to protect "the right to life" and denies that there is "an international right to abortion" and that states have "an international obligation to finance or facilitate abortions" (Geneva Consensus 2021). Its ideological line also affirms the sovereignty of nations, not exclusively to Latin America. The tie between 'traditional values', anti-rights sexual and gender politics, and the sovereigntist narrative that curdles in a kind of neo-patriotism (Sanahuja and López 2020) are central in the geopolitical field. The current Russian intervention in Ukraine is partly explained by this type of dynamic (Edenborg 2022).

A similar split is observed with respect to neoliberalism. Despite the neoliberal transversality of the Latin American Right, they perform a rhetorical operation according to which social movements that defend human rights, especially feminists and LGBTIQ+ militants, are neoliberal because they are unconcerned about the problems of most people. Correspondingly, an anti-neoliberal struggle must also be anti-feminist. Neoconservative religious forces also defend the idea that "anti-neoliberalism can only come hand in hand with the preservation of 'family values' and the discipline of work to which they are intimately associated" (ibid).

Verónica Gago, for example, recalls that in Argentina "a well-known *villero* priest had insisted that abortion is not a popular demand" and argued, trying to appeal to those who discredit neoliberals, that "the IMF [International Monetary Fund] is abortion" (Gago 2019).

In the same vein, the narrative about the people *versus* the elites is appropriated by both the new political rights and neo-conservativisms. Anti-elite discourse is useful for garnering popular support. But here the elites are identified with progressives—to whom a kind of "constitutive hypocrisy" is ascribed (Bergel 2021)—and with feminisms and LGBTIQ+ militants, who they perceive as unconcerned about the people's hunger. For them, the "new left" is the project of intellectuals and privileged minorities, related to this is the line of so-called protection of communities and neighbourhoods via policies to combat insecurity. Through a "post-ideological" framework, governments maintain that "the problems of the people" are central (Giordano 2014) rather than the politics that (re)produce violence and profit from police corruption, narco-states,[12] and racist and misogynistic state violence. The reinforcement of the perception of insecurity is key to generating collective fear as a moral economy (Serrano 2019): it creates the need for private security offered by those who themselves instil fear.

Assemblage 3: (In)security, Violence, and War

The promise of combating insecurity authorizes the use of state violence to produce social control over civil disobedience and, at the same time, serves to garner popular votes, especially from women, who are victims of insecurity. Securitization policies, as well as those that have to do with social reproduction—money transfers, food stamps, etc.—are fundamental to ensuring the support and votes of women, who are primarily responsible for sustaining life. Securitization also justifies xenophobic policies, of which women are often at the centre: Lenín Moreno blamed migrants in Ecuador for violence, and specifically, gender violence (BBC 2019), as did the Macri government in Argentina (Collazo and Pulleiro 2021). Meanwhile, state and parastatal violence, violence against social leaders, and patriarchal pacts between the state, men, and communities that tolerate gender violence, are made invisible.

Religious neoconservatives do politics in a convergent way, coupling the concept of freedom with the concept of security (Brown 2020a) and fuelling moral panic through different themes, such as security and order, immigration, and sexual liberalization (Demirović 2018). The moral panic against 'the other' and the

---

12   Narco-state refers to a persistent association, institutionally verified and reproduced by different actors, between state political institutions and the illegal economies of drug trafficking. In short, to the organization of criminal businesses around the state.

moral economy of fear enable authoritarian neoliberalism and religious neoconservatism to use bellicose language.

In Brazil, for example, Bolsonaro employs the notion of "war" when referring to cultural hegemony in view of the diversification of family models and gender identities (Roth 2020). Applying the rhetorical device of war to talk about these issues is historically present in authoritarian regimes in general. However, as Raphael Hoetmer (2020) argues, the current particularity is that the discourse of war unfolds from democratic institutions and is "naturally" associated with common meanings. In fact, the language of war is central to neo-conservative militances, whish display a broad activism against the "cultural warfare" of feminism and progressivism, and a "spiritual war" against feminists, "cultural Marxism", the homosexualization of the world, and "gender" (Hoetmer 2020). The politicization of religion is a conservative key that ensures as Cristina Vega (2019) argues, in the Ecuadorian case, a fiction of security, order, and private solidarity.

The doctrine of "spiritual warfare" is relatively recent, dating from the 1980s. This framework establishes a narrative about the "forces of good and evil", exacerbates their confrontation and from there extrapolates everything that occurs in social, economic, and natural life (Vega, Castellanos, and Salazar 2021). The 'forces of evil' are consolidated in a very explicit, systematic, and definitive way in gender ideology.

This 'culture war' is also a global assemblage. The Right's use of combat-related words such as "weapon," "battle," "fight", and "threat," in Europe has been flagged and analysed by Agnieszka Graff and Elżbieta Korolczuk (2022).

Assemblage 4: Gender Ideology

Gender ideology is probably the broadest and most powerful device linking the contemporary political Right and religious neoconservatives. In Latin America it has had an unprecedented increase in usage.

In his inauguration speech, Brazilian president Jair Bolsonaro mentioned the fight against "gender ideology" as part of his administration's agenda; "the alleged existence of a 'gay kit' that Haddad would distribute among children in schools was one of the most effective fake news of his campaign" (Stefanoni 2021). When Bolsonaro visited former President Donald Trump in 2019, he emphasized his goal of fighting against the scourge of "political correctness", "fake news", and "gender ideology" (Roth 2020). Gender ideology was central in the No campaign during the Colombian Peace Accords, and thereafter the religious neoconservatives joined forces with Uribe right-wingers (Gil 2020): if the Yes won, the mantle of gender ideology would fall over the country. Nayib Bukele also won the presidency of El Salvador, waving the flag against gender ideology (Gago 2019) at the same time as the coalition that assured the Lacalle Pou triumph in Uruguay in 2019 (Abracinskas,

Álvarez, and Puyol 2022). The anti-gender ideology platform has been vital for the elections in large parts of Latin America, used in the discourses of the political Right. Thus, the fight against gender ideology has served not only to reconfigure gender and sexuality policies but also to obtain political power that arises, is nurtured, and is part of gender and sexuality policies (Serrano 2019).

Conversely, in the field of religious neo-conservatism, gender ideology has served to build alliances between Evangelicals and Catholics, to 'embody' the common internal enemy, create a morality panic, secularize their discourse, and gain universality for their agendas by alluding to non-religious categories. Gender ideology has ended up being an umbrella under which many things fall. Still, a common axis appeals to atavistic and deep fears about the destruction of essential ties and the family, affirming a notion of 'obligation' to gender-sex confusion, homosexuality, contraception, and abortion (Vega 2017).

Ravecca et al. (2022) demonstrate how denouncing gender ideology has been a critical piece of neoconservative action and ensures a sort of right intersectionality (Moragas 2022). In politics around gender ideology, diverse actors articulate programs about different social, economic, and cultural issues. The idea that gender ideology in schools is institutional violence against children and adolescents has been developed by religious neoconservatives and the political Right. Political deployment in this sense takes place inside and outside national borders, for instance, Organization of American States' meetings are one of the most systematic international forums in this regard. A recent analysis reports that neoconservative discourses are characterized by robust semantics against gender ideology and even the 'gender ideology industry' (Moragas 2022).

For all of the above, gender ideology is a political strategy, a discursive and rhetorical device at its core, from which neoconservatism resists the expansion and guarantee of rights. Although gender ideology occupies the foreground of the political discourses of authoritarian neoliberals and religious neoconservatives, other more specific fields of politicization articulate alliances, platforms, and actions, such as family, education, and freedom. The next few pages address those topics.

Assemblage 5: Family and Education

For those on the authoritarian neoliberal right, to defend the family and traditional values is to defend the national community (Hoetmer 2020). However, it is not a conservatism that operates only in the realm of morals. It has economic and political implications: the defence of the traditional family is a main factor of their criticism against the state as guarantor, where there has been, be it in the form of welfare states or, in the case of Latin America, fragile state social policies.

Wendy Brown (2020) underscores that the morality rooted in the heteropatriarchal family, as a vital part of good order and as an essential economic unit, the traditional family that functions as a stabilizer and social controller. Although not necessarily subject to specific disciplinary sexual customs, the neoliberal conception of families allows that unit to "absorb" the withdrawal of the state from its social protection functions and cushion the structural crisis of social reproduction (Alabao 2020; Gago 2019).

Melinda Cooper (2017) studied this phenomenon in the United States and there is evidence of this in Latin America. In Bolsonaro's Brazil, for example, the ministries of the Economy and of Women, Family, and Human Rights are the most important to the institutional fabric and are run by an ultra-neoliberal and a religious neoconservative, respectively (Kalil 2020). The centrality of the traditional family cuts across the different—more or less radical—Right, which converges in their insistence on family-focused policies (Alabao 2020a) and makes a moralizing use of the family institution for their political programs (Gago 2019).

The retraditionalization of the family unit collides with the disruption of the domestic sphere made by feminists and LGBTIQ+ militants. Faced with this, the political Right is committed to the pacification of domestic areas, either by moral means or financial indebtedness (Gago 2019). And that is perfectly met by the neoconservative bent that ensures doctrinal affirmation of tradition and popular bases, since churches are today privileged channels for the redistribution of resources, which is a mechanism by which to foster obedience (ibid.).

The defence of the traditional family is totally related to policies on education, especially comprehensive sexual education. For the neoliberal ethic "education is training for work" (Brown 2020a), a way of developing human capital, not a space for social, political, and human formation. As a primary political tenet, religious neoconservatives put the brakes on sexual education in schools, which they argue endangers the family and children due to the indoctrination of 'gender ideology'. That is why one of their fundamental campaigns throughout Latin America is "Don't mess with my children", an interdenominational platform for Evangelicals and neoconservative Catholics aimed at halting all inclusion of issues related to gender equality and sex education.

Assemblage 6: Freedom

Finally, a key assemblage between religious neoconservatives and authoritarian neoliberals is based on the politicization and instrumentation of notions of freedom. This dispute is about the definition of what freedom is. Religious neoconservatives defend their public voice based on freedom of expression, worship, and individual freedoms, and use the latter to oppose the action of the state—described as totalitarian or communist—and feminist and LGBTIQ+ agendas, posited as a danger to order and tradition.

The freedom the Right defends is specifically individual and negative, as propagated by doctrinal liberalism and authoritarian neoliberalism. That means freedom boils down to "non-interference": no one should be able to interfere in private life which includes not only the family and the domestic, but also property. Meanwhile, exploitation in the world of work, subordination within the family, or dispossession of life resources have nothing to do with freedom. As a result, people are free to "choose", which means free to be exploited or subordinated.

However, whereas religious neoconservatives reject state action because it threatens freedom, they push to gain presence and participate in the state. They do the opposite of what they say, as they recognize the state as a vital territory of social control and therefore, they want to occupy it. Neoliberalism does the same. It discursively promulgates the downsizing of the state while it actually only changes its character, transforming state apparatuses into business ones. Both routes ensure the social engineering model of de-democratization, eliminating the social function of the state, limiting its retributive possibilities of power and resources.

Based on eight analyses of Latin American cases, Sonia Corrêa and Magaly Pazello (2022) warned of a firm and novel activation of the syntagm "freedom". This "freedom" appeal reveals the link between anti-gender agendas and neoliberal rationality, it becomes a political trope of a sort of selective autonomy which is ultra-individualistic and has no consequences for the real structures of subordination and exploitation.

Final Words and the Question about Neoconservatism beyond the Political Right

The six political assemblages analysed in this paper present both a map of places where the politics of de-democratization is played out and its authoritarian drifts. The articulation, sometimes contingent and other times persistent, between the political Right and religious neoconservatives, is vital to understanding the contemporary panorama and sharpening our gaze integrally toward the places where common sense is disputed, along with the organization of reproduction, and the development of political meanings. In these arenas, themes of gender and sexual diversities are central and interconnected with the organization of life, the economy, the state, and moral matters.

Although "the epistemological scene around gender" constitutes an (open) "battlefield" in the discussion on right-win politics (Roth 2020), the analysis can and must go further. Neoconservative religious politics has expanded along the spectrum of the political Left and that is mandatory to consider. The relationship between religious neoconservatives and the new Right(s), authoritarians, populists, and neoliberals, is increasingly analysed (Kalil 2020). However, it is not the same when talking about the pink tide or in contexts with governments self-defined as leftist or progressive.[13] The paucity of analysis in this regard makes it seem that neoconservatisms only operate or feed on the described bridges with the political Right, but this is not the case.

The pink tide became an action platform for the advancement of social and political rights. Feminist sectors, women, and sexual dissidents considered those political processes a window of political opportunity to advance sexual and gender justice, although their participation in them has been described as scarce or conflictive (Rossi and Tabbush 2020). During that period, Latin American women escaped poverty to a greater extent than in previous years because the proportion of women without their own income decreased and they were beneficiaries of social policies (ONU-Mujeres 2017). Participation in parliamentary bodies in state apparatuses increased considerably, especially in countries including Bolivia, Ecuador, and Venezuela. That increase had already been taking place across the region since the 1990s but accelerated during the first decade of the 2000s (ONU-Mujeres 2021).

However, the national pathways of progressivisms were and are deeply brittle and discontinuous. During some periods and with respect to certain issues, advances could be made that were later halted at other junctures. For example, while the general poverty index decreased, the feminization of poverty increased during that period. In other words, there was a general decrease in poverty but women benefited less than men from the policies that ensured that fact (ONU-Mujeres 2017). But above all, it was the policies that question traditional norms of family and sexuality—such as abortion, same-sex marriage, recognition of gender identity and, in some cases, gender-based violence—that were most hampered by the leaders' conservatism and/or directly by alliances between the politicians in power and expanding religious neoconservatism. The evidence in this sense overturns the assumption that, by definition, left-wing politics questions conservative beliefs and hierarchies, with an implicit or explicit religious base.

For example, at the beginning of his administration, the former Ecuadorian President Rafael Correa (2007–2017) supported an explicit decolonial agenda of LGBTIQ+ rights, whereas later Correa ignored women's rights and did not hide his misogyny (Lind 2020). Likewise, in Ecuador gender ideology was installed in political discourse, when Correa himself mentioned it in 2013.[14] Likewise, the deepening of neo-extractivism profoundly affected women—particularly indigenous and peasant women—in places that fell prey to plunder.

---

13   For a discussion about Venezuela and Cuba see works included in the References section by Carosio (2020), Morales (2020), and Torres (2020).
14   Correa said some politicians were trying to impose "gender ideology" on school systems, denying natural laws.

Women played a key role during the presidencies of Evo Morales in Bolivia, and they promoted an agenda of depatriarchalization of society and the state. However, there were also clear processes of consolidation of the patriarchal pact and the unquestionable persistence of macho rhetoric was activated on successive occasions, where different political figures forged alliances with religious neoconservative sectors. In Venezuela, considerable progress was made in the recognition of rights and institutional reforms, which, however, have been stagnant and offer few rights. Other types of issues, such as equal marriage or the right to voluntary abortions, were held back or rejected by Chávez's Catholic discourse (Hernández 2021). In fact, the Catholic Church ensured that the 1999 Constitution would mark the defence of life from conception, as a way to block the right to voluntary abortions.

More recently, in Mexico, the AMLO government has rearranged its discourse and policies around gender. On the one hand, advocating for democratizing policies and, on the other, establishing alliances with conservative forces. At the same time, the National Anti-AMLO Front (FRENAAA), a neoconservative right-wing movement, is constituted as openly "pro-life", anti-feminist, and a defender of religion. The recently elected president of Peru, who represents a celebrated disruption of the regional right turn with a democratization program across many levels, has been against abortion and sexual and reproductive rights. In fact, he came to the presidency with a certain Evangelical element: "His wife and daughter are from the Church of the Nazarene and he often joins in praying" (Semán 2021).

During the pink tide, some progressives achieved important alliances with feminist movements, for example in Uruguay and Argentina, and this implied significant institutional changes. But other governments, including Bolivia, Ecuador, and Venezuela, maligned feminist organizations and on different fronts allied themselves with actors and/or values closer to neoconservatism (Hernández 2021).

Therefore, although the turn to the right has implied a kind of backlash[15] for policies in favour of the rights of women and LGBTIQ+ people, we cannot disregard that the political leftists in power maintained a conflictive relationship and certain restrictive issues, drawing from feminist agendas. Concurrently, religious neoconservatisms are present today in all political regimes.

Now, although the relationship between the left and sexual and gender justice is uncertain and urgently needs to be politicized,[16] there is an organic and institutional link between religious neoconservatives and the neoliberal Right, which is

---

15 The backlash approach should be critically considered because neoconservative actions are not only reactive, they have a proactive and even preventive dimension regarding certain issues.

16 For an excellent comparative analysis of gender and sexuality issues during the pink tide, see Rossi and Tabbush, *Género, sexualidad e izquierdas latinoamericanas. El reclamo de derechos durante la marea rosa*.

more or less authoritarian. That does not disregard the fact that there have been advances in rights under right-wing governments. In fact, there are counterintuitive studies that show that neoliberal, right-wing, and even anti-democratic governments have promoted some policies that positively impact sexual and gender justice (Htun 2003). However, in the current phase of neoliberalism and for all the aforementioned reasons, it is expected that the neoconservative pathway will gain traction, especially although not exclusively under governments on the Right.

All this complexity requires difficult and accurate analyses of what we now see as a course of de-democratization (Corrêa and Kalil 2020). In addition to its authoritarian implications, this process implies a gradual erosion of the democratic structure of politics that potentially transforms or voids the institutional architecture. The analysis of religious neoconservatives and their back-and-forth ties with myriad political forces plays a central role in the construction of a democratic sexual and gender policy. Criticism from the popular camps must be anti-neoliberal but also, and very firmly, anti-neoconservative.

References

Abracinskas, L., P. Álvarez, and S. Puyol (2022), "Políticas antigénero en el contexto pandémico, tendencias en conflicto: Uruguay", *Políticas antigénero en america latina en el contexto pandémico*, Observatorio de Sexualidad y Política.

Alabao, N. (2020), "El 'neoliberalismo progresista' y la izquierda conservadora", July, available at https://nuso.org/articulo/el-neoliberalismo-progresista-y-la-izquierda-conservadora/imprimir/. Last accessed on 13 June 2022.

Alabao, N. (2020a), "La extrema derecha que dice defender a las mujeres", January, available at https://nuso.org/articulo/extrema-derecha-Le-Pen-Europa/. Last accessed on 13 June 2022.

BBC (2019), "Feminicidio en Ecuador: la advertencia del presidente Lenín Moreno a los migrantes venezolanos tras el asesinato de una mujer embarazada a manos de su expareja", *BBC*, 21 January, available at https://www.bbc.com/mundo/noticias-america-latina-46942272. Last accessed on 13 June 2022.

Bergel, M. (2021), "Pensar las nuevas derechas", *Jacobin-Lat*, 31 March, available at https://jacobinlat.com/2021/03/31/pensar-las-nuevas-derechas/. Last accessed on 13 June 2022.

Bringel, B. (2020), "Bolsonaro y el fin del ciclo democrático en Brasil ¿Qué raíces y anclajes tiene el bolsonarismo?" *Nuevas derechas autoritarias. Conversaciones sobre el ciclo político actual en América Latina*, October, Quito: Edición Fundación Rosa Luxemburg/Ediciones Abya-Yala, available at https://rosalux.org.ec/pdfs/IndiceNuevasDerechasAutoritarias2020.pdf. Last accessed on 13 June 2022.

Brown, W. (2020), "Neoliberalismo en ruinas con Wendy Brown", *Jacobin-Lat*, 3 December, available at https://jacobinlat.com/2020/12/03/el-neoliberalismo-en-ruinas/. Last accessed on 13 June 2022.

Brown, W. (2020a), "Entrevista a Wendy Brown "El neoliberalismo es una de las fuentes del ascenso de las formas fascistas y autoritarias", 4 December, available at https://www.eldiplo.org/notas-web/el-neoliberalismo-es-una-de-las-fuentes-del-ascenso-de-las-formas-fascistas-y-autoritarias/. Last accessed on 13 June 2022.

Burak Tansel, C. (2017), "Authoritarian Neoliberalism Towards a New Research Agenda", *States of Discipline: Authoritarian Neoliberalism and the Contested Reproduction of Capitalist Order*, ed. Cemal Burak Tansel, London: Rowman & Littlefield International.

Campos, C. (2021), "El Partido Republicano: el proyecto populista de la derecha radical chilena", *Revista Uruguaya de Ciencia Política*, vol. 30, no.1, pp. 105–34.

Carosio, A. (2020), "Derechos y antiderechos sexuales en la polarización política venezolana", *Derechos en riesgo en América Latina: 11 estudios sobre grupos neoconservadores*, ed. Ailynn Torres Santana, Quito/Bogotá: Fundación Rosa Luxemburgo/Desde Abajo, pp. 201–222.

Collazo, C., and A. Pulleiro (2021), "Los límites de lo decible", *Jacobin-Lat*, 6 October, available at https://jacobinlat.com/2021/10/06/los-limites-de-lo-decible/?fbclid=IwAR3-19QfQ_rMuP08Q1iI6iEEGMkdElCDU93oZCmylbGSUlmP8gth6BMYbGw. Last accessed on 13 June 2022.

Cooper, M. (2017), *Family Values: Between Neoliberalism and the New Social Conservatism*, New York: Zone Books.

Corrêa, S. (2018), "Política do gênero": Um comentário genealógico", *Cadernos Pagu*, no. 53, 5 March, available at https://www.scielo.br/pdf/cpa/n53/1809-4449-cpa-18094449201800530001.pdf. Last accessed on 13 June 2022.

Corrêa, S., and I. Kalil (2020), *Políticas Antigénero en América Latina: Brasil, ¿la catástrofe perfecta?*, Río de Janeiro: ABIA / SPW, available at https://sxpolitics.org/GPAL/uploads/Ebook-Brasil%2020200204.pdf. Last accessed on 13 June 2022.

Corrêa, S., and M. Pazello (2022), *Políticas Antigénero en America Latina en el Contexto Pandémico*, Rio de Janeiro: Observatorio de Sexualidad y Política (SPW)/ABIA, pp. 9–22, available at https://sxpolitics.org/GPAL/uploads/E-book-Covid-ES.pdf. Last accessed on 13 June 2022.

Delgado-Molina, C.A. (2019), "La «irrupción evangélica» en México. Entre las iglesias y la política", *Nueva Sociedad*, no. 280, pp. 91–100.

Demirović, A. (2018), "El populismo autoritario como estrategia neoliberal de gestión de la crisis", *Constelaciones. Revista de Teoría Crítica*, vol. 10, pp. 116–34.

Edenborg, E. (2022), "Putin's Anti-Gay War on Ukraine", *Boston Review*, 14 March, available at https://bostonreview.net/articles/putins-anti-gay-war-on-ukraine/. Last accessed on 13 June 2022.

El País (2018), "El matrimonio no parece ser un derecho para homosexuales", *El País*, March 25, available at https://elpais.com/internacional/2018/03/26/america/1522024297_765736.html. Last accessed on 13 June 2022

El Tiempo, "Diputada santandereana propone marcha por educación sexual en colegios", *El Tiempo*, 8 August, available at https://www.eltiempo.com/colombia/otras-ciudades/proponen-marcha-para-defender-educacion-sexual-en-colegios-50047#:~:text=El%20grupo%20es%20liderado%20por,comunidad%20minoritaria%20a%20la%20mayor%C3%ADa. Last accessed on 13 June 2022.

Gago, V. (2019), "Cartografiar la contraofensiva: el espectro del feminismo", *NUSO*, no. 282, July–August 2019, available at https://nuso.org/articulo/cartografiar-la-contraofensiva-el-espectro-del-feminismo/. Last accessed on 13 June 2022.

Gago, V., and M. Malo (2020), "La Internacional Feminista. Luchas en los territorios y contra el neoliberalismo", *La Internacional Feminista. Luchas en los territorios y contra el neoliberalismo*, Madrid: Traficantes de Sueños.

Geneva Consensus Declaration (2021), *theiwh.org*, 22 October, available at https://www.theiwh.org/wp-content/uploads/2021/11/GCD-Declaration-2021.pdf. Last accessed on 13 June 2022.

Gil, F. (2011), "Relativismo cultural, diferencia co- lonial y derechos de las mujeres", *El Género: una categoría útil para las ciencias sociales*, Bogotá: Universidad Nacional de Colombia, pp. 171–202.

Gil, F. (2020), *Políticas antigénero en América Latina: Colombia*, ABIA / SPW, F. Gil, available at https://sxpolitics.org/GPAL/uploads/Ebook-Colombia%202020203.pdf. Last accessed on 13 June 2022.

Giordano, V. (2014), "¿Qué hay de nuevo en las «nuevas derechas»?", *Nueva Sociedad*, no. 254, November–December, available at https://static.nuso.org/media/articles/downloads/4068_1.pdf. Last accessed on 13 June 2022.

Global Witness (2021), *Last line of defence*, 13 September, available at https://www.globalwitness.org/en/campaigns/environmental-activists/last-line-defence/. Last accessed on 13 June 2022.

Goodfriend, H. (2020), "El Salvador: de la esperanza a la locura", *Revista Común*, 30 November, available at https://revistacomun.com/blog/el-salvador-de-la-esperanza-a-la-locura/. Last accessed on 13 June 2022.

Graff, A., and E. Korolczuk (2020), *Anti-Gender Politics in the Populist Moment*, London and New York: Routledge.

Grzebalska, W., E. Kováts, and A. Pető (2017), "Gender as symbolic glue: how 'gender' became an umbrella term for the rejection of the (neo)liberal order", *Political Critique*, 13 January, available at http://politicalcritique.org/long-read/2017/gender-as-symbolic-glue-how-gender-became-an-umbrella-term-for-the-rejection-of-the-neoliberal-order/. Last accessed on 13 June 2022.

Hernández Castillo, R.A. (2021), "Las izquierdas y los pactos patriarcales", *Rompeviento.tv*, 15 March, available at https://www.rompeviento.tv/las-izquierdas-y-los-pactos-patriarcales/. Last accessed on 13 June 2022.

Htun, M. (2003), *Sex and the State: Abortion, Divorce, and the Family Under Latin American Dictatorships and Democracies*, Cambridge: Cambridge University Press.

Hoetmer, R. (2020), "A modo de introducción. Anatomía del giro autoritario y la derechización", *Nuevas derechas autoritarias. Conversaciones sobre el ciclo político actual en América Latina*, Quito: Fundación Rosa Luxemburgo/Ediciones Abya-Yala.

Kalil, I. (2020), "Políticas antiderechos en Brasil: neoliberalismo y neoconservadurismo en el gobierno de Bolsonaro", *Derechos en riesgo en América Latina: 11 estudios sobre grupos neoconservadores*, Quito/Bogotá: Fundación Rosa Luxemburgo/Desde Abajo, pp. 35–54.

Kováts, E., and M. Põim (2015), *Gender as symbolic glue. The position and role of conservative and far right parties in the anti-gender mobilizations in Europe*, Foundation for European Progressive Studies, available at https://library.fes.de/pdf-files/bueros/budapest/11382.pdf. Last accessed on 13 June 2022.

Lind, A. (2020), "Prólogo", *Género, sexualidad e izquierdas latinoamericanas. El reclamo de derechos durante la marea rosa*, Buenos Aires: CLACSO, pp. 13–16.

Madrid Charter (2020), available at https://fundaciondisenso.org/carta-de-madrid/. Last accessed on 13 June 2022.

Marina, D. L. (2019), "Agustín Laje y Nicolás Márquez recibirán premio por su lucha contra ideología de género", *ACI*, 17 September, available at https://www.aciprensa.com/noticias/agustin-laje-y-nicolas-marquez-recibiran-premio-por-su-lucha-contra-ideologia-de-genero-48207. Last accessed on 13 June 2022.

Márquez, N., and A. Laje (2019), *El libro negro de la nueva izquierda. Ideología de género o subversión cultural (The Black Book of the New Left)*, Buenos Aires: Grupo Unión.

Moragas, M. (2022), "Políticas antigénero en la Asamblea General de la Organización de los Estados Americanos 2019-2021: más de lo mismo, pero ni tanto", *Políticas antigénero en america latina en el contexto pandémico*, Río de Janeiro: Observatorio de Sexualidad y Política, available at https://sxpolitics.org/GPAL/uploads/E-book-Covid-ES.pdf. Last accessed on 13 June 2022.

Murillo, A. (2018), "El matrimonio no parece ser un derecho para homosexuales", *El País*, 26 March, available at https://elpais.com/internacional/2018/03/26/america/1522024297_765736.html. Last accessed on 13 June 2022.

Nehe, B. (2020), "No solo los gobiernos son autoritarios, la sociedad también lo es ¿En qué consiste el auge del autoritarismo en el mundo y qué rol juega América Latina?", *Nuevas derechas autoritarias. Conversaciones sobre el ciclo político actual en América Latina*, Quito: Fundación Rosa Luxemburgo/Ediciones Abya-Yala.

ONU-Mujeres (2017), *El progreso de las mujeres en América Latina y El Caribe*, available at https://lac.unwomen.org/sites/default/files/Field%20Office%20Americ

as/Documentos/Publicaciones/2017/07/UN16017_web.pdf. Last accessed on 13 June 2022.

ONU-Mujeres (2021), *Hacia una participación paritaria e inclusiva en América Latina y el Caribe. Panorama regional y aportes de la CSW65*, February, available at https://www.cepal.org/sites/default/files/document/files/consulta_regional_alc_csw65.pdf. Last accessed on 13 June 2022.

Peck, J., and A. Tickell (2002), "Neoliberalizing Space", *Antipode*, July, pp. 380–404.

Ravecca, P., M. Schenck, B. Fonseca, and D. Forteza (2022), "Interseccionalidad de derecha e ideología de género en América Latina", *Analecta Política*, vol. 12, no. 22, pp. 1–29, available at doi:10.18566/apolit.v12n22.a07. Last accessed on 13 June 2022.

Rossi, F., and C. Tabbush (2020), *Género, sexualidad e izquierdas latinoamericanas. El reclamo de derechos durante la marea rosa*, Buenos Aires: CLACSO.

Roth, J. (2020), "¿Puede el feminismo vencer al populismo? Avances populistas de derecha y contestaciones interseccionales en las Américas", *Ensayos InterAmericanos*, vol. 4, Bielefeld: Kipu-Verlag.

Sanahuja, J.A., and C. López (2020), "Las derechas neopatriotas en América Latina: contestación al orden liberal internacional", *Revista CIDOB d'Afers Internacionals*, no. 126, pp. 41–63.

Semán, P. (2021), "Los evangélicos se volvieron una parte importantísima del mundo popular al que el progresismo busca interpelar", *Contexto*, 24 September, available at https://ctxt.es/es/20210901/Politica/37247/pablo-seman-religiones-america-latina-evangelicos-pablo-stefanoni-pentecostales.htm. Last accessed on 13 June 2022.

Serrano Amaya, J. F. (2019), "Ideología de género", populismo autoritario y políticas sexuales", *Nómadas*, no. 50, pp. 155–173.

Stefanoni, P. (2021), "Las nuevas derechas expresan insatisfacciones y enojos de parte de la sociedad", *telam.com.ar*, 14 March, available at https://www.telam.com.ar/notas/202103/547354-stefanoni-la-rebeldia-se-volvio-de-derecha.html. Last accessed on 13 June 2022.

Stefanoni, P. (2021a), *La rebeldía se volvió de derecha*, Buenos Aires: Siglo XXI.

Svampa, M. (2017), "Populismos Latinoamericanos en el fin del ciclo progresista", *Infraolitica*, 11 April, available at https://infrapolitica.com/2017/04/11/populismos-latinoamericanos-en-el-fin-del-ciclo-progresista-por-maristella-svampa/. Last accessed on 13 June 2022.

Svampa, M. (2018), "Del cambio de época al fin de ciclo", *Maristella Svampa*, 3 December, available at http://maristellasvampa.net/del-cambio-de-epoca-al-fin-de-ciclo-2/. Last accessed on 13 June 2022.

Svampa, M. (2020), "Lo que las derechas traen a la región latinoamericana. Entre lo político y lo social; nuevos campos de disputa", *Nuevas derechas autoritarias. Con-*

versaciones sobre el ciclo político actual en América Latina, ed. Muggenthaler, Quito: Fundación Rosa Luxemburgo/Ediciones Abya-Yala.

Svampa, M., and E. Terán-Mantovani (2019), "En las fronteras del cambio de época: Escenarios de una nueva fase del extractivismo en América Latina", *Cómo se sostiene la vida en América Latina. Feminismos y re-existencias en tiempos de oscuridad.* Quito: Fundación Rosa Luxemburgo.

Torres, A. (2019), "De la marea rosa a la marea conservadora y autoritaria en América Latina: desafíos feministas", *Friedrich Ebert Stiftung*, September, available at http://library.fes.de/pdf-files/bueros/quito/15682.pdf. Last accessed on 13 June 2022.

Torres, A. (2020), *Derechos en riesgo en América Latina: 11 estudios sobre grupos neoconservadores*, Quito/Bogotá: Fundación Rosa Luxemburgo/Desde Abajo, pp. 201–22.

Torres, A. (2020a), "Neoconservadurismos en América Latina: análisis desde la crisis", *Derechos en riesgo en América Latina: 11 estudios sobre grupos neoconservadores*, Quito/Bogotá: Fundación Rosa Luxemburgo / Desde Abajo, pp. 201–22.

Vaggione, J.M. (2009), "Sexualidad, Religión y política en América latina", *trabajo preparado para los diálogos regionales (Río de Janeiro)*, August, available at https://sxpolitics.org/wp-content/uploads/2009/10/sexualidad-religion-y-politica-en-america-latina-juan-vaggione.pdf. Last accessed on 13 June 2022.

Vaggione, J.M. (2012), "La cultura de la vida. Desplazamientos estratégicos del activismo católico conservador frente a los derechos sexuales y reproductivos", *Religião e Sociedade*, vol. 32, no. 2, pp. 57–80.

Vega, C. (2017), "¿Quién teme al feminismo? A propósito de la 'ideología de género' y otras monstruosidades sexuales en Ecuador y América Latina", *Sin Permiso*, 8 December, available at https://www.sinpermiso.info/textos/quien-teme-al-feminismo-a-proposito-de-la-ideologia-de-genero-y-otras-monstruosidades-sexuales-en. Last accessed on 13 June 2022.

Vega, C. (2019), "La "ideología de género" y la renaturalización privatizadora de lo social", *Fundamentalismos religiosos, derechos y democracia*, Quito : FLACSO Ecuador.

Vega, C., L. Castellanos, and J. Salazar (2021), "Poner orden en la familia y en el país. La politización reactiva y la consolidación de la articulación evangélica en Ecuador", *América Latina en Tiempos Revueltos. Claves y luchas renovadas frente al giro conservador*, Montevideo, Cochabamba and Morelos: ZUR.

Exploring the Colonial and Apartheid Roots of Urban Authoritarianism in Postapartheid South Africa

Khanyile Mlotshwa

Introduction

In urban studies, the concept of neoliberal authoritarianism has become central, almost hegemonic, in addressing issues of financialization and commodification in cities across the world. However, central to this chapter contribution is the argument that in cities in the formerly colonized Global South, the neoliberal authoritarianism concept has to be supplemented by the concept of coloniality drawn from decolonial studies. While the concept of neoliberal authoritarianism unmasks issues of class, the concept of coloniality presents issues of race, colonial history, gender, and other intersectional matters as relics or constructs of the colonial period. Stuart Hall conceptualizes 'the postcolonial' as the conjectural moment "in which both the crisis of the uncompleted struggle for 'decolonization' and the crisis of the 'post-independence' state is deeply inscribed" (Hall 1996, 224). Andreas Huyssen calls it a time when the focus shifts from "present futures to present pasts" (2001, 57; see also Gregory 2004). The concept of neoliberal authoritarianism, while exposing issues of class and financialization even in the Global South, needs to be supplemented by the idea of coloniality which powerfully unmasks racist ways of thinking about the world while articulating them to global capitalism. This chapter contribution theorizes the enduring racial inequalities, class inequalities, spatial inequalities, and brutality present in the governance of the poor Black subject in postapartheid South Africa as both urban authoritarianism and coloniality. As a way of discussing two illustrations of urban authoritarianism in postapartheid South Africa, the chapter further opens a debate on the need to decolonize the concept of the right to the city that has become hegemonic in studying urban social movements globally. Henri Lefebvre popularized the concept of the right to the city, a superior form of right, manifesting itself as "a cry and a demand" (1967, 158). As a superior right, it carries within it a sense of the right to the commons, to participation and appropriation (Lefebvre 1996, 174; Mitchell 2003). It is the contention of this chapter that, particularly in Africa, the right to the city is an ideal. This idealism is dealt with in detail as the last section of the chapter that reflects on the two illustrations.

Neoliberal Authoritarianism and Coloniality in the City

The enduring racial, class, and spatial inequalities and brutality in the governance of the poor in postapartheid South Africa is in this chapter analysed through the staging of a debate and dialogue between the concepts of neoliberal authoritarianism and that of coloniality. The concept of coloniality is not used here to displace that of neoliberal authoritarianism but in a spirit of complementarity between the two. Ronaldo Munck's (2013) observations about the concept of precarity in the Global South are also relevant in this study of neoliberal authoritarianism. While Munck feels the concept of the precariat is generally inadequate, he emphasizes that for the Global South it does not name anything new, but "elides the experience of the South in an openly Eurocentric manner" (Munck 2013, 747). The superexploitation and accumulation through dispossession that precarity refers to has always prevailed in the Global South. Similarly, growing state power and the exclusion of a large majority of populations that neoliberal authoritarianism names have been the living conditions for most people in the Global South since colonization. Decolonial thinkers have named these conditions as coloniality, in order to make them visible by reaching as far back as 1652 to the present. In this section, I discuss the concepts of neoliberal authoritarianism and coloniality, and how they can be articulated.

Ian Bruff has argued that under neoliberal conditions it is imperative to look beyond the mere exercise of brute coercive force in order to perceive the ways in which the state and other institutions of power are reconfigured to insulate them from dissent and contestation (2016, 107). Neoliberal violence is legitimated through ideological means (Biebricher 2020; Springer 2016). It is, however, also visible in constitutional debt ceilings, sweeping free trade agreements, direct and violent suppression of political freedoms, austerity measures, increasing support for right-wing and xenophobic sentiments, and the normalization of illicit financial transactions (Fabry and Sandbeck 2018; Ryan 2018). For Cemal Burek Tansel, neoliberal authoritarianism relies upon both coercive state practices that suppress opposition and judicial and administrative state apparatuses that limit the space to challenge this violence (2017, 2). Neoliberal authoritarianism disenfranchises subordinate groups and moves policy making beyond popular contestations (Fabry and Sandbeck 2018, 3). Bruff, however, contends that this strengthening of the state does not insulate it from popular struggles and demands, or discontent the disenfranchised (2016, 108). This has been the case in South Africa where against increasing brutality, such as the police shooting of 34 striking miners in Marikana on

16 August 2012 and the random killing of protestors and activists, strikes have not abated (Swart and Rodney-Gumede 2019; South African Human Rights Commission [SAHRC] 2015). Authoritarian neoliberalism can be categorized into three varieties that include technocracy, populist nationalism, and traditional authoritarianism (Gallo 2021). Across the globe, and in a transnational manner, technocrats are deployed to use "their scholarly and professional reputation to enact fully fledged neoliberal programmes" (Gallo 2021, 5). For Bob Jessop (2014), this expertise is used as a tool for depoliticization, where elected leaders give way to unaccountable bodies, agencies, and committees of experts who push political agendas such as expenditure cuts, liberalizations, and privatizations. Growing populist nationalism has been paralleled by growth in xenophobia. Technocracy and populist nationalism share a claim that they want to enact what is good for the country (Caramani 2017). Hall (1985) names the link between neoliberalism and nationalism as "authoritarian populism". Traditional authoritarianism is seen in the rise of political entrepreneurs who promise to protect countries from world markets (Inglehart and Norris 2017).

Simon Springer (2016) opens up the concept of neoliberal authoritarianism to a dialogue with coloniality, positing that both colonialism and neoliberalism pave "a road to hell with ostensibly good intentions" (2016, 153). His central argument is that neoliberalism has managed to hide its violence and authoritarianism through creating the impression that all violence is 'local' and blaming it on "backward" cultural practices (Springer 2016, 155; see also Kaplan 2000; Huntington 1996). The postcolonial period in Africa has been characterized as marked by dictatorships, coups and ethnic wars. This has occluded external interference such as the recently come to light role of France in the Rwandan genocide of 1994 (BBC 2021; Aljazeera 2021). To Springer, these Orientalist discourses ignore "the 'global' political economy of violence" as encapsulated in neoliberal authoritarianism (Springer 2016, 155; see also Ryan 2018; Bourdieu 1998; Dumenil and Levy 2011; Giroux 2004; Goldberg 2009; MacEwan 1999). We now turn to the concept of coloniality to expose the long history of the colonial presence of authoritarianism in the Global South.

Emerging from the Latin American decolonial school of thought, coloniality refers to the endurance of colonialism and the patterns of its authoritarian violence. It is the "relations of domination that continue even after colonialism has ceased" (Hlabangane 2021, 166). Coloniality represents the technologies of imperialism and colonial matrices of power that still haunt the Global South (Ndlovu-Gatsheni 2013, 11). Derek Gregory would call it the colonial presence which is "the performative force of colonial modernity" (2004, 4). William Mpofu and Melissa Steyn argue that the coloniality of Western modernity has led to extractivism around natural resources, exploitation of labour, and the legal control of 'undesirables' (2021, 2; Grosfoguel 2008; Maldonaldo Torres 2008; Mignolo 2005). This sounds like neoliberal authoritarianism. However, Artuto Escobar notes that coloniality is an analytical tool concerned with understanding modernity basing on colonial difference and from the locus of the enunciation of ex-colonized people (2007, 179–210). Similar to neoliberal authoritarianism, coloniality is part ideological. It has endured more than colonialism "in some part due to the knowledge systems with which it conceives of and engages with the world" (Hlabangane 2021, 168). The concept of coloniality allows us to unmask, resist, and seek to destroy gendered violence and inequality, peripheralization, underdevelopment, displacement, and dispossession (Mpofu and Steyn 2021, 2; Ndlovu-Gatsheni 2013). It challenges those involved in democratic projects to centre the voices of the oppressed (Ndlovu 2021). As a theoretical concept, it reveals how racial and ethnic classifications of people endure as specific and constitutive elements of the global capitalist system (Quijano 2000, 1). While the concept of neoliberal authoritarianism will unmask issues of class, the concept of coloniality will shine light on issues of race, colonial history, gender, and other intersectional matters.

Genealogies of Authoritarian Urbanism in South Africa

In South Africa, the history of urban space appears to be already authoritarian in that it emerges at the crux of colonialism, land dispossessions, and racism, as a zone where Black Indigeneous subjects are excluded. The South African economy was transformed by the discovery of minerals—diamonds and then gold—in the late 1800s, marking the beginning of capitalist urbanization as linked to deepening European conquest, dispossession, discrimination, migration and capitalist economic progress (Feinstein 2005, 3). Two forms of migration are central to the emergence of urban spaces. First, was the increased European migration after the discovery of diamonds and gold in the 1800s, when about 5,000 artisans and labourers were brought to the Cape of Good Hope from the United Kingdom to boost the population in the colony (Feinstein 2005, 28). Second, was the regional migration of Black subjects in order to boost labour in the mines that was encouraged by the mining industry. This migration between South Africa and most of sub-Saharan Africa in the 1870s which persisted in the postapartheid moment was jointly initiated by the colonial South African government and capital (Xulu 2013; Fine 2014). Its genealogy can be traced back to the farm labourers at the time of conquests and land dispossessions in the 1700s and mapped ahead to the present African migrants engaged in precarious jobs in Johannesburg, Cape Town, Durban, and many of the postapartheid cities. A former editor of the Cosatu magazine, Dominic Tweedie, argues that the South African working class comes from a lot of different countries in the African continent (in Hlatshwayo 2010, 7). Harold Wolpe notes the links and continuity in the "ideological foundations of apartheid" especially with regard to "the African reserves and the African migrant labour" (1972,

289). Once the urban space emerged in the combination of the crystallization of colonial capital around mining compounds and a thriving labour migrant system, racist legal developments increased its authoritarianism.

The 1913 Natives Land Act sums up the articulations of land dispossessions, urbanization, inequalities, and subjectivation and primitive accumulation under colonial conditions. The implications of the Act were that the confiscation or expropriation of land from the Black Indigenous peoples left them landless, compelling them to be labourers in farms, in mines, and in the manufacturing industries in emerging urban centres. This landlessness made Black people living in cities perpetual 'squatters', "a native... with no land of his own" who is in a perpetual state of unfreedom (Mabin 1992, 15). While the intention was to grow the reserves, later Bantustans, where black people lived exiled from citizenship, the 1913 Native Land Act had unintended implications in that "from the 1930s, informal settlements on the fringes of the cities and many towns began to become common" (Mabin 1992, 16). After this Act, the colonial and Apartheid authorities instituted further legal instruments to alienate the Black subject from the urban space. The Natives Urban Act of 1923, linked to the 1913 Native Land Act, was supposed to provide for improved conditions of residence for natives in or near urban areas and the better administration of native affairs (Worden 1991; Dyzenhaus 1991; Davenport 1991). The Natives Urban Areas Consolidated Act of 1945, also called the Bantu Urban Areas Consolidation Act, came as a follow-up to the Native Urban Act of 1923 and was meant to tighten "influx controls" of Black African people into urban spaces (Dyzenhaus 1991, 37; Dugard 1978, 422). The Act effectively deemed urban areas in South Africa as 'white' and required all Black African men in cities and towns to carry around permits called 'passes' at all times (Worden 1991; Dyzenhaus 1991; Davenport 1991).

Authoritarianism gives rise to its own resistance, all coloniality is matched by acts of decoloniality. Townships, as specific places where Black people lived in urban South Africa, have emerged as both a mark of this subject's subjugation and resistance. The South Western Townships (Soweto) are an example of how colonial urban policies around health issues and sanitation combined with the desire by Black people to be in the city. In 1904, Black people and Indians were removed from the inner city to Klipspruit Farm about 12 miles out of the city of Johannesburg, after a pneumonic epidemic broke out among Indian communities. The Indians and Africans were compelled to remain at the outskirts of the city even after the epidemic had waned. In 1963, now greatly expanded, it was named Soweto (Phillips 2013, 311). However, the Soweto residents over the ensuing years developed and offered resistance to white rule. James Mpanza's squatter movement in the 1940s and the Asinamali Party's rent boycotts between 1954 and 1958 are some of the examples of early resistance in the townships (Phillips 2013, 311; Sisulu 1998). Alexandra, a township that lies across from Sandton, the richest square mile in Africa, was established in 1912, a year before the 1913 Land Act (Musiker and Musiker 2000).

However, as a result of informal urbanization over the years, the township is now populated by shacks called *imikhukhu* or *imijondolo* in isiZulu. In the early 1960s, to control the population of Black people in Alexandra, the apartheid government decided to implement a programme of demolishing houses in the township, replacing them with hostels. The idea of hostels was to accommodate Black people—especially men—temporarily in the city as labourers. They were not expected to be permanent, and therefore, to have a lease. This is explained in the next section, where I discuss two cases of how urban authoritarianism has manifested itself in postapartheid South Africa, the issue of leases is one of the lingering problems that keep emerging in the many protests around housing.

Urban Authoritarianism and Coloniality in Postapartheid South Africa

Urban authoritarianism and coloniality in postapartheid South Africa manifests in a variety of ways, all of which have a historical genealogy. This section illustrates two such manifestations and their provenance. The first one involves migration and the experiences of alienation that migrants contend with in inner city Johannesburg, where they live crowded and in most cases, dirty, squalid high-rise buildings. The second case involves residents of Soweto, Johannesburg's oldest township, who refused to vote in local government elections on 1 November 2021 but chose to protest at the African National Congress's (ANC) headquarters in the city centre—the ANC is the ruling party. This chapter follows a qualitative methodology to probe ways in which South Africa's postapartheid Black subjects make sense of their situation in urban spaces (Guest, Namey, and Mitchell 2013; Merriam 2009; Marvasti 2004; Denzin and Lincoln 2005). To collect data, the chapter combined archival research and ethnographic methods. This involved participant observation in inner-city Johannesburg where most immigrants live, keeping a notebook, taking pictures on a mobile phone, and conducting interviews. The data collected was subjected to a combination and triangulation of Critical Discourse Analysis (CDA), ideological analysis, and semiotic analysis (Wodak 2001; Thompson 1990; Van Leeuwen and Jewitt 2004). In one way or another, each of these illustrations exemplify the struggle for right to the city.

Migration and Living Under Borders and Coloniality in Urban South Africa

In the postapartheid moment, the Johannesburg that immigrants—both local and from across Africa—come to is a place aspiring to be a global city (Acuto and Steele 2013; Sassen 1991). It is a concrete jungle, described as the "New York of Africa" and the "heartbeat of Africa" (Sihlongonyane 2005, 22). The city is caught up in coloniality and authoritarianism in at least two significant ways. First, Johannesburg has historically been a big city in Sub-Saharan Africa, such that thousands of migrant labourers who flock their every year are caught up in the circuits of capitalism whose roots go all the way back in the 1800s. The second sense of this authoritarianism is cultural, manifesting in how the fingerprints of apartheid are still legible in the streets and buildings that these migrant labourers occupy. For the majority Black people, the spatial arrangements that were obtained under apartheid still persist, where Black people are consigned to cramped in townships. The situation obtained in inner city Johannesburg has an added cultural dimension. Suburbs in central Johannesburg like Hillbrow, Yeoville, and Berea, that under Apartheid were occupied by white migrants mostly from East Europe, are now under the occupation of Black migrants from outside South Africa. However, coloniality persists, for example, in the naming of streets and buildings. It is important to briefly describe this coloniality of the built environment of the inner suburbs of Johannesburg before bringing in the voices of interviewees who discuss how it alienates them.

Fig 1, Fig. 2: Street signs bearing street names in Yeoville.

South African authorities have, over the years, grappled with the politics of naming in terms of streets and buildings. If you go into the city centre in Johannesburg, nearly all the streets and major buildings have been renamed after African liberation heroes including Nelson Mandela, Oliver Tambo, and Reginald Luthuli, to mention a few. The recent addition is the Winnie Mandela House, which is the newly unveiled headquarters of the opposition, the Economic Freedom Fighters

(EFF) party. These are deliberate moves to 'decolonize' the city. However, the streets and buildings in the Yeoville, Berea, and Hillbrow suburbs still bear the names of some key players of the colonial and Apartheid eras, and mostly Black African immigrants live surrounded by this coloniality and colonial presence. This architecture gives those who dwell here specific subject positions as they are constantly confronted with coloniality. This psychologically and culturally positions them in the margins of the city and the economy. The naming of the mostly dilapidated buildings and the streets keeps the immigrants out of the city, even when they are in the city. One interviewee captures how these buildings, streets, and public spaces still mirror a white South Africa, whose image they have carried with them from their home countries and their villages within South Africa. Ncube, an almost 65-year-old man from Zimbabwe, says this is the Johannesburg that they have always called *"e'skhiweni"* (a white place). "This is what we mean", he says. "It is not only because we will be referring to the large number of white people, compared to where we come from, but the city is white, the streets bear white names and even the buildings that we sleep in". Ncube says he intentionally uses "sleep" rather than "live in" because for most of the day they will be at work, as they labour long hours as security guards and in restaurants. In the interviews, it becomes clear that to call a place "a white place" is also to make an economic statement. It means it is a place where capital is concentrated and where it is possible to get a job, no matter how precarious it is. The implications of this cultural rejection by Johannesburg are its subtle bordering which brings us to how, under neoliberal capitalism, the majority of immigrants in cities live under the authoritarianism and coloniality that emerges at the intersection of migration, borders, and urbanism.

In Johannesburg, the immigrant as a Black subject lives as if estranged from the city. Nkosinathi, a 43-year-old Zimbabwean immigrant, explains that, "we are in the city, but we are outside the city. It is like living at the border. These buildings, these streets reject us in many ways. We cannot inhabit them". Nkosinathi, not his real name, is married and lives with his wife and a child in Hillbrow, one of the inner-city suburbs. Ironically, Nkosinathi grew up in Beitbridge, an area at the border of Zimbabwe and South Africa. He notes that when he got to Johannesburg, it was his first time experiencing city life. For some Africans, coming to Johannesburg is coming to the city and migration to Johannesburg can be thought of primarily as 'rural-urban' migration although national borders are involved. He says when he first arrived in Johannesburg, he lived at Park Station, a big bus station in Johannesburg, "sleeping outside" and bathing at a nearby hostel. He was homeless. Nkosinathi's early years of homelessness are not peculiar to him but speaks to what can be characterized as the alienation that most migrant experience in big cities. This is part of living at the border (Wright 2013; Nyers 2010; Ngai 2003; Balibar 2002). Most of the interviewees, especially women, spoke about neglect in many spaces including clinics, police stations, and other public offices. It also means that migrants have marginal access to public services, meaning they cannot get decent paying jobs and as a result, cannot afford decent housing. For Ms. Bibesho, who has worked for nine years as a domestic servant for a Congolese family in Sandton, Johannesburg is a classic diaspora space, where the diaspora is a place of pain that you live in because of fear of returning home. However, Ms. Bibesho says she has not experienced xenophobia, but saw it on television from the comfort of Sandton. This speaks to the geography of xenophobia and the borders that it inscribes within the country. It always takes place in the poor townships and some poor inner-city spaces.

Protesting for Housing on Election Day

Housing struggles articulated as land struggles have continued to be an indication of the marginality of Black subjects in urban South Africa in the postapartheid period. What is starkly revealed as problematic here is the relationship of the people, who long for a piece of land even if it is to build a shack, and the state as a specific authoritarian, colonial, and Apartheid relic that is uncaring (Alexander 2010; Bénit-Gbaffou 2008). The last point is significant because under the postapartheid regimes, the state is mostly constituted by the ANC, a former liberation movement that people looked up to deliver freedom. For most Black Africans, how they come to inhabit the city is through owning a small piece of land where their family house stands. This ownership is important because it also means access to water, electricity, education, health, and other social services. The marginalization of Black subjects in postapartheid South Africa has been a constant struggle that has made South Africa a hotspot in terms of protests. In South Africa, there are numerous service delivery protests every week. According to the Institute for Security Studies, there are about 2.26 protests daily. Until now the highest number of incidents were recorded in 2013 and 2014, with more than three protests a day. This period was followed by reductions to nearly one per day in 2018, when Cyril Ramaphosa became president. The number started growing steadily again in 2019, reaching about 2.5 a day on average (Lancaster and Mulaudzi 2020).

During the local government elections on the 1 November 2021, there were protests on issues of service delivery around the country. Some of the protests were at places designated as polling stations. However, the most significant of these protests was staged by Soweto residents at Luthuli House, the ruling party's headquarters in Central Johannesburg. The more than 1,000 residents from different parts of Soweto marched to Luthuli House after refusing to vote. They wanted to hand a petition to the ruling party. Their main grievance was the long wait for Reconstruction and Development Programme (RDP) houses. The residents, who said they are backyard dwellers, said some of them had been waiting for more than 25 years for houses. Independent South Africa is 27 years old this year. This means the promise of houses was made in the honeymoon years of the country's independence. According to the media, "some of the grey-haired protesters came armed with their C4 housing application forms—some dating as far back as 1996—when then president Nelson Mandela unveiled the Reconstruction and Development Programme (RDP), which culminated in several residents being allocated houses" (Pillay and Ndaba 2021). As earlier alluded to, these residents were directly linking the issue of housing to that of land. This is a link that the ANC had sought to downplay in its messaging. Since the opposition Economic Freedom Front (EFF) party brought the matter to the centre of national politics, the ANC has remained unclear on the issue of land. On several occasions, the ruling party has refused to vote with the EFF on the land issue. The parties disagree on the aspect of expropriation without compensation that the EFF insists on. It was only in the years approaching the party's 2017 congress which elected Cyril Ramaphosa as leader of the movement that the ideas of the Radical Economic Transformation (RET) emerged, their ideas on the land seemed to converge with those of the EFF. Under president Cyril Ramaphosa, a billionaire, the ANC has been hugely ambiguous on the issue of land. This is inspite of the fact that for many residents and citizens, the land issue is real and is central to their citizenship. In recent years, the differences between the ANC and the EFF are that the opposition party wants radical change to ownership patterns whereas the state would own all the land and lease it out according to its judgements. The ANC, while agreeing on the need to reform land ownership still insists on private ownership patterns.

Decolonising the Right to the City

To borrow from Fanon on Marxist analysis in colonial conditions, in Africa, and much of the Global South, the concept of the right to the city must be "slightly stretched" (1963, 40). This is because when conceptualized as a right, it comes with assumptions that become problematic when one acknowledges centuries of colonial and postcolonial history and takes into account the centrality of race in understanding urban inequalities, divisions, and resultant struggles. Lefebvre popularized the concept of the right to the city, a superior form of right, manifesting itself as "a cry and a demand" (1967, 158). As a superior right, it carries within it a sense of the right to the commons, to participation, and appropriation as distinct from the right to property (Lefebvre 1996, 174). According to Don Mitchell, the right to the city is "a work in which all its citizens participate" (2003, 17). In the context of cities across the world and in Africa in particular, this is ideal. Lefebvre has been seen as utopian. For Peter Marcuse (2012), this utopianism carries with it a revolutionary will to imagine a city different from the current neoliberal cities and this means radical and complete change to the capitalist system (see also Purcell 2002,

101). For David Harvey, the right to the city must not only be "a right of access to what the property speculators and state planners define" but must include the right to change the city (2003, 941). In cities in the Global South such as Johannesburg, the majority Black subject emerges out of the ashes of a history of colonialism, Apartheid, and racism, closed out of urban spaces, the right to the city is not pre-given. It comes with a lingering question of the 'human' who is the subject of the (human) right to the city. This human can be recovered by acknowledging the colonial, apartheid, and racist history of the urban space in postapartheid South Africa. For Samara, He, and Chen, the production of urban space in the Global South today is tied to neoliberalism and the right to the city (2013, 2). While neoliberalism is characterized by an emphasis on an urban future of various forms of enclosure, the right to the city emphasizes various forms of justice (Samara, He, and Chen 2013, 12). As shall be discussed in the next paragraph, this overlooks cases when the right to the city is appropriated by neoliberalism to perpetuate its own brand of authoritarianism.

Lucy Earle (2017) argues that there are three reasons for embracing the concept of the right to the city. First, the right to the city concept "tallies with international aid donor concern for decentralization" putting emphasis on devolution of responsibilities from national to city levels (Earle 2017, 8). Appropriated by experts and international donors, the right to the city here straddles a thin line between a right and authoritarianism. In his three varieties of authoritarian neoliberalism, Ernesto Gallo (2021) cites technocracy as the first example. Here, technocrats are characterized as the "organic intellectuals" of neoliberal capital and international agencies penetrating the state from without (Gallo 2021, 5). There are a number of organizations that fight for rights such as the right to housing in South Africa and operate within this neoliberal context of donor funding which includes capital and ideas. There are experts advising these activists. The second reason for embracing the concept of the right to the city is that it presupposes equality and asserts a right for all "city dwellers to benefit from everything that urban life and society has to offer" (Earle 2017, 8). Earle's application of the concept of the right to the city is seen as an ideological and bastardized departure from the way Lefebvre, Mitchell, Harvey, and Marcuse thought about it. To reflect on Earle's arguments, first, assuming equality has been proven to be a fallacy by historical examples and the two illustrations proffered in this chapter. Illegalized migrants and Soweto residents still waiting for an RDP house are not equal in any way to the officials they protest to at Luthuli House, for example. They are not equal to white people in suburbs who cannot be seen protesting over anything. The third reason proffered by Earle is that the right to the city concept "appeals to the rights-based approach to development that has been in vogue over recent years" (2017, 8). We discuss this rights-based approach in the next paragraph from the angle of citizenship.

The right to the city is also conceptualized and argued for in the context of citizenship. Emerging in the context of modernity, citizenship is problematically "bound to the idea of universal equality" (Earle 2017, 33). The limits of universal equality have already been addressed. Citizenship is seen as eroding hierarchies and privileges to install a regime based on the equality of rights and equality before the law (Holston and Appadurai 1999; Scott 1998). Aaron Kamugisha problematizes this by pointing to the coloniality of citizenship as appearing in a "variety of practices, tropes of belonging and identity concerns that frustrate and deny the aspirations of many" (2007, 20). He describes the coloniality of citizenship as "a complex amalgam of elite domination, neoliberalism and the legacy of colonial authoritarianism" (Kamugisha 2007, 20). As in the case of South Africa, this is where existing colonial and Apartheid forms of citizenship persist beyond the independence moment and are kept intact by a middle-class nationalism that kow-tows to the racial order that underlies it. For Manuela Boatca and Julia Roth (2016), the coloniality of citizenship is in the conditions under which it emerged in Europe. Rather than a "modern, progressive institution that helped overcome particularities of unequal social origin", citizenship developed through "the legal (and physical) exclusion of non-European, non-White, and non-Western populations from civic, political, social and cultural rights; these exclusions, and thus citizenship as such, have historically been (en)gendered" (2016, 191). In the Global South, specifically in unequal societies such as South Africa, and as our two case studies attest, low-income residents of cities are not always excluded foreign migrants or members of minority ethnic groups but "national citizens living in a democratic state" (Earle 2017, 34).

Conclusion

A dialogue and debate between the concepts of neoliberal authoritarianism, on one hand, and, coloniality, on the other, is fruitful for the understanding of postapartheid urban authoritarianism in South Africa. While the concept of neoliberal authoritarianism makes apparent the classed nature of the struggles in divided and unequal postapartheid cities like Johannesburg, the concept of coloniality unmasks what this teleological and universalist approach obscures. The concept of neoliberal authoritarianism, with its roots in Europe and European history, could be colonizing in the sense that it reads the situation in Global South cities as similar to that of the West. In naming the struggles in Johannesburg as the struggle of the right to the city, deploying a neoliberal authoritarianism theoretical lens would obscure the fact that the working class in the Global South is population of mostly colonial subjects used for labour, that built cities in which it has always been unwelcome. The argument here is twofold. First, the specificity of the working class and its struggles in the Global South are obscured through an uncritical application of a theoretical approach informed by neoliberal authoritarianism. Second, the uncritical application of this approach imposes European history onto the Global South and imagines the European working class as the revolutionary subject, ('demanding the right to the city') displacing the working class of the Global South as a specific historical subject. Neoliberal authoritarian as a theoretical concept constructs its subject of history as the European working class. The challenge then becomes the normativity, teleology, and universalism of the neoliberal authoritarianism theoretical approach. This is not exceptional to the concept of neoliberal authoritarianism. I argue elsewhere that Antonio Gramsci (1977), who pays attention to the colonial question, for all the important insights he makes on how colonies are exploited to develop the metropolises in Europe, writes the Black African subject out of African history (Mlotshwa 2022, 109–10). While Gramsci posits that colonialism was the expansion of the capitalist system outside the West where the colonies were impoverished for the benefit of European civilization, the problem becomes that it is the European working class that is enthroned as the population that would resolve the problems of capitalism at the centre of this globalizing history (Gramsci 1977, 302). The subject of the right to the city struggles in cities in the Global South, is unclear, and as such the struggles in the Global South are not textured, remaining unclear as part of a global urban struggles. This raises the need for a debate and dialogue between critiques of neoliberal urbanism and Global South epistemologies, such as the concept of coloniality, to make sense of the problems of urban authoritarianism. In postapartheid South Africa, what is at stake is the relationship of the masses who long for a piece of land even if it is to build a shack, and the state as a specific colonial and apartheid relic. Only an approach that takes the concept of coloniality seriously would unmask the tragedy of the fact that the contest between the postapartheid national and local government rulers, on one hand, and the people, on the other hand, not only echoes that of the colonial and Apartheid periods but is the same struggle. Coloniality makes these continuities apparent.

References

Acuto, M., and W. Steele (2013), *Global City Challenges: Debating a Concept, Improving the Practice*, Basingstoke and New York: Palgrave Macmillan.

Al Jazeera (2021), "France 'enabled' 1994 Rwanda genocide, report says", 19 April 2021, available at https://www.aljazeera.com/news/2021/4/19/france-enabled-1994-rwanda-genocide-report-says. Last accessed on 29 July 2022.

Balibar, E. (2002), *Politics and the Other Scene*, London and New York: Verso.

Biebricher, T. (2020), "Neoliberalism and Authoritarianism", *Global Perspectives* vol. 1, no. 1, pp. 1–18; available at https://doi.org/10.1525/001c.11872. Last accessed on 29 July 2022.

Bénit-Gbaffou, C. (2008), "Introduction: the place of participation in South African local democracy", *Transformation: Critical Perspectives on Southern Africa*, vol. 66, no. 1, pp. i–vii.

Boatca, M., and J. Roth (2016), "Unequal and gendered: Notes on the coloniality of citizenship", *Current Sociology Monograph*, vol. 64, no. 2, pp. 191–212.

Bourdieu, P. (1998), "Utopia of endless exploitation: The essence of neoliberalism", *Le Monde Diplomatique*, December: 1–5.

British Broadcasting Corporation (BBC) (2021), "Macron asks Rwanda to forgive France over 1994 genocide role", 27 May, available at https://www.bbc.com/news/world-europe-57270099. Last accessed on 29 July 2022.

Bruff, I. (2016), "Neoliberalism and authoritarianism", The Handbook of Neoliberalism, edited by S. Springer, K. Birch, and J. MacLeavy, New York and London: Routledge, pp. 107–17.

Caramani, D. (2017), "Will vs. reason: The populist and technocratic forms of political representation and their critique to party government", *American Political Science Review*, vol. 111, no. 1, pp. 54–67.

Davenport, T. R. H. (1991), *South Africa: A Modern History*, London: Palgrave Macmillan.

Delius, P. 2017. "The history of migrant labour in South Africa (1800–2014)", *Oxford Research Encyclopaedia of African History*. Available at: https://doi.org/10.1093/acrefore/9780190277734.013.93. Last accessed on 29 July 2022.

Denzin, N. K., and Y. Lincoln (eds.) (2005), "Introduction: The discipline and practice of qualitative research", *The SAGE handbook of qualitative research*, Thousand Oaks, London, and New Delhi: Sage Publications, pp. 1–31.

Dumenil, G., and D. Levy (2011), *The Crisis of Neoliberalism*, Cambridge: Harvard University Press.

Dyzenhaus, D. (1991), *Hard Cases in Wicked Legal Systems: South African Law in the Perspective of Legal Philosophy*, Oxford: Oxford University Press.

Earle, L. (2017), *Transgressive Citizenship and the Struggle for Social Justice: The Right to the City in Sao Paulo*, Cham: Palgrave Macmillan.

Easton, K. (2017), "Southern Africa", *The Routledge Companion to Postcolonial Studies*, J. McLeod (ed.), London and New York: Routledge, pp. 129–38.

Escobar, A. (2007), "Worlds and Knowledges Otherwise: The Latin American Modernity/Coloniality Research Program", *Cultural Studies*, vol. 21, nos. 2–3, pp. 197–210.

Fabry, A., and S. Sandbeck (2018), "Introduction to special issue on 'authoritarian neoliberalism'", *Competition & Change*, vol. 23, no. 2, 109–15, available at https://doi.org/10.1177%2F1024529418813827. Last accessed on 29 July 2022.

Fanon, F. (1963), *The Wretched of the Earth*, New York: Grove.

Feinstein, C. H. (2005), *An Economic History of South Africa: Conquest, Discrimination and Development*, Cambridge, New York, and Melbourne: Cambridge University Press.

Fine, J. (2014), "Migrants and Migrant Workers in the Post-Apartheid era", *Global Labour Journal*, vol. 5, no. 3, pp. 330–46.

Gallo, E. (2021) "Three varieties of Authoritarian Neoliberalism: Rule by the experts, the people, the leader", *Competition & Change*, pp. 1–21, available at https://doi.org/10.1177%2F10245294211038425. Last accessed on 29 July 2022.

Giddens, A., and P. W. Sutton (2014), *Essential Concepts in Sociology*, Cambridge, UK and Malden, MA: Polity.

Giroux, H. A. (2004), *The Terror of Neoliberalism: Authoritarianism and the Eclipse of Democracy*, Boulder, NC: Paradigm.

Gowen, P. (2001), "Neoliberal cosmopolitanism", *New Left Review*, September–October, pp. 79–94.

Gramsci, A. (1977), *Selections from Political Writings, 1910–1920*, London: Lawrence and Wishart.

Gregory, D. (2004), *The Colonial Present: Afghanistan, Palestine, Iraq*, Malden, MA: Blackwell.

Grosfoguel, R. (2008), "Latin@s and the decolonization of the US empire in the 21st century", *Social Science Information: Special Issue on Migrants and Clandestinity*, vol. 47, no. 4, pp. 605–22.

Guest, G., E. Namey, and M. Mitchell (2013), *Collecting Qualitative Data: A Field Manual for Applied Research*, Thousand Oaks, CA: Sage.

Hall, S. (1985), "Authoritarian populism: A reply", *New Left Review*, vol. 1, no. 151, pp. 115–24.

Hall, S. (1996), "When was the 'postcolonial'? Thinking at the limit", *The Postcolonial Question: Common Skies, Divided Horizons*, edited by I. Chambers and L. Curti, London and New York: Routledge, pp. 242–60

Harvey, D. (2003), "The right to the city", *International Journal of Urban and Regional Research*, vol. 27, no. 4, pp. 939–41.

Hlabangane, N. (2021), "The underside of modern knowledge: An epistemic break from western science", *Decolonising the human: Reflections from Africa on difference and oppression*, edited by W. Mpofu, and M. Steyn, Johannesburg: Wits University Press, pp. 164–85.

Hlatshwayo, M. (2010), "Research report on Cosatu's responses to xenophobia", *South African Civil Society and Xenophobia: Synthesis*, edited by D. Everatt, New York: The Atlantic Philanthropies.

Holston, J., and A. Appadurai (1999), "Introduction: Cities and Citizenship", *Cities and Citizenship*, edited by J. Holston, Durham, NC: Duke University Press, pp. 155–73.

Huntington, S. P. (1996), *The Clash of Civilizations and the Remaking of World Order*, New York: Simon and Schuster.

Huyssen, A. (2001), "Present pasts: media, politics, amnesia", *Globalization*, edited by A. Appadurai, Durham, NC: Duke University Press, pp. 57–77

Inglehart, R., and P. Norris, (2017), "Trump and the populist authoritarian parties: The silent revolution in reverse", *Perspectives on Politics*, vol. 15, no. 2, pp. 443–54.

Jessop, B. (2014), "Repoliticising depoliticisation: Theoretical preliminaries on some responses to the American fiscal and Eurozone debt crises", *Policy & Politics*, vol. 42, no. 2, pp. 293–311.

Kamugisha, A. (2007), "The coloniality of citizenship in the contemporary Anglophone Carribean", *Race and Class*, vol. 49, no. 2, pp. 20–40.

Kaplan, R. (2000), *The Coming Anarchy*, New York: Random House.

Kruger, L. (2013), *Imagining the Edgy City: Writing, Performing, and Building Johannesburg*, New York: Oxford University Press.

Lancaster, L., and G. Mulaudzi, (2020), "Rising protests are a warning sign for South Africa's government", Institute for Security Studies (ISS), 6 August, available at https://issafrica.org/iss-today/rising-protests-are-a-warning-sign-for-south-africas-government. Last accessed on 29 July 2022.

Leeuwen, T. van, and C. Jewitt (eds.) (2004), "Introduction", *Handbook of Visual Analysis*, London, Thousand Oaks and New Delhi: Sage Publications, pp. 1–9.

Lefebvre, H. (1996), "Writing on cities", *Writings on Cities*, edited by E. Kofman, and E. Lebas, London: Blackwell, pp. 34–43.

Lefebvre, H. (1996), "The right to the city", *Writings on Cities*, edited by E. Kofman, and E. Lebas, London: Blackwell, pp. 63–184.

Mabin, A. (2000), "Varied legacies of modernism in urban planning", *A Companion to the City*, edited by G. Bridge, and S. Watson, Malden, MA, Oxford, and Victoria: Blackwell Publishers, pp. 555–66.

MacEwan, A. (1999), *Neoliberalism as Democracy? Economic Strategy, Markets, and Alternatives for the 21st Century*, New York: Zed Books.

Maldonado-Torres, N. (2008), *Against War: Views from the Underside of Modernity*, Durham, NC: Duke University Press.

Marcuse, P. (2012), "Whose right(s) to what city?" *Cities for People, Not for Profit: Critical Urban Theory and the Right to the City*, edited by N. Brenner, P. Marcuse, and M. Mayer, London and New York: Routledge, pp. 24–41.

Marvasti, A. B. (2004), *Qualitative Research in Sociology: An Introduction*, London, Thousand Oaks, New Delhi: Sage Publications.

Merriam, S. (2009), *Qualitative Research: A Guide to Design and Implementation*, San Francisco, CA: Jossey-Bass.

Mignolo, W. D. (2005), *The Idea of Latin America*, Oxford: Blackwell Publishing.

Mitchell, D. (2003), *The Right to the City: Social Justice and the Fight for Public Space*, New York: Guildford Press.

Mlotshwa, K. (2022), "Marxist theory, decoloniality and Black African subjectivity", *Marxism and Decolonization in the 21st Century: Living Theories and True Ideas*, edited by S. J. Ndlovu-Gatsheni and M. Ndlovu, Abingdon and New York: Routledge, pp. 109–25.

Mpofu, W., and M. Steyn, (eds.) (2021), "The trouble with the human", *Decolonising the human: Reflections from Africa on difference and oppression*, Johannesburg: Wits University Press, pp. 1–24.

Muller, G. (2013), "The legal-historical context of urban forced evictions in South Africa", *Fundamina*, vol. 19, no. 2, pp. 367–96.

Munck, R. (2013), "The precariat: a view from the South", *Third World Quarterly*, vol. 34, no. 5, pp. 747–62.

Murray, M. J. (2011), *Taming the Disorderly City: The Spatial Landscape of Johannesburg after Apartheid*, New York: Cornell University Press.

Musiker, N., and R. Musiker (2000), *A Concise Historical Dictionary of Greater Johannesburg*, Cape Town: Francolin Publishers.

Ndlovu, S. (2021), "Humanness and ableism: Construction and deconstruction of disability", *Decolonising the human: Reflections from Africa on difference and oppression*, edited by W. Mpofu and M. Steyn, Johannesburg: Wits University Press, pp. 65–85.

Ndlovu-Gatsheni, S. J. (2012), "Beyond the equator there are no sins: Coloniality and violence in Africa", *Journal of Developing Societies*, vol. 28, no. 4, pp. 419–40.

Ndlovu-Gatsheni, S. J. (2013), "Why decoloniality in the 21st century?" *The Thinker*, vol. 48, no. 10, pp. 10–15.

Ngai, M. M. (2003), "The strange career of the illegal alien: Immigration restriction and deportation policy in the United States, 1921–1965", *Law and History Review*, vol. 21, no. 1, pp. 69–107.

Nyers, P. (2012), "No one is illegal between city and nation", *Studies in Social Justice*, vol. 4, no. 2, pp. 127–43.

Phillips, H. (2014), "Locating the location of a South African location: The paradoxical pre-history of Soweto", *Urban History*, vol. 41, no. 2, pp. 311–32.

Pillay, K., and B. Ndaba (2021), "PICS: Soweto residents boycott elections, and give ANC 14 days to respond to their grievances", *IOL*, 1 November, available at https://www.iol.co.za/news/politics/pics-soweto-residents-boycott-elections-and-give-anc-14-days-to-respond-to-their-grievances-87150648-d625-498b-beec-c2e6db74084c. Last accessed on 29 July 2022.

Purcell, M. (2002), "Excavating Lefebvre: The right to the city and its urban politics of the inhabitant", *GeoJournal*, vol. 58, pp. 99–108.

Quijano, A. (2000), "Coloniality of power, eurocentrism, and Latin America", *Nepantla: Views from the South*, vol. 1, no. 3, pp. 533–80.

Ryan, M. D. J. (2018), "Interrogating 'authoritarian neoliberalism': The problem of periodization", *Competition & Change*, pp. 1–22, available at https://doi.org/10.1 177/1024529418797867. Last accessed on 29 July 2022.

Samara T.R., He S., and Chen G. (2013), *Locating right to the city in the global south*, London New York: Routledge.

Sassen, S. (1991), *The Global City: New York, London, Tokyo*, Princeton: Princeton University Press.

Scott, J. C. (1998), *Seeing Like a State: How Certain Schemes to Improve the Human Condition Have Failed*, New Haven: Yale University Press.

Sihlongonyane, M. F. (2005), "The Rhetoric of Africanism in Johannesburg as a World African City", *African Insights*, vol. 34, no. 4, pp. 22–30.

Sisulu, W. (1998), "Foreword", *Soweto: A History*, edited by P. Bronner and L. Segal, Cape Town: David Phillips, pp. 3–8.

Smith, D. M. (ed.) (1992), *The Apartheid City and Beyond: Urbanization and Social Change in South Africa*, New York and Johannesburg: Routledge and Wits University Press.

South African Human Rights Commission (SAHRC) (2015), "Marikana commission of inquiry: Report on matters of public, national and international concern arising out of the tragic incidents at the Lonmin Mine in Marikana, in the North West province", available at https://www.sahrc.org.za/home/21/files/marikana-report-1.pdf. Last accessed on 29 July 2022.

Springer, S. (2016). "The violence of neoliberalism", *The Handbook of Neoliberalism*, edited by S. Springer, K. Birch, and J. MacLeavy, New York and London: Routledge, pp. 153–63.

Strauss, M., and S. Liebenberg (2014), "Contested spaces: Housing rights and evictions law in post-apartheid South Africa", *Planning Theory*, vol. 13, no. 4, pp. 428–48.

Swart, M., and Y. Rodney-Gumede, (eds.) (2019), *Marikana Unresolved: The Massacre, Culpability and Consequences*, Johannesburg: Juta.

Tansel, C. B. (ed.) (2017), *States of Discipline: Authoritarian Neoliberalism and the Contested Reproduction of Capitalist Order*, London: Rowman and Littlefield International.

Thompson, J. B. (1990), *Ideology and Modern Culture: Critical Social Theory in the Era of Mass Communication*, Stanford: Stanford University Press.

Vletter, F. de (1985), "Recent trends and prospects of black migration to South Africa", *The Journal of Modern African Studies*, vol. 23, no. 4, pp. 667–702.

Wodak, R. (2001), "The discourse-historical approach", *Methods of Critical Discourse Analysis*, edited by R. Wodak and M. Meyer, London: Sage.

Wolpe, H. (1972), "Capitalism and cheap labour-power in South Africa. From segregation to apartheid", *Economy and Society*, vol. 1, no. 4, pp. 425–56.

Worden, N. (1991), *The Making of Modern South Africa: Conquest, Apartheid, Democracy*, Basingstoke and London: Macmillan Press Limited.

Wright, C. (2013), "The museum of illegal immigration: Historical perspectives on the production of non-citizens and challenges to immigration control", *Producing and negotiating non-citizenship: Precarious legal status in Canada*, edited by L. Golding and P. Landolt, Toronto: University of Toronto Press, pp. 31–54.

Xulu, N. (2013), "COSATU and Internal Migrant Workers: Old Fault Lines, New Dilemmas", *COSATU's Contested Legacy: South African Trade Unions in the Second Decade of Democracy*, edited by Sakhela Buhlungu and Malehoko Tshoaedi, Leiden and Boston: Brill, pp. 212–27.

(Re)Thinking Authoritarianism in Democracy[1]
The Public Denunciation of State Violence During the Pandemic in Argentina 2020-21

Julieta Mira

> "Antisemitism (not merely hatred of Jews) imperialism (not merely conquest), totalitarianism (not merely dictatorship) … have demonstrated that human dignity needs a new guarantee which can be found only in a new political principle, in a new law on earth, whose validity this time must comprehend the whole of humanity while its power must remain strictly limited, rooted in and controlled by newly defined territorial entities".
> Hannah Arendt, *The Origins of Totalitarianism* (1951)

Introduction: Pandemic, Lockdown, and State Violence

In March 2020, the Argentine government declared a nationwide lockdown to limit the spread of COVID-19. Against this backdrop, which has been referred to as a *state of exception*, the country witnessed renewed acts of state violence, perpetrated by police and security forces against their own population. Though these events are typically referred to by various social actors and by the state itself as 'institutional violence'[2] (a fairly recent category), this chapter attests to the fact that, in public denunciations of such incidents, this conception is contested, and that counter-

---

1 Translation by Michael Dorrity and Joel Scott for Gegensatz Translation Collective.
2 In terms of convention in this paper, native categories are placed within inverted commas to give visibility to the words of relevant actors and to create a distinction between these and the sociological analysis.

positions exist that can contribute to a more complete understanding of this phenomenon.

The research presented here shows that there are other ways of naming and denouncing the phenomenon of state violence within Argentina. These include 'police violence',[3] 'state repression',[4] and complaints about 'trigger-happy' officers.[5] In other words, though one may be speaking about the same social fact in sociological terms, a distinction can be observed regarding its social classification, and this is of particular interest in understanding its impact on society and the ways in which such events are both socially and institutionally processed.

In terms of the concrete facts, I am concerned with the diverse modalities of fundamental human rights abuses which—while nothing new in the history of Argentine democracy since 1983—were produced in this instance against a backdrop of movement restricted by the pandemic, that is, under the guise of securitization (Nunes 2020). Such modalities include intimidation, threats, arbitrary detention, abuse, beatings, torture, forced disappearances, and assassinations. Most of these practices are designated as criminal offences in the Argentine criminal code. Moreover, in various international human rights treaties ratified by the Argentine government, torture and forced disappearances are punishable practices which can in turn lead to the state being held to account by international bodies for non-compliance with treaty commitments.

One further conceptual connection worth examining is the one between the exceptional state violence of authoritarian governments and the long-term state violence that has become habitual in times of democracy (Lvovich 2020). The current situation allows us to expose the continuity or persistence of authoritarian characteristics in a democracy while at the same time grounding the recurring demands for the democratization of the police and security forces in Argentina since 1983 (Frederic 2008; Oyhandy 2013 and 2014). Considering the situation from another perspective, we can confirm that state violence in the Southern Cone transcends the dichotomy of democracy-dictatorship (Lvovich 2020).

This chapter first examines the discursive construction of public denunciations—in the sociological terms proposed by Luc Boltanski (2000)—of these acts

---

3   This category is widely used by sociologists as a direct reference to the concrete facts described, that is, the illegitimate use of violence by public officials.
4   This denomination is not new. Rather, it refers to experiences of the last military dictatorship as a 'repressive state apparatus', highlighting state behaviour toward the population beyond the legitimate use of violence as permitted by law.
5   This expression refers to the irresponsible and abusive use of firearms by public officials, at times with lethal effects. The reference, as such, is to the casualness with which security or police forces are willing to pull the trigger, despite the gravity of the consequences for the population. Events illustrating this phenomenon are described over the following pages (see section 4).

of state violence, which at their height resulted in the violent deaths of the defenceless and vulnerable (Gayol and Kessler 2015 and 2018). These denunciations configured these events as injustices, which thus enable demands for justice to be made. These social discourses of public denunciation form various categories with which to name these social phenomena: institutional violence, police violence, trigger-happy officers, and state repression. In approaching this problem, I focus on state authoritarianism in times of democracy and the questions this generates.

Secondly, this chapter presents the collective movements that crystallized around the public denunciations of often lethal acts of state violence committed by members of the police or security forces during the pandemic. An overview of these denunciations was made possible by examining the diverse reports produced by government institutions as well as reports made by civil society and human rights organizations with different relationships to the state. Some of the most prominent of these are the Permanent Assembly for Human Rights (Asamblea Permanente por los Derechos Humanos, APDH),[6] the Provincial Commission for Memory (Comisión Provincial por la Memoria, CPM),[7] and the Committee against Police and Institutional Repression (Coordinadora contra la Represión Policial e Institucional, CORREPI).[8] Based on these sources, it is possible to gain a sense of the types of practices that make up what is referred to as institutional violence, who carries out these acts of violence, and the individuals and regions that bear the brunt of it, as well as some of the public and social responses it has inspired. All of this occurs against the backdrop of a dispute over the social meaning of these acts of state violence, the resulting tensions of which shall be examined over the following pages.

---

6 Founded in 1975, the APDH is a non-profit civil association dedicated to the defence and promotion of human rights. It grew out of a call from a broad and diverse range of figures from the social, political, intellectual, and religious spheres of Argentina. See https://www.apdh-argentina.org.ar/secretaria/relaciones-internacionales/92.

7 The CPM is an autonomous self-regulated public body. It was created in 1999 by a legislative provision of the Chamber of Deputies of the Province of Buenos Aires and ratified by two provincial laws in 2000. The CPM implements public policies promoting collective memory and human rights. Its objectives and working areas are guided by its commitment to remembering state terrorism and the promotion and defence of human rights in democracy. Since its inception, it has promoted spaces of encounter between the state and civil society. See https://www.comisionporlamemoria.org/la-cpm/historia/.

8 CORREPI was founded in 1992 and defines itself in its mission statement as a political organization in the field of human rights. It seeks to combat "the repressive policies of the state", for which it has proposed to combat police repression and to work toward the release of political prisoners. Its work involves producing reports, communicating through its website, and engaging in various public activities, such as events, demonstrations, festivals, and open radio. Its fundamental principles include the refusal to cooperate with the state and independence from all political forces. See http://www.correpi.org/quienes-somos/.

Thirdly, while examining the case of Brandon Romero, a young man who died as a result of police violence in the city of Mar del Plata, I will explore the social mobilization that emerged around the public denunciation of the event and the activism directed against police violence that it triggered (Pita 2010). All of which sheds light on the legal controversies that occurred during the enquiry into Romero's violent death (Gayol and Kessler 2015). In short, I convey the struggle of his family and friends in their search for justice.

Finally, the concluding section provides some reflections on the relevance of discussing the terms used to name these acts of state violence against young people from within the academy. I focus in particular on the severity of these practices, as arbitrary killings have been occurring with alarming frequency. The situation offers us an opportunity to (re)think authoritarianism in democratic Argentina, and thus also to (re)think the role of social research.

In summary, this chapter examines the expressions of authoritarianism that can occur in non-authoritarian regimes, whereby the most extreme examples are arbitrary killings carried out by public officials. I seek to provoke critical reflections on the need to observe, analyse, and denounce the authoritarianism that persists in democratic countries and which infringes on people's most fundamental rights, such as the right to life or the right to live free from torture. The goal is to offer a means of accounting both for different forms of authoritarianism and for public response strategies in the form public denunciations.

The Sociological Focus: Public Denunciations

The purpose of this chapter is not to discuss institutional violence but rather to outline both how a case that is framed in this way is denounced, as well as its social, political, legal, and media repercussions. From this perspective, we can visualize how a social strategy of responding to authoritarian state practices is generated. The category of institutional violence is used as one means of denunciation, yet other forms of possible enunciation do exist in this field. By examining these, we can identify other actors seeking to make public denunciations of state violence. Upon closer inspection, we see that this concept is highly contested, and this contestation deserves particular attention if we are to understand these phenomena from a reflexive and comprehensive sociological perspective (Vecchioli 2011). It is essentially a question of understanding how we can establish deaths that matter (Gayol and Kessler 2018) in Argentina, both in sociopolitical and in legal terms.

We can thus see the emergence of a social discourse which, as mentioned above, constructs diverse categories to name social facts: institutional violence, police violence, and state repression. From this perspective, it is important to give visibility to—and to adopt—the words and ways of classifying used by those directly engaged in making denunciations. Although the perspective of those seeking to construct different meanings may change, the actions being denounced are fundamentally the same. In anthropological terms, these are native categories, that is, conceptualizations produced and circulated by the relevant actors. Disputes then ensue as to which category is accepted as valid and legitimate when it comes to formulating the denunciation. In this sense, it is important to emphasize that this is guided by a methodology following that of the social actors (Mira 2019) and recovering their voices, in the tradition of ethnography.

Approaching this issue through the conceptual framework developed by Boltanski (2000), we are able to sketch out a theory of the conditions that such a public denunciation of injustice must fulfil in order to be considered legitimate, allowing it to generate socio-legal and political effects. The denunciation first requires someone to enunciate it or, in Boltanskian terms, an author. In order for the author's endeavour to be successful, they need followers. The cause, according to Boltanski, seeks to become exemplary and to generate a transferral between the particular case and the general interest. It does this as it must have the quality of being generalizable, that is, of becoming a collective cause (2000, 238). Boltanski goes on to consider the circumstances under which a denunciation is recognized as normal and valid and under which, by contrast, it is discounted or ignored (2000, 243). This is relevant given that public denunciation presupposes a demand for the perpetrator to be punished.

Boltanski constructs an actantial system of denunciation, establishing "a system of relations between four actors: 1) the person making the denunciation; 2) the person for whose sake the denunciation is made; 3) the person against whom it is made; and 4) the person to whom it is addressed" (2000, 247). In other words, the author claims that four actants are involved: the denouncer, the victim, the accused, and the judge (Boltanski 2000, 247). In the case of forced disappearances and deaths, victims necessarily need to be represented by others, and the condition of victimhood is extended to the family.

It is important to highlight that the victim is "an individual who as one person cannot embody a cause but whose denunciation can link up with a collective cause" (Boltanski 2000, 249). Similarly, it is worth paying particular attention to how the victim is depicted in the different arenas, namely in the attempts to redress the instance of state violence, or by constructing them as '*pibes chorros*'[9] or underserving victims, in a performative move which seeks to divest them of their position as a

---

9   The phenomenon of agenda setting (Varona Gómez 2011) can be seen in the provocative dissemination of news concerning *pibes chorros*, i.e. thieves, which portrays young people as extremely dangerous. Consequently, it fuels the circulation of fear and stigmatization, which shapes public opinion by constructing a sociopolitical agenda of insecurity and a political discourse of security (Oyhandy 2014).

victim and thus their capacity to be recognized within the legal system. I share Ailynn Torres Santana's understanding when she claims that: "it is, to a certain extent, a privilege to be recognized as a victim. It means you exist, you are seen, you are the subject of protection. When an assaulted person is denied the possibility of considering themselves a victim, they are erased from the scene" (2021).

When police violence is publicly denounced according to this actantial system, social mobilization occurs around injustice, moving from the singular axis of the specific case to the general. The goal is to construct a collective cause and to sway public opinion (Boltanski 2000, 248). At the same time, legal documents also constitute a productive space within which denunciation can be pursued (Boltanski 2000, 254), as occurred with the case of Brandon Romero (see section 4).

This approach is reminiscent of Hannah Arendt's maxim of the right to have rights (1951): "we became aware of the existence of a right to have rights ... and a right to belong to some kind of organized community" because only in "completely organized humanity could the loss of home and political status become identical with expulsion from humanity altogether" (Arendt 1951, 297). From this perspective, denunciation serves to remind us that the people who suffer violence or even death possessed rights that were taken away by public officials through the illegitimate use of force. This grounds the urgency of the demand to respect human dignity. The right to have rights is a major driving force behind public denunciations, collective campaigns, and demands directed at the authorities. These demands are expressed by the victims and by various social organizations in response to acts of state violence in democratic Argentina, as is described below.

Dispute for Meanings: The Collective Cause

In analysing state violence, it is worth noting that the term institutional violence has come to be incorporated into the language of the state, so much so that there are now specialized departments dedicated to the matter in diverse public institutions and at various levels of authority and jurisdiction. For this reason the Attorney General's Office against Institutional Violence (Procuradoría Especializada en Violencia Institucional, PROCUVIN 2020),[10] the National Directorate of Policy against Institutional Violence (Dirección Nacional de Políticas contra la Violencia Institucional), part of the Secretariat for Human Rights and National Cultural Pluralism

---

10   Particularly during the pandemic, this institution prepared a document detailing the powers of the security and police forces and what they are prohibited from doing, including details of the rights of individuals in the event of an inspection on suspicion of having contravened lockdown measures, see https://www.fiscales.gob.ar/violencia-institucional/.

(Secretaría de Derechos Humanos y Pluralismo Cultural), in turn part of the Ministry for Justice and Human Rights (Ministerio de Justicia y Derechos Humanos), and the Directorate of Policy against Institutional Violence (Dirección de Política contra la Violencia Institucional) at the Undersecretariat for Human Rights of the Province of Buenos Aires (Subsecretaría de Derechos Humanos de la Provincia de Buenos Aires) were created.[11] Information on the official website of the Argentine government attests to the conceptual—at times vague—breadth of the term, stating that:

> Any structural practice of violating rights committed by members of the security forces, armed forces, prison services, and the healthcare system involving a restriction of autonomy and/or freedom (detention, confinement, custody, guardianship, internment, etc.) must be considered institutional violence. The National Directorate of Policy against Institutional Violence provides legal advice and psycho-social aid to victims of institutional violence and other serious human rights violations.[12]

In the same sense, it is important to note the inauguration of the National Day for the Fight against Institutional Violence in commemoration of the Budge Massacre on 8 May, which was passed into law in 2013.[13] The 1987 massacre consisted in the execution of the three friends who had gathered in the district Ingeniero Budge, and which came to be emblematic of trigger-happy behaviour by officers of the state—a designation that emerged from within civil society and that signals the state's infringement on fundamental rights. The event gave rise to the mobilization of a group of neighbours in the Buenos Aires province, who sought legal action against the public officials implicated in the killings (Gingold 1997). Indeed, the lawyer for the families was one of the founders of CORREPI. The symbolic action of creating a national holiday appropriates the event in a certain sense, with a view—the play on words is fitting—to institutionalizing it, and turning it into public policy. Undoubtedly, this performative act redefines this type of event and can offer a degree of understanding in terms of the different denominations and tensions which become apparent in the demands of certain actors on the ground.

In light of the present analysis and the disputes in this field, it is interesting to note that in recent decades, certain human rights organizations have been using an innovative conceptualization of institutional violence. In this instance, it refers to violence inflicted directly on the body, either physically or psychologically. In this

---

11 See https://www.gba.gob.ar/derechoshumanos/subsecretarias_e_instituto.
12 See https://ppn.gov.ar/index.php/institucional/noticias/1100-dia-nacional-contra-la-violencia-institucional.
13 See https://ppn.gov.ar/index.php/institucional/noticias/1100-dia-nacional-contra-la-violencia-institucional.

chapter, I examine the actions of security forces or the police which—as based on antecedents predating the pandemic—principally target young men in poor neighbourhoods. These actions have been condemned in reports generated during the use of these special measures (APDH 2020; CPM 2020). In its latest report, the CPM revealed that: "of the 150 interviews conducted, the entire sample group reported having witnessed practices of institutional violence in their neighbourhood and identified young men as the target in 86.67 percent of cases" (CPM 2020, 23).

The origin of the category 'institutional violence' can also be considered from this perspective. Sofía Tiscornia traces the trajectory of the term, beginning with its emergence from a dialogue between anthropology and the experience of human rights during the dictatorship, to its conversion into a successful political category. Tiscornia claims that the category—which was still rather new at the time—managed to permeate both public institutions and public policy while at the same time rendering such events as visible, and worthy of respect and due consideration.

Tiscornia argues that: "state violence—in a democratic state—is local violence, violence that has long since been defanged—if you'll permit the oxymoron—by the uses and habits of offices, officials, agencies, basements, and other municipal, provincial, and national bureaucracies" (2017, 26). For their part, Marcela Perelman and Manuel Trufó from the Centre for Legal and Social Studies (Centro de Estudios Legales y Sociales, CELS)[14] define institutional violence as practices, routines, norms, or even design problems that configure the "necessary conditions for the recurrence of different types of human rights violations" (2016, 4).

Against the backdrop of the public health crisis beginning in March 2020, various cases of state violence have exemplified how deeply engrained authoritarianism is in the structures of the security and police forces in Argentina. They also show how lockdowns proved to be a favourable opportunity for bolstering the deployment of such measures, principally against vulnerable and marginalized social groups. That is, such behaviour on the part of public officials is nothing new, but rather forms part of a diverse context within which the interventions were accepted as part of the restriction of movement, particularly during the initial phase of the pandemic.

Following Boltanski's actantial system, we can see how different civil society organizations functioned as denouncing actors, in this role contributing to the construction of a public denunciation of state violence during the pandemic (2020–21). In general, police and security forces have been the denounced actors, and the denunciations have mostly been addressed towards the general public and state authorities. The majority of victims for whom records exist have been young and

---

14   The CELS was created in 1979 during the last military dictatorship with a view to promoting human rights, justice for those who had been forcibly disappeared, and to bolster the democratic system.

generally male. In efforts to generate a collective cause, the individual cases that make up this corpus are presented variously as institutional violence, state repression, and/or as the consequences of trigger-happy police. It is important to note that the designation varies according to the actor making the denunciation, and that this thus contributes to the development of the collective cause.

From the beginning of COVID-19 restrictions, denunciations in the form of reports or public communications were made by Amnesty International Argentina,[15] the APDH,[16] and CORREPI.[17] The reports compile various facts, identifying the victims and perpetrators, with particular attention on the state force involved, the type of violence perpetrated, and the date and location of the event. These documents of public denunciation clearly seek to give detailed accounts of as many instances of institutional violence in Argentina as possible. However, the difficulty that civil society faces in tackling this task is evident, given the notorious lack of any systematic and complete information collected by the state itself, as would be necessary for a significant record of this phenomenon.

It is worth mentioning, however, that a number of denunciations have been made by public institutions. Various documents have been produced on the matter, including the Report on Legal Aid and Institutional Violence[18] issued by the Directorate of Assistance to Persons Deprived of their Liberty (Dirección de Asistencia a las Personas Privadas de su Libertad) of the Public Defender's Office (Ministerio Público de la Defensa) of the Autonomous City of Buenos Aires. The document exposes irregularities and abuses committed by local police at the beginning of the lockdown in Buenos Aires.

The APDH compiled a survey of incidents of state violence gathered by its regional offices located in different parts of Argentina. The conclusions of the report point to consistent data-based police profiling nationwide, i.e. the target focus on male youth. In view of this situation, which for the APDH constitutes a collective cause of combatting state repression, it demanded "an end to these actions, which are illegal, abusive, and contrary to human rights, as well as the punishment of the persons responsible" (2020, 93). Finally, the APDH has stated that in response to these events, they wish "to see ... a democratic culture in the security forces and respect for everybody's human rights, without exception" (2020, 93). Indeed, they note:

---

15 See https://amnistia.org.ar/amnistia-internacional-alerta-sobre-la-actuacion-de-las-fuerzas-de-seguridad-durante-la-cuarentena-por-el-coronavirus/.
16 See https://apdh.org.ar/informes/apdh-informe-violencia-institucional-aspo.
17 See http://www.correpi.org/2020/reporte-no-47-de-aplicacion-del-dnu-297-2020/ y http://www.correpi.org/2020/represion-en-pandemia-al-menos-71-asesinatos-estatales-en-4-meses/.
18 See https://www.mpdefensa.gob.ar/comunicacion/mas-noticias/informe-del-mpd-violencia-institucional-durante-la-cuarentena and https://www.mpdefensa.gob.ar/sites/default/files/informe_mpd.pdf.

We must continue to denounce the impunity with which these repressive practices are carried out in multiple parts of Argentina. There is nothing new about this behaviour nor is it alien to the historical tradition of the Argentine security forces in times of democracy. What's more, there isn't anything new about the discourses that are constructed to legitimize this violence, which call to mind such tragic times in our history. (APDH 2020, 108)

The Case of Brandon Romero in Mar del Plata: The Struggle for Justice

The murder of Brandon Romero[19] provides one example of how Argentine society, its institutions, and the media frame such violent deaths perpetuated by agents of the state, as well as how they construct public denunciations and offer responses which may or may not be satisfactory for the victims. In this particular case, one can see how the arbitrary murder of a young person by members of the police force came to engender a collective cause: a struggle for justice ensued, taking aim at what is framed as institutional violence, trigger-happy police, or state repression, depending on the actor formulating the public denunciation.

Brandon was 18 years old when he left home to hang out with friends in the early hours of the morning of 5 July 2020. He would not return alive. Earlier in the night, Brandon had been riding around the outskirts of the city of Mar del Plata—in the Province of Buenos Aires—with four other young people on motorbikes when they came across the police officer Pedro Arcángel Bogado.

In events that are described very differently according to whom one asks, Brandon ultimately died as a result of seven shots undeniably shot from Bogado's service weapon. In agreement with this is the coroner's report: Brandon had gunshot wounds throughout his body. Two were fatal headshots. Brandon's family denounced his killing as an execution, and CORREPI was of the same opinion.[20] Bogado maintained that it had been an act of legitimate self-defence as the group were intent on robbing and killing him, a claim which was then inscribed into the social narrative of fear of crime (Kessler and Otamendi 2020). The media went so far as to suggest that Brandon had often been in trouble with the law and had a criminal record. His family, by contrast, described him as a worker, a baker who

---

19 Research has been carried out on the basis of the court files, communication with the family's lawyer, and social media.
20 See http://www.correpi.org/2021/a-un-ano-del-fusilamiento-brandon-romero-presente-juicio-y-castigo-para-arcangel-bogado/.

left for work at four in the morning, without once having ended up in a police station.[21]

Figure 1. Poster in Mar del Plata commemorating the anniversary of Brandon Romero's death.

Source: Faculty of Health Sciences, Social Work and the Secretariat of Extension of the National University of Mar del Plata

After filing criminal charges and with a legal investigation underway, the family quickly ran into difficulties accessing justice, with proceedings growing ever more torturous. On the fifth of every month, Brandon's family and friends gather in front of the courts in Mar del Plata to demand justice, even camping out there on one occasion. Significantly, the same event is given different designations even at the same protest. Some signs read "institutional violence", while others decry "state repression", as can be seen in the photographs depicting crowds at various public

---

21 The hour-long video "Sin plata, sin miedo" made by Brandon's family and friends in the Libertad neighbourhood of Mar del Plata—a province of Buenos Aires—when he would have turned 19 years old in 2021, and which relates his story and their access to justice, is available at: https://www.youtube.com/watch?v=klg964Mu8_s.

events for Brandon (see figures 1, 2, and 3 below). This example shows that the use of the notion of trigger-happy police spans those who frame the events as institutional violence and those who frame it as state repression. It becomes clear that the act of denominating is a social operation which depends more on the actors who narrate the events than on the events themselves.

Figure 2. Demonstration in Mar del Plata one year after the death of Brandon Romero, 5 July 2021.

Source: photographer unknown, circulated on social networks in support of the fight for justice

One year after his death, his family continues to fight for legal justice but has been given no response as to the possibility of a trial.[22] The main obstacle originated in the prosecutor's assertion that the facts of the case be classified as legitimate self-defence on the part of the perpetrator. The Buenos Aires policeman accused was thus also acquitted of the crime. The prosecutor sought to prove the accusation of attempted robbery and the victim's responsibility, presenting him as innately criminally inclined. The prosecutor's account distorts the balance of legal interests at stake, the case of a police officer as a public official, and any analysis of reasonableness in cases of legitimate self-defence. In particular, the prosecutor's account obfuscates the police officer's unique responsibility in exercising the power of the state through the use of their service weapon. Clearly, the prosecutor

---

22 See http://www.correpi.org/2021/a-un-ano-del-fusilamiento-brandon-romero-presente-juicio-y-castigo-para-arcangel-bogado/.

Figure 3. "If it's institutional, it's not violence, it's state repression". Collective against trigger-happy police, La Plata.

Source: photographer unknown, circulated on social networks in support of the demand for justice

sought to foreground the robbery and thus a case of legitimate self-defence in the development of events. In point of fact, the murder was the most important event and the perpetrator had suffered no assault at all.

By contrast, the event was characterized by César Sivo, the lawyer representing Brandon Romero's family, as an example of trigger-happy police officers, and part of a broader trend of institutional violence. As such, he requested that it be brought to trial as an aggravated homicide. In his role as the person making the denunciation before the criminal justice system, Sivo's written request of trial dated 21 April 2021 accurately pointed out that the police practices to which Brandon was subjected are reminiscent of the repression experienced during Argentina's last military dictatorship:

> In terms of institutional violence, the task before us is enormous: to undo the legacy of the military dictatorship. Institutional violence is the biggest debt facing the Argentine people. In light of this, living in a democratic system, one would hope that the security forces in Argentina would be subordinate to the political powers elected by the people, rather than being directed at those very people. Institutional violence continues to be a practice within the cultural matrix of the police (and the state in general), who cannot comprehend their role in society and are likely still guided by the principles of impunity and authoritarianism.

On 14 June 2021, Judge Saúl Errandonea decided to bring Brandon's case to trial, with Bogado facing a charge of "aggravated homicide, given that the crime was committed as an abuse of his function or post as a member of the police force and for the use of his firearm", which carries a sentence of life imprisonment. This was made possible by the work of the Romero family's private lawyer, who decided to continue with the prosecution after the prosecutor's office elected to dismiss the case. On 26 August 2021, the first chamber of the court of appeals of Mar del Plata finally granted the request for a trial, although it removed the aggravating circumstances. A court date is still to be set.

Brandon's case gives a name and a history to all the young people murdered under similar circumstances. Such cases frequently occur throughout the country, but very few are ever denounced, and fewer still actually make it to court and ultimately result in a conviction. These stories are evidence of a serious shortcoming in both the lack of accurate official data and exhaustive national registers in Argentina concerning the real number of victims of state violence.

Conclusions: 'Never Again'?

Firstly, it is important to note that the concept of 'institutional violence' is used unquestioningly by certain sections of civil society, by public institutions, and by academics. It could be claimed that 'institutional violence' constitutes a sort of common-sense term in present-day Argentina. It is used to denominate, refer to, categorize, and describe incidents of state violence perpetrated by the police and the other security forces mentioned in this chapter during times of democracy. However, other categories serving to denominate these same injustices committed by public officials do exist, and they conflict with the category of 'institutional violence'. As a consequence, it is crucial to distinguish between these terms in the social sciences, to understand the social conflicts to which they attest, and to use them as formulated by the actual stakeholders seeking to determine their meaning.

In spite of the above, it is worth considering the extent to which the state denounces its own violent and authoritarian actions. And when it does do so, what mechanisms does it use, and how successful are these mechanisms? Specifically, what exactly is the role of public institutions dedicated to addressing institutional violence? The little information that is publicly available on the subject has been referred to here. Similarly, it is also worth considering—with reference to Boltanski's actantial scheme—if the state can act as a denouncing actor of institutional violence, the subject of the denunciation, and at the same time function as the recipient of the denunciation. It is abundantly clear that there is an obvious conflict of interests, regardless of which state agencies or organizations intervene. This question becomes all the more urgent when we consider the impunity afforded, in almost all cases, to trigger-happy police officers.

Undoubtedly, one major area of attention is the legal response to denunciations in the form of criminal complaints brought against members of the police or security forces and the course of those investigations. The treatment of these cases within the criminal justice system is often oriented towards constructing a case of legitimate defence for the police officer concerned. Despite the evidence proving that summary executions have taken place, the authorities seek to quickly resolve such cases by having them dismissed without prejudice. This legal situation is denounced as clear proof of impunity. Thus, contrary to the protection of life and access to justice, this institutional action violates the human rights of the victims and could make the Argentine state guilty of non-compliance with the international human rights treaties of which it is a signatory.

This situation makes clear that neither the police nor other security forces should receive further privileges in the enforcement of public policy during emergency situations such as the COVID-19 pandemic. The events described show that despite their long history, given the slightest opportunity, the repressive practices of state officials in Argentina show their face at every turn. All of this occurs in the absence of any real capacity on the part of state bodies—executive or judiciary—to restrict these illegitimate actions or the suffering thereby inflicted on the population.

The promise of "Never Again"[23]—a centrepiece in the new social-democratic contract—is currently in jeopardy in the wake of these painfully recent and violent deaths in Argentina. Faced with such authoritarian practices, at least one section of Argentine society resists these events by way of public denunciation. They invoke the right to have rights and demand respect for the human dignity of the

---

23   Title of the final report of the National Commission on the Disappearance of Persons (Comisión Nacional sobre la Desaparición de Personas, CONADEP), published in 1984. This phrase was used by the prosecutor Julio César Strassera at the end of his plea in the so-called "Trial of the Military Juntas" in 1985.

victims, but as Arendt (1951) reminds us, every member of humanity should act as a guarantor of these rights.

References

Arendt, Hannah (1951), *The Origins of Totalitarianism*, Cleveland: Meridian.

Asamblea Permanente por los Derechos Humanos (APDH 2020), "Violencia institucional en el aislamiento social preventivo y obligatorio", online publication, pp. 1–100, available at https://apdh.org.ar/informes/apdh-informe-violencia-institucional-aspo. Last accessed on 16 July 2022.

Boltanski, Luc (2000), *El Amor y la Justicia como competencias: Tres ensayos de sociología de la acción*, Buenos Aires: Amorrortu editores.

Comisión Provincial por la Memoria (CPM 2020), "Primer Informe: Violencia Institucional de las Fuerzas de Seguridad hacia las niñeces y juventudes de La Matanza", Buenos Aires, pp. 1–44, available at https://www.comisionporlamemoria.org/archivos/informes/informes-especiales/informeninez.pdf. Last accessed on 16 July 2022.

Frederic, Sabina (2008), *Los usos de la fuerza pública: debates sobre militares y policías en las ciencias sociales de la democracia*, Buenos Aires: Biblioteca Nacional y Universidad Nacional de General Sarmiento.

Gayol, Sandra, and Gabriel Kessler (2015), "Violent death, public problems and changes in Argentina", *Current Sociology*, vol. 65, no. 5, pp. 1–17.

Gayol, Sandra, and Gabriel Kessler (2018), *Muertes que importan: Una mirada sociohistórica de casos que marcaron la Argentina reciente*, Buenos Aires: Siglo XXI.

Gingold, Laura (1997), *Memoria, moral y derecho: El caso de Ingeniero Budge (1987–1994)*, Mexico City: FLACSO.

Kessler, Gabriel, and Alejandra Otamendi (2020), "Sociology of fear of crime in Latin America", *The Oxford Handbook of the Sociology of Latin America*, edited by Xóchitl Bada and Liliana Rivera Sánchez, Oxford: Oxford University Press, pp. 1–23.

Lvovich, Daniel (2020), "La violencia dictatorial y la violencia estatal de largo plazo en el cono sur de América Latina: entre lo excepcional y lo habitual", *História: Questões & Debates*, Curitiba, vol. 68, no. 1 (Jan/June 2020), pp. 85–108.

Maccario, Paula (2019), "Los orígenes del totalitarismo, principios políticos y dignidad humana", VI Jornadas Internacionales Hannah Arendt. Conficto, discurso y política: A 60 años de La condición humana", Centro de Investigaciones en Filosofía, Facultad de Humanidades y Ciencias de Educación, Universidad de La Plata, 22–4 August 2019.

Mira, Julieta (2019), "Follow the actors: Ethnographic keys for understanding legal activism for criminal justice reform in Argentina", *The Age of Human Rights Journal*, vol. 13, pp. 63–74.

Nunes, João (2020), "The COVID-19 pandemic: securitization, neoliberal crisis, and global vulnerabilization", *Cadernos de Saúde Pública*, vol. 36, no. 5, pp. 1–4.

Oyhandy, Angela (2013), "Democracia y violencia estatal: Algunos debates sobre policías y militares en la Argentina desde la post-dictadura hasta la actualidad", *Cuestiones de Sociología*, no. 9, pp. 281–85.

Oyhandy, Angela (2014), "De la Reforma Policial a la Declaración de Emergencia: cambios y continuidades en las políticas de seguridad en la provincia de Buenos Aires", *Cuestiones de Sociología*, no. 10, pp. 1–10.

Perelman, Marcela, and Manuel Tufró (2016), "Informe. Violencia Institucional. Tensiones actuales de una categoría política central", Buenos Aires: Centro de Estudios Legales y Sociales, pp. 1–19.

Pita, María Victoria (2010), *Formas de morir y formas de vivir: El activismo contra la violencia policial*, Buenos Aires: Editores del Puerto.

Public Defence Service (2020), *Public Defence Service Report CABA: Report on Criminal Assistance and Institutional Violence*, online version, pp. 1–5.

Tiscornia, Sofía (2017), "La violencia institucional como tema de trabajo e investigación", *Espacios de crítica y producción*, Dossier Violencia Institucional, no. 53, pp. 25–32.

Torres Santana, Ailynn (2021), "¿A dónde irá Cuba después del 11J? Una sociedad no se rompe con un estallido, es al revés", *Revista Anfibia*, UNSAM.

Varona Gómez, Daniel (2011), "Medios comunicación y punitivismo", *InDret*, no. 1, pp. 1–35.

Vecchioli, Virginia (2011), "Profesionales del derecho, activismo jurídico y creación de nuevos derechos: Hacia una mirada comprensiva del derecho desde las ciencias sociales", *Revista Política*, vol. 49, no. 1, pp. 5–18.

Legal documents concerning the case of Brandon Romero (Mar del Plata, Provincia de Buenos Aires, Argentina)

Errandonea, Saúl, Supervisory Court in Preliminary Proceedings (Juzgado de Garantías) no. 2, Mar del Plata: *Prosecutor's request of trial*, 14 June 2021.

First Chamber of the Court of Appeals (Cámara de Apelaciones y Garantías), Sala I: Case no. 33585 *"Bogado Pedro s/ Homicidio Agravado – IPP 14202, Prosecutor's request of trial*, Mar del Plata, 26 August 2021.

Office of Preliminary Investigations, Trial and Enforcement (Unidad Funcional de Instrucción, Juicio y Ejecución), no. 5, Mar del Plata: *move for acquittal*, 12 March 2021.

Sivo, César, private lawyer of the Romero family: *request of trial*, Mar del Plata, 21 April 2021.

Authoritarianism and Developmentalism Framing 'Progressive' Governments in Mexico and Argentina[1]

Inés Durán Matute and Mariano Féliz

Introduction

In the decade of the 2000s, progressive governments came into the administration of the state apparatus in many Latin American countries. After decades of overt neoliberal governments, these political coalitions put forth a new development discourse that was set to overturn the practice of economic and social adjustment. These governments were only able to sweep under the rug neoliberal reforms without disarticulating their legacy. The authoritarian nature of development policies remained the backbone of progressive politics. Their discourses appealed to the people and presented themselves as the tool needed to move towards egalitarian and inclusive societies. However, under a veil of national interests and popular participation, they continued to foster capitalist accumulation via predatory and violent tactics against people and nature, against life itself. Their time in power came to an end, mostly giving way to right-wing governments.

Still, a new wave of progressive governments emerged on the continent. Andrés Manuel López Obrador (Mexico, 2018), Alberto Fernández (Argentina, 2019), Pedro Castillo (Perú, 2021), and Gabriel Boric (Chile, 2022) present themselves as 'democratic' candidates in opposition to authoritarian and right-wing governments. In the eyes of many, they represent hope, a way to confront oppressions and inequalities, strengthen democracy, promote development, and achieve social justice. Their contradictions or 'betrayals' are seen as errors, individual mishaps, or even as external intrusions; they are never understood as the result of a violent and oppressive process of 'othering' within the logic of accumulation rooted in the capitalist state. Progressive capitalism is a ruse; it disguises the advancement of conservative, aggressive, and authoritarian politics. So, we wonder: do progressive strategies differ from those of the far-right? Does this kind of government impact the form of the

---

1 We are thankful to all the participants in the course "State and Capital" at the Graduate School of Sociology, Institute of Social Sciences and Humanities, Meritorious Autonomous University of Puebla (Mexico) for all their comments, insights, and rich discussions on a previous version.

state differently? Or is it that both progressive and right-wing, are these two facets equally necessary to reproduce capitalist social relations?

The prevailing theory portrays the state as this autonomous, intermediary, impersonal, neutral, and overarching political institution. This interpretation tends to direct hopes to change the world—ending its atrocities, injustices, and oppressions—towards political electoral participation and the seizure of state power. It has created confusion as to what the state exactly is and its role in reproducing capitalism. Thus, our focus is inspired by state derivation theorists who consider the state a form of capitalist social relations. This chapter discusses how authoritarianism and (neo)developmentalism in progressive governments are ingrained within the state form to ensure capital accumulation. The current experiences of Mexico and Argentina show how the practices, strategies, and policies of these governments promote—by action or omission—the exploitation and plundering of peoples and territories while producing a reactionary and authoritarian sociopolitical discourse.

Theoretical Remarks

State as Form

For decades, within the Marxian camp, the state was seen mainly either as an instrument of the capitalist class, as in the theory of state monopoly capitalism, or as a political institution separated from economics, as in neo-Ricardian analyses. However, in the 1970s, the state derivation debate explored the deceit of this separation, the limits of state interventionism, and the illusions of state power (Holloway and Picciotto 1978). Inspired by Pashukanis's Marxist interpretation of the state, the main question was why class domination appears in capitalism as the form of a public, impersonal, autonomous, separated power, that is, the state. The state was seen as a way to guarantee the exchange of commodities for the continuous reproduction of capitalism. For derivationists, states are linked to the processes of accumulation and appear as a separated sphere. So, they encouraged the perception of the unity-in-separation and the separation-in-unity of state and capital to derive this 'separation' from the relations of domination (Holloway 2017).

But do states have 'exactly' the same form? States are not all 'exactly' the same; they are not omnipresent, omnipotent, or absent of contradictions. They are a way to organize social relations to promote capital accumulation, with their differences and ways of interacting and existing within a global system (Holloway 1996). The functions of the state are thus often in contradiction with its form and cannot be derived directly from it but must be analysed based on the concrete historical conditions of capital valorization (Gerstenberger 1978; Bonnet and Piva 2017).

Moreover, the real contradiction between capital and labour in the space of immediate production or circulation of value is mediated not only by the practices of the actors who are directly in conflict but also by the institutional forms that—temporarily—solidify these contradictory relations (Féliz 2017).

All states exist in competition and must attract capital to their territories for their survival, providing the best conditions through, among other things, infrastructure, cheap labour, resources, and tax incentives. In its structure and practices, the state reproduces the hierarchical command of capital, even when appearing in the form of 'democratic' governments (Mészàros 1999). The state as a real abstraction, that is, as the result of the unconscious actions of subjects, assumes a central role in the production and reproduction of the power of capital over society as a whole (Negri 2003; Salama 1979). The state emerges as the guarantor of class domination, with violence always behind the scenes (Hirsch 1977). However, not all actions carried out by the state are consistent with the interests of capital or in favour of the same group of capitalists; they engage in a process of "trial and error" (Álvarez Huwiler and Bonnet 2018). This implies that state personnel react to daily conditions for their self-preservation and that of the state, not necessarily to guarantee the requirements of capitalist reproduction.

State, Colonialism, and the Accumulation of Capital

Capitalist social relations have a historical "a-spatial nature", extending across national borders; however, states seek to territorialize them (Holloway 1996, 362). States act as a situated form to organize these relations based on historical and geographical conditions. Processes of colonization in Latin America thus stained the specific form of states and their paths of incorporation to capitalism. Each state was shaped and is continuously reshaped differently; they have their own characteristics and practices to guarantee capital accumulation. Still, states in the region might share some similarities due to common colonial legacies. This section argues that colonial histories have crafted Latin American states through a deeply violent and oppressive process of 'othering' within the logic of accumulation. To do so, we draw upon the concept of 'primitive accumulation' as an ongoing phenomenon. This perception allows us to see states' limitations and contextual conditions in the competition to accumulate.

We follow Massimo De Angelis's (2001) understanding of primitive accumulation as the continuous process of separating the producer from the means of production "instigated by some social actor", such as the state. Primitive accumulation is a violent process requiring classification, hierarchization, and oppression. It does not impact the so-called Global South exclusively but "affects the global space of contemporary capitalism as it keeps redrawing its geographical coordinates" (Mezzadra 2011, 303). Bordering mechanisms are continuously used to create new geographic and social separations and enclosures that oppress some sectors of the population and territories more intensely in the quest for capital accumulation. There are different degrees in which accumulation operates; not in the sense that it produces less or more surplus value, but in how violence and oppression are daily experienced depending on geographies, times, and societies.

The Latin American specificity is thus embedded in an aggressive form of exploitation for value accumulation where the state actively intervenes. The colonial conditions set the tone for the constitution of states as the unique form to organize social relations and legalize accumulation, shaping the way these societies were integrated to global capitalism by a violent process of conquest. After independence, societies were produced by states through this colonial violence and structuring (Connell and Dados 2014). Histories of slavery, serfdom, marginalization, and discrimination marked social structures and established the ideal of a homogenized citizen (Moncayo 2012, 32). Internal colonialism traversed the process of state formation and gave continuity to the colonial structure by moulding minds, behaviours, practices, and discourses. The state emerged as a tool of colonization where the civilizing mission was renewed, and development persisted as its main purpose (Bonneto 2012). The expansion of capitalism in these 'postcolonial' societies, thus, occurred through an ongoing process of primitive accumulation via the state and shaped a "'stratified' form of development" (Morton 2010, 10). Not only were power relations rearranged, but also visions and ambitions were formed.

This novel configuration articulated the role of states with the construction of alterities (Bermúdez Peña et al. 2016). Gender and racial/ethnic hierarchies were employed in distinctive ways to justify accumulation. As Roswitha Scholz (2019, 41) explains, the value dissociation manifests within the state and politics, as these arenas have been erected through "masculine alliances", denying and repudiating everything considered feminine. Women, Indigenous peoples, Afro-descendants, and nature in Latin America were indeed constructed as internal others to feed the machinery of the capitalist world economy, to make possible the production of value. The region and its people were historically inserted, in a particular and unique way, into the global set of capitalist social relations.

Moreover, social constructions influenced—and continue to influence—the particular form of states. In this context, Latin America has been imagined as part of the 'Third World' and, thus, an exploitative dynamic is maintained by considering some peoples and spaces as in need of 'development'. Furthermore, an extractivist logic has been sustained by the perception of Latin America as a region of immense 'natural resources' from which profit can be generated. In this way, a process of conquest aimed at absorbing life into the global logic of capital was unleashed, where states play a key role in separating and ranking their territories and societies through authoritarian practices and violent mechanisms. The Latin American region is just an example of how this is done through colonial legacies and hierarchies, and how developmentalist ideas, structures, and ambitions are now put forth by progressive governments to secure the reproduction of capital.

State-Form and the Political Regime

The state seeks to create conditions to underpin the political hegemony of socially dominant forces, seeming to separate itself from the social structure through the political system, legitimating its intervention. In this way, capital succeeds in installing its domination and interests as expressions of the general welfare. However, the political legitimacy of capital's dominance and its material accumulation and reproduction capacities are associated with a specific geographic territory and a certain cultural pattern (Féliz and López 2010). Thus, at the level of the political regime we can characterize a multiplicity of expressions of the state-form (Bonnet 2007). Depending on historical, social, political, and geographical circumstances, states assume diverse forms of being. In moments of crisis and radical conflict, the state-form, for instance, can get into a more openly repressive mode, as seen in the 1970s–80s.

The economic crisis provoked great social discontent, and thus the states' interventions increased in violence, repression, and authoritarianism. As neoliberalism surfaced to sustain capital's reproduction, in the UK, Thatcher's government attacked the working class that resisted the loss of rights and the reduction in benefits. Meanwhile, in Mexico, through a 'perfect dictatorship'[2] and in Argentina, with the military dictatorship, overt violence came to the fore as capital advanced its need to restructure society. Neoliberal governance operates from the local to the global, articulating coercion and seduction to favour accumulation and sustain capitalist/colonialist arrangements, structures, meanings, and discourses (Durán Matute 2018). In the Latin American region, neoliberalism emerged as a development strategy that re-weaved capitalist social relations worldwide so the state reorganized its functions but gave continuity to its authoritarian colonial legacy (Connell and Dados 2014).

So, rather than considering that we are now witnessing the rise of authoritarian neoliberalism (Bruff 2014), we must recognize the broader history of authoritarianism and the continuity of authoritarian statism (Ryan 2019). This is the reason why we have drawn the lines between colonialism, state formation, and capitalism. The prior experiences of authoritarianism in the region should be put forth to understand how in different degrees and ways the state—at the level of the political

---

2   This idea was put forth by the writer Mario Vargas Llosa in 1990, and it has come to mean how in Mexico we live(d) under a dictatorship, not ruled by a man, but by a political party that used the Revolution to legitimize itself and simulate a democratic political system to maintain power.

regime—has always resorted to violence, discipline, intimidation, coercion, control, manipulation, and seizure to organize capitalist social relations. We should not disregard the complexities and interconnections of states' experiences, as their actions, policies, and measures can be more or less violent depending on their historical trajectories and the global operation of capitalism. It is not that states are weak or strong, but circumstantial, flexible, innovative, and uncertain in their means for capital accumulation throughout history.

Still, what is the specificity of contemporary authoritarianism? Why are we seeing a rise of authoritarianism with different traits and in diverse milieus? Violence is in fact inherent to the reproduction of the capitalist totality that increases in the long-term crisis to guarantee social order and the narrative that sustains it (González Cruz, Doulos, and Rodríguez Aza 2022). Since the 2008 global crisis, this violence has intensified in conjunction with labour exploitation. Thus, this rise cannot be understood exclusively via politics, but by considering states' techniques of governance as a way to secure the production of surplus value. Furthermore, violence, as an interconnected phenomenon in time and space, provokes a hierarchical design of territories and societies where 'development' appears as a solution (Inclán 2018). However, is the developmentalism promoted by progressive governments a true break in authoritarianism? Or rather, are these governments presenting another authoritarian way to sustain the reproduction of capital in times of crisis? In the following sections, we try to answer these questions.

General Notes on Latin America's Progressive Governments

During the early 2000s, in many Latin American countries, progressive coalitions won national elections.[3] Their strategies were to promote economic growth as the engine of development with the state taking a more active role in the extraction, control, and commercialization of 'resources' to promote 'social justice' (Gudynas 2012). They used a discourse of change and proclaimed themselves as 'post-neoliberal' to endorse a form of 'inclusive' capitalism sustained by neo-developmentalist ideas. Even if these governments have important differences, they all deepened the extractivist role of the state, supported by anti-poverty programmes distributed among peasants and the lower classes (Vergara-Camus and Kay 2017). Besides, through new megaprojects, communities were alienated from their environment and their relationship with nature was disrupted. This combination of developmentalist policies and actions with forms of clientelism and corporatism weakened the

---

3   This turn happened in Venezuela in 1999, in Paraguay in 2003, in Argentina in 2003, in Brazil in 2003, in Uruguay in 2005, in Chile in 2006, in Bolivia in 2006, in Ecuador in 2007, in Nicaragua in 2007, and in El Salvador in 2009. The tide turned sour at different times and at different paces.

autonomy of social organization, whereas its blending with repressive and authoritarian methods criminalized and marginalized social struggles.

The governments of the 'pink tide', this left-wing turn, led to what has been dubbed as passive revolutions, that is, limited structural transformations that have a top-down conservative background and use demobilizing and subalternizing political practices (Modonesi 2015). They incorporated social struggles' ideas into political discourse and leaders into state administration, while capitalist forms and practices remained mostly unchanged (Vergara-Camus and Kay 2017). Social and ecological impacts were largely neglected while states were aligning themselves with transnational corporations. Not surprisingly, the radical Left criticized these governments for their neo-developmentalist vision and paternalistic, authoritarian, anthropocentric, and racist approaches (Gaudichaud, Webber, and Modonesi 2019). The reformist illusion sustained by the liberal Left fell apart as policies of state redistribution showed their limits. Moreover, the revolutionary process—including any possibility of real social change—was absorbed by the logic of power (Holloway 2010). By mixing reform and restoration, they showed an assortment of renewed neo-extractivist practices to boost capitalism in these territories while recreating the myth of development and social inclusion.

This situation and agenda are not exclusive of progressive governments in the region. The idea that extractivism is necessary both for competition in the global market and to overcome 'underdevelopment' has prevailed among governments of all political positions (Navarro Trujillo and Linsalata 2020). However, progressive governments' perverse use of the rhetoric of development provides a 'positive' façade in times of crisis from which to reproduce capitalist social relations. In effect, in different ways states perpetuate a fantasy of development that justifies authoritarian practices and regimes in order to fight the 'enemies' of progress and promote the marketization of the economy (Bloom 2016). Progressive governments through (neo)developmentalism renew the violent and oppressive process of 'othering' within the logic of accumulation. Development appears not just as a discourse, but as lived, internalized, and reproduced practices that naturalize hierarchies and reinforce capitalist structures.

Economic inequality is not the main problem, how a process of othering takes places as a technique of governance is. The exploitation, dispossession, violence, and oppression experienced is justified in these terms while people target 'sell out' governments, transnational corporations, or imperial powers as the culprits. Thus, many advocate for national interests and responses, as if Latin American countries were external to global capitalist organization and operation, as progressive governments usually maintain. At this point, it might be tempting to analyse whether distinctions between the Right and Left matter when some 'concessions' are granted, and 'improvements' made. However, as we argue here, progressive and right-wing governments are expressions of the pendulum of the political hegemony of capital. They evidence how capital needs a third party, a state flexible enough to surpass obstacles in reproducing capitalist social relations in a diversity of contexts and a variety of ways.

Mexico and Argentina: Apart but So Close

Progressive governments are an essential part of Latin America's history, as they have impacted politics in the region and continue to appear as political alternatives. Being thousands of kilometres away, Mexico and Argentina exemplify this particular form of how capitalism operates in Latin America today. These two countries have great historical, social, and political differences but illustrate how the production and reproduction of capital combines violence and extractivism, authoritarianism, and developmentalism via the state's use of 'progressive' rhetoric. Due to their disparities, the two perspectives presented here follow their own narrative, explaining why and how these 'outdated' progressive governments are part of a global authoritarian turn. The intention is not to read them as national cases, but as specific 'leftist' manifestations of the current global logic of accumulation. They shed light on how Latin American states are continuously shaped in order to guarantee the accumulation of capital and exhibit the risk of people being lured by these governments as alternatives to capitalism.

Argentina

After four years of an openly neoliberal government, a (neo)Peronist alliance capable of winning the elections was formed, and Alberto Fernández (AF) was elected president from 2019–23.[4] During Mauricio Macri's government from 2015–19, the crisis of capitalism in Argentina deepened, preventing the economy from surpassing a process of stagnation and exacerbating growing instability initiated by the 2008 global crisis. AF came into office to recover the economy, "turning the economy back on" (Perfil 2019), stimulating growth as a means for social inclusion. His government brought back a neo-developmentalist state driven by previous progressive governments from 2003–15, which now sought to overcome its limits and

---

4   Peronism is a political movement born in the mid-1940s. It expressed the bursting of working people into the political arena, articulated by the nascent developmental state. President Domingo Perón's government which was in power from 1946–51 and 1951–55, represented a process of social inclusion of the masses through open state regulation of social conflict in Argentina's history. The Peronist movement has been the dominant political party ever since. It has been dubbed as populist or national-popular—e.g. Néstor Kirchner, 2003–07 and Cristina Fernández de Kirchner, 2007–15—but it has also been neoliberal—e.g. Carlos Menem, 1989–99.

deepen its structural tendencies.[5] This new progressive government—as it presents itself—has consolidated the concentration and internationalization of capital, via the primary-export matrix and insertion into the global debt system. It did so by denying democratic participation in decisions, with many government officials discrediting criticisms of the new policies by suggesting these voices are "enemies of progress", as explained before.

Previously, neo-developmentalism channelled the systemic tension between the pressure to multiply the valorization of capital in a new context and the popular demands born out of neoliberalism. National governments thus allocated public resources and promoted legislation to expand extractivism (Féliz 2014): legislation favourable to investment in mega-mining, the expansion of genetically modified crops (GMOs), and urban extractivism was consolidated. The frontiers of capital were violently expanded through various forms. In some cases, it appeared via police repression of community and social resistance. In others, it was more subtle, through the violence implicit in monetized relations (Dinerstein 2002), as in the increase in the price of land that displaced settlers—in many cases non-owners—to more remote and precarious places. These forms of violence manifested the unity of state and capital.

Nowadays, the acceleration of the economic crisis and the pandemic led AF's government to fast-track its extractivist agenda. First and foremost, no limits were placed on the expansion of the production of crops, especially soya.[6] The expansion of soya throughout Argentina began in the 1990s when GMOs were approved and came with strings attached, this crop led to a major transformation in the agricultural industry with massive use of agrochemicals and fertilizers. Soya became the star crop and helped previous progressive governments to take advantage of the price surge created by the irruption of China on to the global markets. This process led to the deterritorialization of peasants and small farmers forced into the cities or proletarianized in rural spaces. With bulldozers and a combination of private and public forces, many traditional communities were and continue to be expelled from the lands they have occupied for generations. It has also meant the destruction of native forests, through action or omission, the state—primarily local and provincial governments—keeps 'cleaning' the land to allow agribusiness to flourish.

Since 2010, oil and gas drilling became a new star in the neo-developmentalist sky, and a gigantic new field was put into action. This new shale, oil, and gas formation was called *Vaca Muerta* (Dead Cow) as it is shaped like a dead cow's head. Expected to be one of the biggest of its kind worldwide, it has lured the attention of global corporations, and its exploitation has been promoted by state policies

---

5   For a characterization of neo-developmentalism, see Féliz (2015 and 2019).
6   Soya, together with maize and wheat, are the principal export goods.

through millions of dollars of government subsidies and infrastructural initiatives. AF's government announced new plans to foster this project with the cooperation of Yacimientos Petrolíferos Fiscales (YPF), the state energy company, and foreign corporations, such as Chevron and PowerChina—especially for the construction of pipelines.

Vaca Muerta is situated in the middle of Mapuchean territories, in the northern region of the country's southern provinces, and has advanced despite their opposition. The Mapuche people are in the process of recovering the territories and ways of life that were robbed from them and destroyed in the 19th century during the so-called Conquest of the Desert (1878–1885); that meant the genocide of the original populations of these provinces, as crop and meat production for export needed to grow. Currently, the expansion of production is also resisted because of its proven negative effects on the population's health. Shale production requires massive water use—a scarce resource in this arid region—and contaminates groundwater. Besides, it creates tonnes of waste that is being deposited next to nearby towns. As the exploitation of *Vaca Muerta* increased, resistance has also been mounting, and recently Mapuche communities have started using direct action to protest the situation (Robles 2021).

Crops and fossil fuels have been part of Argentina's popular history of extractivism, but there is a field a bit more hidden: mining. Since Kirchner's government from 2003–07, numerous mining projects have been approved. In the north-western provinces of Jujuy and Salta—on the border with Bolivia and Chile—there are massive lithium deposits. However, this mineral exists within saltwater lakes that provide most of the water for these arid areas on the foothills of the Andes. In cooperation with transnational corporations, the state is now putting the primary source of drinkable water for the local and Indigenous communities at risk. As in other cases, resistance abounds, and so does repression. For instance, the project *Agua Rica* (Tasty Water), a mining project in the province of Catamarca—in the far west of the country—has been stalled for many years by the resistance of a grassroots assembly. In the middle of the pandemic, the Canadian corporation Yamana Gold began operations to extract copper and gold, but the population picketed the access ways to the mining field. As a response, AF's government sent the National Gendarmerie—a national police force in charge of securing borders—to disband the protest, and rapidly and illegally detained several activists that were released more than two weeks later.

Still, resistance prevails, especially that of women and socioecological movements, which are increasingly transversal. Throughout this period, women have been at the forefront of the conflicts against extractivism, putting the reproduction of life at the centre. The government has responded by combining greenwashing and a new discourse of green developmentalism, and creating several underfunded programmes to 'protect' the environment. However, we cannot neglect how women's struggles have helped advance their rights and those of gender diverse people. Recently, the right to identity for the LGBTIQ+ community—that allows for a self-defined gender and name to be recognized in legal documentation—and the right to abortion have been passed into law. This has been a result and response to the long-term mobilization of the feminist movement. In fact, the first time a pro-abortion bill was voted on in Congress was in 2018, under Macri's right-wing government. While at the time it was rejected, a bill was finally passed in 2020.[7] These struggles have also led to the creation of the first Ministry of Women, Genders, and Diversity. This state of affairs has given place to increasing debates about the state's patriarchal and racist nature and its relation to developmentalist strategy. Even if some of the movements have entered an uneasy relationship within the state, many continue to light the fire of change.

Another process of the current neo-developmentalist agenda is urban extractivism (Vázquez Duplat 2017). It is the result of the articulation between the appropriation of ground rent accrued from the other forms of extractivism, especially agricultural production, and the extreme exploitation of labour. The circulation of ground rent to urban settings has spurred landed property prices giving way to a concomitant increase in the price for letting a house. While it is a long-standing process, it has been accelerated through the recent multiplication of financial regulations favouring construction's financialization. Urban extractivism is forcing people out of their homes into more peripheral and precarious settings on the outskirts of cities and towns.

This expulsion process implies not only the violence of money but also the direct violence of the state; an example of this is the mass settlement in Guernica in the province of Buenos Aires. In May 2020, about 3000 families moved into a vacant plot of land in the area. For three months, they organized collectively in assembly and constructed soup kitchens, sanitary stations, and childcare centres. In mid-July, the government of the province—part of the national governing alliance—decided to evict these families and return the land to its previous alleged owners, planning to develop a closed housing cluster. A combination of open repression by the police, the judiciary's support, small subsidies, and vague promises were used to expel these families.

All in all, extractivism is directly linked to the need to repay foreign debt and keep Argentina's territory within the world's debt system (Toussaint 2019). Different governments have defended the need to repay an illegal and illegitimate foreign debt and have systematically indebted the country (Cantamutto and Féliz 2021).

---

7   It should be noted that since 2003, the National Campaign for the Right to Legal, Safe, and Free Abortion pushed for the approval of such a law, which was blocked in Congress for many years by the progressive, developmentalist governing coalition, in power from 2003–15, that is currently at the core of Alberto Fernández's government.

Both Macri's and AF's governments signed deals with the International Monetary Fund (IMF), transforming foreign debt and extractivism into two sides of the same coin in Argentina's development strategy and the backbone of the party system's consensus. Capitalist development led by extractive practices breeds violence and feeds on it. No matter the name of the governing alliance, this is the consensus amongst the dominant classes and their political expressions.

However, sheer violence cannot create political consensus; some level of consent is also needed. Whilst capital needs the state to guarantee the processes of accumulation, it also requires policies and an ideological discursive platform. These can change over time to respond to the contingent demands of oppressed sectors, to channel them as much as possible within the boundaries of capitalist accumulation. In Argentina, since the early 2000s, popular movements have multiplied their demands, and thus, the state has given institutional, political, and ideological responses. For example, it created several massive but basic cash-transfer programmes—including the Universal Child Allowance, AUH in 2009—along with policies to promote the so-called popular economy. These policy interventions were meant to defuse the most radical demands of the movements of the unemployed (MTD), and fragment and divide their organization.

These policies grew in institutional support and became the main component of state social interventions. Even Macri's 2015–19 government reached an agreement with the main movements—organized around the recently created Confederation of Workers of the Popular Economy, CTEP—to pass into law a new Social Supplementary Wage (SSC) that guaranteed a transfer equal to half the minimum wage for workers in the popular economy. AF's government continued these policies with a radical twist: many social movements, most within the UTEP—Union of Workers of the Popular Economy, the new name of the CTEP—became part of the governing coalition and were given positions in areas related to the management of resources and policymaking for these workers. This alliance combines conviction and acceptance of the impossibility of more radical action. These movements agreed to become part of the governing coalition to succeed in their main objective: avoiding a new 'neoliberal' government.

As we have seen, with all their differences, AF's progressive coalition shares similar neoliberal policies and goals. The combination of expanding extractivism, higher foreign debt, and the multiplication of social policies has only increased poverty (Kessler and Assusa 2020),[8] precarization of work and life, and the plundering of common goods (Svampa 2019). No matter the political coalition in government, the political regime has processed capitalism in Argentina in a way that the relationship between debt, plundering, violence, and social control remains.

---

8   These policies guarantee that people can survive poverty but almost never escape it.

Mexico

Andrés Manuel López Obrador (AMLO) took office as the new Mexican president in December 2018. By using 'progressive' rhetoric, he got the endorsement of over half of voters who saw in him 'hope', in a country devastated by neoliberal policies and the war on drugs. In effect, AMLO promised the Fourth Transformation (4T) of the country, a 'post-neoliberal' project where authoritarianism will be eradicated, modernization forged from below, and development built with social justice (Presidencia de México 2019a, 8). For nationals, as well as people abroad, it was a promising turn against the authoritarian history of the country and the global context of far-right politics. However, the 4T government kept the same capitalist direction and deepened its authoritarian approach from its inception.[9] AMLO's arrival instigated the persistence of a 'simulated democracy', where dynamics, practices, and relations of power simulate an encouraging democratic functioning but authoritarianism, clientelism, corporatism, impunity, and paternalism keep tainting politics (Durán Matute 2018, 33–34).

This state of affairs can only be explained by recalling how in 2006, the Mexican government initiated a war against drug cartels. Since then, violence and insecurity have increased to the point that official numbers report more than 350,000 homicides (Instituto Nacional de Estadística y Geografía 2022). Furthermore, there are more than 85,000 missing persons, and 4,000 mass graves have been found (Secretaría de Gobernación 2020 and 2021). Paradoxically, to end the war, the 4T government proposed a constitutional reform to create the National Guard, a 'peace police' of over 100,000 officers who would intervene in civil duties but have military training and structure (Presidencia de México 2019a, 11, 23–24). During the pandemic, the government also granted more power and assigned policing tasks to the armed forces; they now patrol the streets, stop migration, control customs, manage social programmes, survey hospitals, distribute COVID-19 vaccines, expand banking in rural life, and construct and administer megaprojects. The 4T government does not offer an alternate solution to violence and maintains the same approach: increasing militarization and repression.

---

9   It is not a surprize that AMLO's political life was initiated in the hegemonic *Partido Revolucionario Institucional* (PRI) that ruled for 78 years, 1929–2000 and 2012–18. Moreover, AMLO's political party, *Movimiento de Regeneración Nacional* (MORENA), was born from the *Partido de la Revolución Democrática* (PRD) which in turn originated from the PRI, and adopted the same tradition of revolutionary nationalism. Not only that, but to win, MORENA, a supposedly left-wing party, signed pacts with both the *Partido del Trabajo* (PT), a façade of a labour party, and the *Partido Encuentro Social* (PES), a right-wing Christian party. Furthermore, the presidential cabinet is integrated extensively by old PRI, PRD, and PAN (*Partido Acción Nacional*) politicians.

In this context, a report from WOLA, an advocacy organization in the Americas, contends that the armed forces have such extreme influence that a coup might not be necessary for them to exercise high levels of power (Brewer 2021). In this way, authoritarianism, violence, criminalization, racism, and xenophobia are further expanded, as seen, for instance, in the detention and hostility towards Central American migrant caravans. In addition, the country is stained with the blood of enforced disappearances, arbitrary detentions, torture, rape, and extrajudicial killings. If, as asserted by Dawn Paley (2014, 15–17), this war is a remedy to the crises of capitalism that involves and benefits a multiplicity of actors, including the state, then why would the Mexican government change its direction? The promise of taking the military off the streets was forgotten and the accusations against them, of crimes against humanity, disregarded. There is a connection between state and parastate violence that guarantees the accumulation of capital; collusion and impunity protect the use of violence, and uphold a transnational criminal network economically and politically.

Violence in Mexico has dramatically impacted women, from the *muertas de Juárez* beginning in the early 1990s to the murder of 7-year-old Fátima in 2020. And, as for now, violence is still far from being eradicated, and closer to proliferation. During the 4T government, the number of femicides have increased about 13 percent. However, while the president suggests this increase is due to a lack of classification by past governments (Gobierno de México 2021), the truth is that the state is still a perpetrator of macho violence. Not only has AMLO accused the feminist movement of being a 'simulation', 'conservatives in disguise', and 'a violent threat', discrediting women's struggles and demands, but at the beginning of the pandemic, he asserted that 90 percent of calls reporting violence against women were fake, even while shelters increased their occupancy and struggled to access resources (see EQUIS, Intersecta, and Red Nacional de Refugios 2020). As women continue to mobilize and multiply their demands, the state responds through increased violence, as seen in the entrenchment at the national palace and the repression in 2021 of the 8M protest, and the subduing and sexual assaults of students of the Normal Rural Mactumactzá at the hands of police in Chiapas.

In this context, Aída Hernández contends that the 4T government, similarly to other progressive governments in Latin America, does not integrate the demands of women; on the contrary, it becomes an enemy of the feminist movement and an ally to conservative values (Hernández 2021). This attitude was evident in the proposal to have a public consultation to ask whether abortion should be legal and the endorsement of Félix Salgado Macedonio—who was accused of sexual abuse and rape—for governor of Guerrero as the national governing party candidate.[10]

---

10   In the end, Salgado Macedonio was removed by the National Electoral Institute due to irregularities in pre-campaign expenses but was replaced by his daughter, who won the election.

The state does not become feminist by integrating women into public office, as the 4T presumes; the way it continues to organize social relations determines its patriarchal shape. In this case, it does so by patronizing women, disregarding their problems, perpetuating aggressions against them, dividing and discrediting the movement, negotiating rights, silencing victims, and maintaining the monopoly on violence. Additionally, this patriarchal form of the state also drives its extractive thrust.

Not surprisingly, in the 4T agenda, extractivism for national development has been a top priority. Although one of the government's commitments was to impede any project that affects and pollutes the environment (Presidencia de México 2019b), 4T flagship projects have been imposed without the appropriate, consulted, and studied plans. For instance, the construction of the Maya Train, a tourist train accompanied by processes of urbanization, industrialization, and commercialization that will fracture the Yucatan Peninsula, began without an environmental impact assessment. Not only that, but this megaproject is appropriating the culture and identity of the Maya people for tourism purposes, combining their struggles to protect land and life with the market logic. AMLO's ceremony to ask for Mother Earth's permission to build it was just proof of that. This approach has been supplemented with a discourse that looks down on Indigenous communities as being 'abandoned' and needing 'development'.

Furthermore, even if the 4T rhetoric has been based on an idea of the will of and benefit to 'the people', the government has not hesitated to sign pacts with the business sector or to attract foreign capital to finance, advise, and operate megaprojects. The problem is not that foreign corporations are welcomed in the country but that their settlement is facilitated at the expense of 'the people'. The government manipulates and reduces public consultations to a formal requisite (Gasparello 2020), while it co-opts members of communities through handouts and social programmes (e.g. Sembrando Vida, Pensión Universal, and Jóvenes Construyendo Futuro). In this way, the Interoceanic Corridor, a freight train that will cross the Isthmus of Tehuantepec, providing a route for commerce, communication, maquila, and energy and mining production, will convert Indigenous lands into a free economic zone. The aim is to replace the Panama Canal and—in conjunction with the Maya Train—act as a barrier that stops Mexican and Central American migration to the US, by militarizing the zone and integrating people into capitalist production chains.

Desperation to attract capital is such that the government even profited from the pandemic by imposing austerity measures that cut 75 percent of the budget for agencies and services except for megaprojects, oil and energy production, clientelist social programmes, and the National Guard (Diario Oficial de la Federación 2020). This action revealed how the advancement of extractivism is done through co-option and violence. The government priority is to rescue Petróleos Mexicanos

(PEMEX) and the Comisión Federal de Electricidad (CFE), so it bets on hydrocarbons as the means to finance national development while it disregards the environmental and social consequences. The construction of Dos Bocas refinery in the state of Tabasco, in this sense, is in a high-risk area and has repressed workers that demand better conditions. Meanwhile, the Morelos Integral Project, an infrastructure project for electricity production in the centre of Mexico, is being constructed within the volcanic hazard map of Popocatépetl and was approved despite opposition and the assassination of Samir Flores Soberanes, a Nahua land defender, three days before the public consultation.

In effect, the escalation of narco-violence and paramilitary forces in these regions has meant the assassination of more than 40 Indigenous land defenders and the incursion into their territories (Durán Matute and Moreno 2021). Whereas communities are violated and displaced, and territories devastated, the state deploys the armed forces to repress opposition, construct and administer megaprojects and protect corporations, e.g. mining police. A case in point has been the opposition of Choluteca communities to the bottled water company Bonafont, part of the conglomerate Danone, in the state of Puebla. In 2021, these communities organized to stop the theft of their water and occupy the plant. They transformed it into a community centre called Altepelmecalli, that included a health clinic, a library, a women's organizing space, an agriculture programme, alternative media, and diverse workshops. However, in February 2022, almost a year later, the National Guard and the police expelled the defenders and dismantled Altepelmecalli.

Still, strong resistance endures from Indigenous peoples against extractive projects. Communities mainly grouped through the Ejército Zapatista de Liberación Nacional (EZLN) and the Congreso Nacional Indígena (CNI) mobilize, demand, and defend. So, while the state organizes capitalist social relations, elsewhere protests, lawsuits, complaints, events, and investigations are being held to create *other worlds*. The occupation of the Instituto Nacional de Pueblos Indígenas by the Otomi community in Mexico City since 2020, is proof of how Indigenous communities sustain their demands for their rights and autonomy, and struggle against megaprojects and violence. The CNI and EZLN communities, besides, organize not just by themselves but with national and international civil society to impede megaprojects' completion and stop the multiple actions that are leading to a social and environmental collapse. The attacks against them still proliferate, as the 4T developmentalist agenda is suited to a country characterized by war.

In this context, during the president's daily morning conferences, insults and disqualifications abound for people that criticize or disagree with the 4T decisions and actions, whether Indigenous, women, activists, academics, or social organizations. So, not only the state constructs the hegemony of 'the people' by excluding Indigenous peoples (Solorio, Ortega, Romero, and Guzman 2021), but by labelling as 'conservatives' a wide array of sectors that oppose the 'developmentalist' transformation. This strategy criminalizes and fragments opposition to maintain classifications and hierarchies for the exploitation of capital. In this way, AMLO's progressive government keeps its objective of capital accumulation through a deadly combination of extractivism, militarization, social programmes, and a perverse rhetoric.

Conclusions

Through the cases of Mexico and Argentina, we have shown how the capitalist state in Latin America works through a deeply violent and oppressive process of 'othering' within the logic of accumulation. It means that territories and societies are separated and ranked, predominantly based on colonial legacies and histories that keep alive a fantasy of 'development' that shapes visions and ambitions of both rulers and the ruled. We explained that understanding the state as a situated form for organizing capitalist social relations allows us to comprehend why authoritarian traits flow through state policies. These tendencies are present in different political forms and changing government coalitions across both time and space. Both neoliberal and progressive states appear as forms of capitalist states for social reorganization and repression of resistance. Still, progressive governments are not a mere continuation of previous forms of government. Through a renovated discourse, they expand, naturalize, and revitalize the state's ability to organize the accumulation of capital. Their perversity is thus based on how they obscure authoritarian practices within capitalism through a rhetoric of development, change, wellbeing, social justice, and environmental protection.

To put this debate in context, by analysing the current progressive governments of Alberto Fernández and Andrés Manuel López Obrador, we have shown that whilst presenting themselves in opposition to neoliberal rule, they are its necessary alternation. We identified how these governments multiply the historical record of violence and oppression with a colonialist and extractivist agenda. As a new wave of progressive governments seems to be emerging in the region, we warn of how these governments use a variable combination of cohesion—repression and violence—and consensus—co-optation, manipulation, and seduction—to disarticulate social resistance and advance new forms of capitalist development. This situation does not mean that popular action against the system does not persist. However, it explains why conflicts tend to be diverted from radical transformation or violently neutralized. Authoritarianism is the main ingredient of an economy based on a patriarchal configuration and a 'neo-colonial' operation that puts life at risk. This new cycle of progressive governments teaches us, thus, a unique way in which capitalism is invigorated through authoritarianism and developmentalism.

References

Álvarez Huwiler, Laura, and Alberto Bonnet (2018), "Ensayo y error. Un análisis marxista de las políticas públicas", *Revista Mexicana de Ciencias Políticas y Sociales*, vol. 63, no. 233, pp. 169–92.

Bermúdez Peña, Claudia, Marisol Troya, Celina Vacca, and Gabriela Veronelli (2016), "Estado y colonialidad: Preguntas iniciales y primeros avances de investigación", *Estudios Sociales del Estado*, vol. 2, no. 3, pp. 221–31.

Bloom, Peter (2016), *Authoritarian Capitalism in the Age of Globalization*, Cheltenham: Edward Elgar Publishing.

Bonnet, Alberto (2007), "Estado y capital. Los debates sobre la derivación y la reformulación del Estado", *Estado y Marxismo. Un siglo y medio de debates*, edited by Mabel Thwaites Rey, Buenos Aires: Prometeo Libros, pp. 269–97.

Bonnet, Alberto, and Adrián Piva (2017), "Prólogo", *Estado y capital. El debate alemán sobre la derivación del Estado*, edited by Alberto Bonnet and Adrián Piva, Buenos Aires: Herramienta Ediciones, pp. 9–26.

Bonneto, María Susana (2012), "El Estado en la región. La conflictiva discusión de alternativas teóricas", *El Estado en América Latina: Continuidades y rupturas*, edited by Mabel Thwaites Rey, Santiago: CLACSO, pp. 117–39.

Brewer, Stephanie (2021), "Militarized Mexico: A Lost War that has not Brought Peace", *WOLA*, 12 May, available at https://www.wola.org/analysis/militarized-mexico-a-lost-war/. Last accessed on 20 June 2022.

Bruff, Ian (2014), "The Rise of Authoritarian Neoliberalism", *Rethinking Marxism*, vol. 26, no. 1, pp. 113–29.

Cantamutto, Francisco, and Mariano Féliz (2021), "Argentina entre la sostenibilidad de la deuda y la vida", *Revista NuestraAmérica*, vol. 9, no. 7.

Connell, Raewyn, and Nour Dados (2014), "Where in the World Does Neoliberalism Come From?", *Theory and Society*, vol. 43, no. 2, pp. 117–38.

De Angelis, Massimo (2001), "Marx and Primitive Accumulation: The Continuous Character of Capital's 'Enclosures'", *The Commoner*, vol. 2, pp. 1–22.

Diario Oficial de la Federación (2020), "Decreto por el que se establecen las medidas de austeridad que deberán observar las dependencias y entidades de la Administración Pública Federal bajo los criterios que en el mismo se indican", 23 April, available at https://www.dof.gob.mx/nota_detalle.php?codigo=5592205&fecha=23/04/2020. Last accessed on 20 June 2022.

Dinerstein, Ana Cecilia (2002), "Regaining Materiality: Unemployment and the Invisible Subjectivity of Labour", *The Labour Debate: An Investigation into the Theory and Reality of Capitalist Work*, edited by Ana Cecilia Dinerstein and Michael Neary, Ashgate: Aldershot, pp. 203–25.

Durán Matute, Inés (2018), *Indigenous Peoples and the Geographies of Power: Mezcala's Narratives of Neoliberal Governance*, New York: Routledge.

Durán Matute, Inés, and Rocío Moreno (2021), *La lucha por la vida frente a los megaproyectos en México*, Guadalajara: Cátedra Jorge Alonso.

EQUIS, Intersecta, and Red Nacional de Refugios (2020), "Las dos pandemias. Violencia contra las mujeres en México en el contexto de COVID-19", *Informe elaborado para la Relatora Especial de Naciones Unidas sobre la violencia contra la mujer, sus causas y consecuencias*, available at https://equis.org.mx/wp-content/uploads/2020/08/informe-dospandemiasmexico.pdf. Last accessed on 20 June 2022.

Féliz, Mariano (2014), "Neo-Developmentalism, Accumulation by Dispossession and International Rent – Argentina, 2003–2013", *International Critical Thought*, vol. 4, no. 4, pp. 499–509.

Féliz, Mariano (2015), "Limits and Barriers of Neodevelopmentalism: Lessons from Argentina's Experience, 2003–2011", *Review of Radical Political Economics*, vol. 47, no.1, pp. 70–89.

Féliz, Mariano (2017), "Acumulación de capital y lucha de clase(s) en y a través del Estado en la Argentina neodesarrollista", *Revista Theomai. Estudios sobre Sociedad y Desarrollo*, vol. 35, pp. 171–86.

Féliz, Mariano (2019), "Neodevelopmentalism and Dependency in Twenty-First-Century Argentina: Insights from the Work of Ruy Mauro Marini", *Latin American Perspectives*, vol. 46, no. 1, pp. 105–21.

Féliz, Mariano, and Emiliano López (2010), "Políticas sociales y laborales en la Argentina: del Estado 'ausente' al Estado pos-neoliberal", *Pensamiento crítico, organización y cambio social*, edited by Mariano Féliz, Luciana Melina Deledicque, Emiliano López, and Facundo Barrera, Buenos Aires: Editorial El Colectivo, pp. 123–40.

Gasparello, Giovanna (2020), "Megaproyectos a Consulta: ¿Derechos o simulaciones? Experiencias en México", *LiminaR. Estudios Sociales y Humanísticos*, vol. 18, no. 2, pp. 124–41.

Gaudichaud, Franck, Jeffrey Webber, and Massimo Modonesi (2019), *Los gobiernos progresistas latinoamericanos del siglo XXI: Ensayos de interpretación histórica*, Mexico City: UNAM.

Gerstenberger, Heide (1978), "Class Conflict, Competition and State Functions", *State and Capital: A Marxist Debate*, edited by John Holloway and Sol Picciotto, London: Edward Arnold, pp. 148–59.

Gobierno de México (2021), "Versión estenográfica. Tercer Informe 2020–2021", 1 September, available at https://www.gob.mx/presidencia/es/articulos/version-estenografica-tercer-informe-2020-2021?idiom=es. Last accessed on 20 June 2022.

González Cruz, Edith, Panagiotis Doulos, and Milena Rodríguez Aza (2022), "¡Ni perdón, ni olvido!: fragmentos rebeldes, rituales de perdón y crisis", (draft).

Gudynas, Eduardo (2012), "Estado compensador y nuevos extractivismos. Las ambivalencias del progresismo sudamericano", *Nueva Sociedad*, vol. 237, pp. 128–46.

Hernández, Aída (2021), "Las izquierdas y los pactos patriarcales", *Rompeviento TV*, 15 March, available at https://www.rompeviento.tv/las-izquierdas-y-los-pactos-patriarcales/. Last accessed on 20 June 2022.

Hirsch, Joachim (1977), "Observaciones teóricas sobre el Estado burgués y su crisis", *El marxismo y la crisis del Estado*, edited by Nicos Poulantzas, Christine Buci-Glucksmann, Jean-Marie Vincent, Joachim Hirsch, and Suzann de Brunhoff, Puebla: Benemérita Universidad Autónoma de Puebla, pp.117–46.

Holloway, John (1996), "Un capital, muchos estados", *Política y Estado en el pensamiento moderno*, edited by Gerardo Avalos Tenorio and María Dolores París, Mexico City: UAM-Xochimilco.

Holloway, John (2010), *Cambiar el mundo sin tomar el poder*, Mexico City: Sísifo Ediciones.

Holloway, John (2017), "El debate sobre la derivación del Estado. Una reflexión reminiscente", *Estado y capital. El debate alemán sobre la derivación del Estado*, edited by Alberto Bonnet and Adrián Piva, Buenos Aires: Herramienta Ediciones, pp. 39–46.

Holloway, John, and Sol Picciotto (1978), "Introduction: Towards a Materialist Theory of the State", *State and Capital: A Marxist Debate*, edited by John Holloway and Sol Picciotto, London: Edward Arnold, pp. 1–31.

Inclán, Daniel (2018), "Violencia y diseño de territorios. La relación negada de la economía contemporánea en América Latina", *De Raíz Diversa*, vol. 5, no. 9, pp. 21–42.

Instituto Nacional de Estadística y Geografía (2022), "Defunciones por homicidios", available at https://www.inegi.org.mx/sistemas/olap/proyectos/bd/continuas/mortalidad/defuncioneshom.asp. Last accessed on 20 June 2022.

Kessler, Gabriel, and Gonzalo Assusa (2020), *Pobreza desigualdad y exclusión social*, Buenos Aires: Jefatura de Gabinete de Ministros.

Mészàros, Itzvan (1999), *Más allá del capital*, Caracas: Vadell Hnos.

Mezzadra, Sandro (2011), "The Topicality of Prehistory: A New Reading of Marx's Analysis of 'So-Called Primitive Accumulation'", *Rethinking Marxism*, vol. 23, no. 3, pp. 302–21.

Modonesi, Massimo (2015), "Fin de la hegemonía progresista y giro regresivo en América Latina. Una contribución gramsciana al debate sobre el fin de ciclo", *Viento Sur*, vol. 142, pp. 23–30.

Moncayo C., Víctor Manuel (2012), "¿Cómo aproximarnos al Estado en América Latina?", *El Estado en América Latina: Continuidades y rupturas*, edited by Mabel Thwaites Rey, Santiago: CLACSO, pp. 19–49.

Morton, Adam David (2010), "Reflections on Uneven Development: Mexican Revolution, Primitive Accumulation, Passive Revolution", *Latin American Perspectives*, vol. 37, no. 170, pp. 7–34.

Navarro Trujillo, Mina Lorena, and Lucia Linsalata (2020), "Más allá de la retórica anti-neoliberal: ofensiva extractivista y megaproyectos en tiempos de la Cuarta Transformación", *Bajo el Volcán*, vol. 1, no. 2, pp. 329–66.

Negri, Antonio (2003), *La forma-Estado*, Madrid: Akal.

Paley, Dawn (2014), *Drug War Capitalism*, Oakland: AK Press.

Perfil (2019), "Alberto Fernández apunta al bolsillo: 'Tenemos que volver a prender la economía'", 5 July, available at https://www.perfil.com/noticias/politica/alberto-fernandez-apunta-al-bolsillo-tenemos-que-volver-a-prender-la-economia.phtml. Last accessed on 27 June 2022.

Presidencia de México (2019a), "Plan Nacional de Desarrollo 2019-2024", 30 April, available at https://lopezobrador.org.mx/wp-content/uploads/2019/05/PLAN-NACIONAL-DE-DESARROLLO-2019-2024.pdf. Last accessed on 20 June 2022.

Presidencia de México (2019b), "100 compromisos del presidente Andrés Manuel López Obrador a un año del triunfo", available at https://presidente.gob.mx/100-compromisos-del-presidente-andres-manuel-lopez-obrador-a-un-ano-del-triunfo/. Last accessed on 20 June 2022.

Robles, Amelia (2021), "Vaca Muerta. Fracking y sismos: comunidades mapuche cortan acceso a yacimientos", *La Izquierda Diario*, 11 August, available at https://www.laizquierdadiario.com/Fracking-y-sismos-comunidades-mapuche-cortan-acceso-a-yacimientos. Last accessed on 20 June 2022.

Ryan, Matthew DJ (2019), "Interrogating 'Authoritarian Neoliberalism': The Problem of Periodization", *Competition & Change*, vol. 23, no. 2, pp. 116–37.

Salama, Pierre (1979), "El Estado capitalista como abstracción real", *Críticas de la economía política*, Mexico: El Caballito, pp. 117–46.

Scholz, Roswitha (2019), *El patriarcado productor de mercancías y otros textos*, Santiago: Pensamiento & Batalla.

Secretaría de Gobernación (2020), "Búsqueda e identificación de Personas Desaparecidas", 30 September, available at https://www.gob.mx/cnb/documentos/informe-sobre-busqueda-e-identificacion-de-personas-desaparecidas-en-el-pais. Last accessed on 20 June 2022.

Secretaría de Gobernación (2021), "Búsqueda e identificación de Personas Desaparecidas", 8 April, available at http://www.alejandroencinas.mx/wp-content/uploads/2021/04/INFORMEBÚSQUEDA8ABRIL2021.pdf. Last accessed on 20 June 2022.

Solorio, Israel, Joel Ortega, Raúl Romero, and Jorge Guzman (2021), "AMLO's Populism in Mexico and the Framing of the Extractivist Agenda: The Construction of the Hegemony of the People Without the Indigenous Voices", *Zeitschrift für Vergleichende Politikwissenschaft*, vol. 15, pp. 249–73.

Svampa, Maristella (2019), *Neo-extractivism in Latin America: Socio-environmental Conflicts, the Territorial Turn, and New Political Narratives*, Cambridge: Cambridge University Press.

Toussaint, Eric (2019), *The Debt System: A History of Sovereign Debts and their Repudiation*, Chicago: Haymarket Books.

Vázquez, Duplat, Ana María (ed.) (2017), *Extractivismo urbano: debates para una construcción colectiva de las ciudades*, Buenos Aires: Rosa Luxemburg Stiftung.

Vergara-Camus, Leandro, and Cristóbal Kay (2017), "The Agrarian Political Economy of Left-Wing Governments in Latin America: Agribusiness, Peasants, and the Limits of Neo-Developmentalism", *Journal of Agrarian Change*, vol. 17, pp. 415–37.

Agrarian Neoliberalism, Authoritarianism, and the Political Reactions from below in Southern Africa

Boaventura Monjane

Introduction

The current neoliberal moment is characterized by the rise of a new wave of authoritarian and populist politics (Scoones et al. 2017; Chacko 2018; Babones 2018; De la Torre 2018; Halmai 2019). Ian Scoones et al. (2017) noted that a new political moment is underway, characterized by the rise of various forms of authoritarian populism. Torcuato Di Tella (1965) defines populism as a political discourse that "enjoys the support of the mass of the urban working class and/or peasantry, but ... does not result from the autonomous organisational power of either of these two sectors" (ibid., 47). Marc Edelman (2020, 2) notes that authoritarian populism almost always has the following characteristics: (1) a claim to represent or advocate for 'the people', the latter typically defined in exclusionary terms; (2) a political base composed of multiple classes; (3) contempt for traditional political and economic elites and their cultural cosmopolitanism; (4) hatred and repressive policies toward stigmatized others at home; and (5) distrust of opponents abroad who are deemed 'threatening'.

Generally, one of the ways in which populism and authoritarianism are expressed and exercised is through the rise of a powerful 'big man' who mobilizes the masses for racist, misogynistic, xenophobic, and nationalist agendas (Sinha 2021; Bello 2018; Curato 2016). Common features of authoritarian populism are that it often bypasses, undermines, or captures democratic institutions while using them to legitimize its dominance, centralize power, and suppress or severely limit dissent (Scoones et al. 2017, 3).

Although the 'big man' characteristic of authoritarian populism is also observable—in cases such as Zimbabwe's former President Robert Mugabe, Angola's former President José Eduardo dos Santos, Tanzania's late President John Magufuli, and, to a lesser extent, Mozambique's former President Armando Guebuza—authoritarian populism in Southern Africa is generally associated with liberation movements that have secured political power as governments. They are said to like using populist positions as a means of legitimizing their power by appealing to the ongoing struggle against foreign domination, thus marketing themselves as the only true alternative for a better future and keeping themselves in power through authoritarian means. When politically challenged, they employ populist discourse, accusing their opponents of being remote agents of imperialism seeking regime change as an instrument of foreign agendas (Melber 2018; Wesso 2021). However, more than the 'big man', it is usually the 'liberation parties' that exercise authoritarianism in the region: FRELIMO in Mozambique, ZANU-PF in Zimbabwe, the ANC in South Africa, and the MPLA in Angola, to name a few.

This chapter brings a regional perspective from Southern Africa. It places emphasis on the countryside, where a deepening of neoliberal agrarian policies is taking place in an authoritarian way, especially in the enforcement of these policies. Just as public law can be 'weaponized' to incrementally hollow out democratic rule (Daly 2019), agrarian policies are being designed to push neoliberal agendas. This is shaping new agrarian relations and struggles, especially in terms of access to and control of land and other natural resources. Looking at Mozambique, Zimbabwe, and South Africa, the chapter discusses agrarian neoliberalism and develops a concept of agrarian authoritarianism to explore the nuances of another dimension of authoritarianism. The chapter also deals with how agrarian authoritarianism is confronted by agrarian movements. Based on long-term field research in those countries, I look at the work of three agrarian movements, namely UNAC in Mozambique, ZIMSOFF, and the FSC in South Africa. One of the characteristics of the agrarian movements in this study is their theoretical contribution to articulating ideas that challenge the current food regime and propose alternatives to it. One such contribution includes the creation of concepts that arise from struggles (Santos and Meneses, 2014), such as agroecology, family agriculture, and food sovereignty.

The chapter is part of my PhD research, in which I compared these three countries and movements. These countries and movements were chosen for several reasons. The first reason is my epistemic proximity to these movements and their struggles through my previous role as an activist and part of the global peasant movement La Via Campesina, to which these movements belong. The second reason is the fact that in these countries the issue of land and agrarian reform remains central to people's struggles: while UNAC in Mozambique is fighting to preserve the gains of the land reform implemented upon independence and subsequent laws guaranteeing land rights to the peasantry, the struggles in Zimbabwe are focused on preventing the reversal of a land reform implemented in the early 2000s, which resolved a historical exclusion of Indigenous people from access to productive land by white British farmers. In South Africa the struggles centre on the demands of the agrarian movements, including the FSC, for agrarian reform to address the persistent agrarian structure that still exists, based on a dualism in which a few white farming families control almost all productive farmland. The third reason, particularly for this chapter, is my argument that these struggles constitute counter-strategies against agrarian authoritarianism. They seek rural and agrarian emancipation. If we consider the centrality of land in the lives of most people in Southern Africa to their dignity, livelihood, social reproduction, and belonging, struggles to defend or for access to land show the continuing importance of land as a political and economic resource (Yeros 2012).

Figure 1. Map of Southern Africa, including the author's research sites.

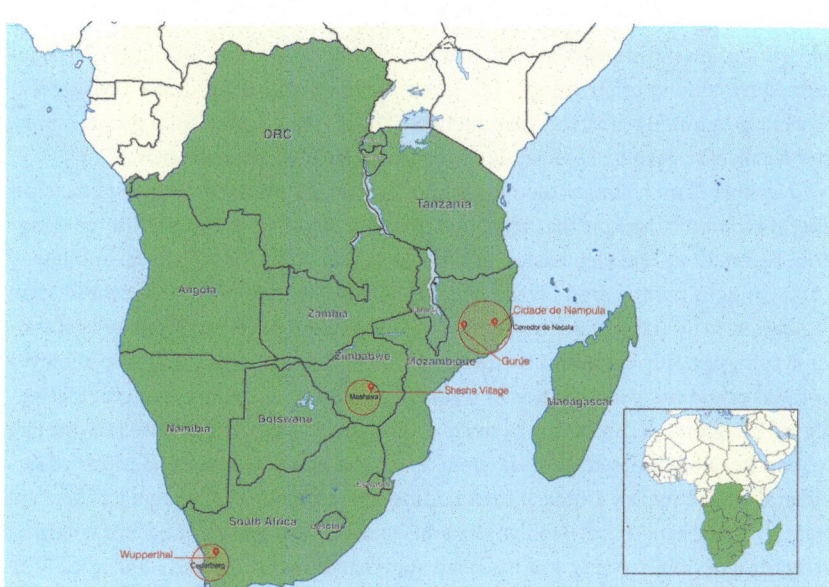

Map illustration: Rubinho Mulungo

After this introduction, I first provide a context for understanding land and agrarian policies in Southern Africa in the context of neoliberalism, which lays the basis for the subsequent section in which I conceptualize agrarian authoritarianism. Third, I show the struggles of the selected agrarian movements in the three countries while discussing how those struggles confront agrarian authoritarianism.

Land and Agrarian Policies under Neoliberalism in Southern Africa

Southern Africa's agrarian structure, class dynamics, and politics have been shaped by successive and interlocking dynamics of colonialism, Apartheid, socialism, civil wars, and the advent of neoliberalism (Van den Berg 1987; O'Laughlin 1996; Saunders and Caramento 2017). Beginning with the adoption of the Washington Consensus starting in the late 1980s—especially in Mozambique and Zimbabwe—the neoliberal process went through several phases. While South Africa's democracy was born neoliberal in nature (with the end of Apartheid in 1994), Mozambique and Zimbabwe experienced the following progression: firstly, the neoliberalism of the 1980s and 1990s, characterized by capitalist restructuring through economic adjustment programmes; then the neoliberalism of the 2000s and 2010s, characterized by, among other things, the intensification of foreign direct investment, especially in mining, and the introduction of large-scale agricultural programmes; and finally, the current neoliberal moment with its authoritarian turn.

Neoliberalism is understood in this chapter as the updated version of classical liberal economic thought that prevailed in the United States and the United Kingdom before the Great Depression of the 1930s (Kotz 2002, 2003; Grewal and Purdy 2014; Quiggin 2018), based on the belief that capitalism requires substantial state regulation to be viable. Neoliberal theory asserts that a largely unregulated capitalist system not only embodies the ideal of free individual choice, but also achieves optimal economic performance in terms of efficiency, economic growth, technological progress, and distributive justice (Kotz 2002). While being a class project relying heavily on the state (Briziarelli 2011), the policy recommendations of neoliberalism are mainly aimed at dismantling the remnants of the regulated welfare state. In Southern Africa, neoliberalism has been characterized by the massive privatization of public assets and has been supported financially and ideologically by the Bretton Woods Institutions (Bond 2008).

In sectors such as energy and agriculture, the introduction and implementation of neoliberal policies has, on the one hand, been accompanied by the process of financialization, and on the other by the promotion of foreign direct investment. In recent years, various agricultural and extractivist-based investment projects have been proposed and/or implemented in the region, leading to conflicts over land and the displacement of rural farming communities, as has been the case in Mozambique (Wise 2016; Rodrigues, Cardoso, and Monjane 2018). Some authors point to the scramble for large tracts of land and water for further expansion of sugar and biofuel production, and later for mineral and energy extraction (coal, natural gas, and oil), guided by a neoliberal compass (Castel-Branco 2014; Manfredi 2017; Moyo, Chambati, and Yeros 2019).

The agrarian sector in Southern Africa is among those that have suffered most from the consequences of neoliberalism.[1] The wedge between governments and small-scale food producers was further reinforced during this neoliberal phase with the implementation of neoliberal agrarian policies. The imposition of land-based agricultural investments in specific regions of the countries concerned resulted in the expropriation of rural people's land. In Mozambique, in the last two decades, megaprojects by multinational companies expropriated hundreds of thousands of hectares from local peasants; consequently, a lot of people were displaced (Monjane and Bruna 2020). Neoliberalism has long dominated the land and agricultural sectors in Zimbabwe. This was partly why attempts to implement land reform in Zimbabwe failed: because it was market-oriented. It was only in the early 2000s that a major break in the agrarian structure occurred, when a popular land occupation movement resulted in radical land reform in the country, which forced a white minority of the agrarian capitalist class to cede land to Indigenous populations who had been landless for a long period (Cliffe et al. 2011; Hanlon, Manjengwa, and Smart 2013).

The land and agrarian structure in South Africa is, to all intents and purposes, much more skewed than in Mozambique and Zimbabwe. A report on land distribution showed that 67 percent of agricultural land belongs to a few white commercial farmers (Monjane 2021a). The South African state has done too little to address this inequality, opting instead to adopt the 'willing buyer- willing seller' market-based land reform. The willing seller-willing buyer approach generally refers to an entirely voluntary transaction between a seller and a buyer. In the South African context, this transaction takes the form of negotiations between landowners who wish to sell their land and government officials acting on behalf of the intended beneficiaries of the land (Dlamini 2007, 9). Edward Lahiff (2007) has demonstrated that the willing buyer-willing seller policy that was adopted at the end of Apartheid was not nearly as successful in redressing the underprivileged position of the peasantry in South Africa. He posits that the country's market-led agrarian reform was influenced by the World Bank and enjoyed the support of landowners and elements within the ruling ANC committed to maintaining the structure of large-scale, capital-intensive farming. This, he adds, contributed to the discrimination

---

1 In Mozambique, for example, the World Bank imposed the liberalization of the cashew sector in 1995 as a condition for granting loans to the country. Mozambique was one of the largest producers of this crop in the world. This condition resulted in the loss of 10,000 jobs, which were never restored despite several attempts in the sector. In this context, the international financial institutions have also imposed constraints to force the implementation of agricultural programmes that give priority to agribusiness and the promotion of industrial inputs (Barroso, Castel-Branco, and Monjane, 2020).

against peasants, most of whom live in poverty which prevents them from producing much to cover their own needs, or forces them to 'depeasantize' or 'semi-proletarianize' on white-owned farms, in mines, and in industries in urban centres. Perhaps more importantly, he adds that, besides the rate of land transfer being so low, where land was transferred, "it has made little positive impact on livelihoods or on the wider rural economy" (ibid., 1577).

The neoliberal state of affairs in South Africa has generated debate among scholars, analysts, and politicians about the future of South Africa amid such glaring (social, economic, racial, and agrarian) imbalances. Some argue that the noncommittal posture taken by the state in South Africa to refuse to implement land reform has led to the rise of radical and populist elements adopting the land reform agenda as a political springboard. For instance, according to Ward Anseeuw and Ntombifuthi Mathebula (2008), the formation and relative popularity of the Economic Freedom Fighters (EFF)[2] and the intensification of the ideas of expropriation of land from white agrarian capitalists without compensation, can be attributed to unresolved issues in South African society. Indeed, the EFF has been riding on the absence of a genuinely nationalist approach to the land and agrarian reform agenda. The party has presented a new model of radicalized land reform ideology, one with great potential to impact South African land reform through its seemingly pro-poor inclination.

The land and policy orientation in (these) countries of Southern Africa is, as we have seen, thoroughly neoliberal and directed against poor, smallholder agriculture and rural areas, even if it takes place in a different political-economic context. We see this in the case of Mozambique, where the government has been "'interventionist,' 'authoritarian,' and 'coercive' for engaging in projects that belittled customary African practices, forcibly relocating people, or threatening the livelihoods of the peasantry" (Pitcher 2012, 19), with policies falling in line with undemocratic forms of governance.

Conceptualizing Agrarian Authoritarianism

As the contemporary world has witnessed an increasing rise of authoritarian politics and a deepening of neoliberalism, itself characterized by a shift in the relationship between the state and the market, recent scholarship has built on these concepts to discuss the extent and impact of populism, authoritarianism, and right-wing politics, as well as their relationship to the countryside. Daniela Andrade (2020) has argued that even in modern democracies, authoritarian populism is

---

2   A new political party, the third biggest in the South African parliament, which uses populist tactics.

much more common, with 21st-century states adopting what the author calls "populism from above and below". With reference to Latin America, Alberto Alonso-Fradejas (2021) posits that the profit motive has led to an alliance between the state and economic elites, whose interests now converge at the expense of the masses. He refers to this as authoritarian corporate populism, which has contributed to the emergence of the state-business axis that increasingly determines and controls the distribution of resources in its favour.

Another way in which political authoritarianism and populism can arguably be exercised is through public policies and legislation that are introduced and enforced in undemocratic ways to impose a particular elite and class agenda. In Southern Africa, this can be observed in the land and agricultural sectors, where the enforcement of neoliberal agrarian policies, and the contradictions that arise from their implementation, are shaping new agrarian relations and struggles in the current neoliberal moment. In light of this, I propose the notion of 'agrarian authoritarianism' to locate neoliberal policymaking and policy imposition. The concept presents an understanding of the current dynamics of the rise of agrarian neoliberalism, characterized by the anti-democratic imposition of exclusionary agrarian policies—policies which are hostile to the majority of small-scale food producers. Grounded in neoliberalism, agrarian authoritarianism is a concerted push to increase productivity through large-scale agricultural interventions at all costs. What is authoritarian about it? Authoritarianism is not in the pro-market policies per se. It is the way in which governments pursue them that is authoritarian. In other words, while neoliberalism is not inherently authoritarian, neoliberalism constitutes a fertile ground for authoritarianism. I therefore subscribe to Thomas Biebricher's account that "neoliberalism and authoritarianism are not intrinsically tied to each other, but even less are they inherently opposed to one another" (Biebricher 2020, 1).

Here, populism is used in the ways in which, discursively and rhetorically, policies are presented to the populations by governmental and political elites, often in a paternalistic manner. It is a populist approach since they claim to benefit small-scale producers when, by and large, they benefit more the agribusiness class and the so-called 'emerging farmers'.

Recently, the Zimbabwean government has been pushing for the return of massive agricultural investments which will likely lead to land concentration by capital and the alienation of smallholder farmers from the land, even though the government claims that this will benefit everyone. Taking a neoliberal and populist stand, the government in Zimbabwe is eager to raise capital via rents and in the process promote industrial capitalist agriculture. This has prompted the government to push for smallholder farmers to embark on joint ventures with foreign capital, while simultaneously crafting a new narrative that land should be given to those who have ample financial and material resources and can fully utilize this, thus promoting the line that the country is now 'open for business' (Monjane and Tramel 2018; Mazwi et al. 2018). This is an example of the triumph of agrarian neoliberalism, which threatens to reverse the land reform from the early 2000s that put an end to unjust colonial land inequality, as will be explored later in this chapter.

Agrarian authoritarianism has been a common trend in other countries of Southern Africa. While promoting the language of investment, governments undermine contentions from grassroots and civil society. Over the last decade, the region of Southern Africa has, in fact, seen civic spaces shrink. In particular, there has been a growing trend for the state to use the criminal justice system to vilify, criminalize, and suppress activists, leaders, and local communities who are fighting for the right to land, denouncing land grabs, exposing corruption, and advocating for inclusive socio-economic development (Monjane 2021b; Wesso 2021).

While neoliberalism provokes resistance (Harris 2003; Lahiff, Borras, and Kay 2007; Stromquist and Sanyal 2013; Tilzey 2020), its authoritarian turn requires new strategies, since neoliberalism has already undermined the class basis for resistance in the countryside. The following section deals with the ways in which agrarian authoritarianism is contested, resisted, and fought against by agrarian movements.

Confronting Agrarian Authoritarianism: The Building of Emancipatory Alternatives

The peasantry has been the major victim of neoliberal agrarian policies, and agrarian movements have organized to object to and challenge them. In fact, contemporary rural movements worldwide are becoming an organizing centre for the masses of rural poor discarded by neoliberalism (Moyo and Yeros 2005, 45). The contradictions inherent to the penetration and development of agrarian capital in the countryside provoke a variety of political reactions from below; in most cases, agrarian movements emerged as a result of these developments in Southern Africa.

The political and social events of the 1980s, with particular attention to the introduction of economic adjustment programmes, sowed the seeds for agrarian movements across Southern Africa, even though rural and peasant organizing and political agency has a longer history prior to neoliberalism. The circumstances surrounding the emergence of these movements are found in the rise and penetration of agrarian capital in the countryside, with the tacit support of governments. This has led to the progressive and systematic rural- and urban-based land struggles to confront agrarian capital. In this section, three cases of resistance to agrarian authoritarianism are discussed.

An Overview of the Movements: UNAC, the FSC, and ZIMSOFF

The National Union of Peasants in Mozambique (UNAC) emerged in the late 1980s, when Mozambique adopted the Bretton Woods structural adjustment programmes (SAPs), where peasants found it necessary to initiate a national movement to defend the interests of the peasantry, as changes in economic strategy threatened the cooperative movement. UNAC has a membership of about 150,000 small and medium-scale farmers, organized in associations and cooperatives across the country.

The Right to Agrarian Reform for Food Sovereignty Campaign (FSC) was launched in 2008, when the world food crisis reached its peak as agrarian capital was intensifying its actions in the countryside, and social and agrarian inequalities were being exacerbated in South Africa. The FSC's interests are broader than just getting access to land for people. "The broad focus of the movement is to challenge neoliberal capitalism and its manifestations at local level, at regional level, at national level. That would include getting access to agricultural land that has been very unequally distributed in South Africa".[3] The FSC constituency consists of landless people, small-scale farmers, women and youth in rural areas, farm-workers, farm dwellers, people with insecure tenure (mostly on municipality and church-owned land), people on forestry land, and landless people in the Western and Northern Cape provinces.

The Zimbabwe Smallholder Organic Farmers' Forum (ZIMSOFF) was founded in 2002, but its origins predate this period. Two crucial ZIMSOFF leaders and founders, Nelson Mudzingwa and Elizabeth Mpofu, worked and played important roles in the Association of Zimbabwe Traditional Environmental Conservationists (AZTREC), a group formed in 1985 around an alliance of spirit mediums, chiefs, and veterans of the liberation struggle. The then-leader of the association, comrade Cosmas Gonese (as he was referred to by the interviewees), served as the secretary-general of the Zimbabwe National Liberation War Veterans Association (ZNLWVA) and was, as is widely recognized, the architect of the land occupation movement that would force land reform in the early 2000s in Zimbabwe. ZIMSOFF seeks to improve the livelihoods of organized and empowered smallholder farmers in Zimbabwe who are practicing sustainable and viable ecological agriculture. It also seeks to strengthen and expand a dynamic alliance of smallholder farmer organizations promoting a movement towards agroecological farming. The ZIMSOFF membership is drawn from farmers who are practising sustainable agriculture, such as agroecology and organic farming, and it has a membership of about 20,000 small to medium-scale farmers all over the country.

---

3   Harry May, programme manager of the Surplus People's Project, interview with the author, Cape Town, March 2018.

Movements in the Struggle against Agrarian Authoritarianism

ProSAVANA in Mozambique

The Programme for Agricultural Development of the Tropical Savannah in Mozambique (ProSAVANA) was a large-scale agrarian programme, introduced in the beginning of the 2010s, aiming to transform the agricultural sector to be more investment and business-friendly (Monjane and Bruna 2020). It was a triangular programme, as it was proposed by the governments of Mozambique, Brazil, and Japan. The idea was that Brazil would transfer technology and its models for agribusiness and monoculture (especially soybeans), that Japan would provide funding and guarantee markets for agricultural products, and that Mozambique would sign off on the project by 'granting' the land.

The main objective of this agrarian programme was to increase agricultural productivity, targeting millions of hectares in north-central Mozambique. The programme was earmarked to have access to 14 million hectares in the Nacala Corridor, and this constituted just half of the total 36 million hectares of arable land in Mozambique (Clements and Fernandes 2013; Monjane and Bruna 2020). The imposition of ProSAVANA in the 2010s sparked debates on whose interest this megaproject was serving. Details revealed that the governments of Japan, Brazil, and Mozambique were secretly paving the way for a massive land grab in Northern Mozambique (Justiça Ambiental et al. 2013, 1). This led to increased agitation and a sense of class solidarity among peasant organizations and other civil society groups. These formed a collective front against the government policy to prioritize agribusiness at the expense of peasant production.

UNAC was at the forefront in the emergence of the Campanha não ao ProSAVANA (No to ProSAVANA Campaign, NPC). The NPC presented an organized and explicit opposition to not only the ProSAVANA project itself, but also to the fundamental paradigm of rural development promoted by the project. The NPC, while demanding the discontinuation of ProSAVANA, also proposed alternatives to rural and agricultural development, such as the push for food sovereignty and support for family farming. The NPC did not limit itself to mobilizing among peasants but kept on incorporating more members from diversified sectors within Mozambique and abroad to include Brazilian agrarian movements and NGOs, as well as Japanese activists and academics, with the campaign soon becoming a transnational movement.

This demonstrates that opposition to neoliberal agrarian policies is taking on a new dimension, one which has a scope which is wider and beyond that of the peasantry. This indicates that the land question in Mozambique, like in Southern Africa, is a highly sensitive and emotive one within the peasant community and broader agrarian civil society. Beyond this, the land question offers interesting insights into a range of wider issues on the policy environment in Mozambique. The land issue therefore overlaps into issues pertaining to political legitimacy and the Mozambican case, much like the land issue in Zimbabwe, demonstrates the complexities of land reform where capital interests are vested, as well as the potential implications in terms of economic performance and political legitimacy. The Mozambican case also emphasizes the negative implications of policymaking from above in the context of land reform. The hibernation—and later termination—of ProSAVANA can be explained as emerging from a combination of tactics intrinsic to the NPC, namely: (1) active agency from below; (2) an inter-sector civil society alliance; (3) communication, publicity, and media strategy; (4) transnationalization of the struggle; and (5) proposal of alternatives to confront the dominant narratives (Monjane and Bruna 2020).

Demands for land reform in South Africa

In South Africa, struggles for land reform are diverse and directed against different actors, but most demands are directed at the state. This is despite the fact that the state owns only tiny portions of the land compared to agrarian capitalists and churches. A case in point is Wupperthal, a village on the west coast of the municipality of Cederberg in the Western Cape. There, a group of landless peasant farmers, members of the Moravian Church (which owns the land), and residents of Wupperthal have been overtly challenging the leadership of the church for more than a decade and pushing for democratization of the land. The fact that churches own immense tracts of land in South Africa does not constitute a novelty. What makes this struggle for land unique is how a small group of believers has dared to protest against a rigid and highly hierarchical faith-based organization, claiming ownership of land in a context where the norm has been for people to relegate their agency to the church's leadership for almost everything. The Concerned Moravians, as the FSC members in Wupperthal call themselves, have on the contrary been articulating their demands very creatively by asking the church's leadership to "take care of the souls and leave the land to the people".[4]

As one land activist put it:

> Generally, the gospel of the church has been a very effective tranquilizer to radical ideas. Partly because they feel that they are a part of [the church]. The first character of their belonging of the church tranquilizes them and they do not see the church as an oppressor. The whole church setup is based on accepting inequal-

---

4   Dennis Bronton, leader of the Concerned Moravians, interview with the author, Wupperthal, March 2018.

ity. How the hierarchy applies in church is much stronger than anywhere else. The issue of resistance can easily be framed as blasphemy.[5]

The tricky part of dealing with the church is that most people generally tend to accept the church as an organizing force, as some sources confirmed to me. This is because churches usually have all kinds of projects that support people in obtaining some form of income; this was the case for the Moravian Church in South Africa (MCSA) in Wupperthal. This equally explains why the Concerned Moravians are few in number (around 20) in a community with around 200 members.

Some would associate neoliberalism with financial institutions and the broader private sector, revealing that there was a blind spot when it came to faith-based organizations like churches. It turns out that churches have strong ties to private investors, to whom land is rented, and to financial institutions. This is the case in Wupperthal, where private landlords are allocated land to grow tea for the markets. As a landowning class, the churches in South Africa (especially the Catholic and Moravian churches) are also promoters and beneficiaries of agrarian authoritarianism.

Among their demands, the Concerned Moravians have always clarified that the fight is not against the church itself but rather the business holding thereof, MCiSA Holdings: "the business side of the church is not allowing us to have full control of the land to do our own thing".[6] This has had a number of consequences for the members. One of these happens to be the refusal of the Cederberg Municipality to support the cooperative that the Concerned Moravians have set up in Wupperthal, because the government cannot implement projects on 'private' land without the church's consent. MCiSA registered a holding in 2011 as an agriculture and tourism company.

Protecting land reform and building an agroecology 'revolution'

Before ZIMSOFF was founded, a number of the current ZIMSOFF leaders settled in Shashe, Zimbabwe as part of the Association of Zimbabwe Traditional Environmental Conservationists (AZTREC) that occupied what used to be a cattle range in the early 2000s. AZTREC had been working with chiefs, traditional leaders, war veterans, ex-combatants, village heads, and government departments for almost two decades prior to the land occupation movement that forced land reform in the early 2000s in Zimbabwe. The group that occupied Shashe was composed of more than 100 people and was led by Cosmas Gonese, the founder and director of

---

5 Siviwe Mdoda, land activist, interview with the author, Cape Town, February 2018.
6 Dennis Bronton, leader of the Concerned Moravians, interview with the author, Wupperthal, March 2018.

AZTREC who was also then secretary-general of the Zimbabwe National Liberation War Veterans Association (ZNLWVA). Today, more than 400 families live in Shashe.

ZIMSOFF is implementing an agroecology project that has been inspiring the Shashe community as well as other farmers' organizations across the country. ZIMSOFF has been showing impressive work in restoring indigenous seeds, especially of grain. The organization has focused on introducing ecologically-sensitive measures to their agriculture. This radical shift towards agriculture demonstrated that land reform transcended the boundaries of mere revolution as it transformed the mindsets of the farming community. This represents a major shift in peasant consciousness beyond encouraging land occupation and reveals the multiple layers of land reform in Zimbabwe.

These projects and activities have led to a considerable transformation in the agroecological outlook of Shashe, and livelihoods have been enhanced. Farmers have turned a ranch into the successful agricultural settlement that it is today. It is now a centre of excellence, an agricultural "college without walls". Shashe has become a successful pilot project which other clusters in Zimbabwe are emulating.[7]

Table 1. Transformation in Shashe, over 20 years

	Before 2000	2010	2020
Land Size	1000 ha arable	3104 ha arable	3104 ha arable
	14,020 ha for grazing	11,916 ha for grazing	11,916 ha for grazing
	Total: 15,020 ha	**Total**: 15,020 ha	**Total**: 15,020 ha
Livestock	Cattle: 3000	Cattle: 6000	Cattle: 7000
	Goats: 200	Goats: 10000	Goats: 10000
	Sheep: 150	Sheep: 500	Sheep: 1000
		Pigs: 500	Pigs: 1000
	Chickens (layers and broilers)	Donkeys, dogs, and poultry	Donkeys, dogs, poultry, rabbits, and fish
Food Crops	Cereals	Cereals (maize, sorghum, millet)	Cereals (maize, sorghum, millet)
	Pulses	Pulses (peanuts, cowpea, beans)	Pulses (peanuts, cowpea, beans)

---

7   Nelson Mudzingwa, ZIMSOFF national coordinator and Shashe resident, interview with the author, Shashe, January 2019.

			Oils (sunflower, soya, sesame)	Oils (sunflower, soya, sesame)
			Vegetables and fruits	Vegetables and fruits
Number of Families		50	400	550
Employment/ Jobs Created		Farmworkers: 50	Plot holders: 400	Plot holders: 500
			Casual workers: 100	Casual workers: 200
			Civil servants: 50	Civil servants: 100
			Total: 550	**Total**: 800
Other Business/ Economic Activities		Beef production	Beef production	Beef production
		Poultry production (chicken and eggs)	Poultry production (chicken and eggs)	Poultry production (chicken and eggs)
		Dairy	Piggery	Piggery
		Sheep and goats	Sheep and goats	Sheep and goats
				Fish production
			Crop production	Crop production
			Entrepreneurship	Entrepreneurship

Source: compiled by Brain Muvindi and the author, based on surveys and data provided by a government official in Mashava village, Masvingo Province

In many ways, livelihoods have been transformed and pre-existing poverty has been considerably reversed. This transformation is to be viewed as part of an emancipatory and counter-strategy to agrarian neoliberalism and authoritarianism. In this way, ZIMSOFF may be viewed as an agent for challenging the neoliberal way of approaching agricultural development and transformation. Furthermore, it is an agent for pushing the agenda of ensuring food sovereignty using local communities and resources. The case of Shashe allows us to look at the capacity for transformation and the resilience of peasant farmers who have come to have access to land (as a result of agrarian reform) to be able to transcend agrarian capital, which dominated the agrarian structure of Shashe prior to the land occupation and subsequent implementation of the land reform programme.

***

I make sense of the data presented above in the conclusion.

Conclusion

As shown in this paper, one of the ways in which authoritarianism is exercised is through the manner in which policy is introduced and imposed, undemocratically, and its implementation forcibly, to push for a certain agenda for the benefit of a certain class (agrarian capital, state elites) to the detriment of the poor. The chapter has presented the struggles of three agrarian movements in Southern Africa. Opposing the hegemony of (agrarian) capitalism (Santos and Rodríguez-Garavito 2003, 23), these struggles confront agrarian authoritarianism, in that they refuse to accept enclosure of their farmland by agrarian capital, either to preserve land reform, to prevent reversals, or to push for an end to landlordship through land democratization. These struggles are equally confronting right-wing tendencies within and outside of governments. In the case of Mozambique, these tendencies can be identified in the form of propaganda by members of the governing FRELIMO party, when promoting the state's efforts to intensify a neoliberal agrarian agenda.

Resistance to agrarian authoritarianism goes beyond resisting unjust agrarian policies, as it also resists authoritarian aspects that are linked to other types of social injustice, such as the denial of the right to say no to large-scale agriculture and agrarian technologies, and hostility towards 'the rural' and 'rural life', as well as the social exclusion of rural populations.

Struggles against agrarian authoritarianism can happen reactively as well as proactively. They are reactive when contradictions arising from the implementation of the activities of (already penetrating) agrarian capital begin to manifest. Those contradictions include the exploitation of the peasantry, land grabs and encroachment on their land, or their exclusion from enjoying the benefits of accessing land (as has been the focus of the FSC in South Africa). They may emerge in a proactive manner, in the absence of agrarian capital, when measures, actions, and activities are implemented by agrarian movements and communities to build an alternative rural life in those communities. This is the case in Shashe where neoliberal agrarian policies and agrarian capital would not find fertile grounds for their imposition. In other words, the presence of rural emancipation expels agrarian authoritarianism. The pursuit of rural emancipation is therefore at the core of the struggle against agrarian authoritarianism. These struggles are, in fact, not merely for access of and control over land. Movements envisage the transformation of society, putting organizational alternatives that allow communities to share available resources. Shashe, in Zimbabwe, is an example of what rural emancipation could look like: today hundreds of families share farming and grazing plots, producing a variety of food crops (grains, cereals, legumes, vegetables, fruit trees), medicinal plants, roots, and livestock (cows, sheep, goats, pigs, chickens, turkeys). A significant number of them save, reproduce, and reuse their own seeds (mostly for grains and cereals). Shashe peasant farmers have more control over both the means and processes of production, as they depend very minimally on external inputs.

References

Alonso-Fradejas, A. (2021), "The Rise of Authoritarian Corporate Populism", *Latin American Perspectives*, 17 May, available at https://journals.sagepub.com/doi/full/10.1177/0094582X211004912. Last accessed on 24 June 2022.

Andrade, D. (2020), "Populism from above and below: the path to regression in Brazil", *The Journal of Peasant Studies*, vol. 47, no. 7, pp. 1–27.

Anseeuw, W., and N. Mathebula (2008), *Evaluating land reform's contribution to South Africa's pro-poor growth pattern*, Pretoria: Cirad, available at https://agritrop.cirad.fr/547917/1/document_547917.pdf. Last accessed on 6 June 2022.

Babones, S. (2018), *The New Authoritarianism: Trump, Populism, and the Tyranny of Experts*, Medford, MA; Cambridge: Polity Press.

Barroso, E., R. Castel-Branco, and B. Monjane (2020), "Fast-tracking Financialization: International Financial Institutions' Responses to the Covid-19 Pandemic in Mozambique", Policy Document, Maputo and Johannesburg: Alternactiva and WoMin, available at https://rightsindevelopment.uwazi.io/api/files/1642438947267zlzycd2ooq.pdf. Last accessed on 25 February 2022.

Bello, W. (2018), "Counterrevolution, the countryside and the middle classes: lessons from five countries", *The Journal of Peasant Studies*, vol. 45, no. 1, pp. 21–58.

Biebricher, T. (2020), "Neoliberalism and Authoritarianism", *Global Perspectives*, vol. 1, no. 1.

Bond, P. (2008), "End of neoliberalism? Sorry, Not Yet", *Monthly Review Press*, 26 December, available at https://mronline.org/2008/12/26/end-of-neoliberalism-sorry-not-yet/. Last accessed on 7 June 2022.

Briziarelli, M. (2011), "Neoliberalism as a State-Centric Class Project: The Italian Case", *Continuum*, vol. 25, no. 1, pp. 5–17.

Castel-Branco, C. N. (2014), "Growth, capital accumulation and economic porosity in Mozambique: social losses, private gains", *Review of African Political Economy*, vol. 41, no. 1, pp. 26–48.

Chacko, P. (2018), "The Right Turn in India: Authoritarianism, Populism and Neoliberalisation", *Journal of Contemporary Asia*, vol. 48, no. 4, pp. 541–65.

Clements, E. A., and B. M. Fernandes (2013), "Land Grabbing, Agribusiness and the Peasantry in Brazil and Mozambique", *Agrarian South: Journal of Political Economy*, vol. 2, no. 1, pp. 41–69.

Cliffe, L., J. Alexander, B. Cousins, and R. Gaidzanwa (2011), "An overview of Fast Track Land Reform in Zimbabwe: Editorial Introduction", *Journal of Peasant Studies*, vol. 38, no. 5, pp. 907–38.

Curato, N. (2016), "Flirting with Authoritarian Fantasies? Rodrigo Duterte and the New Terms of Philippine Populism", *Journal of Contemporary Asia*, vol. 47, no. 1, pp. 142–53.

Daly, T. G. (2019), "Democratic Decay: Conceptualising an Emerging Research Field", *Hague Journal of the Rule of Law*, vol. 11, no. 1, pp. 9–36.

De la Torre, C. (2018), *Routledge Handbook of Global Populism*, 1st edition, Abingdon: Taylor & Francis.

Di Tella, T. (1965), "Populism and Reform in Latin America", *Obstacles to Change in Latin America*, edited by Claudio Veliz, Cambridge: Cambridge University Press.

Dlamini, S. (2007), "Taking land reform seriously: From willing seller-willing buyer to expropriation", master's thesis, University of Cape Town, 2008.

Edelman, M. (2020), "From 'populist moment' to authoritarian era: challenges, dangers, possibilities", *The Journal of Peasant Studies*, vol. 47, no. 7, pp. 1–27.

Edelman, M., and S. M. Borras (2016), *Political Dynamics of Transnational Agrarian Movements*, Rugby: Practical Action Publishing.

Grewal, D., and J. Purdy (2014), "Introduction: Law and Neoliberalism", *Law and Contemporary Problems*, vol. 77, no. 4, pp. 1–24.

Halmai, G. (2019), "Populism, authoritarianism and constitutionalism", *German Law Journal*, vol. 20, no. 3, pp. 296–313.

Hanlon, J., J. Manjengwa, and T. Smart (2013), *Zimbabwe Takes Back Its Land*, Sterling VA: Kumarian Press.

Harris, R. L. (2003), "Popular Resistance to Globalization and Neoliberalism in Latin America", *Journal of Developing Societies*, vol. 19, no. 2/3, pp. 365–426.

Justiça Ambiental et al. (2013), "Joint Statement: Leaked copy of the Master Plan for the ProSAVANA programme in Northern Mozambique confirms the worst", Maputo, 29 April, available at http://cade.cocolog-nifty.com/file/20130429eng.pdf. Last accessed on 24 June 2022.

Kotz, D. (2002), "Globalization and Neoliberalism", *Rethinking Marxism*, vol. 14, no. 2, pp. 64–79.

Kotz, D. (2003), "Neoliberalism and the US Economic Expansion of the 1990s", *Monthly Review*, vol. 54, no. 11, pp. 15–33.

Lahiff, E. (2007), "'Willing buyer, willing seller': South Africa's failed experiment in market-led agrarian reform", *Third World Quarterly*, vol. 28, no. 8, pp. 1577–97.

Lahiff, E., S. M. Borras, and C. Kay (2007), "Market-led agrarian reform: policies, performance and prospects", *Third World Quarterly*, vol. 28, no. 8, pp. 1417–36.

Manfredi, M. (2017), "Foreign Direct Investments in African lands: The Chinese and EU different approach", *DPCE Online*, vol. 30, no. 2, available at http://www.dpceonline.it/index.php/dpceonline/article/view/385. Last accessed on 7 June 2022.

Mazwi, F., N. Tekwa, W. Chambati and G. T. Mudimu (2018), "Locating the position of peasants under the 'New Dispensation'", *Policy Brief*, vol. 3, no. 1, Harare: Sam Moyo African Institute for Agrarian Studies, available at http://aiastrust.org/wp-content/uploads/2015/10/SMAIAS-Policy-Brief_-Locating-the-position-of-peasants-under-the-New-Dispensation.pdf. Last accessed on 29 June 2022.

Melber, H. (2018), "Populism in Southern Africa under liberation movements as governments", *Review of African Political Economy*, vol. 45, no. 158, pp. 678–86.

Monjane, B. (2020), "Confronting State Authoritarianism: Civil Society and Community-Based Solidarity in Southern Africa", *Pandemic Solidarity: Mutual Aid During the Covid-19 Crisis*, edited by Marina Sitrin and Colectiva Sembrar, London: Pluto Press, 2020, pp. 105–20.

Monjane, B. (2021a), "Rural Struggles and Emancipation in Southern Africa: Agrarian Neoliberalism, Peasants' Movements and Rural Politics in Mozambique, South Africa and Zimbabwe", PhD thesis, Faculty of Economics, University of Coimbra, 2021, available at https://estudogeral.uc.pt/bitstream/10316/95250/3/2021%20MONJANE-PhD%20Thesis-Deposited%2015.04.2021.pdf. Last accessed on 7 June 2022.

Monjane, B. (2021b), "Introduction: Land as a Central Element in Rural Organisation and Agency in Southern Africa", *We Rise for Our Land: Land Struggles and Repression in Southern Africa*, Ottawa: Daraja Press, 2021.

Monjane, B., and N. Bruna (2020), "Confronting Agrarian Authoritarianism: Dynamics of Resistance to PROSAVANA in Mozambique", *The Journal of Peasant Studies*, vol. 47, no. 1, pp. 69–94.

Monjane, B., and S. Tramel (2018), "Transforming the politics of food in Southern Africa, from the local to the global", *Amandla Magazine*, 19 October, available at https://aidc.org.za/transforming-politics-food-southern-africa-local-global/. Last accessed on 7 June 2022.

Moyo, S., and P. Yeros (2005), "Introduction", *Reclaiming the Land: The Resurgence of Rural Movements in Africa, Asia and Latin America*, edited by Moyo and Yeros, London: Zed Books, pp. 1–7.

Moyo, S., W. Chambati, and P. Yeros (2019), "Land and Natural Resources in Zimbabwe: Scramble and Resistance", *Reclaiming Africa: Advances in African Economic, Social and Political Development*, edited by Moyo, Yeros, and P. Jha, Singapore: Springer, 2019.

Ntsebeza, L. (2005), "Land tenure reform in South Africa: A focus on the Moravian Church land in the Western Cape", *Competing Jurisdictions: Settling land claims in Africa*, edited by S. Evers, M. Spierenburg, and H. Wels, Leiden: Koninklijke Brill, 2005.

O'Laughlin, B. (1996), "Through a Divided Glass: Dualism, Class and the Agrarian Question in Mozambique", *The Journal of Peasant Studies*, vol. 23, no. 4, pp. 1–39.

Pitcher, M. A. (1996), "Recreating colonialism or reconstructing the state? Privatisation and politics in Mozambique", *Journal of Southern African Studies*, vol. 22, no. 1, pp. 49–74.

Provost, C. (2013), "La Via Campesina celebrates 20 years of standing up for food sovereignty", *The Guardian*, 17 June 2013, available at https://www.theguardian.com/global-development/poverty-matters/2013/jun/17/la-via-campesina-food-sovereignty. Last accessed on 7 June 2022.

Quiggin, J. (2018), "Neoliberalism: Rise, Decline and Future prospects", *The SAGE Handbook of Neoliberalism*, London: Sage, 2018.

Rodrigues, S. da P., D. Cardoso, and B. Monjane (2018), "Moçambique: terra de todos, terra de alguns", *Público*, 19 August, available at https://www.publico.pt/2018/08/19/mundo/reportagem/terra-de-todos-terra-de-alguns-1840612. Last accessed on 24 June 2022.

Santos, B. S., and C. Rodríguez-Garavito (2005), "Law, politics, and the subaltern in counter-hegemonic globalization", *Law and Globalization from Below: Towards a Cosmopolitan Legality*, Cambridge: Cambridge University Press, pp. 1–26.

Santos, B. S., and M. P. Meneses (2014), *Epistemologías del Sur*, Madrid: Akal, 2014.

Saunders, R., and A. Caramento (2017), "An extractive developmental state in Southern Africa? The cases of Zambia and Zimbabwe", *Third World Quarterly*, vol. 39, no. 6, pp. 1166–90.

Scoones, I., M. Edelman, S. M. Borras, R. Hall, W. Wolford, and B. White (2017), "Emancipatory rural politics: confronting authoritarian populism", *The Journal of Peasant Studies*, vol. 45, no 1, pp. 1–20.

Sinha, S. (2021), "'Strong leaders', authoritarian populism and Indian developmentalism: The Modi moment in historical context", *Geoforum*, vol. 124, pp. 320–33.

Stromquist, N. P., and A. Sanyal (2013), "Student resistance to neoliberalism in Chile", *International Studies in Sociology of Education*, vol. 23, no. 2, pp. 152–78.

Tilzey, M. (2020), "From neoliberalism to national developmentalism? Contested agrarian imaginaries of a postneoliberal future for food and farming", *Journal of Agrarian Change*, vol. 21, no. 1, pp. 180–201, available at https://onlinelibrary.wiley.com/doi/abs/10.1111/joac.12379. Last accessed on 29 June 2022.

Van den Berg, J. (1987), "A Peasant Form of Production: Wage-Dependent Agriculture in Southern Mozambique", *Canadian Journal of African Studies / Revue Canadienne Des Études Africaines*, vol. 21, no. 3, pp. 375–89.

Wesso, R. (2021), "Shrinking or Shifting? The Closing of Civil Society Space in Five Countries in Southern Africa", *We Rise for Our Land: Land Struggles and Repression in Southern Africa*, edited by B. Monjane, Ottawa: Daraja Press.

Wise, T. A. (2016), "Land Grab Update: Mozambique, Africa Still in the Crosshairs", *Food Tank*, 2016, available at https://foodtank.com/news/2016/10/land-grab-update-mozambique-africa-still-in-the-crosshairs/. Last accessed on 7 June 2022.

Yeros, P. (2012), "Book Review: Henry Bernstein (2010). *Class Dynamics of Agrarian Change*", *Agrarian South: Journal of Political Economy*, vol. 1 no. 3, pp. 341–46.

Factors of Resilience and Constraint in the Myanmar Resistance Movement

Nwet Kay Khine

The year 2021 was marked by frequent military coups in some parts of the Global South. Democratic decline and backsliding have in general been a rising trend in recent years, but the coup in Myanmar marked a full return to dictatorship and showed what the collapse of democracy looks like. In a global retreat of democracy, regional institutions like the African Union (AU) and the Association of Southeast Asian Nations (ASEAN) are taking multilateral restrictive measures to oppose the unconstitutional attempts to seize power. Despite international pressure, the Myanmar military's actions against the will of its own people suggest that authoritarian-led democratization can soon be reversed, once a democratic experiment designed by authoritarian elites fails to yield an intended result (Ye Myo Hein 2022). Conversely, a taste of democracy which lasted only a decade is driving millions of Myanmar citizens towards a revolutionary fight against the dictators. This paper investigates the trajectory of Myanmar's revolution in the light of Arjun Appadurai's five dimensions of globalization, which are comprised of ethnoscapes, technoscapes, financescapes, mediascapes, and ideoscapes. It argues that multi-layered interactions in all five 'scapes' added some extra layers of resilience to the newfound mass political awakening and unprecedented resistance to the military coup. Likewise, these intertwining processes enable the junta to preserve its "Khaki" or "military capitalism" (McCarthy 2019, 1–2) and allow a shift towards digital authoritarianism for a fascist resurgence. Members of the resistance are aiming to end the hegemonic military rule in society as well as fascist thoughts vehemently fuelled by the military's propaganda, but how close they are to their objectives remains questionable one year after the coup.

Myanmar's People's Resistance in Light of Appadurai's Five Dimensions of Globalization

Since independence, Myanmar has experienced a coup d'état three times. In the previous coups of 1962 and 1988, the military quickly quashed the resistance through arrests, forced disappearances, and persecution. In 1962, the public did not loudly object to the Revolutionary Council led by General Ne Win as the media remained "non-committal on the end of Nu's cabinet" (Taylor 2015, 256), which was then a democratically-elected government. Many leading politicians of the incumbent government were then also arrested (Win Tint Tun 2007), a tactic which was repeated in 2021. Additionally, when the 1988 uprising occurred, the signs of revolt were not as widespread as in the nationwide protests of 2021. Compared with past political awareness, the sheer scale of resistance was in stark contrast to what the junta expected, as they later admitted (Irrawaddy 2021a). For example, *Nway-u*, or Spring Revolution, is a new national movement (Bynum 2021) named after the first month that marks the beginning of *Nway* (spring) in this monsoon region of Southeast Asia (GlobalPost 2011). Mass participation in the Civil Disobedience Movement (CDM) is claimed by the activists as an effective strategy in showing defiance against the military power. People took part in various forms of CDM including banging pots and pans, peaceful street demonstrations, labour strikes, consumer boycotts against the military's industries, withholding the paying of taxes and bills, non-participation in social and religious gatherings arranged by law enforcement bodies, and so on. At the peak of the demonstrations in February and March of 2021, 22 million people took to the streets (Goldman 2021).

Suppressing the resistance, the State Administrative Council, which was newly formed by the coup leaders, continued to impose its will on the people that a fresh election would be held within two years. This time, the politicians guess a new election will look like the one in 2010, in which the Union Solidarity and Development Party (a proxy of the military, USDP) was handed victory without any significant opposition. In forming an alliance with some 30 small political parties, the military has been trying to eliminate the legitimate role of the elected party of the last election, the National League for Democracy (NLD). Prompt actions were taken to prove the alleged voting fraud of the NLD and proposals were made to restructure the political landscape by introducing a proportional representation (PR) system. After being defeated in the last two general elections, the military is now convinced that the USDP cannot compete with the NLD's popularity and thus the best solution will be changing the electoral system. The first-past-the-post (FPTP) system enshrined in the 2008 Constitution turned out to be the wrong pick, and the military Union Election Commission (UEC), which is now in the pocket of the junta, started discussions on switching to the proportional representation system. However, it does not mean that the military will relinquish its permanent quota, 25 percent of the total seats. The majority of Myanmar citizens object to the return of military rule and are pouring their support into insurgency groups, which were immediately founded as a fall-back option for urban protest. Within one year, the number of new groups that have been involved in guerrilla war all over the country has increased to 462 and local data analysts estimate that approximately 35,000 members are waging war (Burma Monitor 2022). Ethnic armed organizations (EAOs) which represented nearly 40 percent of the marginalized ethnic-minority population[1] are trying to seize the moment for strengthening their autonomy; there is however no common strategy. Many of them joined the side of the National Unity Government (NUG) in exile to build a central command for defence, while some are still in the position of waiting and seeing before forging a strategic alliance with either side of the war (ICG 2022).

Since March 2021, thousands of citizens have chosen armed struggle, aiming to put the military atrocities to an end and to develop a common future with various ethnic groups—probably in a newly-defined territory. Armed resistance was indeed not an unfamiliar strategy as Myanmar has seen a different generation of armed resistance especially during the peak of communist insurgency in the 1960s and again during the founding of the students' army after the 1988 uprising. Notwithstanding historical experience, the 2021 resistance seems to have some new enabling factors that have increased citizens' openness to revolutionary ideas and actions. The country's experience during the years of reform featured a new reconfiguration of society which resulted in movements of people, things, and ideas in different aspects of globalization. This sort of mobility can be better explained within the framework of the five 'scapes' coined by Appadurai (1990, 296). It should be stressed that the disjunctive and unpredictable nature of the five dimensions—ethnoscapes, technoscapes, ideoscapes, financescapes, and mediascapes—can help to induce a social climate that gives birth to a brand-new generation of revolutionaries. Nonetheless, it would be wrong to imply that Myanmar is free from the dark side of the kind of global cultural flow that Appadurai mentioned.

Appadurai defines 'ethnoscape' as the landscape of persons who constitute the shifting world in which we live. Such a shifting population appears to affect the politics both within a country and between countries to an unprecedented degree. In his view, 'technoscape' refers to the global configuration of ever-fluid technology, and movements of technologies across national boundaries. A 'financescape' is

---

[1] There are 14 provinces in Myanmar. Seven provinces, known as regions, in central Myanmar are populated by Bamar (also known as Burmans) which is the biggest ethnic group of the country. The other seven provinces, known as states, belong to seven major ethnic groups: Kachin, Karenni, Karen, Chin, Mon, Rakhine, and Shan.

a financial landscape that allows for the movement of currencies, capital, and securities both within national borders and transnationally. In a 'mediascape', we see the flow of images of the world involving many "complicated inflections" through different types of production mode, audiences, and the interests of the owners. Finally, 'ideoscape' is defined as a concept related to the "ideologies of states and the counter-ideologies of movements oriented to capturing state power or a piece of it" (Appadurai 1990, 299). In the early stages of revolution, the impact of global cultural flow that is embodied in Appadurai's notion of 'scape' has a profound impact on the people's participation. Movements of people, things, technology, capital, and ideologies across national boundaries have to a large extent benefitted the people's resistance strategies. The following discussions will highlight how the trajectory of the Spring Revolution is influenced by the flows of the five 'scapes'.

Ethnoscapes

The presence of a Myanmar diaspora across the world is a key factor that complements the forming of domestic resistance. Because of deep poverty at home, emigration from Myanmar grew rapidly in the last three decades. Persecution, landlessness, unemployment, and dispossession of land back home are key reasons for citizens of Myanmar to leave for neighbouring countries and beyond. Although emigration had mostly been concentrated in the ethnic-minority provinces of border areas in the 1990s, it has been spreading to the whole country in the last decade. Many Myanmar people are becoming climate refugees as agriculture no longer offers favourable jobs in the villages of Central Myanmar and the lower part of the Irrawaddy Delta due to the changing weather patterns and frequent incidences of natural disaster. Neoliberal agrarian reform, which sped up after the opening-up of the country, also resulted in a higher degree of landlessness, and foreign remittances have been a survival income for many families (Borras et al. 2020, 20). In 2018, approximately 3.1 million people from Myanmar officially lived outside of the country (Akee and Kapur 2017, 3). Since the coup, Myanmar migrant workers and diaspora communities in various parts of the world have been channelling both moral and financial support back to the resistance movement, although COVID-19 is still another struggle they are facing (Nachemson 2021). Taking advantage of regional proximity, Myanmar migrant workers in Thailand and Singapore often organized monthly donation activities (AAC 2021). Local representatives are also appointed to take care of collecting money in different counties. With the help of social media, these kinds of self-help groups can expand their networks in their respective countries. Similar networks of Myanmar diasporic communities in Europe, the US, the UK, and East Asia are working voluntarily to raise funds that either go to the NUG or are directly distributed through local contacts that link up with recipient communities. In addition to fundraising activities, diasporic communities are also active in advocacy for Myanmar's struggle in the foreign media and directly engaging with policymakers in the host countries regarding support for Myanmar's democracy. While this new politics is taking shape, the members of the exile community—who had to flee the country because of their political activism and participation in different resistance movements—have also contributed to the mass movement. The effort of diasporic communities bore fruit in some cases as they were able to put the Myanmar issue on the international stage through sanction advocacy and cultural activities (Cabot 2022). Back in 1988, Myanmar diasporic communities were almost non-existent in many parts of the world and domestic revolutionaries could hardly expect substantial financial support of the kind recently seen in the mass purchase of NUG bonds from Myanmar nationals abroad. Crowdfunding among the diaspora has been a major source of funds to fulfil the needs of the internally-displaced people as well as weaponry for the revolutionaries. In recent months, the military junta's State Administration Council (SAC) has been targeting the Myanmar diasporic community with threats to withdraw the passports of high-profile dissidents among Myanmar communities, while at the same time attempting to persuade other citizens to come back to the country (Dziedzic 2021). The spirit of self-sacrifice among individuals and collective solidarity in enduring intimidation and repression is the foundation of success in any revolution. Although struggle back home is not an issue which is 'out of sight, out of mind' for the Myanmar diaspora, it is also critical for them not to fall for the usual dictatorship tactics which aim to bring the diasporic communities over to the side of the SAC by bribing, dividing, and co-opting the diasporic opposition forces (De Mesquita, Bueno, and Smith 2011).

Technoscape

Since reintegration with the international community back in 2011, Myanmar had seen rapid changes in mechanical and informational technology. New technological changes are seen by the military as the 'breeding ground' of the rebels. In comparison with past dissidents, the young generation nowadays are hard to control as they are often more familiar with technology which plays an essential role in modern-day living. In previous democratic uprisings, it was easier to silence the domestic voices as it was only necessary to enforce print censorship and stop leaflets and posters from being distributed in universities—which were usually the centre of protest—and on the main streets. In the 1990s, before the internet was introduced, the army's textbook strategy to control all communication devices was simply to control ownership of fax machines and satellite receivers for television. Now one can imagine the impact of the dramatic rise in imported technologies in a rapidly-integrating society. In comparison with the printing machine of the old days, a modern-day smartphone has the capacity to disseminate a message many times faster; on the other hand, it has also served the purposes of hatemongers targeting ethnic minorities in recent years. For the resistance movement, tech transformation offers a better means to cope with authoritarian methods of deterring public mobilization. At the peak of the protests, the mobile data cut imposed for days did not stop protesters from gathering, as they could still receive messages via different kinds of encrypted messages coming through peer-to-peer mesh networks or Bluetooth services. Since 2014, Myanmar has had 'leapfrog' growth in mobile phone penetration and there were 69.43 million mobile connections in Myanmar as of January 2021. The number of internet users dramatically increased from less than 1 percent of the population in 2012 to 53.1 percent of the population (23.65 million) in 2021. It is not surprising to see the surge of social media users, which reached approximately 29 million (Phyo Thiri Lwin 2021). All these figures demonstrate how technology can contribute to the revolutionaries' call for action. It also brought a generation who are ready to challenge the military rule with tech solutions in providing counterstrategies. However, the increase in internet users cannot be automatically interpreted as an increase in digital literacy. In a networked propaganda society (Benkler, Faris, and Roberts 2018, 1), sadly misinformation and disinformation are often applied as weapons by all warring parties to differing degrees (Rao and Atmakuri 2021). A quote which is popularly attributed to US Senator Hiram Johnson is one which is still relevant to the Myanmar battlefield of today: "in war, truth is the first casualty". Still, one of the resilience factors of the revolution is the volunteerism of tech experts who are willing to give tech advice to the NUG and activist communities. Digital security tools are important for the activists to protect themselves from the state-sponsored cyber-attacks[2] when a series of new apps and games are also invented by tech volunteers for various revolutionary purposes—from fundraising and building CDM networks, to scouting and consumer boycotts.

Financescape

The improvement of banking in Myanmar was prioritized for public service reform and gained attention from international financial institutions. In the circumstances surrounding the coup, Myanmar has seen a dramatic decline of banking services because of a brief participation of banking staff in the CDM, and later because of restrictions imposed by the Central Bank to reduce the amount of withdrawable cash—not only at the bank but also at ATMs. The subsequent crisis in the financial sector killed public trust in the banking sector, although the banks forced

---

2   Anonymous interview with representatives from a technical support group to the revolution, virtual meeting, 21 October 2021.

their staff to return to the workplace. Because of the past experiences in three periods of demonetarization—in 1964, 1985, and 1987 respectively—traditionally the Myanmar population has lost trust in saving cash and prefers to invest in gold or property. Only in the last few years could the bank attract more customers as the 2008 Constitution guarantees that the state shall not demonetize the currency that is in legal circulation, according to Section 36 (Myanmar News Agency 2021). However, as the coup itself provided evidence that the military was no longer respecting the Constitution, public trust in government and private institutions dropped overnight and the likelihood of a run on the banks appeared imminent for several weeks. Finally, the banking sector did not collapse as expected, but even by 2022, it had not returned to normal functioning. Yet, it is still a larger sector than the Myanmar banking of the 1990s.

Around the uprising of 1988, there were only four government banks, while no private bank was allowed to operate since the nationalization of private banks (including foreign ones) happened in 1962. Financial transactions across borders were possible only for those who had official income in foreign countries or export-import companies. Myanmar citizens could not use international financial services such as Visa or Mastercard until 2014, and the gradual introduction of ATMs in different cities was only introduced after 2011. Thein Sein's administration (2011–15) decided to allow citizens to receive foreign remittances through private banks. However, with the introduction of online banking and digital purse services in the last five years, people can now move their money more easily than ever. Until the bank crisis caused by the coup, four state-owned banks, 27 domestic private banks, and 13 foreign banks were operating in Myanmar (GIZ 2021). The use of digital payment services, which were newly introduced in 2016, has grown dramatically, with one survey noting an increase from one percent to eighty percent of users within four years (Salai Tun Tun 2020). Fluid financial exchange among the people is considered a threat by the military who want to control transactions and stop people from channelling resources to any resistance groups or individuals. Nevertheless, fundraisers attempted more creative ways to avoid the freezing of accounts, interrupted flow of financing, and seizing of financial assets. Numerous tactics for generating funds for the war are being employed including adopting cryptocurrency, crowdfunding, establishing social media click-to-donate platforms through streaming videos, or simply running grocery stores. The NUG shadow government also introduced a new kind of digital lottery after the people started to boycott the military-run lottery. Some initiated raffle tickets for international sales and later people started buying the revolution bond of the NUG. These are cross-border sales and tickets were mainly purchased through the Myanmar diaspora abroad and their trusted domestic networks. Regardless of user controls and unreliable services, it is impossible that the government can trace every transaction that is involved in funding the anti-junta insurgency.

Mediascapes

The flow of news and information across borders and cultures has been significantly changing society in the last ten years. Before the pre-printing censorship was lifted in 2012, all media outlets were supposed to submit manuscripts to the Press Scrutiny and Registration Division (Fuller 2012), which was then known as the 'butcher of the news'. Censors working under the Ministry of Home Affairs or the Ministry of Information were assigned to scrutinize every line and paragraph, and to block all content which was deemed to harm the interests of the ruling class or to express the views of the dissidents. In those days, it was common that the voice of the foreign press was quickly silenced as foreign correspondents who were critical of the new regime were hardly allowed to report on events in Myanmar. By telling lies to the international community, the military government could hide the real picture on the ground. In 2021, it was harder to hide the local events from international scrutiny as the internet has broken the barrier between foreign journalists and local correspondents. At the local level, a new form of networked media ecosystem has recently emerged and this enables smaller regional media outlets to work together to share inputs and provide effective news distribution channels. In comparison with the state of access to information in the aftermath of the coup in 1988, people certainly have greater access to reliable news and a diverse range of views nowadays. In 1988, the military's suppression of the social movement's media was harsh and diminished all significant opposition voices within the first month of the coup. This kind of curbing of media freedom is no longer feasible in 2021. Nevertheless, the coup leaders are still enthusiastic about telling their version of truth to the public, but the 'official' narrative of the state-run media reports are mocked by anti-coup members of the public through the use of memes on social media platforms.. A decade of freedom without pre-printing censorship seems to have been sufficient experience for the people to see the function of a more pluralistic media landscape. The popularity of digital media outlets, which are largely operated in a clandestine manner, and a dramatic rise in the number of followers are indicators that both the news media and the readers show defiance against the military's censorship and propaganda.

Ideoscapes

Enlightenment worldviews such as freedom, rights, equality, representation, and democracy are embodied in the slogans of the movement as they were pronounced in 1988. However, this time, the meanings of these slogans have become more penetrating in both rural and urban lives. To a large extent, the recent expansion of civil society has played a key role in widening space for discursive forums around values and ideas. The role of civil society organizations (CSOs) became more vi-brant after 2008's Cyclone Nargis demanded an increase in contributions from NGOs and opened the door for the wider participation of local activists and organizations in the humanitarian—and later in the development—sector. The interconnection between Western versions of NGOs and traditional civic organizations in Myanmar became more intensified, although the NGO approaches were often criticized as lacking an in-depth understanding of the local situation, as well as for lacking effectiveness and accountability in their activities. Nevertheless, Myanmar to a certain extent benefitted from the expanding space for debate and discursive culture. In parallel with Western donors' initiatives for public education on human rights, democracy, and civic values, many public intellectuals, organizations, and labour and student unions also sought alternative ideas to counteract neoliberal shortcomings (Bello 2018, 64) brought about by the new government's development agenda. After nascent democratic reform was disturbed by an ultranationalist movement sponsored by the military and Buddhist monks that led to a series of incidents of sectarian violence in 2013, many local groups started to deliberate upon ideas for social justice, human rights, and pluralistic values in society. With constant pressure from the successive governments, their attempts were neither strong nor influential enough to prevent the Rohingya crisis in Rakhine State, nor discrimination in other ethnic-minority areas. Yet, many started to seek out local collaboration and external technical support through expanding networks to ease the right-wing pressure. There were times and opportunities for local groups to promote the importance of the ideas of human rights and human dignity as well as to learn from past mistakes and shortcomings in the face of the complexity of the ultranationalist movement. In 2021, the resistance movement received intellectual input from a collective of activist organizations and human rights defenders which had been working in a range of social justice issues before the coup. Many leaders of the resistance movement came from activist backgrounds, and they were well positioned to use existing networks accumulated throughout the reform years. Some of them had been engaging in anti-racism campaigns, rights for ethnic minorities, environmental justice, protecting human rights, promoting democracy education, and so on, thus 'knitting together' different layers of society.[3] A form of ideological alliance among activists, educators, the CDM, labour unions, politicians, and ethnic-minority leaders later emerged which would be utilized in any future federal democratic country under a newly-drafted Federal Democracy Charter (CRPH 2021) Naturally, all these de-territorialized transformations occurred to the above five dimensions in a way that was disjunctive, undirected, and non-linear (Hannigan 2002).

---

3   Interview with a leader from the General Strike Committee of Nationalities (GSCN), 30 July 2021.

The Flow of Global Interconnectedness and Recent Impact on the Coup Leaders

When it comes to the impacts of globalization, authoritarian governments in many Southeast Asian countries have, for their own survival, embraced different features of interconnectivity within the five 'scapes' (Morgenbesser 2020, 3–4). In Myanmar, the military—which claims to be the custodian of the state—is at the centre of this aforementioned "fundamental disjuncture between economy, culture, and politics" (Appadurai 1990, 328). The transformation of the five 'scapes' serves to sustain the authoritarian leaders' legitimacy and authoritarian power by acquiring new techniques for silencing political opponents. The opening-up of the country after 2010 provided the military with more opportunities to enrich themselves from the greater global economic and technological interconnectedness, while 'khaki capitalism' would provide reliable resources for their attempts to steer towards ultranationalist ideological dominance (Kironska and Peng 2021, 16).

The Military's Silencing of Opposition by Taking Advantage of the Changing Ethnoscape

The coup had resulted in a dramatic increase in the movement of people especially in ethnic-minority areas. The number of internally displaced people in Myanmar has doubled to 800,000 (UN News 2022). After the military killed over 1500 on the streets and arrested another 10,000, many had to flee to the EAO-controlled areas. When the coup happened, the people's resistance near and far has shaken the ethnopolitical landscape as the country started to question where they stand in terms of the revolution. According to Appadurai, ethnoscapes "appear to affect the politics of (and between) nations to a hitherto unprecedented degree" (Appadurai 1990, 297). Under these circumstances, the people begged the EAOs to stand together with the revolutionary cause; many accepted, while others remained committed to neutrality. To reduce the momentum of the resistance, the military leaders have been wooing EAOs while attacking the NUG's legitimacy. The military seems to know how to exploit the existing ethnoscape within the territory of Myanmar and the emerging movement beyond the border.

Throughout the troubled history, 'divide and rule' is the main successful strategy of the army, as it exploits social cracks in ethnic-minority communities. While they allow the pro-ceasefire ethnic-minority elites to exploit natural resources, they continue to undermine the rights of other ethnic minorities who confirmed their continued resistance to the military power. Despite the mediation of foreign organizations such as the Nippon Foundation (Asahi Shimbun 2021) and assistance from the Thai Government (Bangkok Post 2021a), its intended ceasefire never appeared to make sense. In the past, the divide and rule tactics of the military proved effective in slowing down the process of unifying all ethnic minorities to build a federal state. Ardeth Thawnghmung (2021) reminds us that Myanmar's National Unity forces—now winning the support of a majority of the Myanmar population, representing over 60 percent of the population—must overcome the divide and rule tactics of the military. The military has been repeatedly trying to persuade ethnic-minority groups by means of diplomacy through inviting them to bilateral meetings, and official commemorations and ceremonies. However, its heavy-handed practices on the battlefield in areas controlled by EAOs are showing that its propaganda, which promises a more inclusive future for the country, is not genuine.

Buying the support of the EAOs by means of a 'carrot and stick' policy, the military anticipates that the emerging rebel forces led by the NUG can be crushed in a short time and the planned fresh election will provide a result which is to the military's liking. In November 2021, the military's Union Election Commission met with over 50 political parties to convince them that proportional representation would be a legitimate way to strengthen Myanmar's democracy, although the NLD and some influential ethnic-minority parties including the Shan Nationalities League for Democracy (SNLD) were not included. It is believed that now 30 out of over 90 political parties in the country are sided with the junta's rule and their plans for the upcoming election (Irrawaddy 2021b). However the junta's goal to hold an election as planned in August 2023 is unlikely to succeed, provided stability and order cannot be established (Bangkok Post 2021b). The discontent of ethnic minorities with the military does not mean that the NUG is now closer to winning the wholehearted support of all ethnic-minority parties. The NUG, which inherited the reputational risk of the NLD after Aung San Suu Kyi had failed to form an alliance with ethnic-minority groups, is now struggling to convince the ethnic-minority leaders of the sincerity of its enthusiasm for a federal democratic system.

For the hardcore of the armed forces involved in the war, such as the Kachin Independence Army (KIA), Karen National Union (KNU), the Karenni Nationalities Defence Force (KNDF), and the Chin National Defence Force, capitulating to the Tatmadaw (the Myanmar military) was not recognized as an option. Open dialogue with the NUG resulted in a more collaborative central 'command and control' system at a national level, although recent attacks by the military increased the numbers of refugees and resulted in villages burned to ashes. Networks of the Myanmar diaspora and stronger cohesion among all kinds of ethnic minorities across the country have certainly built value-based solidarity for the first time in history. However, it should also be noted that the military has rich experience in the game of divide and rule and is still seeking measures to keep its enemies divided.

The Military's Technoscape Advance: Intense Competition in Virtual and Real Battlefields

In the war with old and new insurgent groups, the military is trying to gain the upper hand, not only in the digital arena, but also 'on the ground' i.e. on the battlefield. The resilience of military rule rested not only on the coercive military might but also on the consent they could trigger in the state-society relationship. Since 2011, the Western world had opened the door wider for engagement with the Myanmar military. Its military-institutional power has been enhanced by different types of collaboration with foreign countries. For instance, while Australia had been supporting the training of Myanmar soldiers in non-combat areas (Stayner and O'Brien 2022), the National Defense Academy of Japan (HRW 2021) had been hosting Myanmar military officials for training in both academic and military courses including combat and arms training. Myanmar has been sending cadets to Russia for weaponry and cybersecurity training. Russia was the source of at least 16 percent of the weaponry procured by Myanmar from 2014–19 (Lukin 2021) and the collaboration has increased even more following the coup. As neither the Parliament nor the executive branch of the NLD government were able to challenge the military's systematic abuses in the last five years, Myanmar had been witnessing increasing violence against civilians even before the coup. Deepening militarization after the coup has led to a dramatic increase in violence with up to a 620 percent increase between 2020 and 2021 (Bynum 2022) reaching the highest civilian death toll from a conflict situation in the last 30 years (Myanmar Media Collective 2022).

Since the outset of war with the Arakan Army which started in 2019, it has been a recurring theme that full internet blackouts have been happening in the combat regions. Since the first month of the coup, the military has banned social media including Facebook and Twitter, and has been restricting web pages by imposing a China-style whitelisting of sites for the general populace. In addition, the SAC has been drafting a new cyber security law that will outlaw the use of VPNs, as seen in many other digital authoritarian states (HRW 2022). To shrink down civic space, the price of a SIM card was subject to a 20-fold increase, and mobile data was charged at a higher price than usual. For some years, the army has been preparing to enhance its online and mobile phone surveillance system by acquiring dual-use technology from Western countries. Even after the Western sanctions following the plight of the Rohingya in 2017, businessmen close to the military circle have in recent years been using their international networks to procure arms and equipment on behalf of the Myanmar military in deals worth millions of dollars. Although the military faced a great loss on the digital battleground, it is trying to defeat the resistance forces through the use of surveillance drones, hacking software, and phone-cracking devices.

Control of the Financescape in a 'Four Cuts' Strategy

In countering armed groups, the coup leaders returned to the 'four cuts' strategy that was persistently applied in the communist counterinsurgency war of the 1960s. In a bid to stamp out the funding, food, intelligence, and recruits that are flowing to the People's Defence Forces, the army is destroying all possible logistical bases owned by civilians. Since the EAOs have limited capacity in terms of combat and logistical support for the People's Defence Forces, the rebels from different regions need direct support from the people, especially for buying weapons and ammunition. A crackdown on the flow of financial support to the rebels came to be effective when the banks chose to cooperate with the junta. Within a few months after the coup they started blocking the financial transactions of those they suspected of being affiliated with the resistance, and even reported these 'suspicious persons' to the security forces (Myanmar Now 2021). As most of the private banks are owned by cronies from military circles, the people do not have many choices, even though they wanted to boycott such services. Once bank accounts and digital wallets of potential donors and fundraisers have been frozen, it also means their personal security is greatly at risk.[4] Meanwhile, the incoming remittance was also closely monitored by the military and a resurgence in the market of illegal remittance has increased the cost of transactions.

The need for fundraisers to be assessed for eligibility by the banks indicates that those who have gained access to capital have a large advantage when it comes to advancing the cause. Although the war has been fought under the leadership of two parallel governments, the weight is with the junta when one takes capital into account as a factor. Historically capital has never been distributed equally "across space and social groups" (Heyman and Campbell 2009, 145). Having unmatched institutional capacity, it is hard for people's movements to survive without a sustainable flow of financing. Hence, it is hard to neglect the fact that the financescape has been given a greater weight among the five 'scapes' and is a vital support for authoritarian resilience. When the NUG had to compete with a ruthless regime that can demand support from crony companies, the NUG itself could hardly manage to mobilize its financial resources in an authorized manner. As Josiah Heyman and Howard Campbell (2009, 140) contended, new patterns of cultural flows suggested by Appadurai should not obscure "new patterns of inequality, especially of political rights while in movement, an inequality that is likely to also affect class relations and social honor". Eventually, the level of risk exposure can also differ between the SAC soldiers and those from the NUG, as financial strength is at the core of formulating war strategies.

---

4 Anonymous interviews with fundraisers, 1 September 2021 to 20 October 2021.

Mediascape for the Dissemination of Far-Right Ideas

Since the coup, the SAC has been steering the ideological state apparatus towards fortifying "Burmanization" (Gray 2018) in a bid for legitimacy. As the military's popularity has sunk to the lowest point in history, Senior General Min Aung Hlaing seriously needed to make efforts to maintain confidence especially within the army. While repeatedly justifying its brutalities as necessary for playing the role of 'the guardian' of the nation and its religion, the core of several speeches of the USDP and army leaders after the coup consisted of the sentiment that the "native Myanmar race, Buddhist religion and cultural identity" are under serious threat by foreign imperialism as well as Islamization.

To sustain its hegemony, Amresh Gunasingham (2019) argued that the Myanmar military has never been hesitant to draw on nationalism to boost its legitimacy through the intrinsic Buddhist majority in society. The military has been exploiting the *Saya-Dagar* (patron-client) relationship by associating with influential Buddhist *Sangha* (clergy) to strengthen its religious and cultural legitimacy. Activities around the pagoda and monasteries have gained more visibility in the media, while the NLD have been blamed for neglecting the Buddhist clergy community in the past five years. Since the NLD did take similar measures to the military, these accusations were unfounded and perhaps also a little ironic (Prasse-Freeman and Ko Kabya 2021, 1–2).

Observing the rise of far-right groups in Myanmar politics, Myat Thu (2021, 201) claims that Myanmar's religious populism never shares the characteristics of left-wing populism. Left-wing populist strategy refers to a process in which politicians incorporate populist ideas as a strategy to address the struggles and demands of society in the name of the people (Venizelos and Stavrakakis 2020). Having a special focus on xenophobia and nativism, Myat Thu insists that the populism utilized by the military is primarily right-wing. When the NLD was dancing to the tune of military appeasement, its leadership failed to acknowledge the consequences of leaning in a far-right direction, especially when it came to dealing with the Rohingya crisis. The military's far-right strategy is indefensible as they stress the continuing exclusion of some ethnic minorities based on their racial purity laws and policies. The perceived threat of a population explosion in neighbouring states was given as justification for restrictive immigration but mobilizing racist monks to preach hate speech has strayed far from the idea of sustaining Buddhist practices and culture as the 'core values' of society. In recent months, the military has been integrating ultranationalist groups into a 'people's militia' strategy. Different brands of ultranationalist groups are being organized in the style of Mussolini's Blackshirts, such as the Pyusawhti militia, to fight against the People's Defence Forces as a paramilitary wing of the army (ICG 2021).

While hundreds of Pyusawhti and military informers are reportedly receiving military training and are heavily involved in tracing the hiding places of the opposition, many new media outlets sprang up from ultranationalist networks. Many of those who are now running the new media outlets and agencies used to work to mobilize the public in anti-NLD rallies in the name of protecting Buddhism. Regular reports on the military-run newspapers and social media channels are targeted at tarnishing the NLD's reputation by labelling them as pro-West, pro-Muslim, and acting as stooges for foreign countries while intentionally degrading Myanmar's culture and national identity. Given this combination of the far-right characteristics of the military regime, Jonathan Saha (2021) even observes that the military's "strategies deployed today recall fascisms past" in different places of the world, although it is still hard to locate Myanmar in the global history and critical discourse of fascism. Nevertheless, he insists "we must name it as fascist". Just as writers like Judith Butler (2017) justify calling Donald Trump a fascist, similar arguments could be levelled at Min Aung Hlaing's plans to move to the far right.

Even before the coup, the army already had a policy of using social media content generators to influence the views of the people. After the coup, the voice of the independent media was silenced. In addition to its monopoly on all branches of the state-run media, military-sponsored racist and anti-democratic content is being distributed widely through social media. The military propaganda agents are well-resourced financially,[5] while independent media outlets are dying as they lack adequate financial resilience, according to media analysts (Burma Monitor 2021). The Tatmadaw also forced their rank and file and associated family members to spread the assigned messages on social media, and even to make attempts to shut down free voices which go against the interests of the military (Reuters 2021). In general, the war makes social media another battlefield. No matter how the regulatory teams of social media companies tried to detect hate speech, through being reported by users, user-generated content during wartime is full of hate messages from every corner of the warring parties, as war—whether for a just purpose or not—is a display of anger. While many major media outlets are being criticized for inciting hate, the reasoning capacity of individual social influencers and public opinion-makers played an important role in shifting from a mob mentality to a crowd with wisdom. The destructive power of social media content cannot be underestimated after Myanmar witnessed the effect of the "We Stand With" campaign (Naw Betty Han 2019) around the time of Aung San Suu Kyi's trip to the International Court of Justice when a majority of the people declared their support for her (Prasse-Freeman and Ko Kabya 2021). The herd mentality in denying accusations

---

5   On 23 October 2021, the SAC announced that they were providing a loan amounting to 15 billion kyat (7 million euros) to the film industry, writers, and media groups who were cooperating with them.

of genocide, killings, and the driving of Rohingya from their homes was later seen as shameful by many social media users, but the cost of ignorance means huge suffering for the Rohingya. Such political manipulation in social media platforms is probable at any time and it triggered a great concern among monitors of online content.

Conclusion

The Myanmar military coup in 2021 marked a new chapter in the relationship between the military and the public. It is impossible to predict the outcome of the people's movement from the current setting of the ongoing revolution. Shifting the balance of power from the military elites to pro-democracy resistance groups is very likely, with a mass awakening in favour of democratic values and anti-racism. The Myanmar people's resistance highlights the fact that globalization fosters some enabling factors (as well as some obstacles) to the pro-democracy movement. Appadurai's theoretical perspective, the five 'scapes'—ethnoscapes, technoscapes, financescapes, mediascapes, and ideoscapes—together serve as an analytical tool to contextualize the effects of the flow of people, finance, technology, and ideas in the ongoing Myanmar revolution. The recent growth of interconnection between Myanmar and abroad energizes the resistance forces from all levels of society. It also creates favourable conditions for the ruling class by facilitating the military's pursuit of eternal supreme power. On the one hand, what will make this revolution succeed or fail is largely influenced by the persistence and tenacity of the Myanmar people living locally and abroad. On the other hand, the military leaders keep sharpening the army's skills, to allow them to play with modern tools and connectivity in order to sustain their ruthless authoritarianism. Upgraded military and information technology help the army to expand its combat capacity as well as its media campaign to scapegoat non-Buddhist, minority-ethnic, and minority-religious groups as part of a populist 'unifying cause' for Myanmar. No matter what the possible revolution's outcome is, it will take time to remove the roots of right-wing authoritarianism as the currently-growing branches gravely threaten the co-existence of different ethnic groups and the independence of the various regions in Myanmar. In a far worse scenario, if the military rule prevails, Myanmar is likely to stand as a breeding ground for new fascism. Alternatively, if civic insurrection can establish a full democracy, Southeast Asia will see that the awakening of the people is the fundamental determinant of the successful anti-authoritarian movement.

References

Aid Alliance Committee (AAC) (2021), "Ye Min appointed by NUG as representative in Thailand", *Facebook*, 14 May, available at https://www.facebook.com/aac.hlakhaing/posts/970209793813787. Last accessed on 17 June 2022.

Akee, Randall, and Devesh Kapur (2017), *Myanmar Remittances*, London: International Growth Centre, available at https://www.theigc.org/wp-content/uploads/2018/06/Akee-and-Kapur-2017-Final-report.pdf. Last accessed on 17 June 2022.

Appadurai, Arjun (1990), "Disjuncture and difference in the global cultural economy", *Theory, Culture & Society*, vol. 7, nos. 2/3, pp. 295–310.

Asahi Shimbun (2021), "Hayashi says government did not arrange Nippon Foundation's Myanmar visit", *The Asahi Shimbun*, 16 November, available at https://www.asahi.com/ajw/articles/14482518. Last accessed on 17 June 2022.

Association for Progressive Communication (2022), "Resist Myanmar's digital coup: Stop the military consolidating digital control", 11 February, available at https://www.apc.org/en/pubs/resist-myanmars-digital-coup-stop-military-consolidating-digital-control. Last accessed on 17 June 2022.

Bangkok Post (2021), "Myanmar Leader writes to PM", 11 February, available at https://www.bangkokpost.com/thailand/politics/2066067/myanmar-leader-writes-to-pm. Last accessed on 17 June 2022.

Bangkok Post (2021), "Myanmar junta says will hold election in August 2023", 24 December, available at https://www.bangkokpost.com/world/2237347/myanmar-junta-says-will-hold-election-in-august-2023. Last accessed on 17 June 2022.

Bello, Walden (2018), *Paradigm Trap*, Yangon, Amsterdam: Transnational Institute, available at https://www.tni.org/files/publication-downloads/paradigmtrap_190718_web.pdf. Last accessed on 17 June 2022.

Benkler, Yochai, Robert Faris, and Hal Roberts (2018), *Network Propaganda: Manipulation, Disinformation, and Radicalization in American Politics*, Oxford University Press.

Borras, Saturnino M., Doi Ra, Jennifer C. Franco, Khu Khu Ju, Khun Oo, Kyar Yin Shell, and Kyaw Thu et al. (2020), *Myanmar's cross-border migrant workers and the Covid-19 pandemic: Their life stories and the social structures shaping them*, Amsterdam: Transnational Institute, available at https://www.tni.org/en/publication/myanmars-cross-border-migrant-workers-and-the-pandemic. Last accessed on 21 June 2022.

Burma Monitor (2021), "Monthly report on social media monitoring", August.

Burma Monitor (2022), "Myanmar Media Update", Zoom presentation, 27 February.

Butler, Judith (2017), "Reflections on Trump", *Society for Cultural Anthropology*, 18 January, available at https://culanth.org/fieldsights/reflections-on-trump. Last accessed on 17 June 2022.

Bynum, Elliott (2021), "Myanmar's Spring Revolution", *Armed Conflict Location & Event Data Project (ACLED)*, 22 July, available at https://acleddata.com/2021/07/22/myanmars-spring-revolution/. Last accessed on 17 June 2022.

Bynum, Elliott (2022), "Continued resistance against the military coup", *Armed Conflict Location & Event Data Project (ACLED)*, available at https://acleddata.com/10-conflicts-to-worry-about-in-2022/myanmar/. Last accessed on 17 June 2022.

Cabot, Cyrielle (2022), "Myanmar coup anniversary: Government in exile urges France to act against junta", *France 24*, 1 February, available at https://www.france24.com/en/asia-pacific/20220201-myanmar-coup-anniversary-government-in-exile-urges-france-to-act-against-junta. Last accessed on 17 June 2022.

CRPH (2021), "Federal Democracy Charter", Committee Representing Pyidaungsu Hluttaw, available at https://crphmyanmar.org/wp-content/uploads/2021/04/Federal-Democracy-Charter-English.pdf. Last accessed on 17 June 2022.

Dziedzic, Stephen (2021), "Myanmar junta cancels passports of high-profile opponents and shadow government figures, documents show", *ABC News*, 2 December, available at https://www.abc.net.au/news/2021-12-03/myanmar-junta-cancels-passports-of-high-profile-opponents/100669294. Last accessed on 17 June 2022.

Fuller, Thomas (2012), "Myanmar to Curb Censorship of Media", *The New York Times*, 20 August, available at https://www.nytimes.com/2012/08/21/world/asia/myanmar-abolishes-censorship-of-private-publications.html. Last accessed on 17 June 2022.

GIZ (2020), *Myanmar's Banking Sector in Stormy Waters: Staying on the reform course before and amidst COVID-19 crisis*, GIZ Banking Report 5th Edition, Bonn and Eschborn: GIZ, available at https://2020.giz-banking-report-myanmar.com/#0. Last accessed on 17 June 2022.

GlobalPost (2011), "Aung San Suu Kyi: Arab Spring is an "inspiration" to the Burmese", *The World*, 28 June, available at https://www.pri.org/stories/2011-06-28/aung-san-suu-kyi-arab-spring-inspiration-burmese. Last accessed on 17 June 2022.

Goldman, Russell (2021), "Myanmar's Coup, Explained", *The New York Times*, 1 February, available at https://www.nytimes.com/article/myanmar-news-protests-coup.html. Last accessed on 17 June 2022.

Gray, Denis D. (2012), "Myanmar's ethnic minorities lament 'Burmanization'", *SFGATE*, 17 March, available at https://www.sfgate.com/world/article/Myanmar-s-ethnic-minorities-lament-12761351.php. Last accessed on 20 June 2022.

Gunasingham, Amresh (2019), "Buddhist Extremism in Sri Lanka and Myanmar: An Examination", *Counter Terrorist Trends and Analyses*, vol. 11, no. 3, pp. 1–6, available at https://www.jstor.org/stable/26617827?seq=1. Last accessed on 28 June 2022.

Hannigan, J. (2002), "Culture, globalization, and social cohesion: toward a deterritorialized, global fluids model", *Canadian Journal of Communication*, vol. 27, no. 2/3, pp. 277–88, available at https://pdfs.semanticscholar.org/87f0/f05c6dba6983cff7197975036e4b87a9941e.pdf?_ga=2.111560388.19849493.1655399283-1444264852.1653065913. Last accessed on 17 June 2022.

Heyman, Josiah, and Howard Campbell (2009), "The anthropology of global flows: A critical reading of Appadurai's Disjuncture and Difference in the Global Cultural Economy", *Anthropological Theory*, vol. 9, no. 2, pp. 131–48.

Human Rights Watch (HRW) (2021), "Japan: Cut Defense Ties with Myanmar Military: Tatmadaw Cadets Receive Training at Japanese Defense Academy", 20 December, available at https://www.hrw.org/news/2021/12/21/japan-cut-defense-ties-myanmar-military. Last accessed on 17 June 2022.

Human Rights Watch (HRW) (2022), "Myanmar: Scrap Draconian Cybersecurity Bill", 15 February, available at https://www.hrw.org/news/2022/02/15/myanmar-scrap-draconian-cybersecurity-bill. Last accessed on 17 June 2022.

International Crisis Group (ICG) (2021), "The Deadly Stalemate in Post-coup Myanmar", 20 October, available at https://www.crisisgroup.org/asia/south-east-asia/myanmar/b170-deadly-stalemate-post-coup-myanmar. Last accessed on 17 June 2022.

International Crisis Group (ICG) (2022), "Myanmar's Coup Shakes Up Its Ethnic Conflicts", 12 January, available at https://www.crisisgroup.org/asia/south-east-asia/myanmar/319-myanmars-coup-shakes-its-ethnic-conflicts. Last accessed on 17 June 2022.

Irrawaddy (2021a) "Myanmar Coup Leader Admits Not in Full Control of Country", 4 June, available at https://www.irrawaddy.com/news/burma/myanmar-coup-leader-admits-not-in-full-control-of-country.html. Last accessed on 17 June 2022.

Irrawaddy (2021b), "Myanmar Political Parties Reject Regime's Proportional Representation System", 9 November, available at https://www.irrawaddy.com/news/burma/myanmar-political-parties-reject-regimes-proportional-representation-system.html. Last accessed on 17 June 2022.

Kemp, Simon (2021), "Digital 2021: Myanmar", *Datareportal*, 12 February, available at https://datareportal.com/reports/digital-2021-myanmar. Last accessed on 17 June 2022.

Kironska, Kristina, and Ni-Ni Peng (2021), "How state-run media shape perceptions: an analysis of the projection of the Rohingya in the *Global New Light of Myanmar*", *South East Asia Research*, vol. 29, no. 1, pp. 16–31.

Lidauer, M., Saw Chit Thet Tun, L. S. Aung, and S. S. Tun (2018), *Unlocking Civil Society and Peace in Myanmar: Opportunities, obstacles and undercurrents*, Yangon: Paung Sie Facility, available at http://themimu.info/sites/themimu.info/files/

documents/Discussion_Paper_Unlocking_Civil_Society_Peace_in_Myanmar_ENG.pdf. Last accessed on 17 June 2022.

Lukin, Artyom (2021),"Why Russia is betting on Myanmar's military junta", *East Asia Forum*, 27 April, available at https://www.eastasiaforum.org/2021/04/27/why-russia-is-betting-on-myanmars-military-junta/. Last accessed on 17 June 2022.

McCarthy, Gerard (2019), *Military Capitalism in Myanmar: Examining the Origins, Continuities and Evolution of "Khaki Capital"*, Trends in Southeast Asia no. 6, Singapore: ISEAS-Yusof Ishak Institute.

Mesquita, Bruce Bueno de, and Alastair Smith (2011), *The Dictator's Handbook: Why Bad Behavior Is Almost Always Good Politics*, New York: PublicAffairs.

Morgenbesser, Lee (2020), *The Rise of Sophisticated Authoritarianism in Southeast Asia*, Cambridge University Press.

Myanmar News Agency (2021), "SAC Information Team Leader dispels rumours of demonetization", *The Global New Light of Myanmar*, 17 September, available at https://www.gnlm.com.mm/sac-information-team-leader-dispels-rumours-of-demonetization/. Last accessed on 21 June 2022.

Myanmar Now (2021), "Blasts target seven KBZ Bank branches in Mandalay", *Myanmar Now*, 28 October, available at https://www.myanmar-now.org/en/news/blasts-target-seven-kbz-bank-branches-in-mandalay. Last accessed on 17 June 2022.

Myanmar Media Collective (2022), "Report: Terrorizing Acts of Myanmar Military", *Facebook*, 11 January, available at https://www.facebook.com/myanmarcdmdonation/photos/a.104744108565490/151072790599288/. Last accessed on 17 June 2022.

Myat Thu (2021), "Populism in Myanmar", *Populism in Asian Democracies*, Leiden and Boston: Brill, pp. 197–210.

Nachemson, Andrew (2021), "Myanmar diaspora in US rally, raise funds in battle against coup", *Al Jazeera*, 24 May, available at https://www.aljazeera.com/news/2021/5/24/myanmar-people-in-us-protest-raise-funds-to-battle-coup-leaders. Last accessed on 17 June 2022.

Naw Betty Han (2019), "Standing with Mother Suu", *Frontier*, 13 December, available at https://www.frontiermyanmar.net/en/standing-with-mother-suu/. Last accessed on 27 June 2022.

Phyo Thiri Lwin (2021), "NetMission Insight: What are Blacklist and Whitelist – A Recent case of Myanmar", *NetMission*, 3 June, available at https://netmission.asia/2021/06/03/netmission-insight-what-are-blacklist-and-whitelist-a-recent-case-of-myanmar/. Last accessed on 17 June 2022.

Prasse-Freeman, Elliott, and Ko Kabya (2021), "Revolutionary responses to the Myanmar coup", *Anthropology Today*, vol. 37, no. 3.

Rao, Anuradha and Archana Atmakuri (2021), "The Role of Social Media in Myanmar's CDM: Strengths, Limitations and Perspectives from India", ISAS

Working Papers, 28 October, available at https://www.isas.nus.edu.sg/papers/the-role-of-social-media-in-myanmars-cdm-strengths-limitations-and-perspectives-from-india/. Last accessed on 17 June 2022.

Reuters (2021), "Myanmar military asks soldiers to create fake profiles and spread misinformation on Facebook, Twitter: Report", *India Today*, 3 November, available at https://www.indiatoday.in/technology/news/story/myanmar-military-asks-soldiers-to-create-fake-profiles-and-spread-misinformation-on-facebook-twitter-report-1872804-2021-11-03. Last accessed on 17 June 2022.

Saha, Jonathan (2021), "Like karaoke fascism all over again: The Military Coup in Myanmar and the Global Rise of the Far Right", *History Workshop*, 1 March, available at https://www.historyworkshop.org.uk/like-karaoke-fascism-all-over-again-the-military-coup-in-myanmar-and-the-global-rise-of-the-far-right/. Last accessed on 17 June 2022.

Salai Tun Tun (2020), "Myanmar sees digital payment growth in 2020: OBG", *Myanmar Times*, 29 September, available at https://www.mmtimes.com/news/myanmar-sees-digital-payment-growth-2020-obg.html. Last accessed on 17 June 2022.

Self, Darin (2021), "Myanmar Lays Bare Challenges of Military-Led Democratization", 3 February, available at https://theglobalobservatory.org/2021/02/myanmar-lays-bare-challenges-military-led-democratization/. Last accessed on 17 June 2022.

Stayner, Tom, and Abbie O'Brien (2022), "Yanghee Lee: Australia, international community must ratchet up response to junta-made crisis", *IPI Global Observatory*, 1 February, available at https://specialadvisorycouncil.org/2022/02/yanghee-lee-australia-international-community-must-ratchet-up-response-to-junta-made-crisis/. Last accessed on 17 June 2022.

Taylor, Robert H. (2015), *General Ne Win: A Political Biography*, Singapore: ISEAS-Yusof Ishak Institute.

Thawnghmung, Ardeth (2021), "Myanmar's National Unity forces must overcome divide and rule tactics", *Nikkei Asia*, 31 July, available at https://asia.nikkei.com/Opinion/Myanmar-s-National-Unity-forces-must-overcome-divide-and-rule-tactics. Last accessed on 17 June 2022.

UN News (2022), "Number of internally displaced in Myanmar doubles, to 800,000", *United Nations*, 11 February, available at https://news.un.org/en/story/2022/02/1111812#:~:text=Internally%20displaced%20people%20receive%20assistance,camp%20in%20Myanmar's%20Kayin%20State. Last accessed on 17 June 2022.

Venizelos, Giorgios, and Yannis Stavrakakis (2020), "Left-Populism Is Down but Not Out", *Jacobin*, 22 March, available at https://jacobin.com/2020/03/left-populism-political-strategy-class-power. Last accessed on 20 June 2022.

Win Tint Tun (2007), *Myanmar under Darkness*, Lu Baung Tit Democrat Party.

Ye Myo Hein (2022), *The Root Causes of Myanmar's Coup Go Deeper*, Washington DC: Wilson Center, available at https://www.wilsoncenter.org/sites/default/files/media/uploads/documents/2022-03-Myanmar_YeMyoHein.pdf. Last accessed on 17 June 2022.

Contentions and Contradictions
The Rise of Duterte's Authoritarianism with Fascist Tendencies Amidst the Hegemonic Crisis of (Neo)Liberal Democracy in the Philippines

Verna Dinah Q. Viajar

Introduction

The pandemic provided an opportunity for Rodrigo Duterte, then president of the Philippines,[1] to tighten his authoritarian grip on power. Aside from expanding his executive powers due to the health emergency crisis, Duterte encroached into the supposedly independent powers of the legislative and judicial branches of government. The Duterte government implemented a highly militarized national pandemic response further integrating the police and the military into politics and governance. After more than one year of constant lockdowns, the Philippines had the worst economic contraction in the Southeast Asian region and shed almost ten million jobs due to the COVID-19 pandemic (Philippine Statistics Office 2020). Before 2020 ended however, Duterte's trust ratings rose to 91 percent in a survey conducted by Pulse Asia in September 2020. Many still believed in his bravado and charismatic personality despite his failures in governance and leadership. Even into 2021, the virus was uncontrolled, corruption scandals into medical supplies had erupted, and Duterte's weekly evening speeches contained mostly rants against his critics. As the Delta COVID-19 variant showed a resurgence in the country in mid-April 2021, the Duterte government focused more on silencing the opposition rather than finding economic and political solutions amid the health emergency.

As the Philippine presidential elections loomed closer in May 2022, new political constellations begin to take shape. A broad opposition movement comprised from the centre-left political groups that supported the previous Aquino government, independent business groups left out by Duterte's rent-seeking

---

1   This article was completed just as the Marcos government assumed office. The analysis into Duterte's legacy in terms of mode of governance and authoritarian practices remains relevant, as they contributed to the rise of the current Marcos-Duterte government.

business cronies, remnants of the Liberal Party, and progressive social movements (i.e. labour unions, professional groups, etc.), gravitated around the sitting Vice President, Leni Robredo. The right-wing religious groups, business groups with dubious track records, the remaining Marcos loyalists,[2] and corrupt traditional politicians threw their support towards Bongbong Marcos Jr., the son of the late dictator Ferdinand Marcos Sr., and Duterte's daughter, Sara Duterte, for president and vice president, respectively. Duterte earlier stated that he intended to stay in power by contemplating running for vice president in the elections to secure himself immunity from lawsuits. This is to subvert his accountability in the ongoing national and international investigations against his bloody war on drugs. In 2021, the International Criminal Court (ICC) through its chief prosecutor moved forward to investigate Duterte for crimes against humanity in the deadly drug war he started in 2016 (BBC 2021). Trumping liberal democratic institutions and ignoring the Philippine Constitution, Duterte projected himself as the bearer of truth without proof or evidence; his words and actions are beyond the law.

In this political moment rife with tensions, contradictions, but also possibilities, it is important to refer to sound conjunctural analysis based on on-the-ground experiences guided by a rigorous analytical framework. Conjunctural analysis is heavily identified with Stuart Hall in his work on cultural studies, who strongly argued that to get the analysis right, critical scholarship and social engagement should "seek to map an entire 'totality of social relations at a given moment'" (Gilbert 2019). This paper utilizes this conceptualization of conjunctural analysis as "broadly defined as the analysis of convergent and divergent tendencies shaping the totality of power relations with a given social field during a particular period of time" (Gilbert 2019, 5). Subsequently influenced by this research track, this paper poses the following overarching questions in the hope that sound analysis of the present may inform the shape of the future: is Duterte's rise to power a historical aberration in the Philippines' political development as a democratic country? Did populist and strongman leaders, such as Estrada[3] and Duterte, come to power due to an unfinished process of democratization in the Philippines? Was Duterte's electoral victory a reflection of a protest vote against a (neo)liberal democratic system that tolerated increasing inequality despite economic growth, but the vote tolerated an authoritarian populist leader? And in what ways is Duterte part of a worldwide trend for

---

2   Supporters of the late dictator, Ferdinand Marcos, whose son, Ferdinand Marcos Jr., won the presidency in the 2022 elections.

3   Joseph Ejercito Estrada, a former actor, served as president from 1998 to 2001, when he was ousted from office due to corruption cases. Indicted for plunder in 2007 and sentenced to lifetime imprisonment in 2007, he was later pardoned by former President Gloria Arroyo. Estrada was elected mayor of Manila City in the 2010 elections and then defeated in the 2016 elections.

the rise of authoritarian populist leaders standing in line with other authoritarian movements across the globe?

As the Philippine state under Duterte experienced political and economic crises exacerbated by the COVID-19 pandemic, this paper sheds some light on Duterte's authoritarianism which unravelled under pressure from the public and progressive movements, demanding accountability for the securitized pandemic response, massive corruption, the economic devastation, and the humanitarian and health crises. These processes deepened Duterte's authoritarian leadership as he tightened his grip on power against his critics, activists, and the political opposition, in general. This paper argues that Duterte's mode of governance embodied authoritarian-populist leadership with fascist tendencies, approached through Stuart Hall's initial coinage of authoritarian populism and deepened through the debates within the Frankfurt school on a critical framework of analyses. This research includes 'fascist tendencies' to characterize the Philippines' experience of authoritarianism drawing from Nicos Poulantzas's discussion on authoritarian statism and Antonio Gramsci's exposition of fascism. The analysis into Duterte's authoritarianism is contextualized within the country's political-economic structures which are embedded within the global neoliberal economic order. Duterte is not only a product of the Philippines' key historical and political moments but also exemplifies the hegemonic crisis of (neo)liberal democracy in the Philippines brought about by the contradictions and the authoritarian turn of neoliberalism on the global scale. This paper utilizes critical theories on neoliberalism, populism, and authoritarianism to interrogate the contradictions and contentions of Duterte's sustained populism in the context of strengthening fascist tendencies. This paper further examines the rise of Duterte through the Gramscian lens on the notion of hegemony.

Background and Context: The Philippine Political Economy and the Rise of Authoritarianism

The Duterte victory in the 2016 presidential elections reconfigured the political forces in the Philippines, allowing the resurgence of the dislodged elites from the previous administrations and establishing new political and economic interests under Duterte. Known for his anti-establishment and irreverent persona, Duterte captured the hearts and minds—which translated into electoral votes—of more than 16 million Filipinos under the banner 'change is coming'. Possibly related to the famous 'winter is coming' quote from the TV series Game of Thrones, the Duterte win heralded the winter of 'yellow politics', dominated by the Aquinos and the heirs to the 1986 People Power democratic uprising.

The first president elected from Mindanao or the southern Philippines,[4] Duterte has commanded majority support from this region given his 20-year stint as Mayor of Davao City. However, it became apparent that he remained a Marcos loyalist, just like his father who became a cabinet minister during the Marcos period, and the junior Duterte maintained control of the city despite political changes and leadership in central Manila.[5] Within the first three months of his presidency, Duterte allowed the Marcoses to bury former president Ferdinand Marcos at the Heroes Cemetery in the face of widespread opposition. He then pardoned former President Gloria Arroyo from plunder (corruption) charges, and launched a violent drug war focused on the street-level rounding-up and arrest of thousands of suspected drug addicts and pushers without due process. Cases of extra-judicial killings (EJKs) continued to pile up among the petty drug dealers and users. However, fear and impunity have been pervasive; not only among petty criminals but more so among human rights and labour activists, the political opposition, critical media, and among the growing critics of the Duterte politics.

Duterte's strongman tactics, violent policies, and anti-human-rights positions likewise put the Philippines on the list of countries which have authoritarian and populist leaders in the ascendant. The Duterte regime (sometimes described loosely as Dutertism) expressed a strong political message that it would not tolerate dissent and critique. Those that have criticized Duterte have either received court summons on trumped-up charges, been maligned in the public media, or received death threats from anonymous armed groups. With his meteoric rise to power and sustained popular support until the mid-term elections in 2019, Duterte continued to consolidate loyalties from the military apparatus and the police, as well as from both newly-formed and traditional political dynasties.

In a patron-client relation characterizing the local regional politics, Duterte consolidated his fiefdom in the last 20 years as city Mayor of Davao. He terrorized activists and criminals alike in his city, the bringer of fear and nightmares for the cause-oriented, critical, and progressive activists. Duterte gained infamy from the rumoured Davao Death Squad (DDS), the vigilante group cleansing the Davao streets of petty criminals via extra-judicial killings. The nameless killings in Davao instilled fear among the petty criminals and those who oppose the status quo. In that fateful 2016 election period, Duterte was the wild card that left everyone guessing until the last moment when he won the presidential elections.

---

4 The second-biggest island, after Luzon, in the Philippines, Mindanao is commonly referred to as 'Southern Philippines'.

5 The people in Visayas and Mindanao would sometimes call it 'imperialist Manila' as a critique of the centralized government system seated in the heart of Luzon, Metropolitan Manila.

The 1986 Uprising against the Marcos Dictatorship

Duterte is a product of the country's historical moments, and the trends that led to his rise to power can be traced back to the unfinished People Power Revolution and the decades of the Marcos dictatorship. From the Left, the growing consensus on the reasons for the presidential victory and continued popularity of the Duterte government points to the disillusionment of the populace with the liberal democratic system. Walden Bello, writing in a 16 July 2019 statement for the group Laban ng Masa ("Fight of the People"),[6] argued that the rise of Duterte became possible because of the people's disappointment in the failure of EDSA[7] or the 1986 People Power promises of empowerment and equality (Bello 2019a; 2019b). The massive gap—between the rights-based, people's empowerment promises, to the reality of widening inequality and continued poverty—frustrated many, which translated into electoral votes for the charismatic and decisive strongman ruler. In Bello's words, a "great deal of the fact of why Duterte is popular is there has been a great deal of disillusionment with the system of liberal democracy here in the Philippines" (Bello 2019c).

The Philippines' People Power Revolution in 1986, a bloodless people's uprising, toppled the dictatorship and corruption of former President Ferdinand Marcos who ruled the country from 1965 to 1986. Marcos was initially elected in 1965 and sought a second term in 1969. Before his term ended in 1972, he had declared martial law, abolished the parliamentary house, and went on to rule with an iron fist for 20 years. Human rights violations, *desaparecidos*, and the repression of opposition figures, militant labour unions, and social movements characterized Marcos's dictatorial rule which at the same time robbed billions from Philippine coffers.

Marcos ruled amidst the rise of post-war 'strongman' leaders in Southeast Asia such as Malaysia's Mahathir, Indonesia's Suharto, and Singapore's Lee Kuan Yew, to name a few. The Cold War between the US and USSR contributed to the longevity of non-democratic governments as the superpowers jousted for influence in the region. In this period, the authoritarian governments became entrenched in the global political economic order characterized by a bipolar arms race. As the developing economies in the 'third world' strove to modernize along a capitalist and liberal development framework, they also became experimental laboratories to the neoliberal turn of capitalist development through structural adjustment programmes (SAPs) enforced by the International Monetary Fund (IMF) and the World Bank

---

6 The broad coalition of leftist organizations in the Philippines who opposed the Duterte administration.
7 Epifanio delos Santos Avenue was the site of two military bases and became the central point of the 1986 People Power Revolution, also referred to simply as EDSA or the EDSA Revolution.

(WB), and masterminded by the Washington Consensus. The dominance of neoliberal policies since the 1980s, through Reaganomics and Thatcherism, propelled the dominance of capital markets, systematically weakening organized labour and influencing ideas and culture towards capitalist competition and consumerism. The markets became unfettered under neoliberalism; many have been left behind.

The 1986 People Power Revolution in the Philippines, when millions mobilized along the EDSA, was perceived as being among the leading moments of democratization in the region. However, Filipino political analysts argued that the People Power Revolution remained unfinished because the revolutionary government[8] led by the first woman president, Corazon Aquino, did not institute transformative and structural change but instead moved towards the "swift restoration of the old liberal elite" (Heydarian 2021). Many perceived that there were not enough transformative policies to counter "predatory political dynasties" wherein the country's economy would remain captured by oligarchies. "As a result, the Philippines, even in subsequent periods of high economic growth, struggled to create truly inclusive development—thus sowing the seeds of long-term discontent, which is fueling authoritarian populism nowadays" (Heydarian 2021). The win for the dictator's son, Ferdinand Marcos Jr., in the 2022 Philippine presidential elections is a setback in the democratization process after the Marcos dictatorship. The current political economic turbulence in the Philippines, with traces of historical revisionism and institutional amnesia, coincides with rising inequality, a cyclical macroeconomic crisis, and poor labour conditions.

The Philippine Political Economy since the Marcos Dictatorship

In the last 30 years, the Philippines further integrated into the global neoliberal economic order, initially taking on protectionist economic policies through import substitution in the 1960s and then moving towards industrialization alongside Japan (Viajar 2009). The country's economic development strategy shifted to export-oriented and a reliance on foreign direct investment towards the beginning of the 1970s, and coupled with Marcos's authoritarianism, plunder, and crony capitalism, the Philippines began to sink into debt. By 1981, the Philippines became one of the first countries to implement SAPs under the IMF towards the liberalization of the country's core economic sectors such as agriculture, finance, and trade (Viajar 2009). However, whilst the neighbouring Southeast Asian countries became emerging industrial economies, the Philippines developed into a service economy,

---

8   Led by former President Corazon Aquino, the widow of opposition leader Benigno Aquino, assassinated in 1983. They were the parents of Noynoy Aquino, who himself was president between 2010–16.

a labour-exporting country, and remained a middle-income economy in the region. Marcos first promoted the labour export policy, establishing an institution to deploy Filipino workers to all corners of the world—the Philippine Overseas Employment Administration (POEA)—to avoid social unrest due to high unemployment rates during the dictatorship.

The Marcos regime left such a huge debt for the succeeding governments that since the early 2000s, debt servicing has been taking up 40 percent of the country's gross domestic product (World Bank 2003). Poverty incidence, even though it decreased from 23.3 percent in 2015 to 16.7 percent in 2018, and income inequality, at 21.6 percent in 2015 despite economic growth, have remained significant problems in the Philippines in the last few years (Philippine Statistics Authority 2020). Inequality in the Philippines remain high. The country's Gini index, the measure of income distribution, has never gone below 40 percent[9] on the index in the last 20 years, measuring 46.2 percent in 2001, 42.2 percent in 2012, 40.1 in 2015, and 42.3 in 2018 (Oxford Business Group 2018; World Bank 2003). The Asian Development Bank 2017 Report mentioned that income inequality in the Philippines is increasing, and equality is not rising in line with GDP growth (Oxford Business Group). With the ongoing effects of the pandemic and the ensuing contraction of the economy at 9.5 percent, poverty and inequality are expected to get worse (Reuters 2021)

The Authoritarian Turn of Neoliberalism

The authoritarian turn of neoliberalism foreshadows the rise of right-wing populist and authoritarian leaders across the globe (Boffo et al. 2019). Neoliberalism as a set of policies, structures, and arrangements that extol the dominance of the 'free market' has far-reaching political, economic, and social ramifications. Neoliberal economic policies promote the primacy of liberalization coupled with privatization and deregulation that signal the minimal role of the state. Such political-economic arrangements promote competition above all else, hyper-consumption, and individualism in the socio-cultural realms. Extolled as the framework of accumulation that can guarantee wealth for the majority, the contradictions of the neoliberal capitalist order arise when only a select few benefit from the wealth generated and the reconfiguration of the state so that it becomes weak and strong at the same time: the authoritarian practices of the governing elite express a strong state by mobilizing its military and police apparatus to restrict freedoms and dissent; in

---

9   A higher Gini Index indicates higher inequality, with 0 percent representing perfect equality and 100 percent representing perfect inequality. With a Gini Index of 40 percent, the Philippines is among those with the highest levels of inequality in Southeast Asia.

turn, the civil and democratic institutions of the state are weakened in the process. Neoliberal globalization was facilitated through the state despite the reduction of its economic role, giving rise to international bodies tasked with facilitating liberalization, privatization, and deregulation through the World Trade Organization (WTO), the IMF, the World Bank, and many others. Saddled with inherent contradictions, the neoliberal framework engendered widespread inequalities and discontent from the many who have been left behind. But what ushered in the authoritarian turn of neoliberalism according to Marco Boffo, Alfredo Saah-Filho, and Ben Fine (2019) was the *"political paradox of neoliberalism"* which "concerns the disintegration of neoliberal democracy under the weight of its own internal contradictions" (2019, 261). The state, despite its diminished economic role, counterintuitively facilitated the "financialized modalities of social reproduction and individualistic subjectivity" (ibid.). The crises of neoliberalism from financialization, starting in the Asian financial crisis of 1997 and followed a decade after in the US and European financial crisis of 2008–09, further cemented the coercive practices of the state to discipline consent from those discontented with neoliberalism.

However, according to Ian Bruff (2014) the rise of authoritarian neoliberalism began in the late 1970s during the golden days of Thatcherism and Reaganomics, when the state became complicit to the "free market" by suppressing "general societal discontent", crushing trade unions and leftist movements, and paving the way for widening socio-economic disparities. Bruff particularly cited Stuart Hall (1979) and Poulantzas (2014) who presciently coined the terms "authoritarian populism" and "authoritarian statism" following the strengthening of neoliberalism in the early 1970s. These debates on the notion of authoritarianism were further traced back by Jeremiah Morelock (2018) to the Frankfurt School referring to authoritarian populism as "the pitting of 'the people' against 'elites' in order to have the power to drive out, wipe out, or otherwise dominate Others who are not 'the people'" (Morelock 2018, xiv). Taken separately, the concept of 'authoritarianism' refers to seeking "social homogeneity through coercion", while 'populism' refers to "defining a section of the population as truly and rightfully 'the people' and aligning with this section against a different group identified as elites" (ibid.). Bruff (2014) however, considering Hall's (1979) and Poulantzas's (2014) arguments, contends that authoritarianism should not be viewed only as "the exercise of brute coercive force" but as "the reconfiguring of the state and institutional power in an attempt to insulate certain policies and institutional practices from social and political dissent" (Bruff 2014, 115).

Through the emergence of populist leaders, the rise of far-right politics or right-wing social forces characterized by "nationalist, racist and xenophobic tendencies" in the West (Stewart 2020, 1208), has been linked as a challenge to the "liberal social and cultural norms" expressed through "multiculturalism, universal human rights and multilateralism" (ibid., 1212). There has been no shortage of authoritarian or 'strongman' leaders in the Southeast Asian region since the Cold War, still seen today with the current authoritarian-populist leaders. During the Cold War, the 1960s–1970s saw the strongman rule of Marcos in the Philippines, Suharto in Indonesia, Hun Sen in Cambodia, Mahathir in Malaysia, and the constant military rules in Thailand and Myanmar/Burma.

The proliferation of authoritarian leaders in the region, even with functioning democratic institutions such as electoral politics, has reshaped the meaning and forms of democracies in Asia. The term 'illiberal democracies' has even emerged in this region, referring to "democratically elected regimes, often ones that have been re-elected or reaffirmed through referenda ... routinely ignoring constitutional limits on their power and depriving their citizens of basic rights and freedoms" (Zakaria 1997, 22). In the recent past, the rise of a 'new wave' of populist-authoritarian leaders in the post-Cold War period, such as Thaksin in Thailand, Duterte in the Philippines, and military rule in Thailand and Myanmar, can be linked to neoliberal globalization and capitalist transformation in the region (see Bello 2021). Neoliberalism has been embedded in the Southeast Asian region since the oil crisis in the early 1970s, putting a majority of the economies in the region in perpetual 'debt crises'. Chained to the conditionalities of the IMF/WB, the countries in the region were among the first implementers of SAPs steeped in neoliberal policies such as the privatization of public assets, the 'opening up' of markets, trade liberalization, fiscal austerity, etc. Whilst some countries such as Malaysia, Singapore, and Thailand followed the export-led, 'state-led development' framework from the 'Asian tigers' (i.e. Japan, South Korea, and Taiwan), wherein the state has a significant economic role, these divergences from the neoliberal playbook were accommodated (Springer 2017). This paper intends to show how neoliberalism has become linked to fascist practices and dimensions.

Deconstructing Duterte: A Gramscian Perspective on Duterte's Authoritarian and Fascist Tendencies[10]

Based on the regional and international context under neoliberalism, Duterte is not only a product of the country's historical and political moments such as the unfinished democratic People Power Revolution that ousted the Marcos dictatorship, but

---

10   Some portions of this section are excerpted from the book chapter entitled "Duterte, COVID-19, and populist-authoritarianism in the Philippines: Contentions and contradictions", submitted to the Rosa-Luxemburg-Stiftung Manila Office for forthcoming publication.

also of the colonial legacies of the Cold War[11] and the embeddedness of neoliberalism in the Philippine economic-political structures. Duterte won the 2016 presidential elections as a 'dark horse' candidate propelled by popular discontent over the ineffective governance of previous governments elected under liberal-democratic institutions. In the 2016 exit polls conducted by the Social Weather Stations (SWS), Duterte garnered the votes from the wealthy and middle classes with 26 points over the next presidential candidate in class ABC, a 17-point lead in class D, and only a 7-point lead in class E (ABS CBN 2016). Duterte also garnered a 28-point lead among college graduates prompting political analysts to say that the "higher the class, the more the appeal of Duterte ... The more the schooling, the more the appeal of Duterte" and that "Duterte's popularity among the country's wealthy and middle classes indicated the emergence of a counter-elite challenging the old elite" (ABS-CBN 2016).

Duterte's popularity also captured the new middle class, those that benefitted from recent economic growth and from working abroad, seeking quick solutions to everyday issues such as crime, drugs, and the horrendous traffic. Campaigning under an anti-elite and anti-establishment message, and at the same time critiquing persistent socio-economic inequalities, Duterte swept the electoral stage with his slogan 'change is coming'. In his campaigns, he promised to single-handedly solve all problems (i.e. crime, corruption, drugs, etc.) within just a few months of being in office. More than 16 million Filipinos believed his rhetoric, entertained by his self-styled bravado and charismatic language. However, after five years of his being in office, the persistent problems—corruption, drugs, crime and traffic—which Duterte had promised to eradicate remain, and have even intensified. A shrewd warlord and politician, Duterte became the bane of the fractured elite who had benefitted from the now-challenged (neo)liberal democratic system.

During the campaign period, Duterte spouted progressive policies, anti-elite rhetoric, and anti-establishment imagery. His penchant for talking in the vernacular, and his humorous speeches, earned him a popular following among the old, the young, and those in between across different social classes. Sections of the radical and progressive Left, such as trade union groups, joined his mostly middle-class and conservative support base. Duterte himself came from a political and well-off family, his father once having been a governor in Cebu Province during the Marcos dictatorship. Despite his affluent background, Duterte preferred to have friends on the streets, mixing with the *lumpens* in his neighbourhood and integrating the personality of the street-smart kid and the foul-mouthed neighbourhood bully. Duterte's gangster-type personality has earned him a cult following from

---

11   Until 1991, the Philippines had maintained huge military bases in Pampanga and Subic in exchange for military and economic support to the Philippines; this is now among the legacies of the Cold War.

the non-elite, anti-establishment crowd. He followed his father's political career as Mayor of Davao City in Mindanao province, taking office in 1988 and ruling for 30 years (BBC 2019). Many were blindsided during the elections, as some segments of the elite thumbed their noses and considered him insignificant when it came to the likely winner of the presidential elections.

Duterte's win sent the Left and progressive groups scrambling to analyse what had happened. When he started baring his authoritarian and fascist tendencies through a series of securitized policies and a crackdown on the Left, many Filipino political analysts debated with each other to try to explain Duterte's rise to power. There were many analytical approaches offered (see Curato 2017) to understand Duterte's form of authoritarianism, such as through the lens of an institutional approach; a personality analysis; and a counter-revolutionary approach. This paper focuses on the debates in the Left on how to analyse Duterte's rise to power, geared towards the search for counter-strategies. Bello (2019) discussed Duterte as a counter-revolutionary of the liberal-democratic order, one who "has excelled in the political improvisation characteristic of skilled counter-revolutionaries like Hitler and Mussolini" (2019, 128). Bello also argues that Duterte is a fascist original, one who is not concerned for "ideological purity" and who does whatever it takes to "defend the nation" (ibid., 129).

Disagreeing with Bello, a splinter group from the Communist Party of the Philippines (CPP), the Partido Manggagawa (PM, Workers' Party), linked with the Fourth International socialist movement, believe that Duterte is not a fascist but a reactionary and a counter-revolutionary of the liberal-democratic movement (Manggagawa 2017). Their main contention against Bello's analysis is that Duterte cannot be a fascist leader due to his lack of a popular movement that is mobilizable. Duterte may have employed social media trolls during his campaign, but they are not organized as a movement. Defining Duterte as a fascist would also force leftist groups to consider armed struggle as a counter-strategy. Since the electoral system is still open for contention, leftist and socialist groups like PM still consider the parliamentary struggle as a counter-strategy option. The CPP and its above-ground allied groups have become the targets of Duterte's bloody red-tagging campaign. Duterte's anti-communist campaign mobilizes the police and the military to weed out communists at the village level. A huge chunk of the national budget has been allotted, more than 16 billion pesos, to the anti-communist task force called the National Task Force to End Local Communist Insurgency (NTF-ELCAC). As the CPP views all state leaders as fascists—based on the ideological view that states are inherently instruments of oppression—henceforth the strategy is to smash the state.

From a different perspective, prominent political analyst Joel Rocamora, who led a popular democracy movement in the 1980s–1990s, has the view that Duterte's populism remain strong but follows the 'demobilized' populism wherein the people are restricted from participating in policy formulation and decision-making (see Rocamora 2020). The popular democracy movement in the 1980s promoted direct participatory democracy wherein ordinary people have voices in governance and the determining of policies that affect their lives and livelihoods. Rocamora analyses Duterte's form of authoritarian rule from the personality perspective, focusing on Duterte's personality formation as a neighbourhood gangster, which characterizes and legitimizes his authoritarian governance. On the other hand, Charmaine Ramos (2021) traces the roots of the neoliberal developmental trajectories of neoliberalism in the Philippines as the root of understanding the emergence of a new wave of "populist politics" with "authoritarian practices" in the return to strongman rule in the Philippines. According to Ramos (2021), the three decades of neoliberal economic expansion have enabled populist politics and the return to strongman rule "as a logical outcome of the neoliberal project of depoliticization, as much as it is a reaction, as suggested in extant literature, to the failures associated with neoliberal economic doctrine" (Ramos 2021, 10).

This paper's contribution in examining Duterte's form of authoritarianism utilizes Gramsci's (1971) notions of hegemony and fascism to argue that Duterte's authoritarian bent embodies fascist tendencies based on Poulantzas's (2014) concept of authoritarian statism. Understanding authoritarianism as dominance, Poulantzas utilizes Gramsci's usage of hegemony which refers to 'leadership' or 'dominance', and the power of ideas, values, and beliefs in a particular historical moment over a particular political-economic context. In looking at Duterte's authoritarian leadership with fascist tendencies, Gramsci's notion of hegemony seems apt, which says that it is about "political leadership based on the consent of the led, a consent which is secured by the diffusion and popularization of the world view of the ruling class" (Bates 1975, 352). Gramsci's analysis reflected the struggle to understand how people can support an irrational fascist political movement, ending up with the most rational analyses of his time and with his analyses geared towards finding a counter-hegemonic strategy and action (Adamson 1980). Useful insights for the understanding of the state under Duterte can also be gleaned from Poulantzas's concept of authoritarian statism, which approaches the analysis of the state corresponding to the phases of capitalism as a state in crisis. Against the backdrop of the expansion of neoliberalism, "fascistic elements or tendencies appear" within the state in crisis (Poulantzas 2014, 209). Authoritarian statism "also involves the establishment of an entire institutional structure serving to prevent a rise in popular struggles and the dangers which that holds for class hegemony" (ibid., 210).

Duterte's rise to power came at a time of hegemonic crisis in the Philippine political economy. This is reminiscent of the Gramscian perspective of "revolutionary politics" (Adamson 1980), that political moment pregnant with change, when a hegemonic crisis occurs. In the Philippine context, the hegemonic crisis refers to the crisis of the (neo)liberal democracy that still regurgitates a semblance of electoral democracy but devoid of genuine participatory governance. The broken system exemplified by the prevalent corruption of political leaders, the widening income and social inequalities, and rising middle-class fear of criminality all fuelled the discontent and the search for change. Duterte captured the imagination of discontented citizens by posing as an anti-elite and anti-establishment figure who would bring the wind of change. According to Gramsci, a hegemonic crisis happens when the ruling class fails to completely dominate or uses force to dominate (i.e. through war), until such time that a broad mass movement puts forward demands and seizes a particular political moment (Adamson 1980). In such a hegemonic crisis, the political field becomes open and "a violent solution led by 'charismatic men of destiny'" may provide the alternative to achieve a "static equilibrium during a hegemonic crisis" (Adamson 1980, 628). Without any strong challenge from other social forces (i.e. the moderates or conservative elites), Gramsci likened the change towards fascism to 'Caesarism' which "refers to a political intervention by some previously dormant or even previously unknown political force capable of asserting domination and thus of restoring a static equilibrium during a hegemonic crisis" (Adamson 1980, 628). In this political moment, according to Gramsci, the fascist takeover may emerge through "the sudden creation of a single heroic figure, or it may be the gradual and institutionalized outcome of a coalition government" (Adamson 1980, 628). The contention of political forces in a crisis of hegemony and the incomplete transformation of new political structures that cannot yet be created have produced a vacuum within which a charismatic leader with fascist tendencies, like Duterte, emerged to fill the void.

Duterte's Authoritarianism with Fascist Tendencies

This paper contends that Duterte's populist-authoritarian rule embodied fascist tendencies. These fascist tendencies can be characterized through the increasingly interventionist state through a heightened economic role or the strengthening of the executive according to Poulantzas's authoritarian statism. The fascist tendencies that appear may also be seen in the presence of support from an organized people's movement; the heightened role of the military; and the persecution of a particular sector or group in society, as seen in Duterte's Philippines in the persecution of drug addicts in the bloody war on drugs. Empirically, Duterte's populist authoritarianism with fascist tendencies is manifested along five dimensions with implications for the role of the state, the military, and the police; its impact on state institutions (i.e. Congress, political parties, electoral bodies, etc.); on the freedom of the press; on the economy, how it is being transformed or untransformed during authoritarian times; and on repression of dissent and people's resistance.

Under Duterte's populist-authoritarian rule, the people were 'demobilized' or excluded from participating in the political process which would determine their future and the future of their communities. Most policies were framed from the top and enforced upon the people. The state policies under Duterte were insulated and removed from the concerns of the people. The state has continued its neoliberal and capitalist developmental trajectory with no significant change in macroeconomic policies or change in the redistributive capacity of the state. Duterte, however, expanded the role of the executive to even encroach on the powers of the legislative and judicial branches of government. In August 2021, Duterte attacked the Commission on Audit (COA) to refrain from auditing the financial management of government agencies. The COA had found billions of anomalous procurements of medical supplies from agencies headed by Duterte executive appointees.

In terms of the economy, it has remained untransformed from its neoliberal economic trajectory under authoritarian times. Duterte would remain hands-off in reforming the neoliberal economic structures of the country to address inequality. He mostly spewed rhetoric against the economic oligarchy, but remained submissive to his allied neoliberal economic masterminds running the economy. His government focused more on allotting increased funds for its anti-communist drive at the village level rather than managing the macroeconomic policies of the country. Over one year into the pandemic, the Philippine economy under Duterte was in freefall, debt had ballooned, and dependence on China's investments was increasing. The devastation of the Philippine economy will be felt in the years to come, bringing hardships to many Filipinos and widening further inequality in the country. The working class have been hit the hardest as unemployment reached an all-time high of 9.8 million jobs lost after a year and a half of intermittent lockdowns.

The role of the military and police was more expansive during the time of Duterte than during the tenures of any other Philippine presidents. The armed apparatus of the state—the police and the military, which possess the legitimate use of state violence—were deployed strongly against Duterte's critics to repress dissent, the enforcement of the deadly drug war, and the implementation of the harsh restrictions during the COVID-19 pandemic. Under the Duterte government, the military and the police were at their most influential, with around 59 ex-military personnel being part of Duterte's executive cabinet. Policies which aimed to fight against communist movements and drugs were both the top priority issues of the government and are also the identified enemies of the military and the police. Based on our history of military and police interventions in politics, as they were politicized during the Marcos dictatorship, successive Philippine presidents must appease the military and police when they take office. In the post-Marcos dictatorship period, the military staged more than a dozen coups d'état in an attempt to wrest power from civilian authority during Corazon Aquino's presidency. The military and the police withdrew their support from former President Joseph Estrada which led to his ouster in January 2001, dubbed the Philippine People Power II. He was later incarcerated and convicted of plunder. Duterte showed the most extreme kind of appeasement by integrating the military and the police into the government.

The wider influence of Duterte's authoritarian policies as head of the executive branch structurally weakened other state institutions, such as the political, economic, and social institutions affected by increasing corruption and the non-meritorious appointment of Duterte loyalists. Under Duterte's authoritarian mode, critical media are under attack. Duterte and his minions in Congress succeeded in shutting down one of the largest independent broadcast networks (ABS-CBN) in the country in the middle of the pandemic. The people's resistance against repression and the critiquing of Duterte's pandemic response and authoritarian policy actions (i.e. the drug war, the Anti-Terrorism Act of 2020) during the health crisis steadily rose, both online and offline. But the narrowing of freedoms and democratic spaces under Duterte restricted popular dissent against authoritarianism. The spate of killings of activists and arrests of critics even during the pandemic multiplied the risks for the opposition movement. More than 65 percent of Filipinos perceive that "it is dangerous to publish anything critical to the administration" based on a survey conducted in November 2020 and published in 2021 (Mercado 2021).

Conclusion: The Search for Counter-Strategies

Duterte's populist-authoritarian rise in the Philippines occurred not only due to the Philippine's key historical and political moments but also exemplified the hegemonic crisis of (neo)liberal democracy in the Philippines brought about by the contradictions and the authoritarian turn of neoliberalism from a global perspective. As part of the country's colonial legacy, the Philippines has been integrated into the global neoliberal economic order since the post-war period, inheriting political-economic and social relations and structures exacerbated during the debt crisis, and by the SAPs since the 1970s. The Philippines experienced authoritarian rule during the Cold War period under the Marcos dictatorship, but democratization processes under the neoliberal economy have advanced since the late 1980s. However, despite the existence of electoral processes, a genuine political and economic democracy has not been achieved under neoliberal capitalist structures. Social and economic inequalities continue to hound the Philippine political economy giving rise to broad discontent. The Left remains fragmented, and the mainstream and centrist elite continues to dominate the political structures. In the last few years of intense neoliberal hegemonic crisis, the right-wing and self-serving conservative forces have captured the discourse of change against (neo)liberal democratic structures in the country. Debates within Philippine leftist movements have been rife in the last five years on how to approach the return of authoritarian rule and right-wing populist politics in the Philippines.

Parliamentary struggle, both in the electoral terrain and on the streets, remain on the table for leftist and progressive movements as a counter-strategy. Significant challenges, however, have hampered a unified opposition movement composed of a broad-based alliance among left-wing, centrist, and progressive forces with the increasingly narrow democratic spaces and attacks on critics and activists under the Duterte regime. A segment of the radical left has been continuing to espouse armed struggle in the countryside for more than five decades, but without success. However, their above-ground radical organizations attained more success in the parliamentary struggle. The political elite in the country remain fragmented based on their various differing examples of self-interest or along progressive and democratic lines. The economic elite can be characterized along the lines of rent-seeking business modality in profit-making and/or the entrepreneurial or professional business modality. There are, however, no illusions that the primary interest of the economic elite in the Philippines coincides with that of the national and transnational capital class who wish to profit from the neoliberal economic order. In the Philippines, the economic and political elites are not mutually exclusive; they may be fragmented but they move along the political and economic realms. Along these lines, the Philippine state is a site of contention and an arena of struggle. Despite the amalgamation of different interests characterizing the modern state and as an instrument for capitalist interests, the state remains a site for struggle within the neoliberal economic order. The imperative towards the search for counter-strategies involves the careful examination of the relations of production, and how they give rise to social forces and shifts in class relations that contend in the formation of the state. It is at this political and economic juncture that the Philippine Left and progressive social forces are crucially important, crafting their bases of unities and rethinking counter-strategies in order to achieve an alternative vision of change, counter to Duterte's populist-authoritarian rule and the return of the Marcos rule.

References

ABS-CBN (2016), "More millennials voted for Duterte, exit poll shows", 14 May, available at https://news.abs-cbn.com/halalan2016/focus/05/14/16/more-millennials-voted-for-duterte-exit-poll-shows. Last accessed on 3 August 2022.

Adamson, W. L. (1980), "Gramsci's Interpretation of Fascism", *Journal of the History of Ideas*, vol. 41, no. 4 (Oct–Dec), pp. 615–33, University of Pennsylvania Press, available at https://www.jstor.org/stable/2709277. Last accessed on 3 August 2022.

Bates, Thomas (1975), "Gramsci and the Theory of Hegemony", *Journal of the History of Ideas*, vol. 36, no. 2 (Apr–Jun), pp. 351–66.

BBC News (2019), "Rodrigo Duterte profile: The provocative but popular Philippines strongman", 22 May, available at https://www.bbc.com/news/world-36659258. Last accessed on 3 August 2022.

BBC News (2021), "Philippines drugs war: ICC prosecutor seeks full investigation", 15 June, available at https://www.bbc.com/news/world-asia-57477802. Last accessed on 3 August 2022.

Bello, W. (2019a), *Counterrevolution: The Global Rise of the Far Right*, Quezon City: Ateneo de Manila University Press.

Bello, W. (2019b), "GISING NA, MAG-ISIP NA, LABAN NA, BAYAN", *Facebook*, 16 July, available at https://www.facebook.com/walden.bello/posts/10156768193889332. Last accessed on 1 August 2022.

Bello, W. (2019c), "Ruthless Philippine President's High Popularity Is the Result of Failed Democracy", *The Real News Network*, 16 July, available at https://therealnews.com/ruthless-philippine-presidents-high-popularity-is-the-result-of-failed-democracy. Last accessed on 1 August 2022.

Bello, W. (2021), "Neoliberalism, Contentious Politics, and the Rise of Authoritarianism in Southeast Asia", *Crisis of Neoliberal Globalization and the Nationalist Response*, edited by B. Berberoglu, pp. 92–115, New York and London: Routledge.

Boffo, M., A. Saad-Filho, and B. Fine (2019), "Neoliberal Capitalism: The Authoritarian Turn", *Socialist Register*, vol. 55, pp. 247–70.

Bruff, I. (2014), "The Rise of Authoritarian Neoliberalism", *Rethinking Marxism*, vol. 26, no. 1, pp. 113–29, available at http://dx.doi.org/10.1080/08935696.2013.843250. Last accessed on 3 August 2022.

Campani, G., and M. Pajnik (2017), "Democracy, post-democracy and the populist challenge", *Understanding the Populist Shift: Othering in a Europe in Crisis*, edited by G. Lazaridis and G. Campani, London and New York: Routledge, 2017, pp. 179–96.

CNN Philippines Staff (2020a), "Duterte approval rating rises to 91% amid pandemic, Cayetano suffers drop – survey", *CNN Philippines*, 5 October, available at https://www.cnnphilippines.com/news/2020/10/5/Duterte-approval-trust-rating-COVID-19-September-2020-Pulse-Asia-survey.html. Last accessed on 3 August 2022.

CNN Philippines Staff (2020b), "P19B NTF-ELCAC fund stays in Congress-approved budget", *CNN Philippines*, 10 December, available at https://www.cnn.ph/news/2020/12/10/P19-billion-NTF-ELCAC-stays-Congress-ratified-budget.html. Last accessed on 3 August 2022.

Cordero, T. (2021), "PSA: 9.8M Filipinos laid off from March 2020 to March 2021 – PSA", *GMA News*, 6 May, available at https://www.gmanetwork.com/news/mo

ney/economy/786448/psa-9-82m-filipinos-laid-off-from-march-2020-to-march-2021-psa/story. Last accessed on 3 August 2022.

Curato, N. (ed.) (2017), *A Duterte Reader: Critical Essays on Rodrigo Duterte's Early Presidency*, Quezon City: Ateneo de Manila University Press.

Gilbert, J. (2019), "This Conjuncture: For Stuart Hall", new formations: a journal of culture/theory/politics, vol. 96–97, pp. 5–37, available at https://www.muse.jhu.edu/article/730832. Last accessed on 3 August 2022.

Gramsci, A. (1971), *Selections from the Prison Notebooks of Antonio Gramsci*, New York: International Publishers.

Gutierrez, J. (2020), "Court Finds Evidence of Crimes Against Humanity in the Philippines", *The New York Times*, 15 December, available at https://www.nytimes.com/2020/12/15/world/asia/philippines-duterte-drugs-icc.html. Last accessed on 3 August 2022.

Hall, S. (1979), "The Great Moving Right Show", *Marxism Today*, January, pp. 14–20.

Heydarian, R. (2021), "Why the Marcos brand remains popular", *Philippine Daily Inquirer*, 26 October, available at https://opinion.inquirer.net/145623/why-the-marcos-brand-remains-popular. Last accessed on 3 August 2022.

Laforga, B. M. (2020), "Philippines to be SE Asia's worst performer this year", BusinessWorld, 11 December, available at https://www.bworldonline.com/philippines-to-be-se-asias-worst-performer-this-year/. Last accessed on 3 August 2022.

Laforga, B. M. (2021), "Philippine GDP shrinks by record 9.5% in 2020", BusinessWorld, 29 January, available at https://www.bworldonline.com/editors-picks/2021/01/29/341581/philippine-gdp-shrinks-by-record-9-5-in-2020/. Last accessed on 3 August 2022.

Manggagawa, Juan (2017), "Duterte is reactionary, counter-revolutionary (to the EDSA revolution), but not fascist – on Walden Bello's definition of a "fascist leader", *International Viewpoint*, 10 December, available at https://internationalviewpoint.org/spip.php?article5262&fbclid=IwAR17a1NrUSWt4_lGnZosYuSHwd2Lvvr-ZIGCwjoEtP9eJJGwr2CVD6UFseU. Last accessed on 3 August 2022.

Mercado, N. A. (2021), "65% of Filipinos believe it's 'dangerous' to publish anything critical of administration – SWS", *Inquirer.net*, 19 March, available at https://internationalviewpoint.org/spip.php?article5262&fbclid=IwAR17a1NrUSWt4_lGnZosYuSHwd2Lvvr-ZIGCwjoEtP9eJJGwr2CVD6UFseU. Last accessed on 3 August 2022.

Morelock, J. (ed.) (2018), "Introduction: The Frankfurt School and Authoritarian Populism – A Historical Outline", *Critical Theory and Authoritarian Populism*, London: University of Westminster Press, pp. xiii–xxxviii.

Oxford Business Group (2018), "Income inequality remains an issue in the Philippines, despite robust economic expansion", *The Report: Philippines 2018*, available at https://oxfordbusinessgroup.com/analysis/lifting-all-boats-government-works-address-persistent-inequality. Last accessed on 3 August 2022.

Philippine Statistics Office (2020), "Updated 2015 and 2018 Full Year Official Poverty Statistics", 4 June, available at https://psa.gov.ph/poverty-press-releases/nid/1 62559. Last accessed on 3 August 2022.

Pobre, Addie, and Cathrine Gonzales (2017), "Looking back at EDSA 11: The political paths of Estrada and Arroyo", *Rappler*, 17 January, available at https://www.rappler.com/newsbreak/158523-look-back-edsa-ii-joseph-estrada-gloria-arroyo/. Last accessed on 3 August 2022.

Poulantzas, N. (2014), *State, Power, Socialism*, London: Verso.

Ramos, C. G. (2021), "The return of strongman rule in the Philippines: Neoliberal roots and developmental implications", *Geoforum*, vol. 124, pp. 310–19, available at https://doi.org/10.1016/j.geoforum.2021.04.001. Last accessed on 3 August 2022.

Reuters (2007), "TIMELINE: Recent coups and attempted coups in the Philippines", 29 November, available at https://www.reuters.com/article/us-phillipines-unrest-idUSSP31116220071129. Last accessed on 3 August 2022.

Reuters (2021), "Pandemic pushes millions in Philippines into poverty", 17 December, available at https://www.reuters.com/markets/asia/pandemic-pushes-millions-philippines-into-poverty-2021-12-17/. Last accessed on 3 August 2022.

Rivas, Ralf (2020), "NTC orders ABS-CBN to stop operations", *Rappler*, 5 May, available at https://www.rappler.com/nation/259974-ntc-orders-abs-cbn-stop-operations-may-5-2020. Last accessed on 3 August 2022.

Rocamora, J. (2020), *Impossible Is Not So Easy: A Life in Politics*, Quezon City: Ateneo de Manila University Press.

See, A. (2021), "Rodrigo Duterte Is Using One of the World's Longest Covid-19 Lockdowns to Strengthen His Grip on the Philippines", *Time*, 15 March, available at https://time.com/5945616/covid-philippines-pandemic-lockdown/. Last accessed on 3 August 2022.

Springer, S. (2017), "Neoliberalism in Southeast Asia", *Routledge Handbook of Southeast Asian Development*, edited by A. McGregor, L. Law, and F. Miller, Abingdon: Routledge, available at https://www.routledgehandbooks.com/doi/10.4324/9781315726106-3. Last accessed on 3 August 2022.

Stewart, B. (2020), "The Rise of Far-Right Civilizationism", *Critical Sociology*, vol. 46, nos. 7–8, pp. 1207–20, available at https://journals.sagepub.com/doi/10.1177/0896920519894051. Last accessed on 3 August 2022.

Talabong, R. (2021), "Mapped: Davao wins big in NTF-ELCAC's P16.4-B barangay program", *Rappler*, 12 February, available at https://www.rappler.com/newsbreak/iq/mapped-davao-wins-big-national-task-force-end-local-communist-armed-conflict-barangay-program. Last accessed on 3 August 2022.

World Bank (2003), "World Development Indicators 2003", Washington, DC: World Bank, available at https://openknowledge.worldbank.org/handle/10986/13920. Last accessed on 3 August 2022.

Viajar, V. Q. (2009), "Implications of Economic Globalization on Labor Market Policies: A Comparative study of the Philippines and Indonesia", *Philippine Political Science Journal*, vol. 30, pp. 89–122, available at https://www.tandfonline.com/doi/abs/10.1080/01154451.2009.9723518. Last accessed on 3 August 2022.

Zakaria, F. (1997), "The Rise of Illiberal Democracy", *Foreign Affairs*, vol. 76, no. 6 (Nov–Dec) pp. 22–43.

Zamora, F., and P. Tubeza (2017), "Duterte hires 59 former AFP, PNP men to Cabinet, agencies", *Inquirer.net*, 27 June, available at https://newsinfo.inquirer.net/908958/duterte-hires-59-former-afp-pnp-men-to-cabinet-agencies. Last accessed on 3 August 2022.

Production of Activism under Authoritarianism
Insights from the Rights-Based Civil Society in Turkey

Ülker Sözen

Introduction

"Do I see hope in civil society? Actually, not much at the moment. I hope I am mistaken".[1] These are the words of one of my respondents, a civil society professional working with victims of torture in a Kurdish city in Turkey, when we discussed their prospects for democratization in the country. This pessimistic take on the potential of civil society activism is understandable given the extent of political repression in Turkey in the last few years, which has been harsher in Kurdish cities and in cases related to the Kurdish issue. This was also a response to the inefficacy of transnational human rights mechanisms in responding to the democratic backsliding in Turkey, which can be read as part of a broader trend affecting other peripheral countries under authoritarian regimes.

Following the general election in June 2015, in which the Adalet ve Kalkınma Partisi (Justice and Development Party, AKP) lost its majority in Parliament for the first time, a political climate of fear dominated Turkey, starting with deadly attacks on members of the public who supported the opposition. Two devastating suicide bombings by ISIS took place in this period, one in Suruç on 20 July 2015 and the other in Ankara on 10 October 2015. In Suruç, a south-eastern town bordering Syria, 33 members of the youth section of a socialist organization were killed in an explosion, members who had been visiting to show solidarity with children living across the border under the threat of ISIS occupation. In Ankara, the capital of Turkey, two bombs killed 104 people at a mass political rally protesting the AKP government's decision to get involved in the war in Syria, organized by labour unions and supported by the left-wing pro-Kurdish Halkların Demokratik Partisi (Peoples' Democratic Party, HDP) and Cumhuriyet Halk Partisi (Republican People's Party, CHP), the main opposition party.

After the June 2015 election, no government could be formed and a general election was held again in November 2015, leading to a de facto coalition of the AKP

---

1 Interview, 5 November 2020.

with the ultra-nationalist Milliyetçi Hareket Partisi (Nationalist Movement Party, MHP). As of early 2022, this coalition is still ruling the country, and is doing so with an intense discourse of securitization. In between the two elections, the peace negotiations between Turkey and the Kurdish movement came to an end, culminating in a counter-insurgency operation in several Kurdish cities that lasted until early 2016. Then in July 2016, there was a failed coup attempt against the AKP rule, after which the government declared a state of emergency, which lasted for two years. This endowed the government with extra-legal executive powers, enabling further repression of civil society and the criminalization of human rights activists and dissident political actors.

These events have led to pessimism among the opposition-aligned public and left-wing circles given the persistence of the AKP's authoritarian rule. The party has found ways to persevere despite its loss in the June 2015 election and the series of political and economic crises and corruption scandals in the last decade.[2] However, civil society activists in Turkey show dedication and commitment despite political repression shrinking the civic space and the discouraging factor of structural problems within the transnational civil society framework.

This article discusses the context within which civil society activism emerges and how civil society actors reflect on and navigate through the hardships they face. The focus is on rights-based and claim-making civil society organizations (CSOs). These are associations that focus on areas such as human rights, women's and LGBTQ rights, impunity, freedom of speech, equal access to justice, and minority rights. They aim to produce activism through advocacy, solidarity-building, lobbying, mobilizing public reaction, and the documentation and monitoring of rights violations. They are largely financed through external funding in the form of project grants since access to public funds is virtually impossible for them. The analysis will explore the transnational networks through which these organizations seek financial assistance and political support, mostly reliant on the human rights and democracy promotion mechanisms of the European Union.

---

2   The public investigation from 17 to 25 December 2013 disclosed massive corruption by high-ranking AKP politicians. Hayrettin Karaman, a pro-government Islamic columnist, issued a fatwa in response, declaring that "corruption is not a theft" (Yilmaz and Bashirov 2018, 1823). The manipulation of Islam has been a common strategy of the AKP to maintain support and prevent public reaction in such cases.

Authoritarian Neoliberalism in Turkey

Turkey has a seemingly unusual history with respect to the rise of authoritarianism in the last decade. The AKP government and its leader Recep Tayyip Erdoğan, who came to power in 2002, were once praised and supported by the liberal international order and the EU as democratizing political forces during the 2000s (Başer and Öztürk 2017, 3). The country was declared a candidate for full membership of the EU in 1999, and the population's motivation to attain EU membership had provided substantial backing to the AKP. Along with the democratic reforms for the EU membership bid, the party pursued a neoliberal agenda from the outset. This entailed the increased privatization of public services and initiatives, the financialization of the economy, the flexibilization of the labour market, and the curtailment of labour rights.

The widespread perspective in the literature is that the AKP played a democratizing role in its first term until 2007 (or, according to some, during its first two terms until 2011) and then took a mostly conservative turn and went down an authoritarian path (McDonald 2011; Özbudun 2014). Cemal Burak Tansel problematizes this narrative of rupture between the early AKP on the one hand, which intended to implement democratic reforms and was committed to the EU membership agenda, and the later AKP on the other, which relied on coercion rather than consent. Accordingly, these two phases should be understood "not as diametrically opposed regimes with inherently contradicting modalities of rule, but as two interlinked nodes on the spectrum of a now-apparent authoritarian governance" (Tansel 2018, 198). That is, the authoritarian practices of the later period of the AKP can be traced back to its early years, if one considers the party's neoliberal restructuring of the economy and other spheres of life since its onset. Tansel analyses the development of the repressive regime in Turkey using the concept of authoritarian neoliberalism, which recognizes the inherent authoritarian dynamics in neoliberal regimes, and argues:

> AKP's recent "authoritarian turn" should be understood as the single facet of an authoritarian model of governance which was already shaped by executive centralisation – at the expense of political oversight and public participation – and sustained by the deployment of the full power of the state in the service of the party's interests. These interests have largely coalesced around neoliberal policies that have increased the scope and pace of commodification and restructured the state's regulatory and distributive roles. (Ibid., 209–10)

Even during its so-called democratic period, the AKP's statecraft relied on governmental decrees and omnibus bills that overrode parliamentary processes and democratic deliberation for changes spanning from accelerated privatization and the weakening of labour rights to increasing political control over the judiciary

(Erol 2018, 3). In this way, the neoliberal transformation led to the corruption of democracy and the erosion of check-and-balance mechanisms, paving the way for the entrenchment of the AKP's authoritarian rule in later years. Furthermore, the AKP's neoliberal policies prevented popular democratic empowerment, especially due to its anti-labour-rights policies and the weakening of labour unions as political actors. This happened through "the collective/institutional exclusion of labouring classes from policy-making processes and their 'disciplining by unmediated/individual incorporation' into AKP's political project as consumers, credit users and social assistance recipients" (Bozkurt-Güngen 2018, 220).

From Opening to Shrinking Civic Space

The government's undemocratic practices concerning economic affairs and labour rights were counterbalanced by the relaxation of state surveillance and controls over civil society during the 2000s as part of the EU harmonization reforms (Zihnioğlu 2020, 124). Moreover, the government and public institutions were open to dialogue and cooperation with claim-making CSOs on projects to improve human rights and the situation of minority groups (Babül 2020). The considerable opening of civic space generated optimism among the left-wing liberals and encouraged them to support the AKP during this period. The support of liberal intellectuals provided the party with ideological legitimization to pursue its neoliberal agenda for almost a decade and helped with discrediting the opposition as anti-democratic and anti-reformist (Ersoy and Üstüner 2016).

However, after the Gezi Protests in 2013, the AKP's stance towards CSOs—especially the rights-based ones that criticized the government's policies—took a negative turn. From that point on, several associations became victims of abuse and harassment in the form of extensive and additional auditing, fines, and even police raids (Yabanci 2019, 291). The closing of civic space intensified after the failed coup attempt in 2016. During the state of emergency rule, hundreds of CSOs and media outlets were shut down with statuary decrees, and many lawsuits were filed against activists, politicians, journalists, and academics under the accusation of supporting terrorism. This led to ongoing imprisonments such as that of Osman Kavala (Bia News Desk 2021), the leading promoter of civil society and human rights activism in Turkey, and Selahattin Demirtaş, the then-co-leader of the HDP.

In July 2017, the police raided a meeting in Büyükada in Istanbul, attended by several human rights CSOs including Amnesty International. 11 civil society activists were detained and put on trial, accused of supporting the coup attempt and terrorism. At the end of the trial in July 2020, four of them were found guilty and given prison sentences (Freedom House 2020). In late 2020, a legislative change was issued that increased control over CSOs, allowing the state to replace the leaders of organizations who face terrorism charges and to seek restrictions on their activities in court (Freedom House 2021). The legislation also allows for annual government inspections of associations, specifically those with international ties. This legislation has been accompanied by an increase in criminalizing discourses by government officials and pro-government media, targeting the dissident CSOs that receive foreign funding and portraying them as enemies of the nation.

Stefan Toepler et al. (2020) define the trend of shrinking civic space which takes place in relation to the global rise of authoritarianism as "attempts by governments to disrupt international funding flows to local CSOs and further reduce their political voice through legal restrictions and other forms of repression" (ibid., 649). The authors discuss the coping strategies of claim-making CSOs, the section of civil society most adversely affected by authoritarianism due to their political activities (ibid., 654–55). Some of the strategies include foregoing foreign support and trying to mobilize domestic resources, reducing their public profile and de facto depoliticization, rebranding and refounding the organization, disbanding and working informally, or continuing activities abroad and/or largely online. For CSOs under authoritarianism it is more important to maintain interaction with and support from their communities, which requires creativity and institutional resilience as part of their strategic plans.

Crackdowns on civil society in the Global South are usually treated as isolated phenomena that are explained by the authoritarian and reactionary tendencies of domestic political forces. Instead, David Sogge (2020) argues for a transnational perspective to understand the worldwide shrinking of civic space and its domestic manifestations. This perspective considers the framework of foreign interests and global power relations, which includes factors such as the repression of organized labour in line with the measures imposed by international institutions like the IMF and the World Bank, and the increasing securitization and anti-terrorism policies that criminalize human rights activism.

Production of Civil Society Activism: Domestic and Transnational Frameworks

Civil society activism is not only an expression of political claims and struggle. I contend that it is also a product whose form, content, and influential capacities are affected by the domestic and transnational political-economic environment and power relations. Furthermore, it entails labour relations insofar as civil society activism becomes a professional activity and there are people who earn their living through this work. Hence, issues related to labour rights and workplace democracy also come into play in organizations that defend human rights and egalitarian values.

In the Turkish context, rights-based CSOs rely largely on foreign funding in the form of project grants, mainly obtained from EU sources enabled by Turkey's candidacy (Zihnioğlu 2020, 125). Especially for the claim-making CSOs, access to national public funds is virtually impossible and there are no tax exemptions. Membership fees are usually insufficient to sustain these associations' activities, as most rights-based CSOs in Turkey are not grassroots organizations and their membership base is quite limited, varying from several dozen to only a few members. Besides, the domestic legal framework is unfavourable, considering the difficulties in and vague eligibility criteria for getting the necessary permissions to collect donations, and the limitations over how donations can be used (TÜSEV 2020).

Under these circumstances, rights-based CSOs have to resort to project grants from foreign donors, mostly linked to the EU and other Global North sources, to secure their existence and realize their activities. "EU funding's short-term, activity-based, measurable outcome and visibility-oriented structure" contributes to some degree of depoliticization of Turkish civil society, even among those CSOs that have a primary focus on advocacy and empowerment, as they shift to service-based activities that better fit the funding framework (Zihnioğlu 2019, 513). In addition, CSOs may shift their mandates and goals to areas where funding is available, such as migration in recent years, which has come to the fore as an aftereffect of the civil war in Syria.

Thereby, dependency on external funding from the EU and other external donors turns out to be a critical problem regarding the transnational framework of civil society activism. Linked to this, the projectification of activism emerges as another significant issue whereby the donors' standard frame for activism is the project form, which serves their expectations regarding efficiency and accountability. The project form potentially causes alienation from grassroots politics and curtails the organic connection of CSOs with claim-making communities, as it requires a professionalized managerial system and a seemingly rationalized special mode of thinking (Buzogány 2011, 81).

The project form is an omnipresent trait guiding many aspects of contemporary human practice. It is characterized by the precedence of activity (as activity has the power to determine and format time, space, and relations), utilitarian networks instead of durable connections, and the treatment of society as isolated functions instead of a web of intertwined institutions (Jensen et al. 2016). Projectification in civil society presupposes the flexibility of operations, short-term time frames, and a fragmented approach to social relations in line with the neoliberal logic of production (Bayraktar 2017). This also refers to a neoliberal structuring of activism which involves the lack of job security for civil society workers and the acute problem of sustainability (that is, the ability of civil society initiatives to run by their own means), whereby short-term grants and time frames are the norm.

Furthermore, this neoliberal organization entails a geographical division of labour between the Global North donors and the Global South civil society actors. Therein, "activism production" is subcontracted by the northern donors which undertake the planning to the southern CSOs and activists who do the groundwork. Paralleling the global neoliberal production networks of goods and services, transnational civil society networks entail fragmentation and involve dynamics that can heighten power differences and exploitation. In this environment, problems such as the political risks that southern activists have to face, the non-democratic practices in CSOs, and the exploitation of voluntary labour are not adequately addressed.

Given the power inequality between northern and southern actors, agenda-setting and gatekeeping are identified as being important complications within the transnational civil society framework (Carpenter 2007). Northern donors have the upper hand because they have the financial resources and better access to political authorities with transnational power. As such, the preferences of large donor bodies such as major foundations and northern states define which needs are supported and in which ways they need to be framed by the southern CSOs seeking their support (Bob 2010, 144). In this environment, southern actors "are largely left out of the agenda-setting process by the more powerful gatekeepers and receive fewer resources and less international attention to alleviate human rights abuses" (Murdie and Polizzi 2017, 727).

Transnational advocacy network (TAN) is a much-referenced concept within civil society literature. It was first discussed by Margaret E. Keck and Kathryn Sikkink, examining cross-national solidarity for civil society activism. The authors describe TAN as a network of civil society actors across various countries which work internationally on a specific political, social, or environmental problem and advocate for change (Keck and Sikkink 1998). These actors are bound together by shared values, a common discourse, and close exchanges of information and services. Ideally, the goal of TANs is to create a boomerang pattern in which the network mobilizes international organizations and powerful liberal states to push the repressive state into paying attention to the demands of domestic CSOs and social movements.

In Turkey, the boomerang pattern led to positive results in areas such as improving women's rights and fighting against torture and human rights violations in the 2000s, when the AKP government was willing to implement reforms for EU membership (Marshall 2009; Şahin and Yıldız 2010). Back then, CSOs in Turkey successfully mobilized EU mechanisms such as the European Court of Human Rights (ECHR) to pressure the Turkish state to take action. This pattern is no longer functioning as the AKP government has practically dropped the EU membership agenda and is pursuing a pragmatic relationship with the EU by concentrating on trade and security. Correspondingly, the EU leadership has set aside the norm-based approach and the agenda of promoting human rights in its relations with Turkey as it prioritizes border security in response to migration flows in the aftermath of the Arab Spring and the civil war in Syria (Thevenin 2021).

In recent years, human rights activists are voicing their disappointment with the EU's passivity regarding the human rights abuses in Turkey, most visibly in the ECHR's handling of the cases regarding the Turkish authorities' violations during the counter-insurgency operation in Kurdish cities in early 2016, and those during the state of emergency rule after the coup attempt (Negrón-Gonzales 2021). This passive stance is arguably linked to the EU's concern over not straining the relationship with the AKP government, which has been using the millions of migrants in Turkey as a bargaining chip. As such, there is a connection between the persistence of the AKP's authoritarian rule and the shrinking civic space in Turkey on the one hand, and the EU's border security agenda on the other.

Perspectives from the Field, Coping Strategies, and the Search for Alternatives

My field research with the rights-based civil society activists in Turkey revealed several key issues concerning not only the political repression that they face but also the civil society framework and transnational advocacy networks. Moreover, I inquired about the activists' strategies and their suggestions for how to maintain resilience under authoritarianism, and how to better use and transform the existing structures for advancing their activism. As expected, feelings of stress and sadness are commonly expressed given the political repression and the threat of persecution. Even if they are not themselves experiencing persecution, many activists bear the emotional toll of monitoring the regular rights abuses as part of their job, and of witnessing many fellow activists having to deal with lawsuits and prison sentences. The quote below, by the director of an association focusing on freedom of speech and founded in the last couple of years, exemplifies these sentiments:

> Fear is something that we discuss a lot [at our association]. I think we need regular therapy sessions. I thought about drafting a grant proposal for such a project [laughs]. A couple of years ago, when there was an intense period of trials against activists, I couldn't read or watch anything, I couldn't concentrate on anything. Everything made me sad. It is really toxic that we scan the news every day on human rights violations as part of our job.[3]

---

3   Interview, 3 September 2020.

In the last few years, this emotional toll has become part of the public conversation in the field of civil society, owing to the influence of feminist and queer interventions emphasizing the connectedness of private and political domains and the importance of emotions in collective action. Some CSOs organize collective therapy sessions and internal meetings for coping with the feelings of burnout and despair in the face of political repression and stressful work schedules.

Moreover, some activists recently addressed this situation with a project on political well-being that involved public workshops and exercises targeting the workers and volunteers in rights-based CSOs and other political organizations, whom they term "political labourers".[4] They start from a critique of the mainstream neoliberal wellness and personal growth industry, as they argue for a collective democratic conception of well-being which both acknowledges and encounters the multi-faceted inequalities dividing society. They adopt a queer feminist perspective proposing mutual care and revolutionary joy as strategies for continuing activism and maintaining resilience under authoritarianism (Equality Studies Association 2021).

At a broader level, criticism regarding the inefficiency of both the EU and international justice mechanisms is a prominent issue raised by civil society activists. This causes disappointment for some, whereas for others it exposes the interest-based realist approach of powerful liberal states that are inconsistent and dishonest. The global human rights regime rests upon the notion of the international liberal order (ILO), which was established after WWII and which reflected the hegemony of the USA, and the assumption that powerful liberal states implement norm-based politics and defend democracy. In the last decade, the rise of Russia and China and the worldwide surge of authoritarian and populist politics have caused a decline of this system, which was already flawed and deceptive, weakening the influence of human rights discourses (Van Lindert 2016).

In this context, international human rights treaties and justice mechanisms have lost their power to enforce democratic norms, contributing to the worldwide shrinking of civic space. A human rights activist who has been in the field for three decades and who has experience working in close contact with international organizations and EU actors expressed their concerns as follows:

> Human rights mechanisms are turning out to be inefficient at the global scale. Even England puts withdrawing from the ECHR on the agenda. International human rights mechanisms are collapsing. They cannot fight off the shrinking of resources, economic inequality, and the growth of racism and xenophobia. Today,

---

4   The project was initiated and conducted by Eşitlik Araştırmaları Derneği (Equality Studies Association) in 2021.

> the human rights issue is being bought off. What will happen to civil society at a global scale, that is the question.[5]

As part of the criticism towards the EU, an officer working at an international donor body operating in Turkey recounted that they viewed the EU's human rights donations as a strategy to whitewash its stance on the migration crisis, a strategy which they considered "completely hypocritical".[6] This interpretation was not uncommon among Turkish civil society activists. The EU's increased financial support for civil society and human rights activism in the aftermath of the coup attempt, which pushed authoritarianism in Turkey to the next level, is seen as an attempt to clear its conscience. That is, the EU has failed to effectively respond to the abundant human rights violations in Turkey since 2016 and has turned a blind eye to the suffering of migrants. This is because its primary concern is securing Turkey's cooperation for the containment of refugees from Syria and other war-stricken countries.

Despite the complaints, some activists think that it is still possible to activate the boomerang pattern, although this would likely not be as successful as in the 2000s. Accordingly, this can be achieved through raising well-framed demands and strategically lobbying EU government actors to influence the Turkish authorities to reverse some of the non-democratic practices:

> The civil society should be realistic in its relationship with the EU. There is no point in asking Germany to stop the weapons trade to Turkey or for the Netherlands to stop investing in hydroelectric dams in Turkey. We should recognize that for the European actors, the issue of human rights and liberties in Turkey is not a priority and their economic and security-related concerns are central. However, we can achieve positive results if we frame our demands precisely. For instance, we can press the EU to introduce the improvement of human rights as a condition for Turkey's long-term request of visa-free travel in the EU.[7]

Criticism towards the funding structure is a much-emphasized topic, pointing to an inadequate understanding of the local context by the EU and donor organizations. The introduction of sub-granting in recent years by the EU Delegation to Turkey—the largest funder of civil society in Turkey—has increased the responsibility of leading rights-based CSOs by burdening them with the heavy workload of reviewing applications, coordinating fund allocation, and monitoring the project cycles of sub-grantee organizations. Moreover, complaints are voiced regarding the short-term and activity-based project grants, which vary from six months to three

---

5 Interview, 4 April 2021.
6 Interview, 9 July 2020.
7 Interview with the director of a human rights association who has been active in the field for over three decades, 10 September 2020.

years at best, and do not allow the CSOs to sustain their capacities and institutional infrastructure.

The project form, and the constant search for funds to keep the CSOs alive, lead to neoliberal labour relations in the rights-based associations. These include short-term work contracts, a lack of job security, flexible work schedules, the giving up of basic labour rights such as severance pay, and exploitation of voluntary labour. It is not uncommon that CSO workers are expected to donate a part of their salary, since project grants are not sufficient to cover all the expenses of organizations. Furthermore, the grants are framed as donors' support for the activism that CSOs produce, with the assumption that these are self-sufficient organizations. The donors expect the CSOs to contribute to the project budget with their own resources. This usually means that workers have to realize some part of the tasks voluntarily without payment. The ethos of activism justifies such practices, wherein the workers are also activists, expected to make sacrifices in order to contribute to a political cause.

Eventually, this situation leads to hierarchical relations and top-down decision making, which ironically generates the conditions for authoritarian management within the CSOs that oppose political authoritarianism. In this regard, an activist who has been employed in different rights-based CSOs for more than a decade reported that:

> The associations [that advocate for human rights and democracy] tend to have a non-democratic self-organization. It is usually a group or a person making the decisions, so there are bosses. Sometimes they are like textile workshops and the workers are expected to give up on their rights. "This is not a job, this is activism" say the bosses and this justifies exploitation ... The boss is the person who brings in the funds, which means the workers' salaries are paid because of them. This results in silence on the part of the workers who face exploitation and mistreatment. And so, demands for more democracy in the workplace are undermined.[8]

Recently, these undemocratic practices have become an issue in civil society circles in Turkey. Worker activists have begun to address exploitation, top-down decision making, and gender and age-based hierarchies in CSOs. There have been public debates about bullying allegations in certain reputable feminist organizations. While the younger activists accused the senior coordinators of overworking the staff and of bullying, the latter brought up the hardship of keeping small organizations alive for many years in the absence of continuous funding sources.

Another key problem regarding the CSOs' claim-making in Turkey is their limitations in reaching out to wider sections of society and raising support. One reason for that is the criminalization and defamation of such organizations by the government. However, another part of the problem relates to their shortcomings

---

8   Interview, 7 March 2021.

in building organic ties with society and engaging in grassroots politics. There is some degree of self-reflection whereby some civil society activists question their established activism perspectives, which include lobbying public authorities and focusing extensively on minority and cultural rights. The quote below, by an activist working for more than a decade in a human rights association focusing on reconciliation, shows how some actors in the field question their strategies and modes of activism:

> I think our association and many CSOs in the field [of human rights] are confused about whom they should address and whom they are trying to influence. Are we talking to the state? Well, there is no possibility of dialogue with the state now. In our association, little by little, we have been discussing ways to change our communication strategy. We are thinking about ways to build an accessible language and address the younger generation.[9]

In connection with the motivation for extending their social influence, some human rights associations have begun to focus more on labour rights, with the perspective that "workers' rights are human rights".[10] Addressing the labour rights abuses, which have evidently intensified under authoritarianism and the recent severe economic crisis prompting dozens of strikes only in the first two months of 2022, might be a way to establish stronger ties with society and gain grassroots support for a rights-based civil society (Osterlund 2022). In this regard, developing rapport with labour organizations and especially with the emergent smaller workers' collectives can be a meaningful strategy to make their struggles visible and to channel the European financial support and leverage to labour causes.

Finally, as an internal strategy for strengthening the stance against authoritarianism, rights-based CSOs seek to enhance dialogue, cooperation, and solidarity among themselves. The Solidarity Network for Human Rights Defenders – Turkey was launched in 2019 to bring together organizations specialized in different causes, such as human rights, media freedoms, access to justice, and women's and LGBTQ rights. Their motivation is to organize a stronger and more unified defence mechanism against the pressures on civil society, such as the detention and trial of activists and the introduction of new legislation that further restricts civic space.

---

9 Interview, 29 July 2020.
10 A recent example is a research report on the workers' rights abuses and preventions of unionization during the state of emergency rule, convened by two important human rights CSOs, Hafıza Merkezi and Eşit Haklar İçin İzleme Derneği: https://hakikatadalethafiza.org/kaynak/ohal-rejiminde-iscilerin-kollektif-haklari-avrupa-kokenli-iliskili-isletmelerde-sendikal-orgutlenme-haklari/.

Conclusion

The rights-based civil society in Turkey is in trouble, being at the intersection of several factors stemming from the domestic context, the transnational civil society framework, and neoliberal work relations. These complications have been aggravated by the authoritarian crackdown on civil society in recent years. The analysis undertaken in this article delineates the main challenges that civil society workers/activists face, their counter-strategies, criticisms, and suggestions to overcome the problems.

To conclude, some key points can be highlighted as ways out of the structural problems and present-day impediments faced by rights-based CSOs in Turkey. These recommendations could also apply to improving the situation of other Global South civil society actors who are struggling against authoritarianism and who are seeking support from transnational networks and mechanisms.

- Developing compelling strategies to connect with broader sections of society and to incorporate the struggles for social and economic rights into human rights activism.
- Along with political authoritarianism, confronting the far-reaching effects of neoliberalism both in society and within CSOs, and improving ties with the labour movement and workers' rights initiatives.
- Addressing the hierarchical relations, undemocratic decision-making patterns, and exploitation within CSOs which amount to intra-organizational authoritarian practices.
- Improving dialogue, cooperation, and solidarity between CSOs working in diverse fields.
- Cultivating a realistic understanding of the EU-oriented transnational advocacy network at play and its contradictions, pragmatic lobbying of EU actors in order to activate the boomerang pattern, and holding the EU donor bodies and justice mechanisms accountable for making change.
- Improving ties with other Global South civil society actors—starting with CSOs in the MENA region that are also clients of European human rights and democracy promotion mechanisms—to put pressure on transnational human rights networks and mechanisms in order to implement effective policies to implement sanctions against authoritarian states.

References

Babül, E. (2020), "Radical once more: the contentious politics of human rights in Turkey", *Social Anthropology*, vol. 28, no. 1, pp. 50–65.

Baser, B., and A. Öztürk (2017), "In Lieu of an Introduction: Is it Curtains for Turkish Democracy?" *Authoritarian Politics in Turkey: Elections, Resistance and the AKP*, edited by B. Başer and A. E. Öztürk, London: I.B. Tauris, pp. 1–20.

Bayraktar, F. (2017), "Neo-liberalleşme, Sivil Toplum Kuruluşları ve 'Projecilik': Eleştirel Bir Bakış", *Amme İdaresi Dergis*, vol. 50, no. 2, pp. 105–42.

Bia News Desk (2021), "Osman Kavala's Fourth Year in Prison", *Bianet*, 2 November, available at https://bianet.org/english/human-rights/252708-osman-kavala-s-fourth-year-in-prison. Last accessed on 28 June 2022.

Bob, C. (2010), "The market for human rights", *Advocacy Organizations and Collective Action*, edited by A. Prakash and M. K. Gugerty, Cambridge: Cambridge University Press, 133–54.

Bozkurt-Güngen, S. (2018), "Labour and authoritarian neoliberalism: Changes and continuities under the AKP governments in Turkey", *South European Society and Politics*, vol. 23, no. 2, pp. 219–38.

Buzogány, Á. (2011), "Stairway to heaven or highway to hell? Ambivalent Europeanisation and civil society in Central and Eastern Europe", *Protest Beyond Borders: Contentious Politics in Europe since 1945*, edited by H. Kouki and E. Romanos, New York: Berghahn Books, pp. 69–85.

Carpenter, R. C. (2007), "Setting the Advocacy Agenda: Theorizing Issue Emergence and Nonemergence in Transnational Advocacy Networks", *International Studies Quarterly*, vol. 51, no. 1, pp. 99–120.

Equality Studies Association, (2021), "White Paper on the Political Well-Being", *Eşitlik Çalışmaları Derneği*, available at https://esitlikcalismalari.org/iyilikhalibasvuru/. Last accessed on 15 November 2021.

Erol, M. (2018), "State and labour under AKP rule in Turkey: An appraisal", *Journal of Balkan and Near Eastern Studies*, vol. 21, no. 6, pp. 1–15.

Ersoy, D., and F. Üstüner (2016), "'Liberal intellectuals' narration of the justice and development party in Turkey", *Turkish Studies*, vol. 17, no. 3, 406–28.

Freedom House (2020), "Turkey: Büyükada Trial Verdict Lays Bare Assault on Human Rights", press release, 9 July, available at https://freedomhouse.org/article/turkey-buyukada-trial-verdict-lays-bare-assault-human-rights. Last accessed on 28 June 2022.

Freedom House (2021), "Turkey: Passage of NGO Law Strips Away Fundamental Rights and Freedoms", press release, 4 January, available at https://freedomhouse.org/article/turkey-passage-ngo-law-strips-away-fundamental-rights-and-freedoms. Last accessed on 28 June 2022.

Jensen, A., C. Thuesen, and J. Geraldi (2016), "The projectification of everything: Projects as a human condition", *Project Management Journal*, vol. 47, no. 3, pp. 21–34.

Keck, M. E., and K. Sikkink (1998), *Activists beyond Borders*, Ithaca: Cornell University Press.

Marshall, G. A. (2009), "Authenticating gender policies through sustained-pressure: The strategy behind the success of Turkish feminists", *Social Politics: International Studies in Gender, State & Society*, vol. 16, no. 3, pp. 358–78.

McDonald, D. (2011), "The AKP story: Turkey's bumpy reform path towards the European Union", *Society and Economy*, vol. 33, no. 3, pp. 525–42.

Murdie, A., and M. Polizzi (2017), "Human Rights and Transnational Advocacy Networks", *The Oxford Handbook of Political Networks*, edited by J. N. Victor, A. H. Montgomery, and M. Lubell, Oxford: Oxford University Press, pp. 715–32.

Negrón-Gonzales, M. (2021), "Countering counterterrorism: Defending human rights and challenging curfews in Turkey", *Turkish Studies*, vol. 22, no. 5, pp. 723–43.

Osterlund, P. B. (2022), "As Turkey's inflation rate climbs, workers strike for pay hikes", *Al Jazeera*, 15 February, available at https://www.aljazeera.com/economy/2022/2/15/as-turkeys-inflation-rate-climbs-workers-strike-for-pay-hikes. Last accessed on 28 June 2022.

Özbudun, E. (2014), "AKP at the crossroads: Erdoğan's majoritarian drift", *South European Society and Politics*, vol. 19, no. 2, pp. 155–67.

Şahin, B., and M. Yıldız (2010), "Transnational Advocacy Networks in Perspective: Democratization, Human Rights and NGOs in Turkey", *Uluslararası İlişkiler Dergisi (International Relations)*, vol. 6, no. 21, pp. 41–65, available at https://www.researchgate.net/publication/290973123_Transnational_advocacy_networks_in_perspective_Democratization_human_rights_and_NGOs_in_turkey. Last accessed on 28 June 2022.

Sogge, D. (2020), "Civic space: Shrinking from the outside in?" *Revista Iberoamericana de Estudios de Desarrollo*, vol. 9, no. 1, pp. 74–98.

Tansel, C. B. (2018), "Authoritarian Neoliberalism and Democratic Backsliding in Turkey: Beyond the Narratives of Progress", *South European Society and Politics*, vol. 23, no. 2, pp. 197–217.

Thevenin, E. (2021), "Between human rights and security concerns: Politicisation of EU-Turkey and EU-Libya agreements on migration in national parliaments", *European Security*, vol. 30, no. 3, pp. 464–84.

Toepler, S., A. Zimmer, and C. Fröhlich (2020), "The changing space for NGOs: Civil society in authoritarian and hybrid regimes", *Voluntas*, vol. 31, no. 4, pp. 649–62.

TÜSEV (2020), "Türkiye'de Yardım Toplama Mevzuatına Dair Değerlendirme: Sorunlar ve Engeller", available at https://www.tusev.org.tr/usrfiles/images/YardimToplamaBilgiNotu_Ulusal.pdf. Last accessed on 28 June 2022.

Van Lindert, T. (2016), "The International Human Rights Regime in a Multipolar World", *Shifting Paradigms*, edited by J. L. Gartner, New York: Humanity in Action Press, pp. 122–30.

Yabanci, B. (2019), "Turkey's tamed civil society: Containment and appropriation under a competitive authoritarian regime", *Journal of Civil Society*, vol. 15, no. 4, pp. 285–306.

Yilmaz, I., and G. Bashirov (2018), "The AKP after 15 years: Emergence of Erdoganism in Turkey", *Third World Quarterly*, vol. 39, no. 9, 1812–30.

Zihnioğlu, Ö. (2019), "European Union Civil Society Support and the Depoliticisation of Turkish Civil Society", *Third World Quarterly*, vol. 40, no. 3, pp. 503–20.

Zihnioğlu, Ö. (2020), "Continuity and change in Turkish civil society", *Turkey in Transition: Politics, society and foreign policy*, edited by E. C. Sokullu, Berlin: Peter Lang, 121–36.

Contributors

Ailynn Torres Santana is an academic and feminist militant. She is currently a Postdoctoral Research Fellow of the Rosa-Luxemburg-Stiftung International Research Group on Authoritarianism and Counterstrategies (IRGAC) and associate researcher at the Latin American Faculty of Social Sciences (FLACSO), Ecuador. Her areas of interest and research include feminist movements, gender inequalities, and neoconservative and anti-gender politics. Among her recent publications is the book "Derechos en riesgo: 11 estudios de grupos neoconservadores" (Rosa Luxemburg Foundation & Desde Abajo, 2020).

Aysegul Can is based at the Department of Urban and Regional Planning, Istanbul Medeniyet University (Turkey). She is a junior lecturer in Urban Studies and holds a PhD in Urban Studies and Planning (University of Sheffield, UK). Her research interests include gentrification, housing policy, urban resistance movements, authoritarian urbanism, social injustice in marginalised areas, and precarity in higher education. Her latest project was titled 'Being an Istanbulite: The Value of Resistance during a Time of Urban Governance through Massive Projects'.

Boaventura Monjane is based at the Institute for Poverty, Land and Agrarian Studies (PLAAS, University of the Western Cape) as a postdoctoral researcher and fellow of the International Research Group on Authoritarianism and Counter-Strategies of the Rosa-Luxemburg-Stiftung. He is also an associate fellow at the Centre for African Studies (CEA, Eduardo Mondlane University). His areas of interest and research include agrarian movements, rural politics, food sovereignty, and climate change.

Börries Nehe coordinates the International Research Group on Authoritarianism and Counter-Strategies. He holds a PhD in Latin American Studies from the National Autonomous University of Mexico (UNAM) and has been working on social movements, state & space theory, and violence and urban conflicts. He has recently published "Geographie der Gewalt. Macht und Gegenmacht in Lateinamerika" (mandelbaum Verlag).

Fábio Luís Franco is a psychoanalyst and holds a PhD in philosophy (University of São Paulo). Since 2006 he has been a member of an interdisciplinary group, the Social Theory, Philosophy, and Psychoanalysis Laboratory (LATESFIP). Over the last few years, he has tried to unite academic research, psychoanalytical practice, and political engagement. Currently, he is a post-doctoral researcher with the Institute of Psychology of the University of Sao Paulo. He is the author of the book "Governar os mortos: necropolíticas, desaparecimento e subjetividade" (Ubu Editora).

Fathima Nizaruddin is an academic and documentary filmmaker from India. She is a post doctoral fellow with the International Research Group on Authoritarianism and Counter-Strategies of the Rosa-Luxemburg-Stiftung. Fathima received a PhD for her practice-based artistic research project from University of Westminster, London in 2017. Her academic works have appeared in journals such as HAU: Journal of Ethnographic Theory, International Journal of Communication, Asiascape: Digital Asia and BioScope: South Asian Screen Studies.

Gustavo Robles is a postdoctoral fellow of the International Research Group on Authoritarianism and Counter-Strategies of the Rosa-Luxemburg-Stiftung and an associate researcher at the Research Institute for Humanities and Social Science (National University of La Plata/CONICET, Argentina). His areas of interest include Critical Theory and contemporary political philosophy and his current research project focuses on the ideological and affective dimensions of authoritarian neoliberalism.

Hugo Fanton is based at the Center for the Study of Citizenship Rights of the Faculty of Philosophy, Languages and Human Sciences (FFLCH) of the University of São Paulo (USP). He holds a PhD in Political Science (University of Campinas - Unicamp) and is the state coordinator of the Central de Movimentos Populares (Popular Movements Central) in São Paulo, Brasil, organisation that articulates urban movements in struggles for social rights. He has been working on social movements, democracy, neoliberalism, authoritarianism and class conflicts.

Hülya Dinçer is a postdoctoral research fellow of the International Research Group on Authoritarianism and Counter-Strategies of the Rosa-Luxemburg-Stiftung and a lecturer at the law faculty, MEF University (Turkey). She holds a PhD in public law from Galatasaray University in Turkey. Her academic research focuses on state violence, transitional justice, authoritarian legalism, social movements and legal mobilization.

Inés Durán Matute is based at the Graduate School of Sociology, Institute of Social Sciences and Humanities, Meritorious Autonomous University of Puebla (Mexico).

She is a postdoctoral fellow of the International Research Group on Authoritarianism and Counter-Strategies of the Rosa-Luxemburg-Stiftung. Her research investigates the impacts of development and democracy while exploring the strategies of anti-capitalist struggles in the context of the socioecological crisis. She is the author of Indigenous Peoples and the Geographies of Power: Mezcala's Narratives of Neoliberal Governance (Routledge, 2018).

Julieta Mira is based at the Institute of Justice and Human Rights of the National University of Lanús (UNLa) and the National Scientific and Technical Research Council (CONICET, Argentina). She holds a PhD in Social Sciences (University of Buenos Aires). She is a postdoctoral fellow at IRGAC, also a visiting scholar at Leuphana Universität Lüneburg and University College Freiburg, Germany. Her areas of research include State Crimes, Social Memory, Legal Activism, Human Rights and Criminal Justice Reform. She is co-founded of the Academic Network Memory, Truth and Justice.

Khanyile Mlotshwa is based at the University of KwaZulu Natal (UKZN)'s Pietermaritzburg campus where he researches and teaches (part time) courses in Cultural Studies. Mlotshwa is also a fellow of the International Research Group on Authoritarianism and Counter-Strategies of the Rosa-Luxemburg-Stiftung. His areas of interest and research include urban cultural studies, black subjectivity in postapartheid South Africa, and migration, among other areas. He recently published an edited book on digital cultures in Zimbabwe with Lexington Books in the US.

Mariano Féliz is based at the Center for Geographical Research of the Institute of Humanities and Social Sciences (CIG-IdIHCS) of the Universidad Nacional de La Plata (UNLP, Argentina) and the Consejo Nacional de Investigaciones Científicas y Técnicas (CONICET, Argentina). He holds a PhD in Economics (Université de Paris XIII/Nord) and a PhD in Social Sciences (University of Buenos Aires). He is a postdoctoral fellow of the International Research Group on Authoritarianism and Counter-Strategies of the Rosa-Luxemburg-Stiftung. He has been working on the contradictions between dependency, development, extractivism and social conflict.

Nwet Kay Khine is a post-doctoral research fellow from International Research Group on Authoritarianism and Counter-Strategies. She is a writer from Myanmar and published several works both in fiction and non-fiction. Her past and present research experiences focus on authoritarianism, media system transformation and environmental justice in transitional democracies. She is currently based in the Chair of Development Politics of Passau University and will join the Passau International Centre for Advanced Interdisciplinary Studies fellowship.

Pedro Salgado is a lecturer in International Relations at the Oxford Brookes University, and postdoctoral fellow of the International Research Group on Authoritarianism and Counter-Strategies of the Rosa-Luxemburg-Stiftung. He is a PhD in International Relations from the University of Sussex, and has also worked previously at Federal University of Uberlandia (UFU), Universität Kassel, and Federal University of Bahia (UFBA). His areas of interest are Historical Sociology and Global Political Economy.

Sabrina Fernandes is a Brazilian sociologist and ecosocialist organizer. She is currently a postdoctoral fellow with the International Research Group on Authoritarianism and Counter-Strategies (IRGAC) of the Rosa-Luxemburg-Stiftung, a guest researcher at Freie Universität Berlin and a contributing editor at Jacobin Magazine. She's the founder of the political education platform Tese Onze and her research interests include depoliticization, ecosocialism and ecofeminism. She's the author of the books Sintomas Mórbidos (2019) and Se quiser mudar o mundo (2020) as well as various texts in Portuguese, English, Spanish and other languages.

Ülker Sözen is a research fellow at IRGAC and a visiting researcher at Alice Salomon Hochschule; she will soon be a postdoctoral researcher at Leipzig University's Religious Studies Institute. She holds a PhD in Sociology from Mimar Sinan University of Fine Arts in Turkey. Her academic research spans identity and memory politics, Kurdish studies, social movements, civil society, and authoritarianism. Her upcoming project tackles youth, religiosity, and secularism in the Turkish digital landscape to analyze the dynamics of polarization and social transformation in contemporary Turkey.

Verna Dinah Q. Viajar is a Postdoctoral Research Fellow of the Rosa-Luxemburg-Stiftung International Research Group on Authoritarianism and Counterstrategies (IRGAC). She is currently based at the University of the Philippines School of Labor and Industrial Relations (UP SOLAIR) as Visiting Research Fellow (VRF). Her area of studies focuses on Southeast Asia labour movements, international political economy, democratization and authoritarianism, migrant domestic work and women in trade unions.